THE NEW YORK TIMES LIVING HISTORY

WORLD WAR II

THE NEW YORK TIMES LIVING HISTORY

WORLD WAR II

The Axis Assault, 1939–1942

Douglas Brinkley,
General Editor

Edited and with chapter introductions by David Rubel

Times Books

Henry Holt and Company

New York

Times Books
Henry Holt and Company, LLC
Publishers since 1866
115 West 18th Street
New York, New York 10011

AN AGINCOURT PRESS BOOK
President: David Rubel
Senior Editor: Julia Rubel
Assistant Editor: Brooke Palmer
Proofreader: Laura Jorstad
Image Research: Erika Rubel

ISBN 0-8050-7246-2 (vol. 1)

Designed by Fritz Metsch

Printed in the United States of America

For text permissions, see p. 335. For illustration credits, see pp. 337-338.

CONTENTS

INTRODUCTION

By Douglas Brinkley

OFFICIAL TRUMAN ANNOUNCES JAPANESE SURREN-DER read the message that circled Times Tower on Times Square in New York City. Since 1928—the pre-television era—moving headlines such as this one had streaked across the building's electric "zipper" sign, conveying important news to passersby twenty-four hours a day, seven days a week. Often, world-shaking events had been reported here before anywhere else. Therefore, all day on August 14, 1945, expectant crowds loitered outside the building, waiting for news from the White House. The tension was palpable. Ever since the dropping of the new atomic bombs on Hiroshima and Nagasaki a week earlier, anticipation had been high that World War II would soon be over. But it was not until early that evening—at 7:04 P.M., to be exact—that *The New York Times* announced to the crowd the arrival of peace.

While surfing my 180-channel home television, I occasionally come across film clips of those fleeting seconds of ecstasy, when joy consumed every face along Broadway. These New Yorkers exuberantly toss their hats high into the air and shout whoops of delight, yet their manner also expresses a deeper truth: relief. During the previous six years, more people had been killed—over fifty-three million—than during any other war in history. An even greater number had been seriously injured, either physically or mentally, by what they had seen, done, or experienced—the soldiers as much as anyone. "Man is stumbling blindly through a spiritual darkness while toying with the precarious

secrets of life and death," Gen. Omar N. Bradley reflected in a speech he delivered in Boston after the close of the war. "The world has achieved brilliance without wisdom, power without conscience. We know more about war than we know about peace, more about killing than we know about living."

It was impossible for those people congregated at Times Tower to comprehend fully the magnitude of the slaughter. The Soviet Union lost 29 million people; Poland, 6.7 million; Germany, 5.6 million; the United States, 413,000. Even tiny Belgium lost 99,000 of its citizens. The manner of their deaths was also unimaginable. For example, Nazi death camps at which 6 million Jews were murdered, along with so many million other "undesirables"; suicidal Japanese kamikaze pilots slamming their planes into U.S. warships; prisoners of war forced to march hundreds of miles without food or water; a single B-29 dropping an atomic bomb to obliterate a city. How efficient death had become, how technological, how widespread. A century earlier, Henry Wadsworth Longfellow had described death in battle as "mysterious," and Henry James called it "the distinguished thing." Yet such high-minded words proved inadequate to describe the grotesqueries of World War II, which gave death a new meaning so atrocious that poets hesitated to define it.

The Jews who survived the war made a collective promise never to forget the Holocaust, and subsequent generations have honored that covenant. Americans, however, far too often delegate the maelstrom of World War II to the past, refusing to see that its causes and effects are still with us. We watch old black-and-white newsreels on The History Channel, buy DVDs of *Band of Brothers* and *Saving Private Ryan*, and vaguely honor the valor of the servicemen who fought in what has become a morality play: the Allies against the Axis, democracy versus fascism, good against evil. Otherwise, World War II exists in the minds of contemporary Americans largely as a swirl of disconnected images, learned by osmosis: those euphoric faces in Times Square, Franklin Roosevelt and Winston Churchill hunkered over a map of Europe, giant swastikas decorating the Chancellery in Berlin, the Higgins boats landing D-day troops on the beaches of Normandy, Lt. Gen. Douglas MacArthur wading ashore as he makes his return to the Philippines, the American flag being raised on Iwo Jima's Mount Suribachi, the towering mushroom cloud expanding over Hiroshima.

These images, forever etched into our minds, have become part of the collective memory of our nation and the world. But they make little sense to most people because what they lack (and understandably so) is a tangible time sequence. Without such a chronology, the jumbled-up images that we all carry around with us serve as little more than hooks for companies marketing World War II nostalgia. Somewhere among the reproduction dog tags and the Andrews Sisters look-alikes and the commemorative T-shirts (many bearing phony company insignia), we've forgotten how to learn about World War II the way it should be studied, chronologically and through documentary evidence.

One of the oldest clichés in my business is that journalism is the first draft of history. Generally, this is true, especially because the best historians use the same source material as journalists—primary documents. These can come in many different forms. They can be campaign speeches, secret government memoranda, invasion plans, private letters, off-the-cuff remarks, folk songs, children's books, accounting ledgers, eyewitness descriptions, oral histories—it's a never-ending list. Yet, for most of us, they are inaccessible because, unlike television images, they can't be beamed into our living room. Furthermore, working with them can be difficult and time-consuming, often requiring trips to libraries, private collections, or the National Archives. So how can we inspect documents without traveling to Washington or struggling with a maze of paperwork at a regional depository? How can we educate our young people about the value of primary sources in understanding out past? How can we re-create a chronology of World War II that puts our national memories in context? It is these questions that *The New York Times* seeks to answer with the Living History series—the first volume of which, about World War II, you are holding.

In this book, the research has been done for you, and you need only read the uniquely powerful results to be impressed with how concise, reliable, and moving such history can be. The May 1940 German invasion of Europe, for example, is described in these pages by a twelve-year-old Dutch boy in Rotterdam. His poignant account, which begins with his father rushing off to battle and ends with his mother dying in an air raid, is the sort of narrative that only a firsthand experience can offer. Similarly, the personal letter that Adolf Hitler wrote to Benito Mussolini on the eve of the German invasion of Russia reveals much about the Nazi dictator's bombastic yet secretive mind-set. It also helps us move beyond the one-dimensional "televised" image of Hitler as simply a strutting, voiceless madman.

Rather than telling history as it's usually told, the insightful and unexpected primary documents found in the Living History series penetrate the cloud cover that has accumulated over the last six decades to reveal the impact of the war on individuals, civilian and military. What was it like to wait out an air raid in the London Underground, accompany a Nazi patrol in occupied Norway, or listen to an American telegrapher in the Philippines tap out the last message from Corregidor as he hears the Japanese bombs burst overhead?

Along with each primary document, the book also includes a contemporary article from the archives of *The New York Times*. These journalistic accounts, often from the scene of the action, impose a measure of objectivity yet still maintain all the drama and uncertainty of the events and their consequences. Unlike professional historians, who have the benefit of hindsight, newspaper correspondents don't know what twists and turns events might take. As a result, their assessments and speculations make fascinating reading. Rough drafts of history they may be, but at the least they tell the same story at the moment it happened.

The paper trail reconstructed in *The Axis Assault* begins in October 1937, when the domestic response to the growing world crisis was a deepening sense of unease and a fierce determination to, in George Washington's phrase, "avoid foreign entanglements." Earlier, Congress had passed strict neutrality laws prohibiting the sale of American arms and making no distinctions between victims and aggressors. Situations evolve, however, and smart politicians evolve with them. Thus, on October 5, 1937, Franklin D. Roosevelt observed in a speech in Chicago that "there is no escape through mere isolation or neutrality.... There is a solidarity and interdependence about the modern world, both technically and morally, which makes it impossible for any nation completely to isolate itself from economic and political upheavals in the rest of the world." The president then explained, voicing a particularly apt metaphor, "When an epidemic of physical disease starts to spread, the community approves and joins in a quarantine of the patients in order to protect the health of the community against the spread of the disease."

Not surprisingly, the Quarantine Speech got a chilly reception, with only one in three of those polled at the time indicating their support. For one thing, Roosevelt had been rather vague as to the nations he had in mind; and for another, he had failed to explain how such a quarantine might work. Meanwhile, a poll taken the following April showed that 54 percent of those surveyed thought the United States should withdraw from Asia entirely—a majority that grew as Japanese aggression in China intensified.

Undaunted, President Roosevelt demonstrated his growing doubts about the international situation by signing on May 17, 1938, a bill authorizing the creation of a two-ocean navy. American isolationists responded with even more outspoken pronouncements. Speaking for many conservative Republicans, Theodore Roosevelt Jr. declared, "We must not permit ourselves to be stampeded in our foreign policy." Even Raymond Moley, one of FDR's original New Deal "brain trusters," predicted that if the United States went to war, "free criticism will be restricted...industries will be nationalized... wages and hours will be fixed...profits will be conscripted." Yet a steadily increasing number of Americans began to believe that war in Europe could not be avoided and that, once it started, the United States would inevitably become involved. They looked more and more to President Roosevelt for guidance.

On New Year's Day, 1941, President Roosevelt worked late into the night in his small study on the second floor of the White House. Accompanied by his close adviser Harry Hopkins and speechwriters Robert Sherwood and Samuel Rosenman, he was putting the final touches on his State of the Union message, to be delivered before a joint session of Congress on January 6. There remained only the question of how to close the speech. After a long silence, the president began dictating what became his famous declaration of hope for "a world founded upon four essential human freedoms"—the freedom of speech and expression, the freedom of religion, the freedom from want, and the freedom from fear. These were, he said, not a vision for "a distant millennium" but "a definite basis for this kind of world attainable in our own time and generation."

Such was the power of Franklin Roosevelt's personality that, over time, he managed to turn America from a country of provincial isolationists into a nation of forward-thinking globalists. As journalist William Allen White wrote at the time with remarkable foresight, the president had given the world "a new magna charta of democracy." According to White, the four freedoms, which became the moral foundation of the United Nations, marked "the opening of a new era for the world." Of course, Roosevelt had a great deal of help from the Axis powers of Europe, whose mounting outrages shocked most Americans.

The war itself finally engulfed the United States on December 7, 1941, when deteriorating U.S.-Japanese relations produced the surprise attack on Pearl Harbor. After another stirring address by the president, Congress approved a war resolution against Japan on December 8, and Roosevelt was spared the politically risky choice of whether to seek a resolution against Germany when Adolf Hitler and Benito Mussolini declared war on December 11. America's sense of security was now thoroughly shattered—a state of affairs that produced oppressive anxiety yet also unified a country that had been deeply fractured. Whereas sizable minorities had opposed every previous U.S. war, virtually every American agreed after December 7, 1941—"a date which will live in infamy"—that the country's war effort must be total.

As *The Axis Assault* makes clear, World War II itself went badly for the Allies until late 1942. The Germans overran France and the Low Countries, invaded the Soviet Union, and advanced across North Africa, while the Japanese captured the Philippines and swept down through the South Pacific, taking New Guinea and threatening Australia, while maintaining their land operations in the China-Burma-India theater. It would not be until the American victory at Midway in June 1942, with which the next volume in the Living History series will begin, that the Allies checked the Axis advance.

This volume ends, therefore, with the outcome of World War II still in the balance. Too often, I believe, we forget what a near thing defeat seemed. No one in June 1942 could yet foresee a D day in Europe or a Hiroshima or Nagasaki in the Pacific. Yet, as you read these documents with the benefit of hindsight, you can sense the momentum starting to shift in the Allies' favor. Meanwhile, your sense of pride will no doubt grow. In a world filled with hatred, death, destruction, deception, and double-dealing, the United States was regarded almost universally in 1942 as a champion of justice, freedom, and democracy. The Times Tower "zipper" might not yet have been flashing VICTORY in June 1942, but certainly the tide of history was turning, and a new world order was in the offing—one in which the Axis assault would be thwarted and, for much of the globe, democracy would reign supreme.

PRELUDE TO WAR

1.

Initial Response to Aggression

October 1937

In October 1937, America was a nation sharply divided between isolationists and interventionists. World War I had been a great disappointment. Pres. Woodrow Wilson had promised in April 1917 that American entry into the war would bring about lasting world peace. Yet the onerous terms of the 1919 Treaty of Versailles, never ratified by the United States, made another European war more, rather than less, likely.

American disillusionment intensified during the mid-1930s, when Sen. Gerald P. Nye of North Dakota sponsored a series of congressional hearings to investigate World War I munition sales. President Wilson had declared that the war was being fought to make the world "safe for democracy," yet Nye showed that the war had also been fought, at least in part, to safeguard U.S.-backed international loans and enrich American war profiteers. Arms manufacturers were Nye's favorite target because, as he revealed, these so-called merchants of death had made huge fortunes before 1917 selling exorbitantly priced munitions to both sides.

The resulting public outrage moved Congress to pass a series of four increasingly restrictive neutrality acts that shackled U.S. foreign policy during the years leading up to World War II. The first of these laws, passed in August 1935, forbade all arms sales to belligerent nations once the president had determined that a state of war existed among them. Because the law made no distinction between

victim and aggressor, there was little the president or his interventionist cabinet could do to counter the expansionism then being practiced by Germany, Italy, and Japan. In fact, in July 1937, when Japan instigated a war with China, the president chose not to acknowledge the conflict formally because doing so would have forced him to bar all weapons sales to our Chinese allies.

Instead, Roosevelt made another sort of public statement. Motivated by Japan's aggression in China (as well as German and Italian adventurism in Spain and elsewhere), the president decided to take on the isolationists directly in his famous "quarantine" speech. It's often forgotten that, when immediate public reaction proved somewhat negative, Roosevelt quickly backed off the strong words he spoke that day in October 1937. Yet the Quarantine Speech nevertheless proved prophetic, expressing thoughts and attitudes that would only grow stronger in Roosevelt's mind as the international situation worsened and war drew near.

German troops assemble at a Nazi party rally in Nuremberg— the Reichsparteitag Erntedankfest—in November 1935.

ROOSEVELT URGES 'CONCERTED ACTION' FOR PEACE AND ARRAIGNS WARMAKERS

President Hits Out; Methods of Undeclared War Menace World, He Says at Chicago

By ROBERT P. POST

CHICAGO, Oct. 5—President Roosevelt today pledged his Administration to a "concerted effort" with other peace-loving nations to "quarantine" aggressor nations.

In a speech studded with warnings that America is menaced by "the present reign of terror and international lawlessness" which has "reached a stage where the very foundations of civilization are threatened," Mr. Roosevelt said that the 90 per cent of the world which wants peace "can and must find some way to make their will prevail."

A new foreign policy for the Administration was presaged with these words at the very close of the last major speech of the President's Western tour:

"America hates war. America hopes for peace. Therefore America actively engages in the search for peace."

No nation was mentioned by name as he indicated that the hands-off policy of the last four years would be reversed and served notice that the United States would join against aggressors and treaty-breakers. But it seemed clear that the speech was aimed at Japan for her attack on China, and Italy and Germany for their activities in Spain. White House attachés said such an interpretation was valid.

It also seemed significant that when Mr. Roosevelt charged violations of the Covenant of the League of Nations, the Kellogg-Briand pact and the Nine-power treaty, he interpolated a reminder that we were signers of the latter two.

The crowd listened intently, remaining silent most of the time, but applauding his demands for world peace. It was evident from comments made in the crowd afterward that the tenor of the address was a surprise, but general approval was heard.

Chicago gave the President a hearty reception, throngs cheering him as he drove through the streets at the head of a parade to dedicate the city's new Outer Drive Bridge, and, later, on his way to luncheon with George Cardinal Mundelein.

The President declared in his address at the bridge ceremonies that "without a declaration of war and without warning or justification of any kind, civilians, including women and children, are being ruthlessly murdered with bombs from the air."

"In times of so-called peace ships are being attacked and sunk by submarines without cause or notice," he continued. "Nations are fomenting and taking sides in civil warfare in nations that have never done them any harm. Nations claiming freedom for themselves deny it to others.

"Innocent peoples and nations are being cruelly sacrificed to a greed for power and supremacy which is devoid of all sense of justice and humane consideration."

While the occasion of the speech was the dedication of the Outer Drive Bridge built with PWA funds, Mr. Roosevelt gave the bridge and the PWA only a scant half-minute before his face set hard, and, speaking very slowly, he went into the major points of the address, every sentence of which showed worry and a determination to take action "against a state of international anarchy and instability from which there is no escape through mere isolation or neutrality."

There was no specific indication as to any steps that might be taken. But Mr. Roosevelt, with an interpolated "mark you well," spoke with even greater seriousness as he said:

"When an epidemic of physical disease starts to spread, the community approves and joins in a quarantine of the patients in order to protect the health of the community against the spread of the disease."

White House attachés said the President was canvassing every possible method of putting the speech into effect, including the possibility of an international conference. They also said that no foreign government had been consulted before the speech was made.

Although pledging himself to every effort to maintain neutrality and keep the nation out of war, Mr. Roosevelt warned that "we cannot have complete protection in a world of disorder in which our confidence and security have broken down."

"If civilization is to survive, the principles of the Prince of Peace must be restored," he said. "Shattered trust between nations must be revived."

Waving farewell to the West at Chicago's La Salle Street Station, the President started for Hyde Park at 2 P.M. (Central standard time) after a triumphal tour which took him through the Pacific Northwest. He will arrive at Hyde Park tomorrow morning at 9:30 o'clock (Eastern standard time).

Mr. Roosevelt's progress through the streets of Chicago was made through a cloud of ticker tape and sheets torn from telephone directories, which rained down on the parade from the time he left Union Station, where his train arrived, until he had passed through the Loop district. Three thousand city and park policemen kept back the crowds.

Later several thousand persons waited patiently outside Cardinal Mundelein's residence at State Street and North Avenue to catch another glimpse of the President as he was escorted by the red-robed Cardinal down a long, enclosed ramp to his automobile.

Their luncheon was private, but newspaper men and a few others were made welcome at a buffet luncheon. The Cardinal and the President posed together for a picture.

The public's generous reception to the President began when the train arrived from St. Paul at 9:30 A.M. He was met at the station by Mayor Edward J. Kelly, Senator William H. Dieterich and Secretary Harold L. Ickes, with hordes of lesser political figures. Many of them were received by Mr. Roosevelt in the hour before the parade started.

At the bridge ceremonies Mayor Kelly and Secretary Ickes paid tribute to Mr. Roosevelt's leadership in pulling the country out of the depression.

Afterward the parade proceeded along the Outer Drive toward the Cardinal's residence.

Japanese soldiers bayonet Chinese prisoners of war in Manchuria (renamed Manchukuo), about 1940.

"The epidemic of world lawlessness is spreading."

The Quarantine Speech of Franklin D. Roosevelt

Franklin D. Roosevelt delivered his Quarantine Speech on October 5, 1937, in Chicago, where he had traveled to celebrate the opening of an important federally sponsored public works project. FDR's choice of Chicago as a venue for his speech defending interventionism was bold because the Midwest was well known as the heartland of isolationism. "By speaking in Chicago," historian David M. Kennedy has written, "Roosevelt was apparently bearding the isolationist lion in his den."

I am glad to come once again to Chicago and especially to have the opportunity of taking part in the dedication of this important project of civic betterment.

On my trip across the continent and back, I have been shown many evidences of the result of common-sense cooperation between municipalities and the federal government, and I have been greeted by tens of thousands of Americans who have told me in every look and word that their material and spiritual well-being has made great strides forward in the past few years.

And yet, as I have seen with my own eyes the prosperous farms, the thriving factories, and the busy railroads—as I have seen the happiness and security and peace which covers our wide land—almost inevitably I have been compelled to contrast our peace with very different scenes being enacted in other parts of the world.

It is because the people of the United States under modern conditions must, for the sake of their own future, give thought to the rest of the world, that I, as the responsible executive head of the nation, have chosen this great inland city and this gala occasion to speak to you on a subject of definite national importance.

The political situation in the world, which of late has been growing progressively worse, is such as to cause grave concern and anxiety to all the peoples and nations who wish to live in peace and amity with their neighbors.

Some fifteen years ago, the hopes of mankind for a continuing era of international peace were raised to great heights when more than sixty nations solemnly pledged themselves not to resort to arms in furtherance of their national aims and policies. The high aspirations expressed in the Briand-Kellogg Peace Pact and the hopes for peace thus raised have of late given way to a haunting fear of calamity. The present reign of terror and international lawlessness began a few years ago.

It began through unjustified interference in the internal affairs of other nations or the invasion of alien territory in violation of treaties; and has now reached a stage where the very foundations of civilization are seriously threatened. The landmarks and traditions which have marked the progress of civilization toward a condition of law, order, and justice are being wiped away.

Without a declaration of war and without warning or justification of any kind, civilians, including vast numbers of women and children, are being ruthlessly murdered with bombs from the air. In times of so-called peace, ships are being attacked and sunk by submarines without cause or notice. Nations

Franklin Roosevelt delivers his Quarantine Speech at the dedication of the Outer Drive Bridge in Chicago on October 5, 1937.

are fomenting and taking sides in civil warfare in nations that have never done them any harm. Nations claiming freedom for themselves deny it to others.

Innocent peoples, innocent nations, are being cruelly sacrificed to a greed for power and supremacy which is devoid of all sense of justice and humane considerations.

To paraphrase a recent author, "perhaps we foresee a time when men, exultant in the technique of homicide, will rage so hotly over the world that every precious thing will be in danger, every book and picture and harmony, every treasure garnered through two millenniums, the small, the delicate, the defenseless—all will be lost or wrecked or utterly destroyed."

If those things come to pass in other parts of the world, let no one imagine that America will escape, that America may expect mercy, that this Western Hemisphere will not be attacked, and that it will continue tranquilly and peacefully to carry on the ethics and the arts of civilization.

If those days come, "there will be no safety by arms, no help from authority, no answer in science. The storm will rage till every flower of culture is trampled, and all human beings are leveled in a vast chaos."

If those days are not to come to pass—if we are to have a world in which we can breathe freely and live in amity without fear—the peace-loving nations must make a concerted effort to uphold laws and principles on which alone peace can rest secure.

The peace-loving nations must make a concerted effort in opposition to those violations of treaties and those ignorings of humane instincts which today are creating a state of international anarchy and instability from which there is no escape through mere isolation or neutrality.

Those who cherish their freedom and recognize and respect the equal right of their neighbors to be free and live in peace must work together for the triumph of law and moral principles in order that peace, justice, and confidence may prevail in the world. There must be a return to a belief in the pledged word, in the value of a signed treaty. There must be recognition of the fact that national morality is as vital as private morality.

A bishop wrote me the other day: "It seems to me that something greatly needs to be said in behalf of ordinary humanity against the present practice of carrying the horrors of war to helpless civilians, especially women and children. It may be that such a protest might be regarded by many, who claim to be realists, as futile, but may it not be that the heart of mankind is so filled with horror at the present needless suffering that that force could be mobilized in sufficient volume to lessen such cruelty in the days ahead. Even though it may take twenty years, which God forbid, for civilization to make effective its corporate protest against this barbarism, surely strong voices may hasten the day."

There is a solidarity and interdependence about the modern world, both technically and morally, which makes it impossible for any nation completely to isolate itself from economic and political upheavals in the rest of the world, especially when such upheavals appear to be spreading and not declining. There can be no stability or peace either within nations or between nations except under laws and moral standards adhered to by all. International anarchy destroys every foundation for peace. It jeopardizes either the immediate or the future security of every nation, large or small. It is, therefore, a matter of vital interest and concern to the people of the United States that the sanctity of international treaties and the maintenance of international morality be restored.

The overwhelming majority of the peoples and nations of the world today want to live in peace. They seek the removal of barriers against trade. They want to exert themselves in industry, in agriculture, and in business, that they may increase their wealth through the production of wealth-producing goods rather than striving to produce military planes and bombs and machine guns and cannon for the destruction of human lives and useful property.

In those nations of the world which seem to be piling armament on armament for purposes of aggression, and those other nations which fear acts of aggression against them and their security, a very high proportion of their national income is being spent directly for armaments. It runs from thirty to as high as fifty percent. We are fortunate. The proportion that we in the United States spend is far less—eleven or twelve percent.

How happy we are that the circumstances of the moment permit us to put our money into bridges and boulevards, dams and reforestation, the conservation of our soil and many other kinds of useful works rather than into huge standing armies and vast supplies of implements of war. I am compelled and you are compelled, nevertheless, to look ahead. The peace, the freedom, and the security of ninety percent of the population of the world is being jeopardized by the remaining ten percent, who are threatening a breakdown of all international order and law. Surely the ninety percent who want to live in peace under law and in accordance with moral standards that have received almost universal acceptance through the centuries can and must find some way to make their will prevail.

The situation is definitely of universal concern. The questions involved relate not merely to violations of specific provisions of particular treaties; they are questions of war and of peace, of international law and especially of principles of humanity. It is true that they involve definite violations of agreements and especially of the Covenant of the League of Nations, the Briand-Kellogg Pact, and the Nine Power Treaty. But they also involve problems of world economy, world security, and world humanity.

It is true that the moral consciousness of the world must recognize the importance of removing injustices and well-founded grievances; but at the same time it must be aroused to the cardinal necessity of honoring sanctity of treaties, of respecting the rights and liberties of others, and of putting an end to acts of international aggression.

It seems to be unfortunately true that the epidemic of world lawlessness is spreading.

When an epidemic of physical disease starts to spread, the community approves and joins in a quarantine of the patients in order to protect the health of the community against the spread of the disease.

It is my determination to pursue a policy of peace. It is my determination to adopt every practicable measure to avoid involvement in war. It ought to be inconceivable that in this modern era, and in the face of experience, any nation could be so foolish and ruthless as to run the risk of plunging the whole world into war by invading and violating, in contravention of solemn treaties, the territory of other nations that have done them no real harm and are too weak to protect themselves adequately. Yet the peace of the world and the welfare and security of every nation, including our own, is today being threatened by that very thing.

No nation which refuses to exercise forbearance and to respect the freedom and rights of others can long remain strong and retain the confidence and respect of other nations. No nation ever loses its dignity or its good standing by conciliating its differences and by exercising great patience with, and consideration for, the rights of other nations.

War is a contagion, whether it be declared or undeclared. It can engulf states and peoples remote from the original scene of hostilities. We are determined to keep out of war, yet we cannot insure ourselves against the disastrous effects of war and the dangers of involvement. We are adopting such measures as will minimize our risk of involvement, but we cannot have complete protection in a world of disorder in which confidence and security have broken down.

If civilization is to survive, the principles of the Prince of Peace must be restored. Trust between nations must be revived.

Most important of all, the will for peace on the part of peace-loving nations must express itself to the end that nations that may be tempted to violate their agreements and the rights of others will desist from such a course. There must be positive endeavors to preserve peace. America hates war. America hopes for peace. Therefore, America actively engages in the search for peace.

2.

German Preparations for War

November 1937

With the surrender of the Central Powers in November 1918, Woodrow Wilson turned all of his energies to the task of brokering a fair and lasting peace. Some of his ideas, such as the creation of a League of Nations, were quickly accepted by Britain and France at the Versailles peace conference; others, however, such as national self-determination for ethnic groups, were just as quickly tabled. Furthermore,

although the United States was willing to give up its share of the spoils of war, the British and French were not. They had just endured four years of horrendous trench warfare and therefore felt completely entitled to strip Germany of its colonies and impose staggeringly high reparations payments.

This humiliation was never forgotten by the Nazis, who eventually used resentment over Versailles to topple the shaky Weimar Republic. Nazi mastermind Adolf Hitler had spent the Great War as a lance corporal, running dispatches for the officers of the Sixteenth Bavarian Reserve Infantry Regiment. As he wrote later in *Mein Kampf,* "The flush of indignation and shame [at Germany's surrender] burned in my cheek...[and] in the next few days I became conscious of my own fate." He had resolved to become a politician.

During the next decade and a half, Hitler skillfully exploited the issue of Germany's prostrate economy—a direct result of Versailles, he insisted—to win ominous gains for the Nazis in the regular parliamentary elections. Finally, on

January 30, 1933, he became German chancellor. Just three weeks later, when a mysterious fire destroyed the Reichstag, a well-prepared Hitler used the crisis as an excuse to assume emergency powers and purge the police. Meanwhile, the private Nazi militia known as the Sturmabteilung (SA) was given "freedom of the streets" to conduct a campaign of political terror that resulted in another Nazi electoral victory on March 5. This victory, in turn, produced the Reichstag votes necessary to pass the Enabling Act, which created a de facto Nazi dictatorship with Hitler at its head.

Thus ended Germany's brief flirtation with democracy. Most Germans initially viewed the Nazi regime as a welcome change from the instability and failure of the Weimar years. They also supported the massive new rearmament program, which not only served the country's economic needs but also helped ease the widely felt "shame" of Versailles. Yet Germany, as Japan, couldn't grow entirely on its own; its needs for food and raw materials were simply too great to be met domestically. Therefore, its *Führer* began looking elsewhere.

Adolf Hitler at a Nazi party rally in Nuremberg, 1928. Eight years later, Hitler remilitarized the Rhineland (in violation of the Locarno treaties of 1925) and, with Benito Mussolini, formed the Berlin-Rome Axis.

NAZIS FURTHER CUT USE OF FOOD FATS

Every Household Required to Report Regularly Its Per Capita Consumption

BERLIN, Nov. 29—The Food Administration issued today two instructions rationing the consumption of butter and other fats "to avoid every unnecessary consumption and generally reduce the present excessive consumption to about pre-war levels."

The present fat consumption is 29.3 per cent per capita above 1913, butter showing an increase of 25.8 per cent, margarine an increase of 124.2 per cent and lard a decrease of 9.5 per cent.

The contemplated curtailment may appear incongruous to the outside world at a time when, in addition to continued rearmament and construction under the Four-Year Plan, Chancellor Adolf Hitler announces grandiose schemes for the reconstruction of Berlin, Hamburg and Munich. But there is nothing incongruous about it to a National Socialist regime, which, moving in the direction of a closed national economy, makes careful differentiation between consumption of domestic materials and consumption of imported goods. Buildings can be produced mostly from domestic materials, but half the fat consumed must still be imported—like many armament raw materials, which come first.

Compared with 1932, net fat imports already have been reduced from 1,157,000 tons to 983,000 tons last year, and will be still lower this year. Most of this reduction has been accomplished, more-over, at the expense of the United States, which in 1932 sold Germany 85,400 tons of lard, and not one pound during the first half of this year.

Under the new rations system, which expands and protects the existing one, each household must fill out two lists, indicating by name, profession and date of birth every person eating regularly within the "boarding community." One list is for butter and the second for lard, bacon and raw fats.

These lists are deposited with butter and meat shops, which become part of the administrative machinery. They issue customers' cards, which permit each household to draw a definite quantity of fat products per capita as fixed from time to time. Butter and other fats produced at home or obtained from other sources must likewise be listed.

According to the National Socialist explanation, this curtailment need not mean further tightening of the belt, because fats can be replaced in the diet by sugar, of which Germany has plenty. The whole increase in fat consumption is, in fact, attributed to a steep rise in the sugar price.

It is pointed out that even such butter-producing countries as Switzerland, Sweden and Denmark consume considerably less butter per capita than Germany but nearly twice as much sugar.

"A problem of space."

The Hossbach Memorandum

Whether Adolf Hitler spent the mid-1930s consciously planning for world war remains a debated topic. Much of that debate focuses on the Hossbach Memorandum—a collection of notes taken by Col. Friedrich Hossbach, Hitler's Wehrmacht adjutant, at a top-secret meeting held on November 5, 1937, at the Reich Chancellery in Berlin. Although Hitler's logic is at times difficult to follow, one cannot miss the basic point that, in his view, Germany's economic survival depended entirely upon its ability to expand its territory by conquest.

Notes on the Conference in the Reichskanzlei on 5 Nov. 1937 from 1615–2030 Hours

Present: The Fuehrer and Reich Chancellor
> The Reichsminister for War, Generalfeldmarschall von Blomberg
> The C-in-C Army, Generaloberst Freiherr von Fritsch
> The C-in-C Navy, Generaladmiral Dr. h. c. Raeder
> The C-in-C Luftwaffe, Generaloberst Goering
> The Reichsminister for Foreign Affairs, Freiherr von Neurath
> Oberst Hossbach

The Fuehrer stated initially that the subject matter of today's conference was of such high importance that its further detailed discussion would probably take place in Cabinet sessions. However, he, the Fuehrer, had decided NOT to discuss this matter in the larger circle of the Reich Cabinet, because of its importance. His subsequent statements were the result of detailed deliberations and of the experiences of his $4^1/_2$ years in government; he desired to explain to those present his fundamental ideas on the possibilities and necessities of expanding our foreign policy and in the interests of a far-sighted policy he requested that his statements be looked upon in the case of his death as his last will and testament.

The Fuehrer then stated:

The aim of German policy is the security and the preservation of the nation and its propagation. This is, consequently, a problem of space.

The German nation is composed of 85 million people, which, because of the number of individuals and the compactness of habitation, form a homogeneous European racial body which cannot be found in any other country. On the other hand, it justifies the demand for larger living space more than for any other nation. If no political body exists in space corresponding to the German racial body, then that is the consequence of several centuries of historical development, and should this political condition continue to exist, it will represent the greatest danger to the preservation of the German nation at its present high level. An arrest of the deterioration of the German element in Austria and Czechoslovakia is just as little possible as the preservation of the present state in Germany itself. Instead of

The banner hoisted by these Nazis, marching in 1927, proclaims, "Death to Marxism."

growth, sterility will be introduced, and as a consequence, tensions of a social nature will appear after a number of years, because political and philosophical ideas are of a permanent nature only as long as they are able to produce the basis for the realization of the actual claim of existence of a nation. The German future is therefore dependent exclusively on the solution of the need for living space. Such a solution can be sought naturally only for a limited period, about 1–3 generations.

Before touching upon the question of solving the need for living space, it must be decided whether a solution of the German position with a good future can be attained, either by way of an autarchy or by way of an increased share in universal commerce and industry.

Autarchy: Execution will be possible only with strict National-Socialist State policy, which is the basis; assuming this can be achieved the results are as follows:

A. In the sphere of raw materials, only limited, but NOT total autarchy can be attained:

    1. Wherever coal can be used for the extraction of raw materials, autarchy is feasible.

    2. In the case of ores, the position is much more difficult. Requirements in iron and light metals can be covered by ourselves. Copper and tin, however, can NOT.

    3. Cellular materials can be covered by ourselves as long as sufficient wood supplies exist. A permanent solution is not possible.

    4. Edible fats—possible.

B. In the case of foods, the question of an autarchy must be answered with a definite "NO."

The general increase of living standards, compared with 30–40 years ago, brought about a simultaneous increase of the demand for an increase of personal consumption—even among the producers, the farmers, themselves. The proceeds from the production increase in agriculture have been used for covering the increase in demands; therefore, they represent no absolute increase in production. A further increase in production by making greater demands on the soil is not possible because it already shows signs of deterioration due to the use of artificial fertilizers, and it is therefore certain that, even with the greatest possible increase in production, participation in the world market could NOT be avoided.

The considerable expenditure of foreign currency to secure food by import, even in periods when harvests are good, increases catastrophically when the harvest is really poor. The possibility of this catastrophe increases correspondingly to the increase in population, and the annual 560,000 excess in births would bring about an increased consumption in bread, because the child is a greater bread-eater than the adult.

Permanently to counter the difficulties of food supplies by lowering the standard of living and by rationalization is impossible in a continent which had developed an approximately equivalent standard of living. As the solving of the unemployment problem has brought into effect the complete power of consumption, some small corrections in our agricultural home production will be possible, but NOT a wholesale alteration of the standard of food consumption. Consequently, autarchy becomes impossible, specifically in the sphere of food supplies as well as generally.

Participation in World Economy: There are limits to this which we are unable to transgress. The market fluctuations would be an obstacle to a secure foundation of the German position; international commercial agreements do NOT offer any guarantee for practical execution. It must be considered on principle that since the World War (1914–18) an industrialization has taken place in countries which formerly exported food. We live in a period of economic empires, in which the tendency to colonize again approaches the condition which originally motivated colonization; in Japan and Italy, economic motives are the basis of their will to expand, and the economic need will also drive Germany to it. Countries outside the great economic empires have special difficulties in expanding economically.

The upward tendency, which has been caused in the world economy due to armament competition, can never form a permanent basis for an economic settlement, and this latter is also hampered by the economic disruption caused by Bolshevism. It is a pronounced military weakness of those States who base their existence on export. As our exports and imports are carried out over those sea lanes which are ruled by Britain, it is more a question of security of transport rather than one of foreign currency, and this explains the great weakness in our food situation in wartime. The only way out, and one which may appear imaginary, is the securing of greater living space, an endeavor which at all times has been the cause of the formation of states and of movements of nations. It is explicable that this tendency finds no interest in Geneva and in satisfied States. Should the security of our food position be our foremost thought, then the space required for this can only be sought in Europe, but we will not copy liberal capitalist policies which rely on exploiting colonies. It is NOT a case of conquering people but of conquering agriculturally useful space. It would also be more to the purpose to seek raw material–producing territory in Europe directly adjoining the Reich and not overseas, and this solution would have to be brought into effect in one or two generations. What would be required at a later date over and above this must be left to subsequent generations. The development of great world-wide national bodies is naturally a slow process and the German people, with its strong racial root, has for this purpose the most favorable foundations in the heart of the European Continent. The history of all times—Roman Empire, British Empire—has proved that every space expansion can only be effected by breaking resistance and taking risks. Even setbacks are unavoidable; neither formerly nor today has space been found without an owner; the attacker always comes up against the proprietor.

The question for Germany is where the greatest possible conquest could be made at lowest cost.

German politics must reckon with its two hateful enemies, England and France, to whom a strong German colossus in the center of Europe would be intolerable. Both these states would oppose a further reinforcement of Germany, both in Europe and overseas, and in this opposition they would have the support of all parties. Both countries would view the building of German military strongpoints overseas as a threat to their overseas communications, as a security measure for German commerce, and retrospectively a strengthening of the German position in Europe....

The German question can be solved only by way of force, and this is never without risk. The battles of Frederick the Great for Silesia and Bismarck's wars against Austria and France had been a tremendous risk, and the speed of Prussian action in 1870 had prevented Austria from participating in the war. If we place the decision to apply force with risk at the head of the following expositions, then we are left to reply to the questions "when" and "how." In this regard, we have to decide upon three different cases:

Case 1. Period 1943–45. After this, we can only expect a change for the worse. The re-arming of the Army, the Navy and the Air Force, as well as the formation of the Officers' Corps, are practically concluded. Our material equipment and armaments are modern; with further delay, the danger of their becoming out-of-date will increase. In particular, the secrecy of "special weapons" cannot always be safeguarded. Enlistment of reserves would be limited to the current recruiting age groups and an addition from older, untrained groups would be no longer available.

In comparison with the re-armament, which will have been carried out at that time by the other nations, we shall decrease in relative power. Should we not act until 1943–45, then, dependent on the absence of reserves, any year could bring about the food crisis, for the countering of which we do NOT possess the necessary foreign currency. This must be considered as a "point of weakness in the regime." Over and above that, the world will anticipate our action and will increase countermeasures yearly. Whilst other nations isolate themselves, we should be forced on the offensive.

What the actual position would be in the years 1943–1945, no one knows today. It is certain, however, that we can wait no longer.

On the one side the large armed forces, with the necessity for securing their upkeep, the aging of the Nazi movement and of its leaders, and on the other side the prospect of a lowering of the standard of living and a drop in the birth rate, leaves us no other choice than to act. If the Fuehrer is still living, then it will be his irrevocable decision to solve the German space problem no later than 1943–45. The necessity for action before 1943–45 will come under consideration in cases 2 and 3.

Case 2. Should the social tensions in France lead to an internal political crisis of such dimensions that it absorbs the French Army and thus renders it incapable for employment in war against Germany, then the time for action against Czechoslovakia has come.

Case 3. It would be equally possible to act against Czechoslovakia if France should be so tied up by a war against another State, that it cannot "proceed" against Germany.

For the improvement of our military-political position, it must be our first aim, in every case of entanglement by war, to conquer Czechoslovakia and Austria simultaneously, in order to remove any threat from the flanks in case of a possible advance westwards. In the case of a conflict with France, it would hardly be necessary to assume that Czechoslovakia would declare war on the same day as France. However, Czechoslovakia's desire to participate in the war will increase proportionally to the degree to which we are being weakened. Its actual participation could make itself felt by an attack on Silesia, either towards the north or the west.

Once Czechoslovakia is conquered—and a mutual frontier, Germany-Hungary, is obtained—then a neutral attitude by Poland in a German-French conflict could more easily be relied upon. Our agreements with Poland remain valid only as long as Germany's strength remains unshakeable; should Germany have any setbacks, then an attack by Poland against East Prussia, perhaps also against Pomerania and Silesia, must be taken into account.

Assuming a development of the situation, which would lead to a planned attack on our part in the years 1943–45, then the behavior of France, Poland, and Russia would probably have to be judged in the following manner:

The Fuehrer believes personally that in all probability England and perhaps also France have already silently written off Czechoslovakia and that they have got used to the idea that this question would one day be cleaned up by Germany. The difficulties in the British Empire and the prospect of being entangled in another long-drawn-out European War, were decisive factors in the non-participation of England in a war against Germany. The British attitude would certainly NOT remain without influence on France's attitude. An attack by France without British support is hardly probable assuming that its offensive would stagnate along our western fortifications. Without England's support, it would also NOT be necessary to take into consideration a march by France through Belgium and Holland, and this would also not have to be reckoned with by us in case of a conflict with France, as in every case it would have as consequence the enmity of Great Britain. Naturally, we should in every case have to bar our frontier during the operation of our attacks against Czechoslovakia and Austria. It must be taken into consideration here that Czechoslovakia's defence measures will increase in strength from year to year and that a consolidation of the inside values of the Austrian army will also be effected in the course of years. Although the population of Czechoslovakia in the first place is not a thin one, the embodiment of Czechoslovakia and Austria would nevertheless constitute the conquest of food for 5–6 million people, on the basis that a compulsory emigration of 2 million from Czechoslovakia and of 1 million from Austria could be carried out. The annexation of the two States to Germany militarily and politically would constitute a considerable relief, owing to shorter and better frontiers, the freeing of fighting personnel for other purposes, and the possi-

An inspector at a German weapons forge performs a final check on some artillery shells, about 1940.

bility of reconstituting new armies up to a strength of about 12 divisions, representing a new division per 1 million population.

No opposition to the removal of Czechoslovakia is expected on the part of Italy; however, it cannot be judged today what would be her attitude in the Austrian question since it would depend largely on whether the Duce were alive at the time or not.

The measure and speed of our action would decide Poland's attitude. Poland will have little inclination to enter the war against a victorious Germany, with Russia in its rear.

Military participation by Russia must be countered by the speed of our operations; it is a question whether this need be taken into consideration at all in view of Japan's attitude.

Should Case 2 occur—paralyzation of France by a civil war—then the situation should be utilized at any time for operations against Czechoslovakia, as Germany's most dangerous enemy would be eliminated.

The Fuehrer sees Case 3 looming nearer; it could develop from the existing tensions in the Mediterranean, and should it occur he has firmly decided to make use of it any time, perhaps even as early as 1938....

Generaloberst von Fritsch mentioned that it was the purpose of a study which he had laid on for this winter to investigate the possibilities of carrying out operations against Czechoslovakia with special consideration of the conquest of the Czechoslovakian system of fortifications; the Generaloberst also stated that owing to the prevailing conditions he would have to relinquish his leave abroad, which was to begin on 10 November. This intention was countermanded by the Fuehrer, who gave as a reason that the possibility of the conflict was not to be regarded as being so imminent. In reply to the remark by the Minister for Foreign Affairs, that an Italian-English-French conflict be not as near as the Fuehrer appeared to assume, the Fuehrer stated that the date which appeared to him to be a possibility was summer 1938. In reply to statements by Generalfeldmarschall von Blomberg and Generaloberst von Fritsch regarding England and France's attitude, the Fuehrer repeated his previous statements and said that he was convinced of Britain's non-participation and that consequently he did not believe in military action by France against Germany. Should the Mediterranean conflict already mentioned lead to a general mobilization in Europe, then we should have to commence operations against Czechoslovakia immediately. If, however, the powers who are not participating in the war should declare their disinterestedness, then Germany would, for the time being, have to side with this attitude.

In view of the information given by the Fuehrer, Generaloberst Goering considered it imperative to think of a reduction or abandonment of our military undertaking in Spain. The Fuehrer agreed to this in so far as he believed this decision should be postponed for a suitable date.

The second part of the discussion concerned material armament questions.

3.

The Rape of Nanking

December 1937

Militarism had been on the rise in Japan since that nation's victory in the Russo-Japanese War of 1904–1905. During the international depression of the early 1930s, however, the political influence of Japan's military leaders became even more pronounced. Like Hitler, they came to believe that their country's economic future depended primarily on its access to raw materials, especially food and oil.

Also like Hitler, they concluded that the only way to ensure such access was through conquest. Beginning as early as 1931 with their annexation of Manchuria, the Japanese set out to create what they later termed a Greater East Asia Co-Prosperity Sphere. This was their euphemism for a military empire that would encompass Chinese rice, Dutch East Indian oil, and Malaysian rubber, among other commodities. Meanwhile, they defended their actions with the claim that they were "liberating" colonized peoples and recovering "Asia for the Asiatics."

During the night of July 7, 1937, Japanese troops skirmished with Chinese units guarding the Marco Polo Bridge about nine miles southwest of Peking. By this time, six years after the annexation of Manchuria, Japan controlled nearly all of northern China—an expansion made much easier by the Chinese civil war being fought between Chiang Kai-shek's Nationalists and the Communists under Mao Tse-tung. By

1937, however, Soviet premier Joseph Stalin, fearing a strong Japanese presence in China, had engineered a reconciliation, permitting the Chinese to present a united front. Feeling empowered, Chiang refused to back down, tensions escalated, and the Japanese soon launched a full-scale invasion. They took Peking by storm in early August and afterward moved their forces south to Shanghai. Chinese defenders held out for three months, but the great port city finally fell in early November. Next, the Japanese moved up the Yangtze Valley to invest the Chinese capital at Nanking.

Determined to block this westward movement into China's interior, Chiang committed hundreds of thousands of soldiers to the defense of Nanking. The final result, however, was no different from that experienced by Chiang's soldiers at Shanghai. The Chinese fought courageously yet could not overcome the Japanese army's superior weaponry—and when the fighting was over, the retribution came.

BUTCHERY MARKED CAPTURE OF NANKING

All Captives Slain; Civilians Also Killed as the Japanese Spread Terror in Nanking

By F. TILLMAN DURDIN

ABOARD THE U.S.S. OAHU at Shanghai, Dec. 17—Through wholesale atrocities and vandalism at Nanking the Japanese Army has thrown away a rare opportunity to gain the respect and confidence of the Chinese inhabitants and of foreign opinion there.

The collapse of Chinese authority and the break-up of the Chinese Army left many Chinese in Nanking ready to respond to order and organization, which seemed in prospect with the entry of the Japanese troops. A tremendous sense of relief over the outlook for a cessation of the fearful bombardment and the elimination of the threat of serious disorders by the Chinese troops pervaded the Chinese populace when the Japanese took over control within the walls.

It was felt Japanese rule might be severe, at least until war conditions were over. Two days of Japanese occupation changed the whole outlook. Wholesale looting, the violation of women, the murder of civilians, the eviction of Chinese from their homes, mass executions of war prisoners and the impressing of able-bodied men turned Nanking into a city of terror.

The killing of civilians was widespread. Foreigners who traveled widely through the city Wednesday found civilian dead on every street. Some of the victims were aged men, women and children.

Policemen and firemen were special objects of attack. Many victims were bayoneted and some of the wounds were barbarously cruel.

Any person who ran because of fear or excitement was likely to be killed on the spot as was any one caught by roving patrols in streets or alleys after dusk. Many slayings were witnessed by foreigners.

The Japanese looting amounted almost to plundering of the entire city. Nearly every building was entered by Japanese soldiers, often under the eyes of their officers, and the men took whatever they wanted. The Japanese soldiers often impressed Chinese to carry their loot.

Food apparently was in first demand. Everything else that was useful or valuable had its turn. Peculiarly disgraceful was the robbing of refugees by soldiers who conducted mass searches in the refugee centers and took money and valuables, often the entire possessions of the unfortunates.

The staff of the American Mission University Hospital was stripped of cash and watches. Other possessions were taken from the nurses' dormitory. The faculty houses of American Ginling College were invaded by soldiers who took food and valuables.

The hospital and the Ginling College buildings were flying American flags and bore on the doors official proclamations in Chinese from the United States Embassy denoting American ownership.

Even the home of the United States Ambassador was invaded. When informed by excited embassy servants of this incursion, Arthur Menken, Paramount newsreel cameraman, and the writer confronted five soldiers in the Ambassador's kitchen and demanded that they leave. The men departed sullenly and sheepishly. Their only loot was a flashlight.

Many Chinese men reported to foreigners the abduction and rape of wives and daughters.

A Japanese machine gunner patrols a street in Shanghai, China, September 1937.

These Chinese appealed for aid, which the foreigners usually were powerless to give.

The mass executions of war prisoners added to the horrors the Japanese brought to Nanking. After killing the Chinese soldiers who threw down their arms and surrendered, the Japanese combed the city for men in civilian garb who were suspected of being former soldiers.

In one building in the refugee zone 400 men were seized. They were marched off, tied in batches of fifty, between lines of riflemen and machine gunners, to the execution ground.

Just before boarding the ship for Shanghai the writer watched the execution of 200 men on the Bund. The killings took ten minutes. The men were lined against a wall and shot. Then a number of Japanese, armed with pistols, trod nonchalantly around the crumpled bodies, pumping bullets into any that were still kicking.

The army men performing the gruesome job had invited navy men from the warships anchored off the Bund to view the scene. A large group of military spectators apparently greatly enjoyed the spectacle.

When the first column of Japanese troops marched from the South Gate up Chungshan Road toward the city's Big Circle, small knots of Chinese civilians broke into scattering cheers, so great was their relief that the siege was over and so high were their hopes that the Japanese would restore peace and order. There are no cheers in Nanking now for the Japanese.

By despoiling the city and population the Japanese have driven deeper into the Chinese a repressed hatred that will smolder through years as forms of the anti-Japanism that Tokyo professes to be fighting to eradicate from China.

The capture of Nanking was the most overwhelming defeat suffered by the Chinese and one of the most tragic military debacles in the history of modern warfare. In attempting to defend Nanking the Chinese allowed themselves to be surrounded and then systematically slaughtered.

The defeat caused the loss of tens of thousands of trained soldiers and millions of dollars' worth of equipment and the demoralization of the Chinese forces in the Yangtze Valley whose courage and spirit in the early phases of the warfare enabled the Chinese troops to hold up the Japanese advance around Shanghai nearly two months. Generalissimo Chiang Kai-shek was responsible to a great degree because against the unanimous counsel of his German military advisers and the opinions of his chief of staff, General Pai Chung-hsi, he permitted the futile defense of the city.

More immediately responsible was General Tang Sheng-chih and associated division commanders who deserted their troops and fled, not even attempting to make the most of a desperate situation following the entry of the first Japanese troops inside the city's walls.

The flight of the many Chinese soldiers was possible by only a few exits. Instead of sticking by their men to hold the invaders at bay with a few strategically placed units while the others withdrew, many army leaders deserted, causing panic among the rank and file.

Those who failed to escape through the gate leading to Hsiakwan and from there across the Yangtze were caught and executed.

The fall of Nanking was predicted in most details two weeks before the Japanese entered. Overwhelming the ill-equipped Chinese troops pitted against them around Kwangteh and northward, the Japanese broke through and captured Wuhu and other points above Nanking on the Yangtze some days before entering the capital. They thus blocked the Chinese Army's chance to retire upriver.

The superficial Chinese defenses some miles around Nanking were passed without great difficulty. By Dec. 9 the Japanese had reached the wall outside Kwanghwa gate. Driven back within the wall, 50,000 Chinese at first put up a stiff resistance. Japanese casualties were heavy as Chinese units on the wall and for miles outside contested the Japanese infiltration.

However, Japanese big guns and airplanes soon wiped out the Chinese near the wall, both outside and inside, shrapnel taking a particularly heavy toll. Meanwhile, the Japanese pushed around the wall, first threatening the Hsiakwan gate from the west.

When the invaders scaled the wall near the west gate Sunday noon behind a heavy barrage they started the Chinese collapse. Raw recruits of the Eighty-eighth Division bolted first and others soon followed. By evening masses of troops were streaming toward Hsiakwan gate, which was still in Chinese hands.

Officers gave up their attempt to handle the situation. Their men threw away their guns, shed their uniforms and donned civilian garb.

Driving through the city Sunday evening, I witnessed the wholesale undressing of an army that was almost comic. Many men shed their uniforms as they marched in formation toward Hsiakwan. Others ran into alleys to transform themselves into civilians. Some soldiers disrobed completely and then robbed civilians of their garments.

While some stubborn regiments continued on Monday to hold up the Japanese, the flight of most of the defenders continued. Hundreds surrendered to foreigners. Dozens of guns were thrust upon me by cowed men who only wanted to know what they could do to be saved from the approaching Japanese.

Hordes surrounded the safety-zone headquarters, turning in their guns, and even throwing them over the gate of the compound in their haste to shed military arms. The foreign committeemen at the safety zone accepted their surrender and interned them in buildings in the zone.

When the Japanese captured Hsiakwan gate they cut off all exit from the city while at least a third of the Chinese Army still was within the walls.

Because of the disorganization of the Chinese a number of units continued fighting Tuesday noon, many of these not realizing the Japanese had surrounded them and that their cause was hopeless. Japanese tank patrols systematically eliminated these.

Tuesday morning, while attempting to motor to Hsiakwan, I encountered a desperate group of about twenty-five Chinese soldiers who were still holding the Ningpo Guild Building in Chungshan Road. They later surrendered.

Thousands of prisoners were executed by the Japanese. Most of the Chinese soldiers who had been interned in the safety zone were shot en masse. The city was combed in a systematic house-to-house search for men having knapsack marks on their shoulders or other signs of having been soldiers. They were herded together and executed.

Many were killed where they were found, including men innocent of any army connection and many wounded soldiers and civilians. I witnessed three mass executions of prisoners within a few hours Wednesday. In one slaughter a tank gun was turned on a group of more than 100 soldiers at a bomb shelter near the Ministry of Communications.

A favorite method of execution was to herd groups of a dozen men at entrances of dugouts and to shoot them so the bodies toppled inside. Dirt then was shoveled in and the men buried.

Since the beginning of the Japanese assault on Nanking the city presented a frightful appearance. The Chinese facilities for the care of army wounded were tragically inadequate, so as early as a week ago injured men were seen often on the streets, some hobbling, others crawling along seeking treatment.

Civilian casualties also were heavy, amounting to thousands. The only hospital open was the American-managed University Hospital, and its facilities were inadequate for even a fraction of those hurt.

Nanking's streets were littered with dead. Sometimes bodies had to be moved before automobiles could pass.

The capture of Hsiakwan gate by the Japanese was accompanied by the mass killing of the defenders, who were piled up among the sandbags, forming a mound six feet high. Late Wednesday the Japanese had not removed the dead, and two days of heavy military traffic had been passing through, grinding over the remains of men, dogs and horses.

The Japanese appear to want the horrors to remain as long as possible, to impress on the Chinese the terrible results of resisting Japan.

Chungshan Road was a long avenue of filth and discarded uniforms, rifles, pistols, machine guns, fieldpieces, knives and knapsacks. In some places the Japanese had to hitch tanks to debris to clear the road.

The Chinese burned nearly all suburbs, including fine buildings and homes in Mausoleum Park. Hsiakwan is a mass of charred ruins. The Japanese seemingly avoided wrecking good buildings. The scarcity of air bombardments in the capture indicated their intention to avoid the destruction of buildings.

The Japanese even avoided bombing Chinese troop concentrations in built-up areas, apparently to preserve the buildings. The fine Ministry of Communications building was the only big government structure destroyed inside the city. It was fired by Chinese.

Nanking today is housing a terrorized population who, under alien domination, live in fear of death, torture and robbery. The graveyard of tens of thousands of Chinese soldiers may also be the graveyard of all Chinese hopes of resisting conquest by Japan.

"They wanted no observers."

George A. Fitch's Nanking diary

As the Japanese approached Nanking, Chiang's government fled upriver to Chungking, and many foreigners also left the capital, some boarding the U.S. gunboat *Panay,* then anchored in the Yangtze River. However, about twenty Europeans and Americans decided to stay, forming an International Committee for the Nanking Safety Zone. The purpose of their group, modeled on a committee set up earlier in Shanghai, was to protect Nanking's civilian population by establishing a demilitarized "safety zone" within the besieged capital. George A. Fitch, author of this account, served as director of the committee after the fall of Nanking on Sunday, December 12. The son of Presbyterian missionaries, Fitch had been born in China in 1883 and returned there after his own ordination to work with the Young Men's Christian Association.

What I am about to relate is anything but a pleasant story; in fact, it is so very unpleasant that I cannot recommend anyone without a strong stomach to read it. For it is a story of such crime and horror as to be almost unbelievable, the story of depredations of a horde of degraded criminals of incredible bestiality, who have been, and now are, working their will, unrestrained, on a peaceful, kindly, law-abiding people. Yet it is a story which I feel must be told, even if it is seen by only a few. I cannot rest until I have told it, and unfortunately, or perhaps fortunately, I am one of a very few who are in a position to tell it. It is not complete for it is only a small part of the whole; and God alone knows when I will be finished. I pray it may be soon—but I am afraid it is going to go on for many months to come, not just here but in other parts of China. I believe it has no parallel in modern history.

It is now Christmas Eve. I shall start with, say, December 10th. In these two short weeks, we here in Nanking have been through a siege; the Chinese army has left, defeated, and the Japanese has come in. On that day Nanking was still the beautiful city we were so proud of, with law and order still prevailing; today it is a city laid waste, ravaged, completely looted, much of it burned. Complete anarchy has reigned for ten days—it has been a hell on earth. Not that my life has been in serious danger at any time—though turning lust-mad, sometimes drunken soldiers out of houses where they were raping the women is not altogether a safe occupation; nor does one feel, perhaps, too sure of himself when he finds a bayonet at his chest or a revolver at his head and knows it is handled by someone who heartily wishes him out of the way. For the Japanese [army] is anything but pleased at our being here after having advised all foreigners to get out. They wanted no observers. But to have to stand by while even the very poor are having their last possessions taken from them—their last coin, their last bit of bedding (and it is freezing weather), the poor ricksha man his ricksha; while thousands of disarmed soldiers who had sought sanctuary with you, together with many hundreds of innocent civilians, are taken out before your eyes to be shot, or used for bayonet practice, and you have to listen to the sound of the guns that are killing them; over a thousand women kneel before you crying hysterically, begging you to save them from the beasts who are preying on them; to stand by and do nothing while your flag is taken down and insulted, not once but a dozen times, and your own home is being looted; and then to watch the city you have come to love and the institutions to which you had planned to devote your best years deliberately and systematically burned by fire—this is a hell I had never before envisaged.

We keep asking ourselves "How long can this last?" Day by day we are assured by the officials that things will be better *soon*, that "we will do our best"—but each day has been worse than the day before. And now we are told that a new division of 20,000 men are arriving. Will they have to have their toll of flesh and loot, of murder and rape? There will be little left to rob, for the city has been well nigh stripped clean. For the past week the soldiers have been busy loading their trucks with what they wanted from the stores and then setting fire to the buildings. And then there is the harrowing realization that we have only enough rice and flour for the 200,000 refugees for another three weeks and coal for ten days. Do you wonder that one awakes in the night in a cold sweat of fear and sleep for the rest of the night is gone? Even if we had food enough for three months, how are they going to be fed after

that? And with their homes burned, where are they going to live? They cannot continue much longer in their present terribly crowded condition; disease and pestilence must soon follow if they do.

Every day we call at the Japanese Embassy and present our protests, our appeals, our lists of authenticated reports of violence and crime. We are met with suave Japanese courtesy, but actually the officials there are powerless. The victorious army must have its rewards—and those rewards are to plunder, murder, rape at will, to commit acts of unbelievable brutality and savagery on the very people whom they have come to protect and befriend, as they have so loudly proclaimed to the world. In all modern history surely there is no page that will stand so black as that of the rape of Nanking.

To tell the whole story of these past ten days would take too long. The tragic thing is that by the time the truth gets out to the rest of the world it will be cold—it will no longer be "news." Anyway, the Japanese have undoubtedly been proclaiming abroad that they have established law and order in a city that had already been looted and burned, and that the downtrodden population had welcomed their benevolent army with open arms and a great flag-waving welcome. However, I am going to record some of the more important events of this period as I have jotted them down in my little diary, for they will at least be of interest to some of my friends and I shall have the satisfaction of having a permanent

Triumphant Japanese soldiers celebrate in front of the Governor's Palace in December 1937 after their occupation of Nanking, China. As many as three hundred thousand civilians were killed. Western protests were strongly worded but empty.

record of these unhappy days. It will probably extend beyond the date of this letter, for I do not antici-pate being able to get this off for some considerable time. The Japanese censorship will see to that! Our own Embassy officials and those of other countries together with some of the business men who went aboard the ill-fated *Panay* and the Standard Oil boats and other ships just before the capture of Nanking, confidently expecting to return within a week when they left, are still cooling their heels (those who haven't been killed or wounded by Japanese bombs and machine guns) out on the river or perhaps in one of the ports. We think it will be another fortnight before any of them is permitted to return, and longer than that before any of us is permitted to leave Nanking. We are virtually prisoners here.

Two weeks before the fall of the city our International Committee for Nanking Safety Zone had been negotiating with both the Chinese and Japanese for the recognition of a certain area in the city which would be kept free of soldiers and all military offices and which would not be bombed or shelled, a place where the remaining two hundred thousand of Nanking's population of one million could take refuge when things became too hot, for it had become quite obvious that the splendid resistance which the Chinese had put up for so long at Shanghai was now broken and their morale largely gone. The ter-rific punishment which they had taken from the superior artillery, tanks, and air force could not be endured forever and the successful landing of Japanese troops on Hangchow Bay attacking their flank and rear was the crowning event in their undoing. It seemed inevitable that Nanking must soon fall....

On Sunday the 12th I was busy at my desk in the Safety Zone all day long. We were using the former residence of Gen. Chang Chun, recently Minister of Foreign Affairs, as headquarters, so were very comfortably fixed, and incidentally had one of the best bomb-proof dugouts in all Nanking. Airplanes had been over us almost constantly for the past two days, but no one heeded them now, and the shell-fire had been terrific. The wall had been breached and the damage in the southern part of the city was tremendous. No one will ever know what the Chinese casualties were, but they must have been enor-mous. The Japanese say they themselves lost forty thousand men taking Nanking. The general rout must have started early that afternoon. Soldiers streamed through the city from the south, many of them passing through the Zone, but they were well behaved and orderly. Gen. Tang asked our assis-tance in arranging a truce with the Japanese and Mr. Sperling agreed to take a flag and message—but it was already too late. He [Tang] fled that evening, and as soon as news got out disorganization became general. There was panic as they [Tang's soldiers] made for the gate to Hsiakwan and the river. The road for miles was strewn with the equipment they cast away—rifles, ammunition, belts, uniforms, cars, trucks—everything in the way of army impedimenta.

Trucks and cars jammed, were overturned, caught fire; at the gate more cars jammed and were burned—a terrible holocaust—and the dead lay feet deep. The gate blocked, terror-mad soldiers scaled the wall and let themselves down on the other side with ropes, puttees and belts tied together, clothing torn in strips. Many fell and were killed. But at the river was perhaps the most appalling scene of all. A fleet of junks was there. It was totally inadequate for the horde that was now in a frenzy to cross to the north side. The overcrowded junks capsized, they sank, thousands drowned. Other thousands tried to make rafts of the lumber on the river front, only to suffer the same fate. Other thousands must have suc-ceeded in getting away, but many of these were probably bombed by Japanese planes a day or two later.

One small detail of three companies rallied under their officers, crossed the San Chia Ho three miles up the river and tried to attack the Japanese forces that were coming in from that direction, but were outnumbered and practically decimated. Only one seems to have succeeded in getting back. He hap-pened to be the brother of a friend of mine and appeared in my office the next morning to report the story. A fellow officer had drowned while the two of them were trying to swim the small tributary to the Yangtze which they had crossed before on rafts, and before daylight he had managed to scale the wall and slip in unobserved.

So ended the happy, peaceful, well-ordered, progressive regime which we had been enjoying here in Nanking and on which we had built our hopes for still better days. For the Japanese were already in the city and with them came terror and destruction and death. They were first reported in the Zone at eleven o'clock that morning, the 13th. I drove down with two of our committee members to meet them, just a small detachment at the southern entrance to the Zone. They showed no hostility, though a few moments later they killed twenty refugees who were frightened by their presence and ran from them. For it seems to be the rule here, as it was in Shanghai in 1932, that any who run must be shot or bayoneted.

Meanwhile we were busy at headquarters disarming soldiers who had been unable to escape and had come into the Zone for protection. We assured them that if they gave up their equipment their lives would be spared by the Japanese. But it was a vain promise. All would have preferred to die fighting, to being taken out and shot or sabred or used for bayonet practice, as they all were later on.

There was still some shell-fire that day, but very little that landed in the Zone. We discovered some fragments of shrapnel in our yard that evening; Dr. Wilson had a narrow escape from shrapnel bits that came through the window of his operating room while he was operating, and a shell passed through one of the new University dormitories; but there were no casualties. The Communications building, the most beautiful in all Nanking, with its superb ceremonial hall, was in flames, but whether from shell-fire or started by the retreating Chinese, we do not know.

On Tuesday the 14th the Japanese were pouring into the city—tanks, artillery, infantry, trucks. The reign of terror commenced, and it was to increase in severity and horror with each of the succeeding ten days. They were the conquerors of China's capital, the seat of the hated Chiang Kai-shek government; they were given free rein to do as they pleased. The proclamation on the handbills which airplanes scattered over the city, saying that the Japanese were the only real friends of the Chinese and would protect the good, of course meant no more than most of their statements. And to show their "sincerity" they raped, looted and killed at will. Men were taken from our refugee camps in droves, as we supposed at the time, for labor—but they have never been heard from again, nor will they be. A colonel and his staff called at my office and spent an hour trying to learn where the "six thousand disarmed soldiers" were. Four times that day Japanese soldiers came and tried to take our cars away. Others in the mean time succeeded in stealing three of our cars that were elsewhere. On Sone's they tore off the American flag and threw it on the ground, broke a window, and managed to get away all within the five minutes he had gone into Prof. C. Smith's house. They tried to steal our trucks—did succeed in getting two—so ever since it has been necessary for two Americans to spend most of their time riding trucks as they delivered rice and coal. Their experience in dealing daily with these Japanese car thieves would make an interesting story in itself. And at the University Hospital they took the watches and fountain pens from the nurses.

Durdin, of *The New York Times*, started for Shanghai by motor that day, though none of us had much faith he would get through, I hurriedly wrote a letter for him to take, but he was turned back at Kuyung. Steele, of the *Chicago Daily News*, managed to get out to the river and reported that a number of Japanese destroyers had just arrived. A lieutenant gave him the news of the sinking of the *Panay* but had no details, nor did he mention the other ships that were sunk. After all their efforts to have us go aboard, finally leaving us with a couple of lengths of rope, by which we could get down over the wall and to the river—it was ironical indeed that the *Panay* should be bombed and we still safe.

Mr. Rabe, our Chairman, Nanking head of Siemens China Company, and Smythe, our secretary, called at military headquarters in the hope of seeing the commanding officer and stopping the intolerable disorder, but had to wait until the next day as he had not yet entered the city. Their calls were quite useless anyway.

On Wednesday I drove around to my house, which is just outside the Zone, to see if everything was all right. Yesterday the gates were intact, but today the side gate was broken in, and the south door open, in spite of the American and Japanese proclamations with which they were sealed. My two American flags had been torn down and destroyed. I had no time to investigate, but asked a friendly looking major who had just moved in across the street to keep an eye on the place, which he promised to do. A staff officer from the Japanese Navy was waiting for me. He expressed his deep concern over the loss of the *Panay* but he too could give no details. The Navy would be glad to send a destroyer to Shanghai with any of the members of the American community who wished to go, also to send radio messages of purely a personal nature. He seemed somewhat disappointed in the brevity of the message I wrote out: "Wilbur, National Committee YMCA, Shanghai: All foreigners Nanking safe and well. Please inform interested parties"; also when I told him that with the exception of a couple of newspapermen the rest of us wished to stay in Nanking.

I offered to drive him back to his ship—he had been obliged to walk the four miles in—but half way we were stopped by an army major who told us that no civilians were allowed further north as they were still rounding up some Chinese soldiers and it was unsafe. We happened to be beside the Ministry of War at the time and it was all too evident that an execution was going on, hundreds of poor disarmed soldiers with many innocent civilians among them—the real reason for his not wanting me to go further. So Mr. Sekiguchi of H.I.J.M.S. *Seta* had to walk the rest of the way. But that afternoon I stole a march on the surly major: I went to Hsiakwan by back roads. At the gate I was stopped, but I had Smith of Reuters and Steele with me who were leaving on that destroyer, so we were finally allowed to pass. I have already described the conditions at that gate—we actually had to drive over masses of dead bodies 2 to 3 feet deep, and 90 feet in length, to get through. But the scene beggars description. I shall never forget that ride.

At the jetty we found Durdin of the *Times* and Art Mencken of Paramount Films, with whom I had just made the trip to the Northwest, to Shansi and Sian, already there, for they were going too, and I had promised to drive Durdin's car back to the American Embassy for him. Mr. Okamura of the Japanese Embassy, just arrived from Shanghai, was also there and gave us the names of the killed and wounded on the *Panay* and the Standard Oil boats, so I offered him a lift back to the city. But at the gate we were stopped again and this time the guard positively refused to let me enter. No foreigners were allowed to enter Nanking and the fact that I had just come from there made no difference. Even Mr. Okamura's appeals were in vain—the Embassy cuts no ice with the army in Japan. The only thing to do was to wait while Okamura took one of the cars to military headquarters and sent back a special pass. It took an hour and a half; but I had the November *Reader's Digest*, the last piece of mail to reach me from the outside, with me, so the time passed quickly. The stench at the gate was awful—and here and there the dogs were gnawing at the corpses.

4.

The *Anschluss*

March 1938

Adolf Hitler began writing *Mein Kampf* while serving a five-year prison term for leading the abortive Beer Hall Putsch of 1923. After only nine months, however, he was released from jail, with his book only half completed. Without giving up the project, Hitler decided to publish what he had, and the first volume of *Mein Kampf (My Struggle)* appeared soon after in 1925. By the time the second volume came

out in 1927, the work had become the standard of the Nazi movement. In it, Hitler sets forth his racial ideology and also proclaims the German need for *Lebensraum* ("living space"). He describes with great detail his vision of a Europe under the leadership of a resurrected Reich and makes plain his desire for an *Anschluss* ("union") of Germany with his native Austria.

At first, Nazi prospects in Austria appeared rather limited. Austrian chancellor Engelbert Dollfuss disliked the Austrian Nazis and strongly opposed any union with Germany (as did France and Italy). When the Austrian Nazis attempted to overthrow Dollfuss's government in July 1934, their coup attempt failed in all respects, except that it did succeed in assassinating the chancellor himself. Although Hitler denied German involvement, few believed him; more to the point, the Führer realized that *Anschluss* would require much more effort and preparation than he had previously anticipated.

Dollfuss's successor, Kurt von Schuschnigg, continued to affirm Austrian independence, yet Hitler's collaborators moved quietly and effectively to undermine Schuschnigg's control.

By February 1938, when Hitler summoned Schuschnigg to his retreat at Berchtesgaden, the Austrian chancellor had no longer the power to resist Hitler's demand that several Nazis be immediately included in Schuschnigg's cabinet. (The most important of these new ministers was Arthur Seyss-Inquart, who took over the interior ministry and thus gained authority over the police.) On March 9, however, Schuschnigg played an unexpected card, announcing that he would hold a plebiscite on March 13 so that the Austrian people could decide for themselves the question of *Anschluss*.

Expecting a sizable majority to vote against union, Hitler acted quickly. He ordered the Austrian Nazis to begin holding public demonstrations and called for Schuschnigg's resignation so that Seyss-Inquart might succeed him. Faced with the threat of an imminent German invasion, Schuschnigg ultimately complied; and in his first official act as Austrian chancellor, Seyss-Inquart requested that Germany send its troops across the border to "restore law and order." The German troops arrived on March 12, and Hitler annexed Austria the following day.

65,000 REICH TROOPS MOVE INTO AUSTRIA

40,000 More Mass Near Border as Planes and Artillery Join the Forces Driving Across

By STANLEY SIMPSON

MUNICH, Germany, March 12—With troops moving throughout the countryside, with innumerable planes roaring overhead and with men called as reservists taking hurried farewell of their families, Bavaria presented today an even more war-like atmosphere than yesterday.

It became obvious that many more units than Munich's Seventh Army Corps had been mobilized and equipped for possible war duty. In well-informed quarters it was estimated that about 65,000 German soldiers were on the way into Austria today—30,000 bound for Vienna and 35,000 for the Austrian provinces.

In place of the Bavarian troops thrown into Austria, reinforcements came into Bavaria from other parts of Germany. About 40,000 were transported today to Rosenheim, Traunstein and other points between Munich and the Austrian frontier.

All day troops continued to march into Austria. Heavy artillery and tanks from Ingolstadt and Coburg were observed as late as 3 o'clock this afternoon moving out on the road to Kufstein, while light artillery was being brought up from Bamberg and Regensburg. In fact, local residents insist that Southern Bavaria is seeing more troops on the move than it ever saw during the World War.

Extraordinary activity was seen all along the road to Simbach, a Bavarian frontier town separated from Braunau, Chancellor Hitler's Austrian birthplace, by a river bridge, and on roads to every other point on the Austrian frontier. Every small town within thirty miles of the frontier has the appearance of a garrison city.

In Muehldorf, about twenty miles from Braunau, large numbers of recruits were leaving in motor buses to join their units at the frontier. Some districts have been denuded of all able-bodied men. In some cases 38-year-old men—of the 1900 class—have been mobilized.

Some of the planes flying overhead, it was learned, carried loads of leaflets to Vienna and other Austrian cities.

Residents of villages and towns in the frontier district have recovered from the acute alarm of yesterday morning, but there is still considerable anxiety. Although reassuring broadcasts were sent all day from the Munich station, that anxiety is subsiding only gradually. Classes in schools were interrupted all morning by fathers who dashed in to take leave of their children before joining reserve regiments.

Contrasting with the frank lack of secrecy yesterday, troop movements were more disguised today. The number plates of military vehicles were covered with sacking, and police cordons surrounded the area of the Munich barracks.

A trainload of Nazi Elite Guards arrived from Berlin early today and continued on toward Austria. This was the first indication here that Hitler would go to his native land.

An indication of the volume of troop movements during the past two days is given by the fact that there is a considerable shortage of gasoline in and around Munich.

It was shortly after 10 o'clock this morning that Hitler arrived by air from Berlin with General Wilhelm Keitel, head of the supreme command of the German armed forces, and

German police enter Imst in the Austrian Tyrol during the Anschluss.

General Sperrle, commander of the Munich air force. Thousands awaited Hitler at the airdrome, and loud cheers accompanied him as he drove into the city.

Heinrich Himmler, chief of all German police, left for Vienna, but Hitler remained in Munich until 3 P.M. Then he left from the military airdrome south of Munich escorted by a squadron of bombers. He landed in the neighborhood of Passau, where an automobile awaited him. Thence he proceeded to Braunau and Linz across the border.

The Munich reaction to the development of the situation is on the whole one of relief. But the fact that troop movements have not halted has given rise to uneasy conjectures. The public is especially struck by the circumstance that in all cases where observation was possible real ammunition, not blanks, was carried and that throughout the day heavy trucks were commandeered and loaded with more ammunition.

People in the streets freely commented that this did not quite agree with press and radio reports that the Austrian reaction to the German measure was one of unmitigated enthusiasm.

It was also learned that a majority of the Bavarian police force had been moved to Austria, being replaced by Prussian policemen—a measure not very popular with the Bavarians.

Local Nazi leaders are making every effort to create enthusiasm for the Austrian adventure, but one sees many skeptical head-shakes, especially among country folk.

The huge scale of the mobilization was noted by everybody, and spokesmen were heard to explain to villagers that it was not only Austria, but a region "beyond it," that was in question.

One Nazi announced today that former chancellor Kurt Schuschnigg of Austria had fled to Czechoslovakia and that Russian troops were in Czechoslovakia preparing to attack the Germans in Austria.

"In five minutes, the troops will march in by my order."

Schuschnigg and Göring on the *Anschluss*

The first of these documents is an affidavit taken from Kurt von Schuschnigg for use at the Nuremberg war crimes trials. The second is the transcript of a telephone call made by Göring to the German embassy in Vienna at 6:28 P.M. on March 11. Göring had intended to speak to German military attaché Muff (M), but delegation secretary Wilhelm Keppler (K) answered instead. Later in this much-interrupted call, Seyss-Inquart (S) himself came to the telephone.

Affidavit

I, Kurt von Schuschnigg, being first duly sworn, depose and say:

That during the first days of March 1938, I was Federal Chancellor of Austria. I then made up my mind that I would hold a plebiscite concerning the independence and sovereignty of Austria, according to the provisions of the Agreement reached with Germany at Berchtesgaden, and, further, according to the Austrian Constitution.

On the evening of the 8th of March, 1938, I informed Dr. Arthur Seyss-Inquart, the then Minister of Interior and Public Security for Austria (who had been previously appointed to such position in compliance with the demands made on Austria at Berchtesgaden), of my intention to hold such a plebiscite. I requested that he, Seyss-Inquart, give me his word of honor that he would keep this information secret until after I had published it, which I intended to do on the evening of March 9, 1938, at Innsbruck. He gave that word of honor. On the evening of the 10th of March, 1938, I had a long conversation with Seyss-Inquart concerning the terms of the plebiscite. He first objected to the procedure which I had proposed. However, when we parted on that occasion, Seyss-Inquart expressed his intention to support the plebiscite as proposed, and declared to me that there would be no difficulty. He, furthermore, expressed his willingness to broadcast a speech favoring the plebiscite and directed to his National Socialist followers. On the night of the 10th of March, 1938, I retired firmly convinced that the plebiscite would be a success for Austria, and that the National Socialists would present no formidable obstacle.

I furthermore state and say that at 5:30 A.M. on the morning of the 11th of March, 1938, I received a telephone call from Dr. Skubl, President of Police for Austria, and Secretary of State for Public Security matters. Skubl informed me that the Austrian-German border was closed—the railway traffic between Germany and Austria had been stopped and movements of German military forces along the Austrian-German border had been reported. I hurried to my office. This news that I had received from Dr. Skubl was confirmed by the Counsel General of Munich, who stated that the German Army Corps of Munich was mobilized, and that Panzer troops were moving toward the Austrian frontier. Dr. Skubl then informed me that the Press Prosecutor for Austria had, on the morning of the 11th of March, 1938, censored an article written by Dr. Hugo Jury, an intimate friend of Seyss-Inquart, which article attacked violently the proposed plebiscite.

I further state and say that I attempted to contact Seyss-Inquart, my Minister for Interior and Security, at once, but every effort to locate him failed, until after 10 o'clock the same morning. Sometime after 10 o'clock, Seyss-Inquart, accompanied Glaise-Horstenau, Minister without Portfolio, appeared in my office. Seyss-Inquart informed me as follows: "I have just come from the airport, where I have met Glaise-Horstenau. Glaise-Horstenau has just now returned from Germany." Glaise-Horstenau then informed me that he had the night before seen Hitler, and that he, Hitler, was very highly excited and in a rage concerning my proposal to hold the plebiscite. "It is my feeling, too, that you should not have done such a thing; it is a big mistake"—Seyss-Inquart was then and there called to the telephone and, upon his return, read to me from a scrap of paper which he held in his hand, the contents of a telephone call which he alleged was just then received by him from Goering in Berlin. The contents as he read it to me was as follows: "The Chancellor must revoke the proposed plebiscite within the time of one hour, and after three or four weeks, Austria must oblige herself to carry out a plebiscite concerning the Anschluss according to the Saar status, otherwise the German Army is ordered to pass the Austrian frontier."

I further state and say that after informing the Federal President of this demand made on Austria by Germany, we decided to recall the plebiscite, and thereupon I informed Seyss-Inquart and Glaise-Horstenau of our intentions.

Seyss-Inquart said that he would go to the telephone and inform Goering in Berlin concerning the decision of the Austrian Government, at that time made. In a few minutes, he, Seyss-Inquart, returned to my office, and informed me further, as follows:

"I have had a telephone conversation with Goering, and Goering has ordered me to inform the Federal Chancellor Schuschnigg, as follows:

" 'The situation can only be saved for Austria when Schuschnigg resigns as the Chancellor of Austria within two hours and Seyss-Inquart is appointed as the new Chief of the Austrian Government. If Seyss-Inquart does not inform me, Goering, within two hours, I, Goering, will suppose that you are hindered from doing so.' "

I then reported to the Federal President the new developments, and, after some conversation with him and other members of the Government, I decided to resign. The Federal President reluctantly accepted my resignation at 3:30 P.M. on the afternoon of the 11th of March, 1938. He expressed himself unwilling to appoint Seyss-Inquart as the Federal Chancellor—he therefore asked me to continue my duties as the "caretaker Chancellor" until he had decided who would succeed me as Federal Chancellor. I accepted and remained as caretaker Chancellor from 3:30 P.M. 11 March 1938 until about 11:30 P.M. the same night, when Seyss-Inquart was appointed to the position of Federal Chancellor.

I further state and say that at about 3:30 P.M. on the afternoon of 11 March 1938, the Foreign Office of the Austrian Government contacted the Embassy of Germany in Vienna, to ascertain if the demands that had been then and there made by Goering on Austria were the official demands of the German Government. The Military Attaché of Germany in Vienna, one Lieutenant General Muff, came before the Austrian Federal President, and repeated the contents of the German ultimatums that had previously been delivered to us by Seyss-Inquart.

I furthermore state and say that the Federal President at about 7:30 or 8:00 o'clock P.M. on the night of 11 March 1938 ordered me, as caretaker Chancellor, to broadcast the events of the day and to protest against the demands made on Austria during that day by Germany. Furthermore, to inform the world that Austria had been forced to give in to those demands of Germany through superior force.

Previously to the above incident, I had been informed that Engineer Keppler had on the afternoon of the 11th of March, 1938, arrived in Vienna from Berlin. That he had set up an office in the Austrian Chancery without my consent or the consent of the Austrian Government. While seeking my Secretary of State and Police President I went into the office occupied by Keppler, and Keppler made the following remark to me:

"You see that if you would have followed my advice that I gave to you a week ago, you would have had an entirely different situation. Do you have now any personal wishes?"

I further state and say that at about 10:00 o'clock P.M. on the night of March 11, 1938, Seyss-Inquart entered the room where I was having a conversation with the Federal President, and informed us as follows:

"Just now, Goering called me by telephone and said: 'You, Seyss-Inquart, must send me a telegram asking for German military assistance owing to the fact that the communists and others in Austria have caused great riots—there is great bloodshed in the Austrian cities and the Austrian Government is no longer able to maintain order with her own forces.' "

I further state and say it was after eleven o'clock P.M. on the night of 11 March 1938 that the Federal President Miklas made up his mind to appoint Seyss-Inquart as Federal Chancellor of Austria and sometime between eleven o'clock P.M. and midnight on the night of 11 March 1938, Seyss-Inquart was appointed by the Federal President of Austria as Chancellor of Austria but not before.

I furthermore state and say that I departed the Chancery building of Austria at midnight on the 11th of March, 1938, and at that time the building was guarded by SS troops, I returned to my home. Upon awakening the morning of the 12th of March, 1938, I found the door of my home blocked and guarded by large numbers of armed SA men. From the date last mentioned until 4 May 1945, I was a prisoner of the German Reich, under continuous guard.

Further the Affiant sayeth not.

Kurt von Schuschnigg.

◆　◆　◆

K: I just spoke to Muff. The Muff action was going on at the same time as mine was, so I did not know about it. Muff just saw the President, but he also refused. I shall call once more to find out whether or not the President wants to speak to me at this last minute.

G: Where is Muff now?

K: Muff just came down; his action was unsuccessful.

G: But, what does he have to say?

K: Well, he would not agree with it.

G: Well, then Seyss-Inquart has to dismiss him; just go upstairs again and just tell him plainly that S-I shall call on the National Socialist guards and in 5 minutes the troops will march in by my order.

[Muff is called to the phone.]

M: It is a fact that Schuschnigg tried to prove to the world that the National Socialists do not have any majority, and only by the threat of German arms—

[The conversation is interrupted for about 3 minutes; interruption comes from Vienna; G remains at the phone.]

Unknown voice (male): Hello?

G: Is that Secretary of the State Keppler?

U: No, he is just in conference with the Federal Chancellor.

G: With the Federal President—

U: No, with the Federal Chancellor, they are all together, Federal President and Federal Chancellor.

G: Who is speaking?

U: Fehsemeier(?), Adjutant of—

G: Has he gone upstairs?

U: Yes, just now.

G: Who is with him, upstairs?

U: The Federal President, the Federal Chancellor, and Mayor Schmiz.

G: Yes, I hold on—Fehsemeier, you have to hurry, we have just 3 minutes left—

U: Yes, I know—

[Goering waits a while at the phone.]

[Keppler comes first to the phone.]

K: Well, I just saw the President again, but he has not given his consent.

G: He refused? Well, then Seyss shall call immediately.

[Seyss-Inquart comes to the telephone.]

G: Well, how do we stand?

S: Please, Fieldmarshal, yes.

G: Well, what is going on?

S: Yes, ah, the Federal President sticks to his old viewpoint....

G: But do you think it possible that we shall come to a decision in the next few minutes?

S: Well, the conversation cannot take longer than 5 to 10 minutes; it will not take any longer, I guess.

G: Listen, so I shall wait a few more minutes, till he comes back, then you inform me via Blitz conversation in the Reich Chancery as usual, but it has to be done fast. I hardly can justify it as a matter of fact. I am not entitled to do so; if it cannot be done, then you have to take over the power, all right?

S: But if he threatens?

G: Yes.

S: Well, I see, then we shall be ready.

G: Call me via Blitz.

5.

The Munich Conference

September 1938

The disintegration of Austria-Hungary following its defeat in World War I led to not only the separation of these two countries but also the creation of two additional states: the Kingdom of Serbs, Croats, and Slovenes (later Yugoslavia); and Czechoslovakia, which included not only Czechs and Slovaks but also three million ethnic Germans living in a border region known as the Sudetenland.

Not long after the *Anschluss*, Hitler began agitating for German annexation of the Sudetenland—by force, if necessary—because, he charged, the Sudeten Germans were being mistreated. The Czechs under Pres. Eduard Beneš were prepared to respond with force themselves, but not so their European allies. As the October 1 deadline set by Hitler approached, the British and French buckled. The French had a military alliance with the Czechs that required them to defend Czechoslovakia's borders, yet French premier Edouard Daladier wasn't sure that either his army or his economy was up to the task. Nor did he believe that Great Britain would offer any aid because of Prime Minister Neville Chamberlain's policy of appeasement—that is, Chamberlain believed that annexing lands dominated by fellow Germans would satisfy Hitler and preserve the peace. In Chamberlain's view, the Sudetenland seemed hardly a suitable cause for war, and he had his own doubts about the ability of the recovering British economy to support rearmament.

With Hitler's rhetoric growing ever more belligerent, Chamberlain traveled to Berchtesgaden on September 15 to ask the German dictator what he wanted. Hitler said the Sudetenland. However, once Chamberlain pressured the Czechs into accepting this and returned to Godesberg on September 22 to close the deal, he found that Hitler had, in the meantime, upped his demands to include further territorial concessions for Poland and Hungary. At this point, the French refused to go along, British public opinion turned briefly against the prime minister, and war seemed imminent. The sudden conclusion of the Munich Pact, of course, made Chamberlain temporarily a hero—until the world learned that Hitler was lying when he pledged that this would be his "last territorial demand in Europe." To the German High Command, Hitler soon issued a directive titled, "Liquidation of the rest of Czechoslovakia," in which he wrote that "preparations for this eventuality are to continue on the assumption that no resistance worth mentioning is to be expected."

A tearful Sudeten woman dutifully acknowledges the ascendancy of Hitler following her region's annexation by Nazi Germany shortly after the Munich Conference.

FOUR POWERS REACH A PEACEABLE AGREEMENT; GERMANS TO ENTER SUDETEN AREA TOMORROW AND WILL COMPLETE OCCUPATION IN TEN DAYS

Nazi Demands Met; Hitler Gets Almost All He Asked as Munich Conferees Agree

By FREDERICK T. BIRCHALL

MUNICH, Germany, Friday, Sept. 30—The four-power conference to decide the fate of Czechoslovakia and avert a general European war by bringing pressure to bear on her to accept its decisions has met here, reached an agreement and adjourned.

In something less than nine hours of actual conversation time it has settled everything to the satisfaction—more or less—of the conferees.

It may be said at once that the decisions give Germany just about all she has demanded except the total extinction of Czechoslovakia as an independent State, which has never in fact been among her formulated demands, although that has been implied.

The decisions indicate, moreover, that the Poles and Hungarians will receive their shares of the spoils of Czechoslovak dismemberment.

The only change discernible from Chancellor Adolf Hitler's Godesberg memorandum is in the period allowed for the fulfillment of the demand. That has been slightly extended and beginning tomorrow the predominantly German territories are to be evacuated and occupied progressively until Oct. 10.

The four governments—Britain, France, Germany and Italy—agree that the evacuation must be completed "without any existing installations being destroyed." This covers the German demand, previously objected to by the British, that Czech farmers in Sudeten territory must leave their farms, stock and crops intact behind them when they evacuate, without compensation for them.

The territories to be evacuated are divided into four categories designated on maps appended to the agreement. The first category will be occupied on Oct. 1 and 2, the second category on Oct. 2 and 3, the third category on Oct. 3, 4 and 5, the fourth category on Oct. 6 and 7 and the remainder, to be determined by an international commission that will lay down the conditions governing the evacuation, by Oct. 10.

This indicates that the incoming German troops will not reach the Czech border fortifications until several days after the begining of the occupation.

[A British spokesman, according to the Associated Press, said the four zones were roughly as follows: Zone One, the smallest, takes in Krumau, along the Czechoslovak–Austrian German border. Zone Two includes Asch, Eger, Karlsbad and Marienbad. Zone Three is along the Silesian border, and Zone Four is along the Saxon border. How deep these zones go into Czechoslovakia was not explained.]

All that Czechoslovakia gains, provided she makes the sacrifices demanded from her, is an immediate guarantee by France and Great Britain of the integrity and frontiers of the territory she has left. This guarantee is to be supplemented by Germany and Italy after the demands by the Poles and Hungarians have been met. A new four-power meeting will be

At the Munich Conference, from left to right: Neville Chamberlain, Edouard Daladier, Hitler, Mussolini, and Count Ciano.

called if those demands are not settled within three months.

An international commission is to decide in doubtful territories whether plebiscites are necessary to determine their future, and if plebiscites are held they will be under international control. In the meantime, international "bodies" will hold the disputed territories.

The final determination of frontiers is also to be carried out by the international commission, and the right of option into and out of transferred territories shall be granted to the inhabitants.

Within four weeks all Sudeten Germans shall be released by the military or police service and the Czech Government shall also agree to release all Sudeten prisoners.

The agreement to this effect was signed by the four powers in the conference room at the Fuehrerhaus, Chancellor Hitler's personal headquarters in Munich, at 1 o'clock this morning [7 P.M. Thursday, Eastern standard time]. The leave-taking afterward was most cordial.

Herr Hitler, "on behalf of the German people," thanked Prime Minister Neville Chamberlain of Britain and Premier Edouard Daladier of France for their efforts for European peace. They responded in kind and will return home by air later today. Premier Benito Mussolini of Italy has already departed by special train.

Mr. Chamberlain spent an hour in the early morning discussing the agreement with the two Czech representatives sent from Prague at his suggestion to receive it.

Much stress is laid on the unanimity obtained in the conference and the mutual friendliness exhibited by the conferees.

"I am not going to quibble about a village," Herr Hitler is said to have told the others when doubtful areas were being discussed and the main points of his demands had been conceded.

A duplicate of the agreement had been prepared for the Czechs and their two representatives will carry it to Prague by air this morning. No doubt seems to exist about their accepting it. What else could they do?

From its outset this conference has proceeded with a smoothness and celerity that must have surprised its participants as much as it has astonished neutral observers. Agreed upon in desperation when the threat of war hung over Europe more threatinglty than at any time since 1914, it has been marked by a spirit of mutual accord inconceivable forty-eight hours ago.

It was the first time the two great European democracies had faced the two leading dictatorships at a conference table. It was Mr. Chamberlain's first meeting with Signor Mussolini and only his third with Herr Hitler. It was the first meeting of M. Daladier with either of the two.

Yet all four seem to have worked together with the thoroughness of purpose and speed in execution that restore to the practice of conferences some of its lost prestige.

One effect of this gathering now beginning to be perceptible is that Premier Mussolini's dream of a four-power combination to try for a general European settlement has been brought appreciably nearer. It really seems that not only has the peril of immediate war been removed but the general atmosphere is being cleared for a much larger adjustment.

The "Big Four" met first yesterday at a buffet luncheon in the Fuehrerhaus.

Herr Hitler had been the first on the scene. Arriving early in the morning from Berlin, he had motored out of Kufstein, on the old Austrian frontier, and there boarded the special train that brought Premier Mussolini and Count Galeazzo Ciano, the Italian Foreign Minister, from Rome. The two dictators, therefore, spent more than an hour together before making their triumphal entry.

For that the school children had recieved a holiday and they formed cheering parties along the streets between the railroad station and the Fuehrerhaus. The streets were lined with black-uniformed Elite Guards and the populace was out in force.

The Duce and the Fuehrer were warmly cheered as they drove to the old ducal palace, where Signor Mussolini is lodged. The Italian Premier wore his fascist uniform and Herr Hitler his customary brown. At the station they had been recieved by Field Marshall Hermann Goering, Dr. Robert Ley, leader of the German Labor Front and General Franz Ritter von Epp, Governor of Bavaria.

Premier Daladier and his French entourage arrived by plane at the airfield outside Munich about an hour later. Joachim von Ribbentrop, the German Foreign Minister, and a Foreign Office delegation awaited them, and more cheering parties of school children and more special guards had been assembled to provide a popular greeting. The French drove away feeling that they had been recieved as friends. The famous old Hotel of the Four Seasons had been set aside for them.

Twenty minutes later two British planes dropped out of the sky to the airfield bringing Prime Minister Chamberlain; Sir Horace Wilson; William Strang, chief of the Central European division of the Foreign Office; Frank Ashton-Gwatkin, who was a member of the Runcim commission to Czechoslovakia; Sir William Malkin; and several Foreign Office specialists. Amid renewed cheers they drove through hurriedly decorated streets to the Regina Palace Hotel.

Before 2 P.M. all had arrived at the Fuehrerhaus. The greeting and formal presentations were over and the ice had been broken at Chancellor Hitler's informal luncheon. At 3 o'clock the "Big Four" moved into Herr Hitler's private office, while minor personages gathered in his conference room, for the serious business of their meeting.

The first hour was devoted to planning the basis for discussion and the order in which the various points should be dealt with. Signor Mussolini had brought a plan for it based on Herr Hitler's Godesberg memorandum. Its essentials were accepted on the theory that the way to Munich had led first through Berchtesgaden and then through Godesberg.

It was also agreed that as fast as one problem had been settled in principle the four chief conferees' assistants should be called in and set to work upon arranging the details of its application while the four proceeded to take up the next point.

This was found to produce speedy action and it had been agreed initially that speed was necessary in view of the fact that the German time limit for the Czech evacuation of Sudeten territory left only three days more.

Upon this one point alone Herr Hitler proved adamant. Evacuation of the Sudeten territory by Saturday night, he contended, was essential to prove to the Sudetens that they were really to have their aspirations fulfilled.

However, about the extent of the territory to be evacuated by the Czechs and occupied by German troops immediately Herr Hitler was in a mood for concession. The result was agreement upon a sort of symbolic evacuation and initial occupation covering only a border strip varying from five to fifteen kilometers [3.1 to 9.3 miles] in depth.

In the meantime, at Mr. Chamberlain's suggestion that the presence of some Czech representatives in Munich was necessary to receive and pass on to their government the decisions of the conference, the four agreed that Prague should be asked to send two to hold themselves in readiness. Accordingly, Huber Masaryk of the Czech Foreign Office and Dr. Vojtech Mastny, the Czech minister to Berlin, who had been consulting his government, arrived by air to await results.

By 4:30 P.M. these preliminaries had been completed and the "Big Four" began to take up point by point the real questions at issue. A symbolic evacuation having been agreed upon, the point on which the discussion centered and on which for a brief period a deadlock seemed immi-

nent was how to get the Czechs out of the "symbolic" strip before Saturday night and enable the Germans to go in without giving the notification the effect of an ultimatum.

Upon this point Mr. Chamberlain and M. Daladier were as insistent as Herr Hitler had been about keeping the evacuation date he had originally set. The dictators did not think that it mattered very much. But a formula was finally devised to cover this also.

Just as Herr Hitler had been willing to take account of the physical difficulties involved in evacuating an extensive Czech zone in those three days still remaining and on that account had consented to reduce the evacuation area, so Mr. Chamberlain and M. Daladier agreed to retain the ultimatum date while softening the tone of the ultimatum itself.

Dealing thus with one point after another, the four chieftains kept hard at it for four hours. In the meantime their assistants were equally hard at work framing the terms of evacuation, drawing maps for the districts to be evacuated and agreeing to the technical details of the process.

At 8:30 P.M. the conference adjourned for dinner. The Germans and the Italians dined together at the Ducal Mansion and the French and British seperately at their hotels. At 10 o'clock the discussions were resumed.

From time to time there came from the council room in the Fueherhaus intimations as to the progress of deliberations, and all these were optimistic, although as the day wore on it seemed certain that this was too large a field to be covered in a single day.

After the resumption, the smaller and more intimate conference agreeing on principles and the larger one laying out details for the application of those principles went on concurrently as in the afternoon. When difficulties arose in the larger conference, the "Big Four" intervened to smooth them out.

Thus, as a whole, this conference has been carried on by:

On the German side, Herr Hitler, Herr von Ribbentrop and Count Ernst von Weiszaecker, Foreign Under-Secretary; for the British, Mr. Chamberlain, Sir Horace Wilson, Mr. Strang and Sir Nevile Henderson, British Ambassador to Berlin; representing Italy, Signor Mussolini, Count Ciano and Don Bernardo Attolico, Ambassador to Berlin; for the French, Mr. Daladier, Charles Rochat, foreign affairs expert, Alexis Léger, secretary general of the Foreign Office, and André François-Poncet, Ambassador to Berlin.

One interesting rumor from the conference room was that in the discussions the French turned out to be even more accommodating and amenable than the British. The Italians, moreover, did not prove to be unreservedly pro-German, but apparently desired to play the part of the disinterested conciliators whenever difficulty arose.

A change in the international atmosphere such as has occurred, and especially such a sudden modification of Germany's rigid viewpoint, could not take place without creating eager speculation as to its causes.

On the outskirts of the conference there were heard a great many sensational rumors, allegedly based upon confidential information as to preceeding developments in Berlin. The purport of it all, while crediting Mr. Chamberlain with supplying the initiative and President Roosevelt's messages with helping to bring about results, is that Herr Hitler was actually brought into acquiescence by the arguments of a German group of curiously assorted personalities.

Baron Constantin von Neurath, former Foreign Minister, Admiral-General Erich Raeder, General Wilhelm Keitel and Marshall Goering were mentioned as among those composing this conservative group that urged Chancellor Hitler to modify an intransigence that was certain to plunge Germany into a European war. Their arguments, according to this story, were that Germany had neither armament materials nor a sufficient number of trained reserves to face a war with three great powers simultaneously and that the impression given to the Chancellor by other advisers that Great Britain would not fight beside France and Russia on the present issue was wholly incorrect.

Events abroad, particularly preparations in London and strong manifestations of British public opinion, undoubtedly supported such arguments and confounded party leaders who had been telling Herr Hitler that neither France nor Britain would fight for Czechoslovakia, that Russia was negligible and that Germany could now "lick the world" anyway.

Unfortunately there are some differences in the list of personalities who have been urging Herr Hitler and those who have been trying to restrain him. It is odd after Marshall Goering's speech at Nuremberg to hear it contended that he became a leader of the conservative element. It is equally strange to hear that another personality whose opportunity for appraisal of foreign sentiment is among the best is included in the other group.

"Do not let us blind ourselves."

William L. Shirer's Berlin diary

Journalist William L. Shirer began his career as a foreign correspondent in Europe during the 1920s. He wrote for the *Chicago Tribune* and the Universal News Service and later broadcast for CBS. In 1941, he published the contents of the journal he kept during his seven years in the German capital. Excerpted here, *Berlin Diary* immediately found an international audience and alerted many Americans to the danger posed by Nazi aggression.

Godesberg, September 23–4, 4 A.M.

War seems very near after this strange day. All the British and French correspondents and Birchall of *The New York Times*, who is an English subject, scurrying off at dawn—in about an hour now—for the French, Belgian, or Dutch frontier. It seems that Hitler has given Chamberlain the double-cross. And the old owl is hurt. All day long he sulked in his rooms at the Petershof up on the Petersberg on the other side of the Rhine, refusing to come over and talk with the dictator. At five P.M. he sent Sir Horace Wilson, his "confidential" adviser, and Sir Nevile Henderson, the British Ambassador in Berlin (both of whom, we feel, would sell out Czecho for five cents), over the river to see Ribbentrop. Result: Chamberlain and Hitler met at ten-thirty P.M. This meeting which is the last, broke up at one-thirty A.M. without agreement and now it looks like war, though from my "studio" in the porter's lodge twenty-five feet away I could not discern any strain or particular displeasure in Chamberlain's birdy face as he said his farewell to Hitler, who also was smiling and gracious. Still the Germans are plunged in deep gloom tonight, as if they really are afraid of war now that it's facing them. They are gloomy and yet feverishly excited. Just as I was about to go on the air at two A.M. with the day's story and the official communiqué, Goebbels and Hadamovsky, the latter Nazi boss of German radio, came rushing in and forbade Jordan and me to say anything over the air except to read the official communiqué. Later I grabbed a bit of supper in the Dreesen lobby. Goebbels, Ribbentrop, Göring, Keitel, and others walked in and out, all of them looking as if they had been hit over the head with a sledgehammer. This rather surprised me, since it's a war of *their* making. The communiqué merely says that Chamberlain has undertaken to deliver to Prague a German memorandum containing Germany's "final attitude" concerning the Sudeten question. The point is that Chamberlain came here all prepared to turn over Sudetenland to Hitler, but in a "British" way—with an international commission to supervise the business. He found Hitler's appetite had increased. Hitler wants to take over *his* way—that is, right away, with no nonsense of an international commission. Actually, it's not an important point for either, but they seem to have stuck to their positions.

In the meantime, word that the Czechs have *at last* ordered mobilization.

Five A.M. now. Shall lie down on a table here in the lobby, as I must be off at six for Cologne to catch the Berlin plane.

Berlin, September 24

Today's story is in my broadcast made at midnight tonight. I said: "There was some confusion among us all at Godesberg this morning…but tonight, as seen from Berlin, the position is this: Hitler has demanded that Czechoslovakia not later than Saturday, October 1, agree to the handing over of Sudetenland to Germany. Mr. Chamberlain has agreed to convey this demand to the Czechoslovak Government. The very fact that he, with all the authority of a man who is political leader of the British Empire, has taken upon himself this task is accepted here, and I believe elsewhere, as meaning that Mr. Chamberlain backs Hitler up.

"That's why the German people I talked with in the streets of Cologne this morning, and in Berlin this evening, believe there'll be peace. As a matter of fact, what do you think the new slogan in Berlin is tonight? It's in the evening papers. It's this: 'With Hitler and Chamberlain for peace!' "

Berlin, September 25

Hitler to make a speech tomorrow evening at the Sportpalast. Seems he is furious at the reports from Prague, Paris, and London that his Godesberg Memorandum goes beyond his original agreement with Chamberlain at Berchtesgaden. He claims not. No war fever, not even any anti-Czech feeling, discernible here on this quiet Sabbath day. In the old days on the eve of wars, I believe, crowds used to demonstrate angrily before the embassies of the enemy countries. Today I walked past the Czech Legation. Not a soul outside, not even a policeman. Warm and sunny, the last summer Sunday of the year probably, and half the population of Berlin seems to have spent it at the near-by lakes or in the woods of the Grunewald. Hard to believe there will be war.

Berlin, September 26

Hitler has finally burned his last bridges. Shouting and shrieking in the worst state of excitement I've ever seen him in, he stated in the Sportpalast tonight that he would have his Sudetenland by October 1— next Saturday, today being Monday. If Beneš doesn't hand it over to him he will go to war.…Curious audience, the fifteen thousand party *Bonzen* packed into the hall. They applauded his words with the usual enthusiasm. Yet there was no war fever. The crowd was *good-natured*, as if it didn't realize what his words meant. The old man full of more venom than even he has ever shown, hurling personal insults at Beneš . Twice Hitler screamed that *this* is absolutely his last territorial demand in Europe. Speaking of his assurances to Chamberlain, he said: "I further assured him that when the Czechs have reconciled themselves with their other minorities, the Czech state no longer interests me and that, if you please, I would give him another guarantee: We do not want any Czechs." At the end Hitler had the impudence to place responsibility for peace or war exclusively on Beneš!

I broadcast the scene from a seat in the balcony just above Hitler. He's still got that nervous tic. All during his speech he kept cocking his shoulder, and the opposite leg from the knee down would bounce up. Audience couldn't see it, but I could. As a matter of fact, for the first time in all the years I've observed him he seemed tonight to have completely lost control of himself. When he sat down after his talk, Goebbels sprang up and shouted: "One thing is sure: 1918 will never be repeated!" Hitler looked up to him, a wild, eager expression in his eyes, as if those were the words which he had been searching for all evening and hadn't quite found. He leaped to his feet and with a fanatical fire in his eyes that I shall never forget brought his right hand, after a grand sweep, pounding down on the table and yelled with all the power in his mighty lungs: *"Ja!"* Then he slumped into his chair, exhausted.

Berlin, September 27

A motorized division rolled through the city's streets just at dusk this evening in the direction of the Czech frontier. I went out to the corner of the Linden where the column was turning down the Wilhelmstrasse, expecting to see a tremendous demonstration. I pictured the scenes I had read of in 1914 when the cheering throngs on this same street tossed flowers at the marching soldiers, and the girls ran up and kissed them. The hour was undoubtedly chosen today to catch the hundreds of thousands of Berliners pouring out of their offices at the end of the day's work. But they ducked into the subways, refused to look on, and the handful that did stood at the curb in utter silence unable to find a word of cheer for the flower of their youth going away to the glorious war. It has been the most striking demonstration against war I've ever seen. Hitler himself reported furious. I had not been standing long at the corner when a policeman came up the Wilhelmstrasse from the direction of the Chancellery and shouted to the few of us standing at the curb that the Führer was on his balcony reviewing the troops. Few moved. I went down to have a look. Hitler stood there, and there weren't two hundred people in the street or the great square of the Wilhelmsplatz. Hitler looked grim, then angry, and soon went inside, leaving his troops to parade by unreviewed. What I've seen tonight almost rekindles a little faith in the German people. They are dead set against war.

Berlin, September 28

There is to be no war! Hitler has invited Mussolini, Chamberlain, and Daladier to meet him in Munich tomorrow. The latter three will rescue Hitler from his limb and he will get his Sudetenland without war, if a couple of days later than he boasted. The people in the streets greatly relieved, and if I judge correctly, the people in the Wilhelmstrasse and the Bendlerstrasse (War Department) also. Leaving right after my broadcast tonight for Munich.

Munich, September 30

It's all over. At twelve-thirty this morning—thirty minutes after midnight—Hitler, Mussolini, Chamberlain, and Daladier signed a pact turning over Sudetenland to Germany. The German occupation begins tomorrow, Saturday, October 1, and will be completed by October 10. Thus the two "democracies" even assent to letting Hitler get by with his Sportpalast boast that he would get his Sudetenland by October 1. He gets everything he wanted, except that he has to wait a few days longer for *all* of it. His waiting ten short days has saved the peace of Europe—a curious commentary on this sick, decadent continent.

So far as I've been able to observe during these last, strangely unreal twenty-four hours, Daladier and Chamberlain never pressed for a single concession from Hitler. They never got together alone once and made no effort to present some kind of common "democratic" front to the two Caesars. Hitler met Mussolini early yesterday morning at Kufstein and they made their plans. Daladier and Chamberlain arrived by separate planes and didn't even deem it useful to lunch together yesterday to map out their strategy, though the two dictators did.

Czechoslovakia, which is asked to make all the sacrifices so that Europe may have peace, was not consulted here at any stage of the talks. Their two representatives, Dr. Mastny, the intelligent and honest Czech Minister in Berlin, and a Dr. Masaryk of the Prague Foreign Office, were told at one-thirty A.M. that Czechoslovakia would *have* to accept, told not by Hitler, but by Chamberlain and Daladier! Their protests, we hear, were practically laughed off by the elder statesman. Chamberlain—looking more like some bird, like the black vultures I've seen over the Parsi dead in Bombay—looked particularly pleased with himself when he returned to the Regina Palace Hotel after the signing early this morning, though he was a bit sleepy, *pleasantly* sleepy.

Daladier, on the other hand, looked a completely beaten and broken man. He came over to the Regina to say good-bye to Chamberlain. A bunch of us were waiting as he came down the stairs. Someone asked, or started to ask: "*Monsieur le Président*, are you satisfied with the agreement?..." He turned as if to say something, but he was too tired and defeated and the words did not come out and he stumbled out the door in silence. The French say he fears to return to Paris, thinks a hostile mob will get him. Can only hope they're right. For France has sacrificed her whole Continental position and lost her main prop in eastern Europe. For France this day has been disastrous.

How different Hitler at two this morning! After being blocked from the Führerhaus all evening, I finally broke in just as he was leaving. Followed by Göring, Ribbentrop, Goebbels, Hess, and Keitel, he brushed past me like the conqueror he is this morning. I noticed his swagger. The tic was gone! As for Mussolini, he pulled out early, cocky as a rooster.

Incidentally, I've been badly scooped this night. Max Jordan of NBC got on the air a full hour ahead of me with the *text* of the agreement—one of the worst beatings I've ever taken. Because of his company's special position in Germany, he was allowed exclusive use of Hitler's radio studio in the Führerhaus, where the conference has been taking place. Wiegand, who also was in the house, tells me Max cornered Sir Horace Wilson of the British delegation as he stepped out of the conference room, procured an English text from him, rushed to the Führer's studio, and in a few moments was on the air. Unable to use this studio on the spot, I stayed close to the only other outlet, the studio of the Munich station, and arranged with several English and American friends to get me the document, if possible immediately after the meeting itself, if not from one of the delegations. Demaree Bess was first to arrive with a copy, but, alas, we were late. New York kindly phoned about two-thirty this morning to tell me not to mind—damned decent of them. Actually at eleven-thirty P.M. I had gone on the air announcing that an agreement had been reached. I gave them all the essential details of the accord, stating that the occupation would begin Saturday, that it would be completed in ten days, et cetera. But I should have greatly liked to have had the official text first. Fortunately for CBS, Ed Murrow in London was the first to flash the official news to America that the agreement had been signed thirty minutes after midnight. He picked it up from the Munich radio station in the midst of a talk.

LATER—Chamberlain, apparently realizing his diplomatic annihilation, has pulled a very clever face-saving stunt. He saw Hitler again this morning before leaving and afterwards a joint communiqué was issued. Essential part: "We regard the agreement signed last night and the Anglo-German naval accord as symbolic of the desire of our two peoples never to go to war with one another again." And a final paragraph saying they will consult about further questions which may concern the two countries and are "determined to continue our efforts to remove possible sources of difference and thus to contribute to the assurance of peace in Europe."

.　　.　　.

LATER. *On Train, Munich–Berlin*—Most of the leading German editors on the train and tossing down the champagne and not trying to disguise any more their elation over Hitler's terrific victory over Britain and France. On the diner Halfeld of the *Hamburger Fremdenblatt*, Otto Kriegk of the *Nachtausgabe*, Dr. Boehmer, the foreign press chief of the Propaganda Ministry, gloating over it, buying out all the champagne in the diner, gloating, boasting, bragging....When a German feels big he feels *big*. Shall have two hours in Berlin this evening to get my army passes and a bath and then off by night train to Passau to go into Sudetenland with the German army—a sad assignment for me.

LATER—And Chamberlain will go back to London and from the balcony of 10 Downing Street that night will boast: "My good friends, this is the second time in our history" (do the crowds shouting: "Good old Neville" and singing "For he's a jolly good fellow" remember Disraeli, the Congress of Berlin, 1878?) "that there has come back from Germany to Downing Street peace with honour. I believe it is peace for our time." Peace with honour! And Czechoslovakia? And only Duff Cooper will resign from the Cabinet, saying: "It was not for Serbia or Belgium we fought in 1414...but...in order that one great power should not be allowed, in disregard of treaty obligations and the laws of nations and against all morality, to dominate by brutal force the continent of Europe....Throughout these days the Prime Minister has believed in addressing Herr Hitler with the language of sweet reasonableness. I have believed he was more open to the language of the mailed fist...." Only Winston Churchill, a voice in the wilderness all these years, will say, addressing the Commons: "We have sustained a total, unmitigated defeat....Do not let us blind ourselves. We must expect that all the countries of central and eastern Europe will make the best terms they can with the triumphant Nazi power....The road down the Danube...the road to the Black Sea and Turkey, has been broken. It seems to me that all the countries of Mittel Europa and the Danube Valley, one after the other, will be drawn into the vast system of Nazi politics, not only power military politics, but power economic politics, radiating from Berlin." Churchill—the lone unheeded prophet in the British land.

The SA organize a boycott of Jewish businesses in Berlin, 1933. Their large sign reads, "Germans! Avoid the fox! Don't buy from Jews!"

6.

Kristallnacht
November 1938

Adolf Hitler considered Jews "parasites," and from the time he came to power, it was clear that he intended to expel them all from Germany. The Nazis' initial plan was to make life so unbearable for them that they would all leave voluntarily. The Nuremberg Laws of 1935, for example, deprived Jews of their citizenship and forbade their intermarriage and sexual relations with Aryans. As a result, many wealthy

German Jews did leave, but no nation, including the United States, proved willing to accept poorer Jewish refugees, who might become public burdens. Hungary and Poland even refused to permit the return of Jews who had emigrated to Germany years earlier to escape the anti-Semitism in those countries.

Zindel Grynszpan was one such Polish Jew, who had settled in Hanover in 1911. On the night of October 27, 1938, he and his family were turned out of their home, stripped of their possessions, and forced over the Polish border—penniless, hungry, and freezing. Zindel's seventeen-year-old son Herschel was living in Paris at the time and soon received a letter from his father detailing the expulsion. Seeking to exact revenge, he decided to assassinate the German ambassador to France; when that proved impossible, he settled on Third Secretary Ernst vom Rath. Shot by Herschel Grynszpan on November 7, Rath died a day later.

Propaganda Minister Joseph Goebbels quickly recognized Rath's death as an opportunity to express German outrage at the "international Jewish conspiracy." With Hitler's approval, SS security chief Reinhard Heydrich sent out an "urgent telegram" at 1:20 A.M. on November 10 to all local police chiefs, ordering them to contact the party leaders in their districts so that they could immediately make arrangements for the demonstrations against Jews "expected in all parts of the Reich" later that night.

Heydrich specifically ordered that "only such measures are to be taken as do not endanger German lives or property (i.e., synagogues are to be burned down only where there is no danger of fire in neighboring buildings)." He also commanded that "places of business and apartments belonging to Jews may be destroyed but not looted." Even with police supervision, however, it was folly to believe that order could be maintained. Fires, of course, spread, and inflation-stressed Germans helped themselves to Jewish merchandise as they could. The next morning, so much broken glass glittered in the streets that the riot came to be known as *Kristallnacht* ("Crystal Night"), a term coined by Economics Minister Walther Funk.

NAZIS SMASH, LOOT AND BURN JEWISH SHOPS AND TEMPLES UNTIL GOEBBELS CALLS HALT

Bands Rove Cities; Thousands Arrested for 'Protection' as Gangs Avenge Paris Death

By OTTO D. TOLISCHUS

BERLIN, Nov. 10—A wave of destruction, looting and incendiarism unparalleled in Germany since the Thirty Years War and in Europe generally since the Bolshevist revolution swept over Great Germany today as National Socialist cohorts took vengeance on Jewish shops, offices and synagogues for the murder by a young Polish Jew of Ernst vom Rath, third secretary of the German Embassy in Paris.

Beginning systematically in the early morning hours in almost every town and city in the country, the wrecking, looting and burning continued all day. Huge but mostly silent crowds looked on and the police confined themselves to regulating traffic and making wholesale arrests of Jews "for their own protection."

All day the main shopping districts as well as the side streets of Berlin and innumerable other places resounded to the shattering of shop windows falling to the pavement, the dull thuds of furniture and fittings being pounded to pieces and the clamor of fire brigades rushing to burning shops and synagogues. Although shop fires were quickly extinguished, synagogue fires were merely kept from spreading to adjoining buildings.

As far as could be ascertained the violence was mainly confined to property. Although individuals were beaten, reports so far tell of the death of only two persons—a Jew in Polzin, Pomerania, and another in Bunzdorf.

In extent, intensity and total damage, however, the day's outbreaks exceeded even those of the 1918 revolution and by nightfall there was scarcely a Jewish shop, cafe, office or synagogue in the country that was not either wrecked, burned severely or damaged.

Thereupon Propaganda Minister Joseph Goebbels issued the following proclamation:

"The justified and understandable anger of the German people over the cowardly Jewish murder of a German diplomat in Paris found extensive expression during last night. In numerous cities and towns of the Reich retaliatory action has been undertaken against Jewish buildings and businesses.

"Now a strict request is issued to the entire population to cease immediately all further demonstrations and actions against Jewry, no matter what kind. A final answer to the Jewish assassination in Paris will be given to Jewry by way of legislation and ordinance."

What this legal action is going to be remains to be seen. It is known, however, that measures for the extensive expulsion of foreign Jews are already being prepared in the Interior Ministry, and some towns, like Munich, have ordered all Jews to leave within forty-eight hours. All Jewish organizational, cultural and publishing activity has been suspended. It is assumed that the Jews, who have now lost most of their possessions and livelihood, will either be thrown into the streets or put into ghettos and concentration camps, or impressed into labor brigades and put to work for the Third Reich, as the children of Israel were once before for the Pharaohs.

In any case, all day in Berlin, as throughout the country, thousands of Jews, mostly men, were being taken from their homes and arrested—in particular prominent Jewish leaders, who in some cases, it is understood, were told they were being held as hostages for the good behavior of Jewry outside Germany.

In Breslau they were hunted out even in the homes of non-Jews where they might have been hiding.

Foreign embassies in Berlin and consulates throughout the country were besieged by frantic telephone calls and by persons, particularly weeping women and children, begging help that could not be given them. Incidentally, in Breslau the United States Consulate had to shut down for some time during the day because of fumes coming from a burning synagogue near by.

All pretense—maintained during previous comparatively minor anti-Jewish outbreaks—to the effect that the day's deeds had been the work of irresponsible, even Communist, elements was dropped this time and the official German News Bureau, as well as newspapers that hitherto had ignored such happenings, frankly reported on them. The bureau said specifically:

"Continued anti-Jewish demonstrations occurred in numerous places. In most cities the synagogue was fired by the population. The fire department in many cases was able merely to save adjoining buildings. In addition, in many cities the windows of Jewish shops were smashed.

"Occasionally fires occurred and because of the population's extraordinary excitement the contents of the shops were partly destroyed. Jewish shop owners were taken into custody by the police for their own protection."

Berlin papers also mention many cities and towns in which anti-Jewish excesses occurred, including Potsdam, Stettin, Frankfort on the Main, Leipzig, Luebeck, Cologne, Nuremberg, Essen, Duesseldorf, Konstanz, Landsberg, Kottbus and Eberswalde. In most of them, it is reported, synagogues were raided and burned and shops were demolished. But in general the press follows a system of reporting only local excesses so as to disguise the national extent of

A Jewish shopkeeper clears away broken glass from in front of his Berlin store in the wake of Kristallnacht. *Thirty-five Jews were killed in the rioting, and seventy-five hundred businesses destroyed. Germans who came to the defense of Jews were either beaten themselves or imprisoned.*

the outbreak, the full spread of which probably never will be known.

On the other hand, the German press already warns the world that if the day's events lead to another agitation campaign against Germany "the improvised and spontaneous outbreaks of today will be replaced with even more drastic authoritative action." No doubt is left that the contemplated "authoritative action" would have a retaliatory character.

"For every suffering, every crime and every injury that this criminal [the Jewish community] inflicts on a German anywhere, every individual Jew will be held responsible. All Judah wants is war with us and it can have this war according to its own moral law: an eye for an eye and a tooth for a tooth."

One of the first legal measures issued was an order by Heinrich Himmler, commander of all German police, forbidding Jews to possess any weapons whatever and imposing a penalty of twenty years' confinement in a concentration camp upon every Jew found in possession of a weapon hereafter.

The dropping of all pretense in the outbreak is also illustrated by the fact that although shops and synagogues were wrecked or burned by so-called Rollkommandos, or wrecking crews, dressed in what the Nazis themselves call "Raeuberzivil," or "bandit mufti," consisting of leather coats or raincoats over uniform boots or trousers, these squads often performed the work in the presence and under the protection of uniformed Nazis or police.

The wrecking work was thoroughly organized, sometimes proceeding under the direct orders of a controlling person in the street on whose command the wreckers ceased, lined up and proceeded to another place.

In the fashionable Tauenzienstrasse the writer saw a wrecking crew at work in one shop while the police stood outside telling a vast crowd watching the proceeding to keep moving.

"Move on," said the policemen, "there are young Volksgenossen [racial comrades] inside who have some work to do."

At other shops during the wrecking process uniformed Storm Troopers and Elite Guards were seen entering and emerging while soldiers passed by outside.

Generally the crowds were silent and the majority seemed gravely disturbed by the proceedings. Only members of the wrecking squads shouted occasionally, "Perish Jewry!" and "Kill the Jews" and in one case a person in the crowd shouted, "Why not hang the owner in the window?"

In one case on the Kurfuerstendamm actual violence was observed by an American girl who saw one Jew with his face bandaged dragged from a shop, beaten and chased by a crowd while a sec-ond Jew was dragged from the same shop by a single man who beat him as the crowd looked on.

One Jewish shopowner, arriving at his wrecked store, exclaimed, "Terrible," and was arrested on the spot.

In some cases on the other hand crowds were observed making passages for Jews to leave their stores unmolested.

Some persons in the crowds—peculiarly enough, mostly women—expressed the view that it was only right that the Jews should suffer what the Germans suffered in 1918. But there were also men and women who expressed protests. Most of them said something about Bolshevism. One man—obviously a worker—watching the burning of the synagogue in Fasanenstrasse exclaimed, "Arson remains arson." The protesters, however, were quickly silenced by the wrecking crews with threats of violence.

To some extent—at least during the day—efforts were made to prevent looting. Crowds were warned they might destroy but must not plunder, and in individual cases looters either were beaten up on the spot by uniformed Nazis or arrested. But for the most part, looting was general, particularly during the night and in the poorer quarters. And in at least one case the wreckers themselves tossed goods out to the crowd with the shout "Here are some cheap Christmas presents."

Children were observed with their mouths smeared with candy from wrecked candy shops or flaunting toys from wrecked toy shops until one elderly woman watching the spectacle exclaimed, "So that is how they teach our children how to steal."

Foreign Jewish shops, it appears, were not at first marked for destruction and were passed over by the first wrecking crews. But in their destructive enthusiasm others took them on as well and even wrecked some "Aryan" shops by mistake.

Among the foreign wrecked establishments were three American-owned shops—the Loewenstein jewelery shop in Kanonierstrasse, near the office of The New York Times, the owner of which shop is now in America; the Leipzig fur shop in Rosenthalerstrasse, owned by C. G. Schultz, who is also in America; and the Rose Bach rug shop in the Hauptstrasse.

Also wrecked were the Warner corset shop on the Kurfuerstendamm, which is partly American owned; a Jewish Ford dealer's off Unter den Linden; and a large, well-known deparment store that has considerable British capital invested in it.

The Leipzig fur shop displayed a large American flag in its window but the manager reported that the wreckers had shouted that they did not care whether the place was American or not and went to work. This shop reported the loss of three silver fox capes and other furs; the Bach rug shop reported the loss of goods valued at 2,000 marks.

No photographing of the wreckage was permitted and Anton Celler, American tourist, of Hamden, Conn., was arrested while trying to take such pictures, although he was soon released. Members of a South American diplomatic mission likewise got into trouble on that account.

Grave doubt prevails whether insurance companies will honor the policies. Some are reported to have flatly refused to reimburse for the damage because of its extent, and, considering the standing the Jew enjoys in German courts today, there is little likelihood of his collecting by suing. But there still remains to be settled the damage done to "Aryan" houses and other property.

"The Jews shall pay for it."

Excerpt from the stenographic report of the Conference on the Jewish Question

The four-hour Conference on the Jewish Question that Hermann Göring, Hitler's second-in-command, convened two days after *Kristallnacht* dealt primarily with the riot's unforeseen consequences. It also marked a major escalation in the Nazis' dehumanization of Jews. Their political liberties had already been eliminated, but now, in the wake of *Kristallnacht,* their economic rights would be taken away as well, leaving them much more vulnerable to exploitation. Göring's new directives also widened the rift between Germany and the Western democracies. As the American consul in Leipzig reported, "This flagitious attack upon a helpless minority very probably has had no counterpart in the course of the civilized world."

GOERING: Gentlemen! Today's meeting is of a decisive nature. I have received a letter written on the Fuehrer's orders by the Stabsleiter of the Fuehrer's deputy Bormann, requesting that the Jewish question be now, once and for all, coordinated and solved one way or another. And yesterday once again did the Fuehrer request by phone for me to take coordinated action in the matter.

Since the problem is mainly an economic one, it is from the economic angle that it shall have to be tackled. Naturally, a number of legal measures shall have to be taken which fall into the sphere of the Minister for Justice and into that of the Minister of the Interior; and certain propaganda measures shall be taken care of by the office of the Minister for Propaganda. The Minister for Finance and the Minister for Economic Affairs shall take care of problems falling into their respective resorts.

The meeting in which we first talked about this question and came to the decision to Aryanize the German economy, to take the Jew out of it and put him into our debit ledger, was one in which, to our shame, we only made pretty plans, which were executed very slowly. We then had a demonstration, right here in Berlin; we told the people that something decisive would be done, but again nothing happened. We have had this affair in Paris now, more demonstrations followed and this time something decisive must be done!

Because, gentlemen, I have had enough of these demonstrations! They don't harm the Jew but me, who is the last authority for coordinating the German economy.

If today a Jewish shop is destroyed, if goods are thrown into the street, the insurance company will pay for the damages, which the Jew does not even have; and furthermore goods of the consumer, goods belonging to the people, are destroyed. If, in the future, demonstrations which are necessary occur, then I pray that they be directed so as not to hurt us.

Because it's insane to burn out and destroy a Jewish warehouse, then have a German insurance company making good the loss. And the goods which I need desperately, whole bales of clothing and whatnot, are being burned, and I miss them everywhere.

I may as well burn the raw materials before they arrive. The people, of course, do not understand that; therefore, we must make laws which will show the people, once and for all, that something is being done.

Hermann Göring greets crowds of cheering Austrians in Vienna two weeks after the Anschluss.

I should appreciate it very much if for once our propaganda could make it clear that it is unfortunately not the Jew who has to suffer in all this but the German insurance companies.

I am not going to tolerate a situation in which the insurance companies are the ones who suffer. Under the authority invested in me, I shall issue a decree, and I am, of course, requesting the support of the competent government agencies, so that everything shall be processed through the right channels, and the insurance companies will not be the ones who suffer.

It may be, though, that these insurance companies may have insurance in foreign countries. If that is the case, foreign bills of exchange would be available which I would not want to lose. That shall have to be checked. For that reason, I have asked Mr. Hilgard of the insurance company to attend, since he is best qualified to tell us to what extent the insurance companies are protected against damage, by having taken out insurance with other companies. I would not want to miss this, under any circumstances.

I should not want to leave any doubt, gentlemen, as to the aim of today's meeting. We have not come together merely to talk again but to make decisions, and I implore the competent agencies to take all measures for the elimination of the Jew from German economy and to submit them to me, as far as it is necessary....

FUNK: That is quite a decisive question for us: Shall the Jewish stores be re-opened?

GOEBBELS: If they will be re-opened is another question. The question is will they be restored? I have set the deadline for Monday.

GOERING: You don't have to ask whether they'll be re-opened. That is up to us to decide.

GOEBBELS: Number 2. In almost all German cities synagogues were burned. New, various possibilities exist to utilize the space where the synagogues stood. Some cities want to build parks in their place; others want to put up new buildings.

GOERING: How many synagogues were actually burned?

HEYDRICH: Altogether there are 101 synagogues destroyed by fire, 76 synagogues demolished, and 7,500 stores ruined in the Reich.

GOERING: What do you mean, "destroyed by fire"?

HEYDRICH: Partly they are razed, and partly gutted.

GOEBBELS: I am of the opinion that this is our chance to dissolve the synagogues. All those not completely intact shall be razed by the Jews. The Jews shall pay for it. There, in Berlin, the Jews are ready to do that. The synagogues which burned in Berlin are being levelled by the Jews themselves. We shall build parking lots in their places or new buildings. That ought to be the criterion for the whole country; the Jews shall have to remove the damaged or burned synagogues and shall have to provide us with ready free space.

Number 3: I deem it necessary to issue a decree forbidding the Jews to enter German theaters, movie houses and circuses. I have already issued such a decree under the authority of the law of the

Chamber for Culture. Considering the present situation of the theaters, I believe we can afford that. Our theaters are overcrowded; we have hardly any room. I am of the opinion that it is not possible to have Jews sitting next to Germans in varieties, movies and theaters. One might consider, later on, to let the Jews have one or two movie houses here in Berlin, where they may see Jewish movies. But in German theaters they have no business anymore.

Furthermore, I advocate that the Jews be eliminated from all positions in public life in which they may prove to be provocative. It is still possible today that a Jew shares a compartment in a sleeping car with a German. Therefore, we need a decree by the Reich Ministry for Communications stating that separate compartments for Jews shall be available; in cases where compartments are filled up, Jews cannot claim a seat. They shall be given a separate compartment only after all Germans have secured seats. They shall not mix with Germans, and if there is no more room, they shall have to stand in the corridor.

GOERING: In that case, I think it would make more sense to give them separate compartments.

GOEBBELS: Not if the train is overcrowded!

GOERING: Just a moment. There'll be only one Jewish coach. If that is filled up, the other Jews will have to stay at home.

GOEBBELS: Suppose, though, there won't be many Jews going on the express train to Munich, suppose there would be two Jews in the train and the other compartments would be overcrowded. These two Jews would then have a compartment all to themselves. Therefore, Jews may claim a seat only after all Germans have secured a seat.

GOERING: I'd give the Jews one coach or one compartment. And should a case like you mention arise and the train be overcrowded, believe me, we won't need a law. We'll kick him out and he'll have to sit all alone in the toilet all the way!

GOEBBELS: I don't agree. I don't believe in this. There ought to be a law. Furthermore, there ought to be a decree barring Jews from German beaches and resorts. Last summer—

GOERING: Particularly here in the Admiralspalast very disgusting things have happened lately.

GOEBBELS: Also at the Wannsee beach. A law which definitely forbids the Jews to visit German resorts!

GOERING: We could give them their own.

GOEBBELS: It would have to be considered whether we'd give them their own or whether we should turn a few German resorts over to them, but not the finest and the best, so we cannot say the Jews go there for recreation. It'll also have to be considered if it might not become necessary to forbid the Jews to enter the German forest. In the Grunewald, whole herds of them are running around. It is a constant provocation and we are having incidents all the time. The behavior of the Jews is so inciting and provocative that brawls are a daily routine.

GOERING: We shall give the Jews a certain part of the forest, and the Alpers shall take care of it that various animals that look damned much like Jews—the elk has such a crooked nose—get there also and become acclimated.

GOEBBELS: I think this behavior is provocative. Furthermore, Jews should not be allowed to sit around in German parks. I am thinking of the whispering campaign on the part of Jewish women in the public gardens at Fehrbelliner Platz. They go and sit with German mothers and their children and begin to gossip and incite. I see in this a particularly grave danger. I think it is imperative to give the Jews certain public parks, not the best ones, and tell them: "You may sit on these benches"; these benches shall be marked "For Jews only." Besides that, they have no business in German parks. Furthermore, Jewish children are still allowed in German schools. That's impossible. It is out of the question that any boy should sit beside a Jewish boy in a German gymnasium and receive lessons in German history. Jews ought to be eliminated completely from German schools; they may take care of their own education in their own communities.

GOERING: I suggest that Mr. Hilgard from the insurance company be called in; he is waiting outside. As soon as he finishes with his report, he may go, and we can continue to talk....

[Hilgard appears.]

The following is our case. Because of the justified anger of the people against the Jew, the Reich has suffered a certain amount of damage. Windows were broken, goods were damaged and people hurt, synagogues burned, etc. I suppose that the Jews—many of them are also insured against damage committed by public disorder, etc.

[Hilgard: "Yes."]

If that is so, the following situation arises: The people, in their justified anger, meant to harm the Jew; but it is the German insurance companies that will compensate the Jew for damage. This situation is simple enough; I'd only have to issue a decree to the effect that damage resulting from these risks shall not have to be paid by the insurance companies. But the question that interests me primarily, and because of which I have asked you to come here, is this one: In case of reinsurance policies in foreign countries, I should not like to lose these, and that is why I'd like to discuss with you ways and means by which profit from reinsurance, possibly in foreign currency, will go to the German economy, instead of the Jew. I'd like to hear from you, and that is the first question I want to ask: In your opinion, are the Jews insured against such damage to a large extent?

HILGARD: Permit me to answer right away. We are concerned with three kinds of insurances. Not with the insurance against damage resulting from revolt or from risks. But with the ordinary fire insurance, the ordinary glass insurance, and the ordinary insurance against theft. The people, because of their contracts, who have a right to claim compensation are partly Jews, partly Aryans. As for the fire insurance, they are practically all Jewish, I suppose. As for the department stores, the victim is identical with the Jew, the owner, and that applies more to the synagogues, except for neighbors to whose places the fire may have spread—although the damage done to the latter's property seems to be rather slight, according to the inquiries I made late last night. As for the glass insurance, which plays a very important part in this, the situation is completely different. The majority of the victims, mostly the owners of the buildings, are Aryans; the Jew has usually rented the store, a procedure which you may observe all over, for example on Kurfuerstendamm.

GOERING: That is what we've said.

GOEBBELS: In these cases, the Jew will have to pay.

GOERING: It doesn't make sense; we have no raw materials. It is all glass imported from foreign countries and has to be paid for in foreign currency! One could go nuts.

HILGARD: May I draw your attention to the following facts: The glass for the shop windows is not being manufactured by the Bohemian, but by the Belgian glass industry. In my estimation, the approximate money value to which these damages amount is 6,000,000 marks—that includes the broken glass, glass which we shall have to replace, mainly to Aryans because they have the insurance policies. Of course I have to reserve final judgement in all this, Your Excellency, because I have had only one day to make my inquiries. Even counting on about half of the 6,000,000 being spent in transacting the business—specialists from the Industry itself are more confident in this matter than I am—we might well have to import glass for approximately 3,000,000. Incidentally, the amount of the damage equals about half of the whole year's production of the Belgian glass industry. We believe that half a year will be necessary for the manufacturers to deliver the glass.

GOERING: The people will have to be enlightened on this.

GOEBBELS: We cannot do this right now.

GOERING: This cannot continue! We won't be able to last with all this. Impossible! Go on then! You suggest that the Aryan is the one who suffers the damage; is that right?

HILGARD: Yes, to a large extent, as far as the glass insurance goes.

Hitler and Mussolini exchange farewells as the Duce leaves Berlin for Italy following a September 1937 visit to Germany.

7.

The Pact of Steel

May 1939

Following the signing of the Pact of Steel between Germany and Italy in May 1939, Benito Mussolini became, in most respects, an echo of Adolf Hitler. Consequently, history has tended to fuse the two dictators together, rendering Mussolini nearly indistinguishable from his more famous ally. Yet the temperaments, situations, and political movements of the two men were all quite different. Mussolini, for

example, encountered relatively few obstacles in his rise to power; yet, even after his Fascist dictatorship became well established, the Duce had difficulty governing Italy—unaccustomed as the country was to coordinated, top-down rule. Hitler, on the other hand, had much more difficulty obtaining power; but once he seized control of the German government, he immediately benefited from Germany's traditional respect for authoritarian rule and its highly obedient, highly motivated, highly efficient bureaucracy.

Hitler and Mussolini first began working closely together after the outbreak of war in Spain in July 1936. The Spanish Civil War began when colonial troops in Morocco rose up against the left-wing Popular Front government in Madrid. Needing to move his troops somehow across the Strait of Gibraltar, the revolt's leader, Gen. Francisco Franco, appealed to Germany and Italy for the necessary aircraft. Eager to gain

an ally on France's southern flank, Hitler and Mussolini readily complied.

So began a partnership that seemed extremely cozy at times, such as when the Duce announced the advent of a diplomatic "Rome-Berlin Axis" in November 1936 or when Italy in November 1937 joined the Anti-Comintern Pact, signed a year earlier by Germany and Japan. Nevertheless, Mussolini still retained during the late 1930s a strong desire to find for Italy a middle path between Germany and the Western democracies. For example, the Duce opposed the *Anschluss* and at Munich presented himself as best he could as a disinterested arbiter of peace.

Yet, despite these misgivings and his resentment at becoming Hitler's junior partner, Mussolini signed the Pact of Steel because his attempts to improve Italian relations with Great Britain had failed and, as war approached, Germany remained his government's most dependable and compatible ally.

AXIS POWERS SIGN TEN-YEAR ALLIANCE TO REMAKE EUROPE

Pact Is Sweeping; Automatic Action in War, Regardless of Origin, Is Called For in Treaty

By OTTO B. TOLISCHUS

BERLIN, May 22—Amid sumptuous ceremonies and an elaborate display of organized popular enthusiasm, Greater Germany and the Italian Empire today signed an unconditional and automatic offensive-defensive alliance. This pact provides for the closest political, economic and military collaboration and support in peace and war, with the declared objective of reorganizing Europe and promoting aggrandizement of the two nations and thereby creating a "just peace" throughout the world.

The alliance converts the Rome-Berlin Axis into a union of "two nations, one will," which, in the words of accompanying speeches, statements and exchanges of congratulatory telegrams, creates an invincible bloc of 150,000,000 people, raised to 300,000,000 by their anti-Comintern friends. Signatures to the pact were affixed at 11 A.M. by Joachim von Ribbentrop, German Foreign Minister, and Count Galeazzo Ciano, Italian Foreign Minister, in the festively decorated Ambassadors Hall of the new Reich Chancellery.

The momentous event was witnessed by Chancellor Adolf Hitler, clad in his simple brown uniform. He looked especially grim and determined as he sat between the two gorgeously uniformed Foreign Ministers.

The equally gorgeously attired assemblage, including Field Marshal Hermann Goering; Col. Gen. Walther von Brauchitsch, Commander in Chief of the German Army; Col. Gen. Wilhelm Keitel, head of the supreme command of the German armed forces; Grand Admiral

Erich Raeder, Commander in Chief of the German Navy; General Alberto Pariani, Italian Under-Secretary for War; and many other high representatives of both partners, lined up behind the German Chancellor and the two Ministers.

When the signatures had been completed, however, Hitler's face lighted up in a broad smile, and grasping Count Ciano's hand with both of his he nearly lifted the Italian off his feet with the warmth of his congratulations. Then the Chancellor presented to him the highest German decoration, the grand cross of the German Eagle in gold.

Inasmuch as the day had not been declared a legal holiday the crowd that usually provides background for such occasions did not, perhaps, come up to standard size. But a thousand boys and girls from the Hitler Youth and some crews of factories and offices had been marched to the Chancellery in a body, and they cheered lustily outside, the cheers rising to a tumultuous roar when Herr Hitler and Count Ciano and their suites appeared on the Chancellery balcony afterward.

At the last minute even the foreign press had been invited inside the sacred precincts of the Chancellery to watch the historic scene and proclaim it to the world.

And historic scene it was, for it produced the most candid and most sweeping alliance in modern times. Discarding with what Count Ciano called "honest openness" all diplomatic provisos, which usually make the casus foederis of such alliances depend upon unprovoked aggression against one or both alliance partners, the German-Italian pact provides:

> In peace constant contact between the two governments in all matters affecting their common interests or the European situation.
>
> In case of danger, immediate consultation on and full political and diplomatic support for counter-measures to meet the danger.
>
> Finally, in case of war involving one partner, no matter how started, full mutual support with all military forces by land, sea and air.

In these and many other respects the new German-Italian pact goes far beyond the pre-war triple alliance of Germany, Austria-Hungary and Italy, for it precludes the possibility of neutrality such as Italy adopted in 1914, preliminary to joining the other side, and it also specifically excludes a separate armistice or peace.

Moreover, this pact provides for immediate technical collaboration "in the military field and the field of war economy" and all other measures necessary for the execution of the pact under standing German-Italian commissions.

According to well-informed sources, it has already been agreed in case of war that Germany shall furnish the supreme command on land while Italy takes command on the seas. Accordingly, it is assumed that the technical collaboration, which has already begun, is taking into account that eventuality and that many German officers and technical experts recently sent to Italy are preparing the organizational ground for joint operations of the German and Italian armies under German command.

Just how Germany will reciprocate on the seas is still not clear, but it is held not unlikely that Italy may demand rapid expansion of the German navy, perhaps even the creation of a German Mediterranean fleet, to assist the Italian fleet in case of trouble.

In explaining the aims of the new pact both Herr von Ribbentrop and Count Ciano, as well as the German and Italian press, emphasized it was a demonstrative answer to the democracies' "encirclement policy," and it is considered more than an accident that the equivalent of the pre-war Triple Alliance was signed on the day on which Britain, France and Russia met at Geneva to seek ways and means of creating an equivalent of the pre-war Triple Entente.

However, although the anti-Comintern pact partners are included in an extended bloc of 300,000,000, nevertheless the stated objective of the new alliance is not to combat bolshevism, all mention of which is carefully omitted today as in the recent past. Rather the alliance is openly proclaimed to be the Instrument of further revision of the Versailles system and therewith European and colonial borders.

In Count Ciano's words, it is designed to place the two nations "at the head of European history, whose highest aims always will be to maintain peace but who are firmly determined to defend their rights to life and ascendancy and to march united into the future."

Herr von Ribbentrop, especially, though the author of the anti-Comintern pact, declared in his speech, which in tone sounded much more aggressive than Count Ciano's, that the whole Rome-Berlin Axis had grown from their "joint defense against the beneficiaries of the Versailles status quo and from the determination of both States to give the European continent a just peace...which in the end will assure the world the blessings of a permanent and firmly founded order."

Both Foreign Ministers asserted there was no problem in Europe that could not be solved by peaceful means, but while Count Ciano refrained from attacking any nation in particular and merely warned that there was no cause justifying war but that any war in Europe would of necessity become a world war, Herr von Ribbentrop went tooth-and-nail after the "so-called democracies."

He violently denounced "democratic war agitators and intrigue mongers who play an irresponsible game with war and war panics in order to preserve old wrongs and deny Germany and Italy their proper place in the world and their proper share of the riches of this earth."

Both nations, he said, are willing to stretch out their hands to a friend, but, he concluded:

"They are determined not to go back one step, but rather to defend the living rights of their nations with all their strength and with all the means at their disposal. Every interference with Italian or German rights will be met in the future with the solidary power of both countries. Every foot of German and Italian soil will henceforth be defended by Italian and German soldiers."

Herr von Ribbentrop did not state whether German soil included Danzig, but the Diplomatisch-Politische Korrespondenz, organ of the Foreign Office, discussing the Danzig incident of yesterday, suggests it does and that it falls under alliance consultations.

The preamble of the pact says that by reason of their "inner kinship, their ideologies and the comprehensive solidarity of their interests, both the German and Italian peoples are determined to stand up with all their united forces for the assurance of their Lebensraum ["living space"] and the maintenance of peace."

Following the signing of the pact, Herr Hitler exchanged telegrams of congratulation with Premier Mussolini and King Victor Emmanuel which repeated the sentiments that Herr von Ribbentrop and Count Ciano already had expressed.

At the same time the Japanese Government, which so far has refused all invitations to join a military alliance, sent the Reich Government a cable message in which it congratulated its "intimate friends" on a "world historic event" and expressed the conviction that the new pact would give "firm support to the highly uncertain European situation and therewith form a valuable contribution to the maintenance and strengthening of world peace."

The signing of the pact was the climax of Count Ciano's two-day state visit, which was the occasion of numerous festivities and banquets that ended tonight with a banquet given by Herr von Ribbentrop at his home. On this occasion the German Foreign Minister received from Count Ciano the Collar of Annunciata, the highest Italian order, which makes Herr von Ribbentrop the King's cousin.

But, in between, Count Ciano also had many conferences with Herr Hitler and Herr von Ribbentrop on details of the new collaboration, which, while putting more power behind the decisions of the alliance, nevertheless also limits the freedom of action of either partner.

The next state visit to Berlin will be that of Prince Paul, Yugoslav Regent, who, having visited Italy, will now visit the other ally, beginning June 1. The Italian King's visit, originally planned to follow soon after, apparently has been postponed until late Summer.

Herr Hitler's own interpretation of the alliance is likely to come in the speech he is scheduled to deliver June 6, following a victory parade of the Condor Legion on its return from the Spanish war, in which German and Italian collaboration was first cemented on the battlefield.

"There are marked differences of character."

A firsthand comparison of Hitler and Mussolini

Writing for the *Daily Mail and Sunday Dispatch,* British war correspondent G. Ward Price began covering international conflicts in 1912, when his editors assigned him to report on the First Balkan War. By 1938, when he wrote this account of his personal observations of Hitler and Mussolini, he had become one of the most respected foreign affairs journalists of his generation.

Despite resemblances in career, achievement, and situation, there are marked differences of character between the two dictators.

This dissimilarity is well reflected in their respective senses of humor. Mussolini has a keen, sardonic wit, which is freely applied to his political preoccupations. His lively eyes dilate still wider when some caustic comment on the international situation suggests itself to his active mind.

Hitler's humor is more ingenuous and personal. He is gay and whimsical in the circle of his close friends, but too earnest in his attitude towards public affairs to be jocular about them.

Mussolini gives the greater impression of vitality. He uses a high arm-chair, but seldom leans back in it. His temperament is too vigorous for him to remain long seated at all. Springing up from behind his heavy oaken work-table, he will carry on a conversation for half an hour standing—his stocky figure bolt upright, sturdy legs straddling wide apart, and massive head held so high that its heavy chin and full, pursed lips are thrust aggressively forward.

Whereas Hitler speaks only German, Mussolini talks to all foreigners in French, which he uses with ease and fluency. Sometimes he will express himself for a few sentences in English, but he began to learn that language after coming to power, and has to talk it slowly and deliberately. He speaks German well, having learned it during the time he spent as a young man in what was then the Austrian province of the Trentino.

Personal contact with him does not reveal the arrogance and megalomania which many people in other countries believe to be his chief characteristics, unless those terms are to be applied to the emphatic tone and positive manner of one accustomed to impose his point of view. His masterful bearing is a genuine quality of nature and habit, not a pose, and he is too good-humoredly cynical to be a victim of folie de grandeur. Businesslike, quick-witted, instantaneous and apt in his replies, he conveys the impression of a successful man of the world who is an expert at his job and enjoys doing it.

The demeanor of Hitler is very different. He does not lend himself so readily as Mussolini to the give-and-take of question and answer, rejoinder and comment. Intercourse with him rather resembles the Socratic form of dialogue; the inquirer propounds a theme, and Hitler enlarges upon it. When more than two people are present, even though they are of his intimate circle, there is no general discourse. Either Hitler talks and they all listen, or else they talk among themselves and Hitler sits silent.

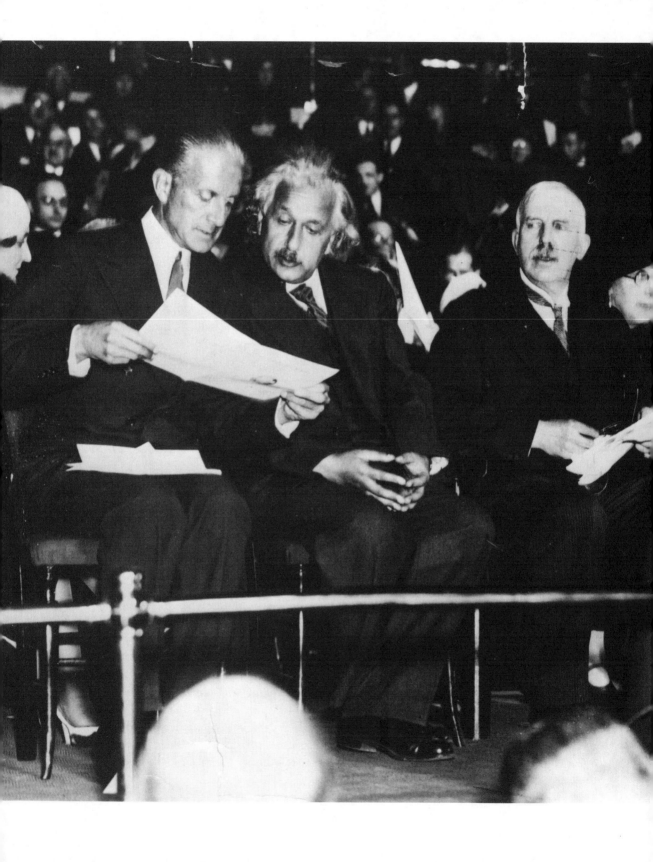

8.

Atomic Possibilities

August 1939

With the discovery of radioactivity in the late 1890s, scientists began to apprehend the fantastic amount of energy contained in a single atomic nucleus. They also began to recognize its potential military importance. Under normal circumstances, radioactive elements released their energy slowly, over millions of years; if, however, one could discharge all of this energy at once, the result would be an

unimaginably powerful explosion. Using Albert Einstein's $E=mc^2$ formula, one physicist estimated that the energy produced by converting the hydrogen atoms in a glass of water into helium "would drive the *Queen Mary* across the Atlantic and back at full speed."

When British physicist James Chadwick discovered the neutron in 1932, the pace of the work accelerated. Because neutrons contained no electrical charge, they could be shot into nuclei and used to probe their secrets. In 1933, Jewish émigré physicist Leo Szilard realized while pausing at a London traffic light that neutron bombardment could itself hold the key to a bomb. "As the light changed to green and I crossed the street," Szilard recalled, "it...suddenly occurred to me that if we could find an element which is split by neutrons and which would emit *two* neutrons when it absorbs *one* neutron, such an element, if assembled in sufficiently large mass, could sustain a nuclear chain reaction" and thus produce an explosion.

Confirmation of Szilard's hypothesis came in January 1939, when Otto Hahn and Fritz Strass-

man of the Kaiser Wilhelm Institute in Berlin published the results of their recent experiments with atom smashers. Using neutron bombardment, they had split atoms of uranium, producing several hundred million volts of electricity. Three months later, a secret German War Office report stated that "the newest developments in nuclear physics...will probably make it possible to produce an explosive many orders of magnitude more powerful than the conventional ones....That country which first makes use of it has an unsurpassable advantage over the others."

Immediately, Szilard and fellow refugee Enrico Fermi of Italy began lobbying the government of their newly adopted country, the United States, to recognize the possibility of an atomic bomb and the danger should Germany possess one first. Fermi met with officers of the army's Bureau of Ordnance and the Naval Research Laboratory in March 1939 with little result. However, Szilard fared better, persuading his eminent friend Einstein to write a letter directly to President Roosevelt in August 1939. The message had the desired result.

Albert Einstein attends a 1933 benefit at the Royal Albert Hall in London to raise funds for German Jewish refugees. Seated with Einstein are, from left to right, Oliver Locker-Lampson, who offered Einstein himself a place of safety in England, and physicist Ernest Rutherford.

HITLER IS 'GREATEST' IN PRINCETON POLL

Freshmen Put Einstein Second and Chamberlain Third

PRINCETON, N.J., Nov. 27—Princeton's freshmen again have chosen Adolf Hitler as "the greatest living person" in the annual poll of their class conducted by The Daily Princetonian. Ninety-three votes were given to the German Chancellor, as compared with twenty-seven to Albert Einstein in second position and fifteen to Neville Chamberlain in third.

In answer to a criticism, which suggested the use of the word "important" rather than "great" for the poll, The Nassau Daily pointed out editorially that the dictionary defines "great" as "eminent or distinguished by rank, power or moral character."

The Princeton yearlings gave most votes to President Roosevelt as the greatest living American, with Charles Evans Hughes and Herbert Hoover in second and third positions, respectively. President Roosevelt ranked fifth, behind Mahatma Gandhi, as "the greatest living person."

A third term for the President, however, was opposed by 368 votes, while only sixty favored it. Most believed he would run but would not be re-elected.

Only 120 Nassau first-year men said they would fight overseas, but 413 would defend this country against invasion. The present war is considered "imperialistic" by 199, "ideological" by only fifty-nine.

The class preferred a Phi Beta Kappa key to a varsity letter in athletics, and thought the chairmanship of The Daily Princetonian was the most desirable campus position.

"It may become possible to set up a nuclear chain reaction."

Albert Einstein's warning letter to President Roosevelt

Einstein's famous August 22, 1939, letter to Roosevelt was drafted by the so-called Hungarian Conspiracy—émigré physicists Leo Szilard, Edward Teller, and Eugene Wigner—during a visit to Einstein's Long Island vacation home. The letter was then entrusted to Alexander Sachs, an economist with White House connections. Sachs, however, found it difficult to obtain a personal appointment with Roosevelt and so had to wait until October 11 before hand-delivering the letter to the president.

> Albert Einstein
> Old Grove Road
> Nassau Point
> Peconic, Long Island

August 2, 1939

F. D. Roosevelt,
President of the United States,
White House
Washington, D. C.

Sir:

Some recent work by E. Fermi and L. Szilard, which has been communicated to me in a manuscript, leads me to expect that the element uranium may be turned into a new and important source of energy in the immediate future. Certain aspects of this situation which has arisen seem to call for watchfulness and, if necessary, quick action on the part of the administration. I believe therefore that it is my duty to bring to your attention the following facts and recommendations:

In the course of the last four months it has been made probable—through the work of Joliot in France as well as Fermi and Szilard in America—that it may become possible to set up a nuclear chain reaction in a large mass of uranium, by which vast amounts of power and large quantities of new radium-like elements would be generated. Now it appears almost certain that this could be achieved in the immediate future.

This new phenomenon would also lead to the construction of bombs, and it is conceivable—though much less certain—that extremely powerful bombs of a new type may thus be constructed. A single bomb of this type, carried by boat and exploded in a port, might very well destroy the whole port together with some of the surrounding territory. However, such bombs might very well prove to be too heavy for transportation by air.

The United States has only very poor ores of uranium in moderate quantities. There is some good ore in Canada and the former Czechoslovakia, while the most important source of uranium is Belgian Congo.

In view of this situation you may think it desirable to have some permanent contact maintained between the administration and the group of physicists working on chain reactions in America. One possible way of achieving this might be for you to entrust with this task a person who has your confidence and who could perhaps serve in an inofficial capacity. His task might comprise the following:

a) to approach Government Departments, keep them informed of the further development, and put forward recommendations for Government action, giving particular attention to the problem of securing a supply of uranium ore for the United States;

b) to speed up the experimental work, which is at present being carried on within the limits of the budgets of University Laboratories, by providing funds, if such funds be required, through his contacts with private persons who are willing to make contributions for this cause, and perhaps also by obtaining the co-operation of industrial laboratories which have the necessary equipment.

I understand that Germany has actually stopped the sale of uranium from the Czechoslovakian mines which she has taken over. That she should have taken such an early action might perhaps be understood on the ground that the son of the German Under-Secretary of State, von Weizsacker, is attached to the Kaiser-Wilhelm-Institute in Berlin, where some of the American work on uranium is now being repeated.

Yours very truly,
Albert Einstein

9.

The Nazi-Soviet Nonaggression Pact

August 1939

After Munich, British prime minister Neville Chamberlain looked forward to a general settlement with Hitler of all Versailles-related European boundary questions, believing that such an agreement was possible and that it would promote a lasting peace. Germany's preeminent role in the March 1939 dismemberment of Czechoslovakia, however, gave the lie to Hitler's claim that he was merely seeking to

protect the interests of fellow ethnic Germans.

On March 23, moreover, Hitler seized Memel, a Lithuanian port on the Baltic that the League of Nations had established as an autonomous territory similar to that existing in the Free City of Danzig. Woodrow Wilson had insisted that the newly reconstituted Poland be given access to the sea. Therefore, the Treaty of Versailles created the Polish Corridor, a strip of West Prussia about thirty miles wide that joined the rest of Poland to the German port of Danzig, which was then placed under Polish administration. Hitler's seizure of Memel and his accompanying demands for the return of the Polish Corridor and Danzig finally persuaded Chamberlain to reconsider his appeasement policy, and on March 31 the prime minister announced to Parliament that his government, joined by France, had guaranteed Poland's borders against German attack.

Although Chamberlain still hoped for a negotiated settlement (and therefore made few military preparations), his announcement stiffened Polish resolve. Ironically, as late as January 1939,

Hitler had hoped to ally himself with Poland against the Soviet Union, whose Communist government he despised. Yet the Poles rejected each of his advances, and finally, after Chamberlain's announcement, he simply gave up.

Meanwhile, in April, Soviet leader Joseph Stalin began hinting his willingness to consider an agreement with Germany that might provide for Soviet neutrality in the event of war. (Although the Soviets were simultaneously holding talks with Britain and France concerning a possible alliance, Stalin fundamentally mistrusted the Western democracies and feared that they would merely take the defensive in a war, leaving his nation to face the full onslaught of German might on its own.) In May, the two sides began formal trade talks, and these eventually led to the political agreement concluded with the Nazi-Soviet Nonaggression Pact. What neither leader revealed, however, was the secret protocol providing for a specific division of Poland "in the even of a territorial and political rearrangement."

GERMANY AND RUSSIA AGREE ON NON-AGGRESSION; RIBBENTROP GOING TO MOSCOW TO DRAFT PACT; BERLIN SEES QUICK SHOWDOWN WITH POLAND

Germans Elated; Amity Treaty With Soviet Lifts Fear

By OTTO D. TOLISCHUS

BERLIN, Tuesday, Aug. 22—Chancellor Adolf Hitler threw another bombshell into the camp of those trying to halt him when it was officially announced here last night that Germany and Soviet Russia had agreed to conclude a non-aggression pact and that Foreign Minister Joachim von Ribbentrop, author of the anti-Comintern pact, would arrive in Moscow Wednesday to "conclude the negotiations."

This announcement, distributed throughout the country by extra editions of newspapers, was hailed here with supreme elation as a great diplomatic victory over Britain because it was taken to mean the end of the Anglo-French-Russian alliance negotiations and the collapse of Britain's "encirclement" policy, lifting from German minds the specter of the Russian steam-roller in case of a new war.

It is still too early to judge the implications of this new coup, repeatedly predicted in these dispatches, because it affects the alignment of many powers, particularly Japan. But one immediate significance revealed itself when German quarters spread the rumor that Herr Hitler was also determined to force a solution this week of the Polish-German conflict, which started over Danzig and now involves the fate of Poland and the issue of a new world war. A German solution will be sought by diplomacy if possible; if not, by the German Army.

According to usually well-informed sources, the German General Staff has orders to be ready for immediate military action by Thursday, and these, perhaps, are not unintentional revelations. This information is taken as a German warning that unless diplomacy finds a way out of the deadlock by that time Herr Hitler is determined to break the deadlock by force of arms.

Before the Russo-German nonaggression pact was announced, some circles were still inclined to regard this threat as merely another move in the "war of nerves," and Polish circles in particular characterized it as "bluff." But the Russian pact, which completely isolates Poland in the east and holds over her the menace of a new partition between her mighty neighbors, puts a different light on matters, and this threat is also backed up by troop concentrations on both sides of the entire German-Polish frontier.

On the German side East Prussia—where most able-bodied men up to 55 are mobilized—is virtually an armed camp. Considerable troop concentrations are also reported in Pomerania, Silesia and Slovakia. According to the best military opinion, these troops are still insufficient for an invasion of Poland, but they are rapidly being increased and preparations are being made to rush flying divisions to their aid.

Some bombing squadrons and tank contingents—the latter painted black with a white cross for identification—are passing through Berlin itself, heading east, and trucks and automobiles are being concentrated at strategic points to move troops quickly. Extensive Polish

Soviet foreign minister Vyacheslav M. Molotov signs the Nazi-Soviet Nonaggression Pact with Stalin, Ribbentrop, and others looking on.

troop concentrations, admitted in Warsaw, now take big headlines in the German press.

The entire German press with inspired unanimity took the stand yesterday that the decision regarding Poland was at hand. The semi-official news service, Dienst aus Deutschland, said:

"The impression prevails in Wilhelmstrasse as well that a decision is ripening quickly."

And though that service said that "all competent authorities anticipate this decision with great calm, based on confidence that the Fuehrer's policy will be successful and will again bring home to the German people a gain as peaceful as it will be substantial," other publications emphasized that Germany would not shrink from any alternative. They pointed to the expansion of Germany's military might and her excellent strategic position created by the Westwall, which in pages of pictures and description was again presented as a death trap to all French and British soldiers.

At the same time all German quarters and publications continued to emphasize that only immediate Polish acceptance of the German demands, which now aim at complete revision of eastern borders to remove all the "injustices of Versailles," can save the situation, and they continued to hammer at London to persuade the Poles to accept.

"It is now up to London"—that is the stand of Wilhelmstrasse, which while preparing for emergencies to the extent of establishing a special night service, yet holds that diplomacy still has a chance and also hints that many moves are also under way behind the scenes. What these moves may be, aside from the new Russo-German pact, are not revealed, but a few of the visible or prospective ones are as follows:

Josef Lipski, Polish Ambassador to Germany, took a plane for Warsaw yesterday to consult his government, presumably on the Russo-German pact, but whether he also took a message from the German Government was not disclosed.

Franz von Papen, Herr Hitler's special Ambassador in particularly delicate situations, was received by the Chancellor at Berchtesgaden yesterday and entrusted with a secret mission on which Herr von Papen left immediately by plane for an undisclosed destination—assumed to be London, but it may be Rome.

Today, presumably after the British Cabinet meeting, Ambassador Sir Nevile Henderson is scheduled to go to Salzburg, and no pretense is being made in such a case that he would merely go to attend motor races.

In addition, diplomatic quarters paid serious attention to a rumor current here that Premier Mussolini of Italy had made an offer to London to remain neutral if Britain remained neutral in a purely Polish-German conflict. That rumor may form the basis of a report abroad that Bernardo Attolico, Italian Ambassador, has brought to Herr Hitler a "negative" answer from Signor Mussolini, which was hotly denied here as another "British lie manoeuvre."

Whether these diplomatic moves will produce a solution remains to be seen, but it is a fact that the new crisis is developing so much like an oft-rehearsed and now almost hackneyed stage play that nobody is quite able to take it seriously and inevitably looks forward to diplomatic intervention that will again "save peace in our time" and give Germany what she wants. And in that confidence may lurk danger.

Meanwhile, the German press spreads the Russo-German pact in huge headlines across the front page, together with Polish troop movements, which are declared to be an intolerable provocation to a big power like Germany, as well as further charges about Polish atrocities that must be halted and halted immediately.

In German military circles an isolated Poland is not considered a major military obstacle, especially since the Westwall permits Germany to throw the major part of her massed army against the country. They give Poland not more than a fortnight before she would be overrun.

For that reason Germany confidently expects today that Poland will throw up her hands and yield and therewith Eastern Europe and all its riches will soon be opened to German organizing efficiency, bringing Herr Hitler's dream of empire close to reality.

As regards the new German-Russian agreement, it actually merely revitalizes and strengthens the already existing Russo-German Treaty of Rapallo and the Pact of Berlin, which provide for the neutrality of one partner in case the other is attacked. The terms of the new agreement apparently are still to be fixed, but if Germany has her way the non-aggression pact will be unconditional, and the new Russo-German trade agreement, announced yesterday, suggests that Russian neutrality might even be friendly neutrality.

As a feat in appeasement Herr Hitler's "appeasement" of Joseph Stalin is unique, considering the former National Socialist campaign against bolshevism. The only question diplomats are asking now is: "Has Stalin also succeeded in appeasing Hitler?"

"Now Poland is in the position in which I wanted her."

Adolf Hitler's speech to his generals on the conclusion
of the Nazi-Soviet Pact

Adolf Hitler made the speech excerpted here to his commanders in chief at Obersalzberg on August 22, 1939, the day that the Nazi-Soviet Nonaggression Pact was announced. After the war, Allied investigators found a transcript in the files of the Oberkommando der Wehrmacht (OKW), or German High Command.

I have called you together to give you a picture of the political situation, in order that you may have some insight into the individual factors on which I have based my decision to act and in order to strengthen your confidence.

After this we shall discuss military details.

It was clear to me that a conflict with Poland had to come sooner or later. I had already made this decision in the spring, but I thought that I would first turn against the West in a few years, and only after that against the East. But the sequence of these things cannot be fixed. Nor should one close one's eyes to threatening situations. I wanted first of all to establish a tolerable relationship with Poland in order to fight first against the West. But this plan, which appealed to me, could not be executed, as fundamental points had changed. It became clear to me that, in the event of a conflict with the West, Poland would attack us. Poland is striving for access to the sea. The further development appeared after the occupation of the Memel Territory, and it became clear to me that in certain circumstances a conflict with Poland might come at an inopportune moment. I give as reasons for this conclusion:

First of all, two personal factors: My own personality and that of Mussolini.

Essentially, all depends on me, on my existence, because of my political talents. Furthermore, the fact that probably no one will ever again have the confidence of the whole German people as I have. There will probably never again in the future be a man with more authority than I have. My existence is therefore a factor of great value. But I can be eliminated at any time by a criminal or a lunatic.

The second personal factor is the Duce. His existence is also decisive. If anything happens to him, Italy's loyalty to the alliance will no longer be certain. The Italian Court is fundamentally opposed to the Duce. Above all, the Court regards the expansion of the empire as an encumbrance. The Duce is the man with the strongest nerves in Italy.

The third personal factor in our favour is Franco. We can ask only for benevolent neutrality from Spain. But this depends on Franco's personality. He guarantees a certain uniformity and stability in the present system in Spain. We must accept the fact that Spain does not as yet have a Fascist party with our internal unity.

The other side presents a negative picture as far as authoritative persons are concerned. There is no outstanding personality in England and France.

It is easy for us to make decisions. We have nothing to lose; we have everything to gain. Because of our restrictions, our economic situation is such that we can only hold out for a few more years. Göring can confirm this. We have no other choice; we must act. Our opponents will be risking a great deal and can gain only a little. Britain's stake in a war is inconceivably great. Our enemies have leaders who are below the average. No personalities. No masters. No men of action.

Besides the personal factors, the political situation is favourable for us: in the Mediterranean, rivalry between Italy, France, and England; in the Far East, tension between Japan and England; in the Middle East, tension which causes alarm in the Mohammedan world.

The English Empire did not emerge stronger from the last war. Nothing was achieved from the maritime point of view. Strife between England and Ireland. The Union of South Africa has become more independent. Concessions have had to be made to India. England is in the utmost peril. Unhealthy industrialization. A British statesman can only view the future with concern.

France's position has also deteriorated, above all in the Mediterranean.

Further factors in our favour are these:

Since Albania, there has been a balance of power in the Balkans. Yugoslavia is infected with the fatal germ of decay because of her internal situation.

Rumania has not grown stronger. She is open to attack and vulnerable. She is threatened by Hungary and Bulgaria. Since Kemal's death, Turkey has been ruled by petty minds, unsteady, weak men.

All these favourable circumstances will no longer prevail in two or three years' time. No one knows how much longer I shall live. Therefore, better a conflict now.

The creation of Greater Germany was a great achievement politically, but militarily it was doubtful, since it was achieved by bluff on the part of the political leaders. It is necessary to test the military [machine]. If at all possible, not in a general reckoning, but by the accomplishment of individual tasks.

The relationship with Poland has become unbearable. My Polish policy hitherto was contrary to the views of the people. My proposals to Poland (Danzig and the Corridor) were frustrated by England's intervention. Poland changed her tone towards us. A permanent state of tension is intolerable. The power of initiative cannot be allowed to pass to others. The present moment is more favourable than in two or three years' time. An attempt on my life or Mussolini's could change the situation to our disadvantage. One cannot forever face one another with rifles cocked. One compromise solution suggested to us was that we should change our convictions and make kind gestures. They talked to us again in the language of Versailles. There was a danger of losing prestige. Now the probability is still great that the West will not intervene. We must take the risk with ruthless determination. The politician must take a risk just as much as the general. We are faced with the harsh alternatives of striking or of certain annihilation sooner or later.

(Reference to previous hazardous undertakings.)

I should have been stoned if I had not been proved right. The most dangerous step was the entry into the neutral zone. Only a week before, I got a warning through France. I have always taken a great risk in the conviction that it would succeed.

Now it is also a great risk. Iron nerves, iron resolution.

The following special reasons fortify me in my view. England and France have undertaken obligations which neither is in a position to fulfill. There is no real rearmament in England, but only propaganda. A great deal of harm was done by many Germans, who were not in agreement with me, saying and writing to English people after the solution of the Czech question: The Führer succeeded because you lost your nerve, because you capitulated too soon. This explains the present propaganda war. The English speak of a war of nerves. One factor in this war of nerves is to boost the increase of armaments. But what are the real facts about British rearmament? The naval construction programme for

1938 has not yet been completed. Only the reserve fleet has been mobilized. Purchase of trawlers. No substantial strengthening of the Navy before 1941 or 1942.

Little has been done on land. England will be able to send at most three divisions to the Continent. A little has been done for the Air Force, but it is only a beginning. Anti-aircraft defense is in its initial stages. At the moment England has only 150 anti-aircraft guns. The new anti-aircraft gun has been ordered. It will take a long time before sufficient numbers have been produced. There is a shortage of predictors. England is still vulnerable from the air. This can change in two or three years. At the moment, the English Air Force has only 130,000 men, France 72,000, Poland 15,000. England does not want the conflict to break out for two or three years.

The following is typical of England: Poland wanted a loan from England for her rearmament. England, however, only granted credits in order to make sure that Poland buys in England, although England cannot make deliveries. This suggests that England does not really want to support Poland. She is not risking eight million pounds in Poland, although she poured five hundred millions into China. England's position in the world is very precarious. She will not take any risks.

France is short of men (decline in the birth rate). Little has been done for rearmament. The artillery is obsolete. France did not want to embark on this adventure. The West has only two possibilities for fighting against us:

1. Blockade: It will not be effective because of our autarchy and because we have sources of supply in Eastern Europe.

2. Attack in the West from the Maginot line: I consider this impossible.

Another possibility would be the violation of Dutch, Belgian, and Swiss neutrality. I have no doubt that all these States, as well as Scandinavia, will defend their neutrality with all available means. England and France will not violate the neutrality of these countries. Thus, in actual fact, England cannot help Poland. There still remains an attack on Italy. Military intervention is out of the question. No one is counting on a long war. If Herr von Brauchitsch had told me that I would need four years to conquer Poland, I would have replied: "Then it cannot be done." It is nonsense to say that England wants to wage a long war.

We will hold our position in the West until we have conquered Poland. We must bear in mind our great production capacity. It is much greater than in 1914–1918.

The enemy had another hope, that Russia would become our enemy after the conquest of Poland. The enemy did not reckon with my great strength of purpose. Our enemies are small fry. I saw them in Munich.

I was convinced that Stalin would never accept the English offer. Russia has no interest in preserving Poland, and Stalin knows that it would mean the end of his regime, no matter whether his soldiers emerged from a war victorious or vanquished. Litvinov's replacement was decisive. I brought about the change towards Russia gradually. In connection with the commercial treaty we got into political conversations. Proposal for a non-aggression pact. Then came a comprehensive proposal from Russia. Four days ago, I took a special step, which led to Russia replying yesterday that she is prepared to sign. Personal contact with Stalin is established. The day after tomorrow, von Ribbentrop will conclude the treaty. Now Poland is in the position in which I wanted her.

We need not be afraid of a blockade. The East will supply us with grain, cattle, coal, lead, and zinc. It is a mighty aim, which demands great efforts. I am only afraid that at the last moment some swine or other will yet submit to me a plan for mediation.

The political objective goes further. A start has been made on the destruction of England's hegemony. The way will be open for the soldiers after I have made the political preparations.

A German Messerschmitt Me100 overflies Poland during the September 1939 Blitzkrieg.

10.

The Invasion of Poland

September 1939

The lesson that most British, French, and even German generals learned from the carnage of World War I was that strong defenses prevailed. French marshal Philippe Pétain, for example, learned from his successful defense of Verdun against repeated German attack that well-prepared fortifications and heavy artillery could disrupt any offensive formation. After the war, therefore, most French and British

war planning centered on defensive strategies.

Yet some military men saw the situation differently: In Great Britain, Maj. Gen. J. F. C. Fuller promoted the use of tanks and other mechanized equipment—insisting that, used in large formations, they would be the weapons of the future. Following Fuller's lead, former infantry captain B. H. Liddell Hart developed his "expanding torrent" theory, which favored swift, deep tank penetrations behind enemy lines. In France, Col. Charles de Gaulle put forth similar ideas in *The Army of the Future* (1934). Unfortunately, none of these men effected any change in policy—except in Germany, where Heinz Guderian, who had served as an intelligence officer at Verdun, persuaded Hitler that tanks supported by aircraft could prove decisive in battle. In his 1937 book *Attention! Tanks!*, Guderian made extensive use of the ideas of Fuller, Liddell Hart, and de Gaulle in outlining the basics of *Blitzkrieg* ("lightning war"). With this revolutionary new strategy, Germany was able to overrun much of Europe by the fall of 1941.

At 4:45 A.M. on September 1, Hitler sent fifty-two divisions (about a million men) across the Polish border. Following Guderian's advice, the Germans' Case White plan called for six tank divisions to smash through the Polish border defenses and penetrate the interior as quickly and deeply as possible. With their flanks protected by new Stuka dive-bombers and with mechanized infantry following in their wake, the German Panzer columns soon joined up inside Poland, encircling their enemies and forcing them to surrender.

The poorly equipped Poles were no match. Within two days, their entire air force was destroyed by the Luftwaffe; and a week later, the Panzer divisions completed their first pincer movement, trapping 170,000 Polish troops. On September 17, the Soviet Union invaded Poland from the east to secure the territory promised it under the secret protocol to the Nazi-Soviet Pact, signed four weeks earlier. On September 27, the Warsaw garrison surrendered, and Poland was no more.

GERMAN ARMY ATTACKS POLAND; CITIES BOMBED, PORT BLOCKADED

Hitler Gives Word; In a Proclamation He Accuses Warsaw of Appeal to Arms

By OTTO D. TOLISCHUS

BERLIN, Friday, Sept. 1—Charging that Germany had been attacked, Chancellor Hitler at 5:11 o'clock this morning issued a proclamation to the army declaring that from now on force will be met with force and calling on the armed forces "to fulfill their duty to the end."

The text of the proclamation reads:

To the defense forces:
The Polish nation refused my efforts for a peaceful regulation of neighborly relations; instead it has appealed to weapons.

Germans in Poland are persecuted with a bloody terror and are driven from their homes. The series of border violations, which are unbearable to a great power, prove that the Poles no longer are willing to respect the German frontier. In order to put an end to this frantic activity no other means is left to me now than to meet force with force.

German defense forces will carry on the battle for the honor of the living rights of the reawakened German people with firm determination.

I expect every German soldier, in view of the great tradition of eternal German soldiery, to do his duty until the end.

Remember always in all situations you are the representatives of National Socialist Greater Germany!

Long live our people and our Reich!

Berlin, Sept. 1, 1939.

ADOLF HITLER

The commander-in-chief of the air force issued a decree effective immediately prohibiting the passage of any airplanes over German territory excepting those of the Reich air force or the government.

This morning the naval authorities ordered all German mercantile ships in the Baltic Sea not to run to Danzig or Polish ports.

Anti–air raid defenses were mobilized throughout the country early this morning.

A formal declaration of war against Poland had not yet been declared up to 8 o'clock [3 A.M. New York time] this morning and the question of whether the two countries are in a state of active belligerency is still open.

Foreign correspondents at an official conference at the Reich Press Ministry at 8:30 o'clock [3:30 A.M. New York time] were told that they would receive every opportunity to facilitate the transmission of dispatches. Wireless stations have been instructed to speed up communications and the Ministry is installing additional batteries of telephones.

The Reichstag has been summoned to meet at 10 o'clock [5 A.M. New York time] to receive a more formal declaration from Herr Hitler.

The Hitler army order is interpreted as providing, for the time being, armed defense of the German frontiers against aggression. The action is also suspected of forcing international diplomatic action.

The Germans announced that foreigners remain in Polish territory at their own risk.

Flying over Polish territory as well as the

German wagons pass a signpost during the September 1939 invasion of Poland.

maritime areas is forbidden by the German authorities and any violators will be shot down.

When Herr Hitler made his announcement Berlin's streets were still deserted except for the conventional early traffic, and there were no outward signs that the nation was finding itself in the first stages of war.

The government area was completely deserted, and the two guards doing sentry duty in front of the Chancellery remained their usual mute symbol of authority. It was only when official placards containing the orders to the populace began to appear on the billboards that early workers became aware of the situation.

"The opening of war by surprise and for quick success."

The German military orders for Case White

This military planning document was prepared in June 1939, about two months after Hitler's initial order that the German High Command develop an invasion plan for Poland.

THIRD ARMY GROUP
Ia Nr. 150/39 g.K. Chiefs
Re: Case White

Top Secret
"Only by officer"
Dresden 6.14.1939

20 Copies
Control No. 8

1. The commander-in-chief of the army has ordered the working out of a *plan of deployment against Poland* which takes into account the demands of the political leadership for the opening of war by surprise and for quick success.
2. The order of deployment by the High Command, "Case White" authorizes the Third Army Group (in Case White 8th Army Headquarters) to give necessary directions and orders to all commands subordinated to it for "Case White."
3. Enclosed are sent:
   a. Aims of the operation (Enclosure 1).
   b. Organization of the forces (Enclosure 2).
   c. Survey of arrival (Enclosure 3).
   d. Signal Communication (Enclosure 4).
   e. Regulations for the supply (Enclosure 5 will follow).
   f. Enemy situation (Enclosure 6).
   g. Directions for execution (Enclosure 7).
4. The order of deployment "Case White" will be put into operation on 20 August 1939; all preparations have to be concluded by this date.

   The former deployments "Case West" and "Case East" are valid until 19 August 1939.
5. For the instruction on the tasks due to this order for deployment, the principles of order OKH Genstb d.H—I Division (Ib Nr. 2000/36 top secret of 12.19.36) are to be applied.

   The instruction can be carried down to the responsible officers of the corps commands to the Division Commanders G-3 (Ia) and G-4 (Ib) of the divisions and the commandants and staff officers of the Garrison Headquarters. Permission to inform further persons must be requested by names.

Communication with the SS-Leibstandarte Adolf Hitler must be instituted only by special order. The order for their commitment is to be prepared.

6. Tenth Corps Command (Gen KdX) and XIII Corps and Io. Div. can perform the necessary reconnaissance in Silesia while observing the appropriate precautionary measures (civilian clothes, motor vehicle, with civilian license number).

7. The whole correspondence on "Case White" has to be conducted under the classification Top Secret. This is to be disregarded only if the content of a document, in the judgment of the chief of the responsible command, is harmless in every way—even in connection with other documents.

8. For the middle of July, a conference is planned where details on the execution will be discussed. Time and place will be ordered later on. Special requests are to be communicated to Third Army Group before 10 July.

9. I declare it the duty of the Commanding Generals, the divisional commanders and the commandants to limit as much as possible the number of persons who will be informed, and to limit the extent of the information, and ask that all suitable measures be taken to prevent persons not concerned from getting information.

Commander-in-Chief of Army Group 3
F. Blaskowitz

11

Britain and France Declare War

September 1939

Having shrewdly engineered Soviet neutrality, Hitler didn't expect either Britain or France to honor its guarantees to Poland. Instead, he believed that Chamberlain and Daladier would simply back down and abandon their ally in the East, just as they had Czechoslovakia. Therefore, it came as a surprise when, in response to the German invasion of Poland, the Western democracies actually declared war.

At first, Britain and France made only oblique threats. Upon learning of the Polish invasion, Chamberlain sent a relatively guarded message to Hitler, requiring him to withdraw from Poland yet offering little in the way of specific consequences should Hitler refuse. Later on September 1, Chamberlain attended a cabinet meeting at which he and his ministers discussed ways that Hitler might yet be pacified, while apparently waiting for Mussolini to intervene and restrain his bellicose German ally.

On September 2, still waiting for a German response, Chamberlain and Daladier agreed that, should the Germans withdraw from Poland, they would attend a peace conference sponsored by Mussolini to reconsider the status of Danzig and the Polish Corridor. That evening, however, the mood in Parliament shifted, and a bloc of Conservative members informed Chamberlain that they would initiate a vote of confidence against him if he didn't shortly declare war. At 9 A.M. London time on September 3, the prime minister sent a final ultimatum to Hitler, giving the Führer (who

had still not replied to Chamberlain's September 1 note) just two additional hours to respond. When no answer came, Chamberlain informed the House of Commons shortly after 11 A.M. that a state of war now existed between Britain and Germany. Meanwhile, France issued its own ultimatum at noon Paris time and joined the war at 5 P.M.

By then, of course, it was already much too late to save Poland, so the British and French concentrated on improving their own defensive positions—much as Stalin had anticipated they would. (Neither, for example, moved to exploit Germany's weakened western defenses, manned only by twenty-five reserve divisions while the strength of the Wehrmacht rampaged in Poland.) Hitler, it seems, would have preferred that the conquest of Poland remain an isolated, contained stratagem. But the ensuing declarations of war by Britain and France did little to perturb him. He had known for years that war with the Western democracies would have to come sooner or later, and he considered the effect on his timetable hardly significant.

A newspaper poster in the Whitehall section of London announces the British declaration of war on Germany.

BRITAIN AND FRANCE IN WAR AT 6 A.M.; HITLER WON'T HALT ATTACK ON POLES; CHAMBERLAIN CALLS EMPIRE TO FIGHT

Premier Calls It 'Bitter Blow' That Efforts for Peace Have Failed

Prime Minister Neville Chamberlain announced to the world at 6:10 o'clock this morning that Great Britain and France were at war with Germany. He made the announcement over the radio, with short waves carrying the measured tones of his voice throughout all continents, from 10 Downing Street in London.

Mr. Chamberlain disclosed that Great Britain and France had taken concurrent action, announcing that "we and France are, today, in fulfillment of our obligations, going to the aid of Poland."

France, however, had not made any announcement beyond stating that the French Ambassador to Berlin would make a final call upon Foreign Minister Joachim von Ribbentrop at 6 o'clock this morning, and it was assumed the French had proclaimed the existence of the state of war.

With the greatest solemnity Mr. Chamberlain began his declaration by reporting that the British Ambassador to Berlin had handed in Great Britain's final ultimatum and that it had not been accepted. Without hesitation he announced Britain's decision and, after touching briefly on the background of the crisis, he expressed the highest confidence that "injustice, oppression and persecution" would be vanquished and that his cause would triumph.

Mr. Chamberlain appealed to his people, schooled during the last year as the crisis deepened in measures of defense and offense, to carry on with their jobs and begged a blessing upon them, warning that "we shall be fighting against brute force."

The declaration came after Great Britain had given Chancellor Adolf Hitler of Germany extended time in which to answer the British Government's final ultimatum of Friday. In the final ultimatum Herr Hitler had been told that unless German aggression in Poland ceased, Britain was prepared to fulfill her obligations to Poland.

Britain's last warning at 4 o'clock this morning, New York time, left no doubt of her stand, for the phrase, "fulfillment of Britain's obligations to Poland," was replaced by a flat statement that a state of war would exist between the two countries as of the hour of the deadline.

After Mr. Chamberlain had finished his statement, which had been introduced as "an announcement of national importance," the announcer warned the British people not to gather together, broadcast an order that all meeting places for entertainment be closed, and gave precautions to prepare the people against air bombings and poison gas attacks.

Mr. Chamberlain began his declaration by reporting that the British Ambassador to Berlin, Sir Nevile Henderson, had two hours before handed a final ultimatum to the German Government that unless the Reich was prepared to withdraw its troops from Polish territory, a state of war would exist between the two countries.

"I have to tell you now that no such undertaking has been received and consequently this country is at war with Germany," he said solemnly.

"You can imagine," the Prime Minister said, "what a bitter blow this is to me."

He cited his "long struggle for peace."

"I cannot believe there was anything more or anything different I could have done," he said.

"Up to the very last," he said, speaking in a low but firm tone, "I worked for peace. But Hitler would not have it."

"Although Hitler now says he put forth reasonable terms to the Poles," continued the Prime Minister, "this is not a true statement." He reiterated the British assertion that Germany's sixteen points were never shown to Poland or to England.

Hitler's actions, Mr. Chamberlain said, show clearly that he will never give up the use of force to attain his ends.

"He can only be stopped by force," the Prime Minister continued. "We and the French have come to that conclusion."

Britain's conscience is clear, the Prime Minister declared.

When it became apparent, he continued, that no word given by Hitler could be "trusted" the "situation became intolerable."

"I know," he told his empire listeners, "that you will all play your parts with courage." Reports from all parts of the empire were, he said, "very encouraging."

In concluding his brief address the Prime Minister explained that government war announcements were to follow. Under the plans laid, he explained, most Britons would be called for service in the fighting units or the auxiliaries. He urged all Britons to follow instructions.

"Report duly according to instructions," he said.

Following the Prime Minister's address a British Broadcasting announcer issued instructions for protection against air raids. These instructions were that theatres and motion picture houses were to be closed until further notice. In some areas, however, it might be possible for them to reopen.

Large sports gatherings were prohibited until further notice. The orders against the gathering of crowds did not apply to churches which, the announcer said, "will not be closed."

In the event of air raids the announcer said that warning notes would be sounded, "every few seconds," on sirens and by short blasts from police whistles. In the event of an air raid all persons were urged to take immediate shelter and were warned against leaving them until they heard the clear signal which would constitute a blast from sirens lasting two minutes.

If poison gas was used rifle shots would be fired, the announcer said. All citizens were warned not to leave their shelter until the clearing signals, which would be given by "hand bells," were sounded.

In regard to schools the announcer said that all schools would be closed at least "for a week from today." He explained that as soon as arrangements could be made the schools would be reopened in the areas where children have been evacuated from the principal cities. The precise date of the reopening of all schools will be decided by the school authorities.

In general instructions to all British subjects the announcer warned them to keep off the streets "as much as you can," to carry their gas masks at all times and to be sure that each person carried an identification tag giving name and address.

The final set of instructions was addressed to recipients of unemployment benefits, instructing them in the procedure they should follow to avoid congestion at the local offices of the Ministry of Labor.

"Everything that I have worked for has crashed into ruins."

Remarks by Neville Chamberlain to the House of Commons

The first set of remarks excerpted here was delivered by Prime Minister Neville Chamberlain at an emergency meeting of the House of Commons on September 2, 1939. The second was delivered by Chamberlain the following morning.

September 2

Sir Nevile Henderson was received by Herr von Ribbentrop at half past nine last night, and he delivered the warning message which was read to the House yesterday. Herr von Ribbentrop replied that he must submit the communication to the German Chancellor. Our Ambassador declared his readiness to receive the Chancellor's reply. Up to the present, no reply has been received.

It may be that the delay is caused by consideration of a proposal which, meanwhile, had been put forward by the Italian Government, that hostilities should cease and that there should then immediately be a conference between the five powers: Great Britain, France, Poland, Germany and Italy. While appreciating the efforts of the Italian Government, His Majesty's Government, for their part, would find it impossible to take part in a conference while Poland is being subjected to invasion, her towns are under bombardment and Danzig is being made the subject of a unilateral settlement by force. His Majesty's Government will, as stated yesterday, be bound to take action unless the German forces are withdrawn from Polish territory. They are in communication with the French Government as to the limit of time within which it would be necessary for the British and French Governments to know whether the German Government were prepared to effect such a withdrawal. If the German Government should agree to withdraw their forces, then His Majesty's Government would be willing to regard the position as being the same as it was before the German forces crossed the Polish frontier. That is to say, the way would be open to discussion between the German and Polish Governments on the matters at issue between them, on the understanding that the settlement arrived at was one that safeguarded the vital interests of Poland and was secured by an international guarantee. If the German and Polish Governments wished that other Powers should be associated with them in the discussion, His Majesty's Government, for their part, would be willing to agree.

There is one other matter to which allusion should be made in order that the present situation may be perfectly clear. Yesterday, Herr Forster who, on 23rd August, had, in contravention of the Danzig constitution, become the head of the State, decreed the incorporation of Danzig into the Reich and the dissolution of the Constitution. Herr Hitler was asked to give effect to this decree by German law. At a meeting of the Reichstag yesterday morning, a law was passed for the reunion of Danzig with the Reich. The international status of Danzig as a Free City is established by a treaty of which His Majesty's Government are a signatory, and the Free City was placed under the protection of the League of Nations. The rights given to Poland in Danzig by treaty are defined and confirmed by agreement concluded between Danzig and Poland. The action taken by the Danzig authorities and the Reichstag yesterday is the final step in the unilateral repudiation of these international instruments, which could only be modified by negotiation. His Majesty's Government do not, therefore, recognise either the validity of the grounds on which the action of the Danzig authorities was based, the validity of this action itself, or of the effect given to it by the German Government.

◆ ◆ ◆

September 3

When I spoke last night to the House, I could not but be aware that in some parts of the House there were doubts and some bewilderment as to whether there had been any weakening, hesitation or vacillation on the part of His Majesty's Government. In the circumstances, I make no reproach, for if I had been in the same position as honourable members not sitting on this bench and not in possession of all the information which we have, I should very likely have felt the same. The statement which I have to make this morning will show that there were no grounds for doubt. We were in consultation all day yesterday with the French Government, and we felt that the intensified action which the Germans were taking against Poland allowed no delay in making our own position clear. Accordingly, we decided to send to our Ambassador in Berlin instructions which he was to hand at 9 o'clock this morning to the German Foreign Secretary and which read as follows:

Neville Chamberlain leaves his 10 Downing Street residence in London on October 1, 1939. The British prime minister is on his way to Rome, where he will meet with Mussolini, but first he intends to stop over in Paris for talks with the French government.

Sir,
In the communication which I had the honour to make to you on the 1st September, I informed you, on the instructions of His Majesty's Principal Secretary of State for Foreign Affairs, that unless the German Government were prepared to give His Majesty's Government in the United Kingdom satisfactory assurances that the German Government had suspended all aggressive action against Poland and were prepared promptly to withdraw their forces from Polish territory, His Majesty's Government in the United Kingdom would, without hesitation, fulfil their obligations to Poland.

Although this communication was made more than twenty-four hours ago, no reply has been received but German attacks upon Poland have been continued and intensified. I have accordingly the honour to inform you that, unless not later than 11 A.M., British Summer Time, to-day 3rd September, satisfactory assurances to the above effect have been given by the German Government and have reached His Majesty's Government in London, a state of war will exist between the two countries as from that hour.

That was the final note. No such undertaking was received by the time stipulated, and, consequently, this country is at war with Germany. I am in a position to inform the House that, according to arrangements made between the British and French Governments, the French Ambassador in Berlin is at this moment making a similar démarche, accompanied also by a definite time limit. The House has already been made aware of our plans. As I said the other day, we are ready.

This is a sad day for all of us, and to none is it sadder than to me. Everything that I have worked for, everything that I have hoped for, everything that I have believed in during my public life, has crashed into ruins. There is only one thing left for me to do; that is, to devote what strength and powers I have to forwarding the victory of the cause for which we have to sacrifice so much. I cannot tell what part I may be allowed to play myself; I trust I may live to see the day when Hitlerism has been destroyed and a liberated Europe has been re-established.

12.

The Phony War
September 1939–May 1940

During the September 1938 Sudetenland crisis, a group of German generals, believing that war with Britain and France would be madness, decided that, for the good of Germany, Hitler would have to be removed from power. Although the Führer's triumph at Munich temporarily ended this plotting, his decision to attack the West in the fall of 1939 renewed the conspiracy. Chief of the General Staff Franz

Halder began carrying a pistol with him to meetings with the Führer yet couldn't quite bring himself to shoot an unarmed man. Still, the talk of assassination continued, most of it centered in the Abwehr, the intelligence branch of the German military.

What agitated Halder and his colleagues so much was their knowledge that the Wehrmacht's Panzer divisions couldn't be transferred from Poland to the West until at least November; therefore, any invasion (code-named Case Yellow) would have to take place during the winter months—a potentially disastrous blunder, they believed. Nevertheless, Hitler stubbornly ignored their repeated warnings; he asserted his own primacy and insisted that plans for Case Yellow move ahead as quickly as possible. Bad weather, however, led to several postponements. Then, in January 1940, the forced landing in Belgium of an off-course courier plane resulted in the capture by the Allies of top-secret documents

relating to the German invasion. No one on the Allied side could be sure that the documents weren't misinformation; but the Germans, knowing them to be real, had to revise their plans accordingly. This required a further postponement of the invasion until May—much to Halder's relief—and again the plot collapsed.

Meanwhile, the defensive-minded British and French converted their factories to military use and waited for something to happen. In England, this period was known as the Phony War; in France, it was the *drôle de guerre*. (The Germans called it *Sitzkrieg*.) The British put their faith in the Royal Navy's ability to defend the English Channel and in the capacity of the Royal Air Force to shoot down Luftwaffe bombers before they could raze British cities. The French, for their part, entrusted their fate to their army—on paper, nearly the equal of the German military—and the Maginot line, the most impressive system of fortifications ever built.

PARIS LIFE ALMOST BACK TO NORMAL; FOOD PLENTIFUL, THEATRES CROWDED

Most of the Shops Have Been Reopened—Army Releases 100,000

By P. J. PHILIP

PARIS, Oct. 28—Except for a few minor inconveniences, no one arriving in Paris today would know there was a war going on at the frontier. Tomorrow it will enter its third month, and all prophets in the past predicted that long before then the French capital would be bombed out of recognition, or that at least the French Government and most of the population would have been bombed out of Paris.

Yet things go on almost without change. The weather is everybody's worst grumble, for it rains almost incessantly and last night there was snow for the first time this season—exceptionally early snow.

More and more restaurants keep opening and are crowded.

Those who listened to an American broadcast the other evening were surprised to hear that eggs, milk and butter were very scarce here. One found the same news in Spanish and some other neutral newspapers. It had been "made in Germany" and the source was not quoted by the American radio speaker. It just isn't true. There is not only no shortage of these things, but in Paris the usual seasonal price rise has not occurred because the supply is greater than the population, depleted by men mobilized, many of their families and nearly all foreigners, requires.

What is most characteristic of the city is that it has gone French again. Restaurants are filled with French people and one scarcely hears any foreign language except, occasionally, English. During the last weeks lighting has been so much improved and restored that there is now little or no danger at night. Automobiles are required to drive at no more than fifteen miles an hour, but that rule is observed only when the police are heard whistling at speeding drivers.

More and more theatres and music halls are giving early shows, and cinemas now remain open until 11 P.M. Telephone restrictions have been or are being removed. Although permits are still necessary for travel in certain directions, these permits are now more easily obtainable, or it is discovered on arrival that they were not really necessary at all.

Except in cases where employers and employed have all been mobilized, nearly all shops have reopened. Schools are at work again, although incompletely because so many teachers are in the army.

One of the most welcome improvements in the situation from the viewpoint of the French people is an announcement that certain classes and categories of reservists are being demobilized. Not only has the whole 1910 class been set free, but exceptions are being made for fathers of four children to whatever class they belong and fathers of three and two children in certain classes.

The only place in which the war really is being felt is the newspaper offices, for their readers keep clamoring for news and there is no news. It is true there exists here in Paris a Commissariat of Information but if it has any information, which is doubtful, it is being extremely careful to keep it to itself.

Too much importance is, perhaps, attached

British troops enter a fortified position in France, December 1939.

abroad to the censorship, which in reality is now working benevolently except in cases where some particular censor's experience is limited. Thus a telegram sent to The New York Times's Paris office two days ago from Amsterdam had its first three lines deleted. The censor's ink, however, was not heavy enough to prevent the words being deciphered. They read:

"Grover Whalen arrived at The Hague from Brussels and says he is satisfied with the results of his talks in Switzerland, France and Rome. Poland and Czecho-Slovakia are ready to exhibit at the Fair."

It seems that the censor had never heard of Grover Whalen and came to the conclusion that a man who traveled so much and had so many international contacts at a time like this must be a first class international spy.

"Simply nothing has happened."

A. J. Liebling's October 22, 1939, "Letter from Paris"

In the fall of 1939, *New Yorker* editor Harold Ross decided that Paris had become too dangerous for Janet Flanner, his correspondent there. (Flanner had been covering France for *The New Yorker* using the pseudonym Genêt.) To replace her, Ross sent over A. J. Liebling, a relatively recent addition to his staff. The thirty-four-year-old Liebling, however, had lived in Paris for a year during his early twenties and was familiar with the French. He flew to neutral Lisbon on a Pan American Clipper, thence made his way to Paris, arriving on October 12. Ten days later, he wrote the "Letter from Paris" reprinted here.

Paris at this writing is a city in which people are tentatively picking up the threads of ordinary existence—tentatively, and a little sheepishly, as if ashamed of their initial agitation. Theoretically, there is as much danger from the air this week as on the first day of War '39, as Frenchmen call this one to distinguish it from the other, but habit is stronger than reason. Wives who were rushed to the country at the outbreak now want to come back to rejoin their husbands in Paris, and in most cases the women are having their way. People buy newspapers as mechanically as they light cigarettes and, after looking at the headlines, leave them on café tables virtually unread because there is no news. The public at first blamed censorship but has now begun to sense that simply nothing has happened, and in the French fashion it has begun to make fun of the baffled journalists. One of the favorite butts is Mlle. Genevieve Tabouis, of *L'Oeuvre*, who writes circumstantially every day of events in Germany, where, of course, she isn't. She has many less eminent imitators.

Paris newspapers have never carried so much German news as now, when the sources of this news are inaccessible. One reported Monday that Hitler had confided his testament of thirty pages to Göring, who presumably was decent enough to count them for the Allied press. Havas announced later that the Führer was practicing revolver shooting at moving targets, a sign he feared assassination. Another journalistic genre, already hackneyed, is the conducted visit of illustrious correspondents to the front. The correspondents, often members of the Académie Française or Goncourt, are invariably taken to Strasbourg, which was cleared of inhabitants when the war began. Each Academician compares Strasbourg to a dead city or a sleeping beauty, according to his taste, and professes to have been startled by the sound of his own footsteps in the empty streets. One columnist wrote, after reading a series of these *rapportages*, "Monsieur X was not frightened by his own footsteps, but by the fourteen correspondents behind him." Serious editorialists, like Gallus, of *Paris-Soir*, have felt impelled to reprove such public levity and to warn their readers that the situation remains potentially grave.

The French have an enormous confidence in their army, especially now that the Germans have let slip the opportunity for a surprise attack. They suspect that the German High Command will not attempt a great offensive unless its hand is forced by *ce fou d'Hitler*, and discussions of strategy in the cafés invariably hinge on just how *fou* Hitler is. As for air raids on great cities, the public senses now that the Germans are loath to begin; while waiting, people say, it is no use torturing oneself.

A few theatres have reopened. The Comédie-Française gives several performances a week, the evening ones beginning at six-fifteen, and the companies of the Opéra and Opéra-Comique share the latter's home on the Rue Favart, each on a one-show-a-week basis. Several music halls have begun their season, and night clubs are struggling against the handicap of an eleven-o'clock closing. Les Halles, where restaurateurs used to go to market long before dawn, now operate in daylight from noon to three in the afternoon, but there is all the old profusion of *primeurs* and game, rock lobsters and oysters. Nothing reassures Parisians more than this gastronomic normality. As they eat, lovingly and with discrimination, they like to talk about the short rations *chez l'ennemi;* it is that, they are convinced, which will provoke a German revolution.

To the visitor returning to Paris for the first time since the beginning of War '39, no major change is apparent in the city by day. There are the air-raid-shelter signs, the strips of paper pasted over shop windows to stop glass from flying in case of an air raid, and sandbags around some public buildings; one soon becomes accustomed to these. The streets are well filled and those favorite subjects for watercolorists, the fishermen and book merchants of the Seine, pursue the placid, meagre tenor of their lives. There are a great many uniforms everywhere, but uniforms never were rare in Paris, and a French soldier seems a normal enough feature of civilian life.

At night, of course, all this changes; windows and street lights cast only the dimmest of rays. Behind the café fronts, however, shrouded by blue paper, one finds groups of people made sociable by the war, consuming their beer and coffee and demonstrating with matches on the tables the strategies that could quickly win War '39. This willingness to talk to almost anybody resembles the fraternization of speakeasy days in New York.

Parisians, always grumblers, are beginning to complain about the air-raid restrictions now that they realize the first alarms were only for practice. "Let's have the lights again," one owner of a *bistro* said to a group of customers a day or so ago. "Light is like the butterflies and the verdure that lifts the spirits." "And if the light attracts the bombers of Monsieur Hitler?" a customer asked. "Then turn off the light," the *bistro* man said. "All you have to do is press a button."

Paul Revere Sentinals from Massachusetts visit the U.S. Capitol in September 1939 to find out how their representatives stand on the neutrality question. The Sentinals oppose any change in the neutrality law. One of their congressmen, Thomas A. Flaherty (his back to the camera), refuses to reveal how he will vote.

13

The Neutrality Act of 1939

November 1939

By the time Britain and France went to war with Germany, the U.S. Neutrality Act of 1935 had been renewed and extended twice. The first renewal, passed in February 1936, included a provision limiting American loans to belligerent nations. The second, signed by President Roosevelt In May 1937, added even more stringent conditions: Countries at war, already prohibited from buying U.S. arms, now had to

pay cash for all their nonmilitary purchases and then transport those goods away in their own ships, so that U.S. vessels wouldn't have to enter war zones. Because of these provisions, the Neutrality Act of 1937 came to be known as the "cash and carry law." (It also extended the list of embargoed commodities to include strategic materials such as steel and oil and made illegal travel by Americans on the ships of belligerents.)

On the evening of September 3, 1939, after the British and French had issued their declarations of war, Franklin Roosevelt announced in one of his fireside chats that the United States would "remain a neutral nation." But, Roosevelt added, "I cannot ask that every American remain neutral in thought as well....Even a neutral cannot be asked to close his mind or close his conscience." The president knew that, by this time, American public opinion had turned decidedly against Germany. However, he also knew that the country would not support mobilization of another American Expeditionary Force similar to that sent to Europe in 1917.

Therefore, he continued to explore containment of the Nazis using "all methods short of war."

Because such a policy necessitated the arming of Britain and France, the existing neutrality law loomed as an insurmountable obstacle. Therefore, on September 13, Roosevelt called for a special session of Congress to consider its revision. Notable isolationists, such as Charles Lindbergh and Father Charles Coughlin, immediately went on the air, calling the special session an interventionist plot and insisting that any weakening of the neutrality law would surely lead to the sending of American troops to Europe. A torrent of letters, postcards, and telegrams soon flooded congressional offices, expressing strongly worded opinions on both sides. These produced a great deal of cantankerous debate on the floors of the House and Senate, which continued for six weeks until Congress finally settled o a compromise. Interventionists succeeded in lifting the arms embargo, but isolationists were able to reimpose the cash-and-carry provision, which had expired six months earlier in May 1939.

ROOSEVELT ESTABLISHES COMBAT AREA; U.S. NATIONALS AND SHIPS BARRED IN IT

Trade Bans Set Up; Vessels Excluded From Europe Except in Arctic and Mediterranean

By BERTRAM D. HULEN

WASHINGTON, Nov. 4—The United States embargo against sale of arms, ammunition and implements of war to belligerents was legally lifted at 12:04 o'clock this afternoon when President Roosevelt, at a ceremony attended in his office by Congressional leaders, signed the joint resolution adopted by Congress after its historic six weeks' debate.

Within a minute afterward the President signed two proclamations designed to protect the United States in the new situation. A later proclamation established a combat area in the European war zones into which American nationals and ships will not be permitted to proceed except under conditions that the President will lay down in rules and regulations to be issued early next week. Through one of the first two proclamations he reiterated his previous order closing United States ports to submarines.

Only one combat area was defined, extending from Norway, south of Bergen, and the Baltic Sea to Spain and taking in Great Britain, Ireland and the English Channel. The Mediterranean was not included, for reasons which were considered obvious although they went unexplained officially.

The Amended Neutrality Law itself forbids American vessels to carry cargoes to the belligerent countries, England, France and Germany. The combat zone proclamation forbids our ships to go in areas which German submarines or British warships may make dangerous.

The combat zone proclamation has the effect of barring trade in American vessels with the neutral nations Belgium, Holland, Denmark, Sweden, Estonia, Lithuania and Latvia. It also shuts off this commerce with Finland and Russia through the Baltic Sea, but permits it with them through the Arctic, while Russian Black Sea ports are also open to our ships.

Cargoes in American ships may still be carried to Italy, Spain, Portugal, Yugoslavia, Greece, Turkey, Rumania and Bulgaria, and also to Norway, north of Bergen.

The President in an accompanying statement said that combat areas may be changed with a changed situation. Some zones now dangerous may become safe and vice versa.

It appeared that there had not been sufficient naval activity in the Mediterranean to warrant a ban being placed on the movement of American traffic in that area, in view of the well-known circumstances that the President does not want to interfere with such movement except when and where necessary. There was also the implication that the United States did not wish to cause undue interference with trade to Italy, whose position toward her German Axis partner is of constant concern to the nations. It was considered obvious by observers that anything preventing needless concern to Italy would be to the advantage of peace.

The neutrality resolution signed today specifies that American ships may not go to belligerent ports in Europe or Africa as far south as the Canary Islands. The President defined the combat area in his explanatory statement issued simultaneously with the proclamation.

Members of the German-American Bund parade on East 86th Street in New York City, October 1937.

"This combat area," the President said, "takes in the whole Bay of Biscay, except waters on the north coast of Spain so close to the Spanish coast as to make danger of attack unlikely. It also takes in all the waters around Great Britain, Ireland and the adjacent islands, including the English Channel. It takes in the whole North Sea, running up the Norwegian coast to a point south of Bergen. It takes in all the Baltic Sea and its dependent waters."

The area was defined more precisely in the proclamation as follows:

"Beginning at the intersection of the north coast of Spain with the Meridian of 2 degrees 45 minutes longitude west of Greenwich;

"Thence due north to a point in 43 degrees 54 minutes north latitude;

"Thence by rhumb line to a point in 45 degrees 00 minutes north latitude, 20 degrees 00 minutes west longitude;

"Thence due north to 58 degrees 00 minutes north latitude;

"Thence by a rhumb line to latitude 62 degrees north, longitude 2 degrees east;

"Thence by rhumb line to latitude 60 degrees north, longitude 5 degrees east;

"Thence due east to the mainland of Norway;

"Thence along the coastline of Norway, Sweden, the Baltic Sea and dependent waters thereof, Germany, Denmark, the Netherlands, Belgium, France and Spain to the point of beginning."

President Roosevelt pointed out in his statement that the Pacific and Indian Oceans were not affected by the combat area ban, nor Africa south of the Canaries. Moreover, certain exceptions will be made by regulation so as not to impose undue hardship on ships or persons now in the combat areas, while ships that cleared for the area before the action was taken will be allowed to complete their voyages.

A routine proclamation repealed formally the previous neutrality proclamations under which arms embargoes were imposed, specifically lifted the embargo, and enjoined all officers of the government to prevent violations of the neutrality of the United States.

This proclamation did not list the categories of arms, ammunition and implements of war, so that the categories previously defined, under the terms of the law, continue to stand. This is important not only because the list is the one used by the State Department in registering domestic manufacturers and exporters and in granting licenses for export to neutral countries, but because the ban under the new law against granting credit for munitions purposes will apply to these categories, unless or until it is changed. The list is the one commonly accepted by the nations as covering armaments and has long been so employed by the League of Nations.

The submarine proclamation was issued solely for legal reasons. It banned the use of American ports or territorial waters to foreign belligerent submarines and was similar to the one issued on the same subject by the President on Oct. 18.

The President signed the resolution and issued his proclamations without any statement of policy, other than that contained in his definition of the combat area. As for policy, he stood on his statement at his press conference yesterday that the new law returned the United States to its traditional position of neutrality.

Secretary Hull, however, had not spoken formally on the subject and so today, shortly before the ceremony of signing took place in the White House, he issued a statement which was widely interpreted as a pledge to keep this nation at peace.

"I am naturally gratified with the basic changes made in the so-called neutrality legislation," he said. "Throughout this year the Executive Department has urged the prompt enactment of these basic changes and prior to the outbreak of the war pleaded with all nations to preserve peace and refrain from war.

"I desire to repeat with emphasis what I have consistently said heretofore, to the effect that our first and most sacred task is to keep our country secure and at peace, and that it is my firm belief that we shall succeed in this endeavor. I am satisfied that the new act will greatly assist in this undertaking."

Preparation of the proclamations and the ceremony of signing the joint Neutrality Resolution occupied most of the President's day. When he finally closed his desk he went to the Executive Mansion. Late tonight he left for Hyde Park, where he will vote on Tuesday. He will return to the capital probably on Wednesday.

The proclamations of the neutrality of the United States and submarine ban were issued immediately after signing of the resolution. The one defining the combat area was not completed until late this afternoon, with the assistance of A. A. Berle Jr., Assistant Secretary of State. When it had also been signed by Secretary Hull it was made public, along with the explanatory Presidential statement.

The proclamations issued today are the essential ones under the law, but rules and regulations to cover various policies under them will be drafted and issued in the next few days.

There were present at the ceremony of signing in the executive offices Vice President Garner; Secretary Hull; Senators Pittman, Barkley, Byrnes and McNary; Speaker Bankhead; and Representatives Rayburn, Bloom and Boland. Senator Austin and Representative Wadsworth, who had supported the legislation in Congress, and Representative Martin, the Republican House leader, had also been invited, but were prevented from being present by what was explained as other engagements. So Senator McNary, the minority leader, was the only Republican present.

As the signing took place news cameras recorded the scene. The President used two pens, one of which he gave to Senator Pittman, as chairman of the Senate Committee on Foreign Relations, and the other to Representative Bloom, as chairman of the House Committee on Foreign Affairs.

Representative Bloom described the ceremony as a very jovial affair. The President remarked facetiously, he said, that he had embarrassed Secretary Hull by asking him where the great seal of the United States was and the Secretary of State could not tell him. So Mr. Hull replied that he did not want to embarrass the President by asking him where it was. It was well known to be in the custody of the State Department.

The ceremony required but ten minutes, and those present filed out, but the Congressional leaders of both parties—Senators Barkley and McNary and Representative Rayburn—remained for five minutes for a talk with the President on foreign affairs. This conversation concerned plans Mr. Roosevelt has announced for keeping the legislative leaders informed of foreign policy developments in connection with the war, since Congress, at his behest, voted not to remain in session after adopting the neutrality legislation.

Senator Barkley also discussed prospects for the regular session of Congress with the President at lunch. Afterward he said that the leaders would not remain in the capital but would be kept informed of events, and, if their presence was required here, would come to the capital by airplane. Mr. Barkley is leaving for Kentucky to vote Tuesday in the Governorship election, and Representative Rayburn is leaving for Texas.

Senator Pittman, upon leaving the White House, was inclined to minimize the possibility of incidents surrounding American shipping under the new arrangements. He added that a country did not go to war every time there was an incident. Moreover, while American ships will not be armed, he said, they will have clear identifications, so there would be no excuse for a submarine sinking one without notice.

State Department officials said the moral embargo against shipping airplanes to nations which bomb civilian populations still stood and was not affected by the lifting of the embargo. Consequently it is assumed that if a belligerent indulges in this practice the government will urge manufacturers not to sell it bombing planes. This appeal has been made in the case of Japan and has been observed unreservedly, according to officials.

With Congress adjourned and most of its members having gone to their homes, the final chapter of the long neutrality fight produced little comment from that quarter. An exception was Representative Fish, who led the fight against repeal in the House. He declared in a statement that it was now up to the Administration to keep the country out of war.

But he expressed his own doubts and said he looked "for the Democratic party to be gradually turned into a war party by the Administration."

"I confess," he stated, "I have no faith in the sincerity of President Roosevelt's efforts to keep us out of war. Only time will tell the story."

"Let your conscience be your guide."

Constituent postcards sent to congressmen during the Neutrality Act debate

Among the innumerable sacks of mail delivered to congressional offices during the 1939 special session were these two postcards, one strongly advocating revision of the 1937 neutrality law, and the other just as strongly against.

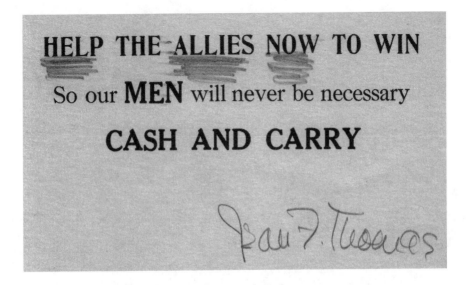

HELP THE ALLIES NOW TO WIN

So our **MEN** will never be necessary

CASH AND CARRY

[signature]

Milwaukee, Wisconsin
November 1st, 1939

Dear Congressman:

Two-thirds of our senators voted in favor of the **BLOOD THIRSTY WAR MONGERS AND MONEY CHANGERS.**

Mr. Congressman, it is up to **YOU** to show them their mistakes. Vote to retain the present embargo bill thereby definitely keeping us out of war.

Let your conscience be your guide.

Yours for faith in God and your fellow men,
L. HAWTIN

Finnish soldiers take part in winter maneuvers in October 1939, six weeks before the Soviet invasion, when strung-out Red Army columns made attractive targets for Finns wearing white camouflage uniforms and traveling on skis. Meanwhile, the ill-prepared Soviets lacked mittens with trigger fingers.

14.

The Winter War

November 1939–March 1940

While the Phony War dragged on in the West, world attention turned to an escalating border conflict in the East. Following the Soviet occupation of eastern Poland in late September 1939, Stalin's government began pressuring Finland to make territorial concessions on the Karelian Isthmus. At the time, the Soviet-Finnish border crossed this strip of land between the Gulf of Finland and Lake Ladoga just twenty

miles north of Leningrad—well within the range of Finnish artillery—and Stalin was concerned that, should Finland fall under German control, Leningrad's safety would be compromised. The Soviet dictator further requested that Finland grant him a thirty-year lease on the port at Hangö, about a hundred miles west of Helsinki, so that the Soviets could establish a naval base there. In exchange, he offered twice as much Soviet territory north of Lake Ladoga.

The Finns agreed to everything except the Hangö lease, which they claimed would violate their neutrality and compromise their independence. The Soviets next began a propaganda offensive, and when that also failed to win them Hangö, they invaded. Stalin initially threw thirty infantry divisions and six tank brigades against the nine Finnish divisions defending Karelia. Later, he sent even more troops north of Lake Ladoga to attack Finland from the east. This latter move showed especially poor judgment.

In general, the Soviets had made the same mistake that Franz Halder was then contemplating

killing Hitler to prevent: They had invaded Finland in winter, when conditions were simply not suitable for offensive operations. Their mechanized units quickly bogged down in thickly forested, snow-clogged terrain, and thousands of frozen Soviet corpses soon lined the few rough tracks along which tanks could pass. Finally, in January 1940, the Red Army pulled back from its lines north of Lake Ladoga and concentrated its vastly superior firepower on the Karelian front. Outnumbering the Finns there fifty to one, the Soviet troops eventually broke through the Finnish lines and threatened Helsinki. On March 12, the Finnish government asked for an armistice. The fighting ended two days later.

Thus the Red Army won the Winter War but hardly in a satisfactory manner. In Berlin, Hitler took careful notice of the numerous blunders the Soviets made and the great difficulty they had subjugating what was, by anyone's measure, a considerably inferior Finnish military. How could the Red Army, the Führer must have wondered, possibly stand up to the Wehrmacht?

RUSSIANS START THEIR INVASION OF FINLAND; PLANES DROP BOMBS ON AIRFIELD AT HELSKINKI

Border Is Crossed; Soviet Artillery Opens Fire as Troops March in Karelian Sector

By G. E. R. GEDYE

MOSCOW, Thursday, Nov. 30—Premier Vyacheslaff M. Molotoff announced in a thirteen-minute radio speech last midnight the breaking off of diplomatic relations with Finland by the Soviet Union through the recall of all Soviet diplomatic, consular and economic representatives in Finland. At the same time he warned all units of the Red Army and Red Navy to stand ready for every emergency.

In contrast to the last Soviet note to Finland and in glaring contrast to the abusive violence of the inspired press and radio campaign, Mr. Molotoff's speech, except for one important particular, conformed entirely to international usage.

Although it accepted, of course, without any effort to substantiate their accuracy, all the Soviet charges concerning the alleged extraordinary violations of the frontier by the Finns in the last few days, the language was restrained and contained indications that the Soviet was prepared to grant concessions to reach a settlement with the "Finnish people." In that, however, lay the important exception to conformity with international usage.

Despite the sentences asserting no desire to interfere in internal Finnish affairs and that the Finnish regime's relations with other States was exclusively the affair of Finland, the speech directly appealed over the heads of the present Finnish Government "to the Finnish people." Thus it confirmed the belief expressed more than once that the Soviet Union intended to try to force the surrender of the bases demanded from Finland through a change in the Finnish Government rather than through involving the Soviet Union in an invasion of Finnish territory.

By these passages of his speech Mr. Molotoff would seem to have confronted the Finnish Government with the alternatives of immediately recalling its diplomatic mission from Moscow at the peril of a still further increase in Soviet military pressure, if not of invasion, or of resignation. If the latter alternative were chosen, it would open the way for the Finnish President to appoint a more amenable government to send a mission to Moscow empowered to accept the Soviet demands in return for the proffered concessions.

One may feel tempted to say that Finland has been told to produce her President Hacha. [Dr. Emil Hacha became President of Czecho-Slovakia when Dr. Eduard Benes resigned under German pressure.] But in justice to the Soviet Union it must be recalled that Chancellor Hitler expressed no desire to compensate the Czecho-Slovak people for the surrender of a few isolated bases by ceding a slice of German territory of greater area but coupled abuse of the Czecho-Slovak Government with abuse of the Czech race and appeared overnight as an invader in the Czecho-Slovak capital.

Mr. Molotoff, whose speech was broadcast by every radio station in the Soviet Union, said "the hostility of the present government of Finland" had obliged the Soviet Union to take measures to guarantee its external safety. He described his demands on Finland as "under the present alarming situation essential to the security of the Soviet Union, especially Leningrad."

Instead of seeking a basis of agreement, he said, the Finnish Government took another course. During the last few days, he charged, Finnish provocations had caused loss of life on the frontier. He said the Finnish Government had received the practical proposals of the Soviet Union to prevent repetition of these incidents "with hostility, with brazen denial," and with a threat to hold Leningrad under the menace of their troops.

Entangled with imperialist powers, he charged, the Finnish Government had rejected a normal solution and had sought a continuance of hostile relations with the Soviet Union. This, he explained, had forced abrogation of the non-aggression pact and subsequent provocations had obliged the Soviet Government to suspend normal relations with Finland.

He announced that the commands of the Soviet land and sea forces had been ordered to prepare for any contingency and suppress all attempted Finnish provocations.

He complained that the foreign press had accused the Soviet Union of designs to seize Finnish territory. This was untrue, he declared. On the contrary, the Soviet Union was prepared to exchange a considerable portion of Karelia for certain strips of territory and showed a friendly attitude toward corresponding vital interests of the Finnish people.

Other foreign observers, he said, had charged that the Soviet Union wanted to interfere in the internal affairs of Finland, which he branded as a lie, affirming that Finland was a sovereign power and the character of her government was for the Finnish people to decide.

He insisted the Soviet Union had done its best in the past to make the Finnish people independent and was ready to help them in the future.

Relations between Finland and other countries were purely Finland's affair in which his government had no right to interfere, he went on, but in the present extremely dangerous situation Moscow could not leave the Finns' safety dependent on the will of their present rulers. Issues with Finland must be solved by friendly cooperation with the Finnish people in order to prolong such cooperation.

Mystery surrounds the assumed connection between Mr. Molotoff's speech and the delayed Finnish reply to last night's Soviet note cancelling the treaty of non-aggression. Certainly Mr. Molotoff's speech was incomprehensibly postponed and the Finnish note was equally incomprehensibly delayed.

Early this evening diplomatic circles suspected that despite Finnish denials the note received here for transmission to the Kremlin was delayed because the Finnish Legation had an inkling of Mr. Molotoff's intended speech before it was delivered. Until 2 A.M. it was impossible to ascertain if any Finnish reply had been received.

Later, however, it appeared that there must have been much movement behind the scenes. Secretary of State Cordell Hull's offer of medi-

These two armed Helsinki residents were among the many civilians mobilized by the Finns to guard schools and public monuments in anticipation of the Soviet assault.

ation probably played a considerable part. Doubtless the knowledge of it caused the Finns to delay presentation of their note, and it is equally probable that the Soviet Union took the American offer into consideration before Mr. Molotoff's speech was drafted in its outwardly reasonable phrasing.

Equally, however, it must have precipitated the delivery of the Soviet note to the Finns embodying the breaking off of diplomatic relations before it was possible for the Finns to present their note.

Throughout yesterday tension over the Finnish crisis was unrelaxed. Diplomatic circles especially awaited impatiently the arrival of the Finnish note in reply to the Soviet Government's denunciation of the Finnish-Soviet non-aggression pact. While many foreigners still believe a peaceful solution might be found, the terms of Premier Molotoff's note of Tuesday, together with the fact of the denunciation of the non-aggression treaty, resulted in a decrease of hopeful spirits.

Many qualified observers began to feel that the Soviet leaders had gone so far as to have deliberately made it impossible for themselves to accept any compromise, and so fears that denunciation of the non-aggression pact might prove an immediate prelude to invasion of Finland increased.

A foreign radio announcement that the Finnish reply was handed to Mr. Molotoff yesterday morning was not true. The Finnish Legation here waited in vain until the evening for the text of the reply to be delivered to Mr. Molotoff, which, it was understood, had been cabled to Moscow from Helsinki in the morning.

Strong rumors circulated that Mr. Molotoff would broadcast to the people at 3 P.M.—according to a subsequent version, 4:45 P.M.—increased the feeling of tension, but both times passed without any broadcast. Foreign reports said that the Finns had agreed to the Soviet terms and would say so in the note to Russia—that is, Finland would withdraw her troops some distance from the frontier without pressing for a parallel step by the Soviet Union—and these reports were generally regarded here as probably true since it was felt the Soviet Union's attitude was becoming so menacing that Finland would be in a desperate position unless she made some such definite gesture of appeasement.

But it was also recalled that Mr. Molotoff on Tuesday declared the demand for Finnish withdrawal of twenty to twenty-five kilometers was a minimum and that anything short of this would fail to placate the Russians. [A kilometer is .621 of a mile.]

Among foreigners there was a general feeling that the Kremlin's handling of the Finnish question had been as clumsy as its policy toward the three Baltic States—Estonia, Latvia and Lithuania—which came to terms with Russia, and toward Turkey, which failed to do so, was tactful and adroit.

It was more than once remarked that the Soviet Union might have expected more understanding of its attitude had it said, when it became clear that the Finns were unwilling to accept the Soviet minimum terms, that world events obliged the Soviet Government to insist that the policy of collective security that Russia had long vainly advocated had become a dead letter and that with the world ablaze Russia must take exceptional measures to secure her frontiers.

It is argued that Russia might have said that if Finland agreed she would receive generous treatment, especially in matters of trade, but that, if she refused, the Soviet Union in the interests of its own security would be obliged to treat the refusal as a hostile act. Though this might have been subjected to criticism as overriding the formal independence of a small neighbor, many felt it would have created a better impression than the methods actually adopted, of alleging frontier incidents without offering any opportunity for impartial investigation, insisting on the correctness of the Soviet Union's own versions and brushing aside all explanations and disavowals while carrying on a campaign of unrestrained vituperation in the press, attributing incredible dreams of conquest to the Finns, and organizing inflammatory meetings of Russian workers, which could hardly fail to meet an unsympathetic reception in the outside world generally.

The violence with which this campaign was carried on yesterday is best indicated by quoting a few outstanding headlines. Most of them were used over accounts of further indignation meetings of Soviet citizens. Says Pravda:

"Sweep Finnish adventurers off the face of the earth—verdict of the Kiroff Electrical Plant in Leningrad. The Red Army will destroy reckless bandits."

The slogan of the Kaganovitch Shoe Factory in Minsk is:

"Woe to those who arouse the fury of the Soviet people."

The government newspaper Izvestia's heads are even more vigorous, thus:

"Annihilate the infamous band. Finnish rulers' answer is lying and insolent. Immeasurable insolence. Chop off the hand hovering over the city of Lenin."

The same paper carries big banner heads:

"Insolent lying note of Finnish Government caused explosion of rage and indignation. The day of reckoning is near. Bring the reckless war provocateurs to book. The mad dogs will be destroyed."

The headline demanding the "chopping off of the threatening hand" introduces an article from Izvestia's special correspondent in Soviet Karelia, who alleges that speeches of Soviet Finns of Karelia are filled with bitterness toward the heads of the present Finnish regime.

"In every village here are living witnesses of the brutal vengeance taken by Finnish White Guards on the Karelian population."

The correspondent relates stories told by these refugees from Finland of murder, rape and torture by Finnish counter-revolutionary bands twenty years ago. That writer speaks of the certainty of victory "in the event the Finnish White regime forces war" on the Soviet Union.

"Farmers, workers, soldiers and intellectuals ask the government to chop off the sword in the hand holding it over Leningrad and are supported by the enraged voices of Finnish workers of Soviet Karelia, who are volunteering in shoals, demanding to be placed in the ranks of the Red Army," the article says.

"A flagrant violation of the American tradition of neutrality."

Franklin Roosevelt's statement concerning the Soviet invasion of Finland and the Soviet ambassador's reaction

The first document reprinted here is the text of President Roosevelt's December 1 statement concerning the Soviet invasion of Finland. The second is the text of a telegram sent by Soviet ambassador Konstantin Oumansky to the People's Commissariat for Foreign Affairs, assessing the current state of U.S.-U.S.S.R. relations. The People's Government to which Oumansky refers was a puppet regime composed of Finnish émigré Communists set up by the Soviets in Terijoki shortly after their invasion.

The news of the Soviet naval and military bombings within Finnish territory has come as a profound shock to the Government and people of the United States. Despite efforts made to solve the dispute by peaceful methods to which no reasonable objection could be offered, one power has chosen to resort to force of arms. It is tragic to see the policy of force spreading, and to realize that wanton disregard for law is still on the march. All peace-loving peoples in those nations that are still hoping for the continuance of relations throughout the world on the basis of law and order will unanimously condemn this new resort to military force as the arbiter of international differences.

To the great misfortune of the world, the present trend to force makes insecure the independent existence of small nations in every continent and jeopardizes the rights of mankind to self-government. The people and government of Finland have a long, honorable and wholly peaceful record which has won for them the respect and warm regard of the people and Government of the United States.

◆　◆　◆

2 December 1939
Top Secret

Today's statement by Roosevelt against us and the Finns is itself a flagrant violation of the American tradition of ostentatious neutrality during the whole Roosevelt administration.

The statement gives new stimulus to an aggravated anti-Soviet pursuit in the press and to blackmailing us with breaking off relations, which is favored by a number of right-wing senators. In conformity with Roosevelt's statement about the threat to small countries' independence, the press writes a lot on the threat from our side, especially to the Norwegian Arctic coast (even though this is refuted in Oslo, which could be of some use when unmasking this provocation in our press) and also of a threat to Rumania and other Balkan countries, and in this connection all sorts of anti-Soviet appearances in Italy are advertised as a "guardian" of the Balkans. There have also been [according to the press] some attempts by us to intimidate Japan and also a tendency to frighten the Germans with our hegemony in the Baltics.

In the official bulletins the State Department sends out to the press, reports from the U.S. legation in Helsinki contain false information from the Finnish leadership. It looks like the American government fosters an illusion that the comedy of "cabinet reform" [in Finland] might lead to a compromise. The creation of the People's Government evokes a new upsurge of class hatred against us. However, for the present, Roosevelt and Hull are adapting themselves to the encouragement of anti-Soviet blackmail and are making excuses in response to journalists' questions about clarification of relations with the U.S.S.R., the employment of the Neutrality Act, the appeal of the U.S. government to the aviation industry not to sell to us and so forth.

The "New York Herald Tribune" asserts that Roosevelt is for, but Hull against, [breaking off relations] because in his opinion the rupture does not help the Finns but draws the U.S. into a European conflict. I do my best in trying to check this, but I have a great deal of doubt about the present line-up of forces. On the basis of a number of indications, I assume that there are, within the American government and among the cliques in the State Department, disagreements over possible measures against the Soviet Union. In a private discussion with two journalists, as told to me by an eyewitness, one of Hull's assistants, Berle, lamented today that the U.S. cannot undertake "anything practical" for Finland. Following an obvious advice by the State Department, the Finnish envoy Procopé made it known that the Finnish government declared a situation of war, not a state of war, thus giving a hint of the undesirability of using the Neutrality Act in the present conflict, because it would cause no damage on the whole to us, who pay the U.S. in cash, but to the bourgeois Finns who, over the last weeks, have been conducting negotiations for a credit of 15 Mill. from the Export-Import Bank of the U.S. However, when the illusions about the duration of resistance of old Finland are crushed, these considerations against the employment of the Act disappear and it is, possibly, put into effect.

In spite of the aggravating campaign to break off relations, I regard this, as before, as extremely improbable. In addition to interpretations of earlier reasons, this impression is supported by a report from London, where at least a part of the British cabinet is against an American-Soviet break-off, which would promote an even closer rapprochement of the U.S.S.R. and Germany.

So, most probably, the anti-Soviet pursuit will be further stimulated, [U.S. ambassador to the U.S.S.R. Laurence A.] Steinhardt will be recalled, we will be accused of intervening in internal affairs, all sorts of faults will be picked with our economic organizations, "recommendations" to refrain from bargaining with us will probably be given to the aviation industry, and furthermore the People's Government will not be recognised and Helsinki will be encouraged to resist. Hull has not yet summoned me.

The instructions in your telegram of 2 December 1939 have been taken as the guiding principles. In connection with the atmosphere of pursuit and threats created around the legation, I have taken all precautionary measures here and in the consulates.

Oumansky

15.

The German Invasion of Denmark and Norway

April 1940

Winston Churchill never got on well with Neville Chamberlain, and as war approached, their relationship became particularly barbed. Repeatedly, Churchill predicted with great accuracy the Germans' aggressive intentions; yet, even as events confirmed Churchill's judgment, Chamberlain refused to listen. Finally, when war came, Chamberlain had to admit his error and include Churchill in his

government, naming him first lord of the admiralty. On the news of this appointment, a brief signal went out to the fleet: "Winston is back."

Churchill had previously served as first lord between 1911 and 1915, when he campaigned successfully for the largest naval expenditures in British history. Yet his support for the disastrous Dardanelles campaign of 1915 led to his removal. Nevertheless, Churchill took up his World War II duties with the same restless energy he had always brought to his leadership roles.

At the outbreak of the war, Norway, Denmark, and Sweden all declared their neutrality, but the situation in Scandinavia remained uneasy. Germany had particularly important trade relations with Sweden, which produced high-grade iron ore vital to the Nazi war effort. During the warmer months, this ore was transported to Germany through the northern Swedish port of Lulea on the Gulf of Bothnia, an arm of the Baltic Sea. For months during the winter, however, Lulea was icebound, requiring that the ore first be shipped by rail to Narvik on Norway's Atlantic coast before being transferred to German freighters.

Beginning in late 1939, Churchill began advocating a plan to mine Norwegian territorial waters so that these ore shipments might be halted.

Of course, such an operation would grossly violate Norwegian sovereignty, yet Churchill had little regard for that nation's neutrality. On February 16, 1940, the crew of the British destroyer *Cossack* boarded a German tanker in Norwegian waters in order to rescue British prisoners being held on board. Norwegian diplomats protested this action vigorously, yet neither they, nor Hitler, believed that the British would change their behavior. On February 18, therefore, Hitler ordered that development of invasion plans for Scandinavia be accelerated. Meanwhile, Chamberlain reluctantly agreed to the mine-laying, which began on April 8. The next day, aided by near-total surprise, German invaders overran Denmark in a matter of hours while simultaneously landing troops at five key Norwegian ports. Even with elements of their fleet already in the area, the British were unable to stop these landings and, later, Germany's complete conquest of Norway.

Smoke from the wreckage of warships clouds the harbor at Narvik, Norway. British troops landed there on April 14 but proceeded so cautiously that, by the time they drove out the Germans in late May, the rest of the country was already lost. Accepting their failure, the British left Narvik in early June.

GERMANS OCCUPY DENMARK, ATTACK OSLO; NORWAY THEN JOINS WAR AGAINST HITLER

Copenhagen Taken; Troops Cross Border as Ships Debark Others in Sudden Nazi Blow

By SVEND CARSTENSEN

COPENHAGEN, Denmark, Tuesday, April 9— German troops crossed the Danish frontier at 5 o'clock this morning.

Three German cruisers arrived at that same hour at Middelfart and troops immediately occupied streets of the town.

Copenhagen was also occupied by German troops this morning.

The invasion came without warning. For some hours before the crossing of the border reports had circulated here that the Germans of South Jutland were expecting German troop trains carrying 45,000 men to arrive at the town of Flensburg during the night. That German town on the border was characterized as a convenient port for shipping troops northward, and although Danish border guards had been put in the highest state of preparedness it was not thought that there would be any threat to Denmark

This belief had been bolstered by the fact that the fleet of more than a hundred German warships that passed through the Great Belt into the Kattegat and Skagerrak yesterday and early today included troopships—and it was presumed that this fleet was on the way to Norway to retaliate against the British Navy.

Mr. Carstensen left Copenhagen after the entry of German forces and went to Kolding, where he filed the following dispatch:

SPECIAL CABLE TO *The New York Times*
KOLDING, Denmark, Tuesday, April 9—The German occupation continues here. It is reported that two ferry points on the Great Belt—Nyborg and Korsoer—have been occupied.

Troops have landed at Middelfart on a large scale. A Little Belt bridge has been reported seized and the city of Aalborg in North Jutland has been occupied.

Although there were no reports of clashes between Danish troops and the invaders today, military resistance was expected at Hadersleben, about thirty miles north of the German border. The placing of guns and erection of barricades were reported from that town.

After leaving Copenhagen I observed from my automobile swarms of fast German planes flying over towns dropping badly printed leaflets that laid responsibility for Germany's invading Denmark and Norway to what was termed a British intention to make Scandinavia a theatre of war.

The leaflets termed Winston Churchill, Britain's First Lord of the Admiralty, "the century's greatest warmonger," who planned to police Norwegian and Danish waters against the wills of the two countries.

The statement said that, since Norway and Denmark were unable to resist effectively, Germany had resolved to act in advance of a British attack and by her own forces take over "protection" of Danish and Norwegian neutrality and "guard" the countries during the war. It was asserted that Germany did not intend to obtain bases for her fight against Britain but solely aimed at preventing Scandinavia from being a battlefield for "British expansion of the war."

According to the statement, negotiations were going on between the German and Danish Governments to make Denmark "secure" and assure that her army and navy were maintained and the Danish people's freedom respected. The country's independence, it was said, is fully secured. The proclamation concluded with an appeal to the army and the population to understand the situation and avoid acts of passive or active resistance which would be useless and be broken by all available means.

The people were asked to continue their daily work and keep order. The German Army and Navy, it was said, from now on will guard the country against "British encroachments."

The statement was signed by General Kauprisch of the German Army.

Children board a train that will evacuate them from Oslo to a safer location in northern Norway, January 1940.

"The conquerors were under a terrible spiritual siege."

An excerpt from John Steinbeck's novel *The Moon Is Down*

John Steinbeck once wrote that he intended his brief 1942 novel, *The Moon Is Down,* to celebrate the "durability of democracy." The book's fable-like plot concerns a small European democracy (not unlike Norway) that finds itself overrun by a powerful authoritarian neighbor (not unlike Nazi Germany). At first, the local people are demoralized, but they gradually recover their spirit and eventually form an effective resistance movement.

The days and the weeks dragged on, and the months dragged on. The snow fell and melted and fell and melted and finally fell and stuck. The dark buildings of the little town wore bells and hats and eyebrows of white and there were trenches through the snow to the doorways. In the harbor the coal barges came empty and went away loaded, but the coal did not come out of the ground easily. The good miners made mistakes. They were clumsy and slow. Machinery broke and took a long time to fix. The people of the conquered country settled in a slow, silent, waiting revenge. The men who had been traitors, who had helped the invaders—and many of them believed it was for a better state and an ideal way of life—found that the control they took was insecure, that the people they had known looked at them coldly and never spoke.

And there was death in the air, hovering and waiting. Accidents happened on the railroad, which clung to the mountains and connected the little town with the rest of the nation. Avalanches poured down on the tracks and rails were spread. No train could move unless the tracks were first inspected. People were shot in reprisal and it made no difference. Now and then a group of young men escaped and went to England. And the English bombed the coal mine and did some damage and killed some of both their friends and their enemies. And it did no good. The cold hatred grew with the winter, the silent, sullen hatred, the waiting hatred. The food supply was controlled—issued to the obedient and withheld from the disobedient—so that the whole population turned coldly obedient. There was a point where food could not be withheld, for a starving man cannot mine coal, cannot lift and carry. And the hatred was deep in the eyes of the people, beneath the surface.

Now it was that the conqueror was surrounded, the men of the battalion alone among silent enemies, and no man might relax his guard for even a moment. If he did, he disappeared, and some snowdrift received his body. If he went alone to a woman, he disappeared, and some snowdrift received his body. If he drank, he disappeared. The men of the battalion could sing only together, could dance only together, and dancing gradually stopped and the singing expressed a longing for home. Their talk was of friends and relatives who loved them and their longings were for warmth and love, because a man can be a soldier for only so many hours a day and for only so many months in a year, and then he wants to be a man again, wants girls and drinks and music and laughter and ease, and when these are cut off, they become irresistibly desirable.

And the men thought always of home. The men of the battalion came to detest the place they had conquered, and they were curt with the people and the people were curt with them, and gradually a little fear began to grow in the conquerors, a fear that it would never be over, that they could never relax or go home, a fear that one day they would crack and be hunted through the mountains like rabbits, for the conquered never relaxed their hatred. The patrols, seeing lights, hearing laughter, would be drawn as to a fire, and when they came near, the laughter stopped, the warmth went out, and the people were cold and obedient. And the soldiers, smelling warm food from the little restaurants, went in and ordered the warm food and found that it was oversalted or overpeppered.

Then the soldiers read the news from home and from the other conquered countries, and the news was always good, and for a little while they believed it, and then after a while they did not believe it any more. And every man carried in his heart the terror. "If home crumbled, they would not tell us, and then it would be too late. These people will not spare us. They will kill us all." They remembered stories of their men retreating through Belgium and retreating out of Russia. And the more literate remembered the frantic, tragic retreat from Moscow, when every peasant's pitchfork tasted blood and the snow was rotten with bodies.

And they knew when they cracked, or relaxed, or slept too long, it would be the same here, and their sleep was restless and their days were nervous. They asked questions their officers could not answer because they did not know. They were not told, either. They did not believe the reports from home, either.

Thus it came about that the conquerors grew afraid of the conquered and their nerves wore thin and they shot at shadows in the night. The cold, sullen silence was with them always. Then three soldiers went insane in a week and cried all night and all day until they were sent away home. And others might have gone insane if they had not heard that mercy deaths awaited the insane at home, and a mercy death is a terrible thing to think of. Fear crept in on the men in their billets and it made them sad, and it crept into the patrols and it made them cruel.

The year turned and the nights grew long. It was dark at three o'clock in the afternoon and not light again until nine in the morning. The jolly lights did not shine out on the snow, for by law every window must be black against the bombers. And yet when the English bombers came over, some light always appeared near the coal mine. Sometimes the sentries shot a man with a lantern and once a girl with a flashlight.

And it did no good. Nothing was cured by the shooting.

And the officers were a reflection of their men, more restrained because their training was more complete, more resourceful because they had more responsibility, but the same fears were a little deeper buried in them, the same longings were more tightly locked in their hearts. And they were under a double strain, for the conquered people watched them for mistakes and their own men watched them for weakness, so that their spirits were taut to the breaking-point. The conquerors were under a terrible spiritual siege and everyone knew, conquered and conquerors, what would happen when the first crack appeared.

THE MARCH THROUGH EUROPE

16.

Germany Invades the West

May 1940

At the time the Germans put their Case Yellow invasion plan into effect on May 10, 1940, they were actually outnumbered on the western front. Not counting the 19 divisions they had deployed defensively along the Maginot line and the 42 divisions they were holding in reserve, the Germans had 75 divisions available for their invasion of the Low Countries. Opposing them were 144 Allied divisions: 101 French,

22 Belgian, 11 British, and 10 Dutch. Even with 36 of the French divisions also tied down on the Maginot line (which the Germans didn't attack), the Allies were still able to commit 81 divisions, excluding reserves, to the German assault. The Allied weaknesses, therefore, weren't manpower, or even equipment, but inferior strategy, leadership, and training.

Both sides had about the same number and quality of tanks, yet the Allies dispersed theirs to support individual infantry formations, while the Germans concentrated their tanks in irresistible armored divisions, which spearheaded the German attack. Receiving little help from the Allies, the Netherlands fell within five days, as Nazi paratroopers quickly seized control of the canal and river bridges that were the key to the Dutch defenses. The Belgians, meanwhile, with a larger army and stronger fortifications, proved more resistant, but they, too, succumbed to German speed, daring, and cleverness. The anchor of Belgium's eastern defenses, for example, was the reputedly impregnable Fort Eben Emael, near

Liège. Because its heavy guns commanded several important invasion routes, the Germans had to neutralize its firepower. Hitler himself provided the solution. "The top is like a meadow," he said of the mostly buried fortress. "Gliders can land on it." Indeed, they could, and fewer than one hundred airborne troops were able to stage a surprise landing, trap the fort's 750 defenders underground, and blow up its big guns.

According to a previously arranged plan, thousands of French and British soldiers moved rapidly into Belgium to take up defensive positions on the Meuse and Dyle Rivers—only to find themselves outflanked by German forces pushing through Luxembourg and the lightly defended Belgian Ardennes. A Panzer corps led personally by Lt. Gen. Heinz Guderian, the father of *Blitzkrieg*, crossed the Meuse near Sedan and dashed to the coast, reaching the English Channel near the mouth of the Somme on May 20. From this point on, the Allied forces in Belgium and northern France were trapped.

German paratroopers at a machine-gun post in the Netherlands, May 1940. This photograph was taken out of a camera found in the possession of a captured paratrooper.

NAZIS INVADE HOLLAND, BELGIUM, LUXEMBOURG BY LAND AND AIR

Air Fields Bombed; Nazi Parachute Troops Land at Key Centers as Flooding Starts

AMSTERDAM, The Netherlands, Friday, May 10—Germany invaded the Netherlands early today, land troops being preceded by widespread air attacks on airdromes and by the landing of parachute troops.

The Netherlands resisted and announced she was at war with Germany. Anti-aircraft batteries and fighter planes engaged swarms of German aircraft when they appeared simultaneously over a score of Netherland cities.

An official proclamation said:

"Since 3 A.M. German troops have crossed the Netherland frontier and German planes have tried to attack airports. Inundations are effective according to plans. The army anti-aircraft batteries were found prepared. So far as is known six German planes have been shot down."

[French, Belgian and British planes were sighted over the Netherlands this morning, a Reuters (British news agency) dispatch said in quoting the Netherland radio station at Hilversum, near Amsterdam.]

German troops were first reported crossing the Netherland frontier near Roermond, eight miles north of the Belgian frontier. German planes landed troops by parachute at strategic points near Rotterdam, The Hague, Amsterdam and other large cities.

A large number of the German troops landed by parachute were said to be dressed in Netherland military uniforms.

Other Germans crossed the Maas River in rubber boats to Netherland territory. They were said to be reaching the Netherland side in "considerable numbers."

A fierce air battle raged over Amsterdam as Netherland fighter planes dived repeatedly on German bombers and troop transport planes with chattering machine guns.

Schiphol Airdrome outside Amsterdam, the nation's largest, was heavily bombed. Military authorities immediately threw a heavy guard around the airdrome in an effort to defend it against German parachute troops.

Planes identified as German Heinkels bombed Schiphol Airdrome repeatedly, loosing some thirty heavy caliber bombs on the landing field between 5:15 and 5:30 A.M.

Reports poured in of planes in great numbers over a score of Netherland cities. Netherland authorities, hurriedly organizing defense, flashed orders to the whole country to be on the alert against parachute troops.

Fifty planes were over Nijmegen, sixty miles southeast of Amsterdam on the German border.

A number of parachute troops reportedly landed at Sliedrecht, Delft and several other points. Delft is twelve and a half miles from The Hague. About 100 parachute troops were landed near Dordrecht, thirty-eight miles southwest of Amsterdam.

Hundreds of troops were landed at Hoogezwaluwe, whose big bridge is the major communicating link between the northern and southern parts of the country. A large number of German troops landed by parachute at Leiden. Others landed at Waalhaven, major airport of Rotterdam, and at Rozenburg Island, near Rotterdam.

The lightning attack did not take the Netherlanders completely by surprise as the country

Hitler poses with some of the paratroopers who captured Belgium's Fort Eben Emael, then considered the strongest fortress in the world.

had been in intense fear of invasion for days and defense measures had been taken.

The Amsterdam radio announced that Netherland troops had captured a number of German parachute troops, wearing German uniforms, near The Hague.

Twenty-four planes appeared over Rotterdam, biggest port in the Netherlands, at 5:50 A.M.

Among towns throughout the country where foreign planes were sighted, including planes identified as German bombers in flights ranging from one to fifty, were Den Haag, Rotterdam, Hook of Holland, Haarlem, Tilburg, Zalt Bommel, Geldermalsen, Venloo, Alkmaar, Maastricht, Hengelo, Scheveningen, Arnhem, Leiden and Emmen.

The descent of swarms of foreign war planes on the Netherlands came after a night of alarms and a week-long period of tension bred by fear the country would be invaded. All public communications between the Netherlands and the outside world were taken over by the government last night, canals were locked and extraordinary measures taken for national safety.

The first aerial activity began at 2:41 A.M., Netherland time, when Amsterdam anti-aircraft batteries first fired at foreign planes.

When the Amsterdam anti-aircraft batteries opened up they fired for four minutes at planes whose motors could be heard plainly over the residential section of South Amsterdam. Reports coming into Amsterdam from various points said numbers of planes crossed the northern half of the Netherlands and the Frisian Islands, flying from east to west.

Amsterdam's anti-aircraft guns blazed again at 4:05 A.M. Intense activity in the air was reported from points throughout the Netherlands, with huge squadrons of foreign planes crossing back and forth.

A squadron of foreign planes was reported circling over Helder, Netherland naval base on the northwest coast at the entrance to Ysselmeer, and six German seaplanes were reported circling over Ijmuiden in Central Holland.

At 5:40 A.M. twelve Heinkel planes and five seaplanes were sighted over Sliedrecht flying westward.

It was said that the parachute troops who had floated down near Haagscheschouw, between Leiden and The Hague, were dressed in Netherland military uniforms. At 5:50 A.M. informants said:

"A great number of parachute troops are landing at many places. All of them are clad in Netherland Army uniforms."

It was reported that one German plane had been shot down near the Schiphol Airdrome.

A number of German parachute troops in German uniforms were captured by patrols on the outskirts of The Hague, it was reported.

It was reported without confirmation that German Messerschmitt planes had "landed" at the Schiphol Airdrome. It could not be ascertained immediately whether the planes had been shot down or whether they had landed of their own accord.

At 6 A.M. more parachute troops were dropped near Ravesteyn, close to Nijmegen.

Fifteen Heinkel bombers were sighted over Delft at 5:50 A.M. A few minutes later an additional twenty-one German planes passed over Rotterdam, apparently heading for the Ypenburg Airport.

At 6:20 A.M. the official radio for the first time said "foreign planes" were landing "enemy" parachute troops. The official announcer said a large formation of planes had just been sighted near The Hague.

At 6:30 A.M. the official radio said:

"New and large formations of planes are arriving constantly from Germany."

At 6:40 A.M. twenty-two German planes were observed flying westward at Rhenen near Utrecht.

It was reported that at least two Netherland planes had been set on fire and destroyed on the ground during the bombing of the Schiphol Airdrome.

Roads leading out of Amsterdam were choked with automobiles soon after daylight. They were heaped with household goods as residents fled in fear of German aerial bombing of the city.

Parachutists began landing in increasing numbers after 7:30 A.M. in the southern part of the country, particularly in the Eindhoven area.

"He didn't find Mother because she is dead."

Excerpt from the diary of a Dutch boy

Dirk van der Heide (a pseudonym) was twelve years old and living in Rotterdam, the Netherlands' largest port, when the Germans attacked. He kept a diary of his experiences during the five-day *Blitzkrieg* and carried it with him to America, where he was sent as a refugee. His text, with a bit of retrospective embellishment, was published in 1941 under the title *My Sister and I.*

Friday, May 10, 1940

Something terrible happened last night. War began!!! Uncle Pieter was *right*. The city has been *bombed* all day. Am writing this in the Baron's air-raid shelter. There are not many air-raid shelters here but the Baron and Father and Mevrouw Klaes had this one built for us and all our neighbors said it was a waste of money. This has been a terrible day and everything is upset and people are very sad and excited. This is what happened. Before daylight I woke up and for several minutes did not know what had happened. I could hear explosions and people were shouting under our windows. Mother came running in in her nightie and dressing gown and told me to get my coat on and come quickly. On the way downstairs she told me there was bombing going on but no one knew yet what it meant but she supposed it was war all right. The noise seemed very near. Father had Keetje in his arms and we hurried across the street to the Baron's and went down into his air-raid shelter. Betje and Brenda and Grietje, Mother said, were already gone to the Baron's. Father pointed toward the city and Mother nodded. There were great flames shooting up into the sky and beams of light from the searchlights and the sirens were going very loud. They are on the tops of buildings and have things on them to make them very loud. We could see bullets going up from our guns. The Baron's air-raid shelter was full of people, all our neighbors and some people I didn't know. They were all talking loudly and no one was dressed, just coats over their nightclothes. Keetje began to cry and Father whispered something to her and kissed her and she stopped. Finally she went to sleep in his arms. We waited about two hours. At first most people thought the noise was only practice. All the time people kept running outside and coming back with news. It was war all right and the radio was giving the alarm and calling all the time for all men in the reserves to report for duty at the nearest place. The radio said this over and over. It was very exciting. The bombing kept on all the time, boom-boom-boom, and everyone said they were falling on Waalhaven, the airport, which is only about five miles away. The Baron went upstairs and began telephoning. The voices on the radio sounded strange and terribly excited. Father put Keetje into Mother's arms and went away. A few minutes later he came back dressed and carrying a gas mask and a knapsack. He kissed Mother and Keetje and me very hard and then hurried out. He shouted back something about taking care of his animals and Mother nodded and told him to be careful, *please.*

After the radio called for the men they all left the shelter and there was no one but the old men and the women and children. At six-thirty the radio said the bombing was over. We all went outside and were glad to get out. I wasn't tired or sleepy now but I wanted to see what was going on. Everything was just the same outside. The sun was beginning to come up and we could see it was going to be a fine day. We went home and Grietje made us some hot porridge and some hot milk and cheese. We ate very little. Mother did not eat at all. She was busy telephoning the hospital and other people. When she came into the dining room she looked sad. Are the Germans coming I asked. Yes, but don't worry, we'll stop them Mother said. I have just talked to Uncle Pieter and he is all right she said but now I must go to the hospital. I want you to get dressed and go with Keetje and Brenda and Betje to the Baron's. Be sure you mind and stay in the shelter when the Baron asks you to. Keetje asked if we were to go to school and Mother said no, not today. She promised to come home as soon as she could. Betje and Brenda and Grietje all began to talk after Mother left and Betje telephoned her family and they were all right too except her brothers had gone away to fight. I went outside as soon as I was dressed. There was much smoke in the air and it made me feel sick for a minute. Brenda and Betje took me over to the Baron's and Grietje came a little later.

We did not go into the air-shelter at once. There was too much to do. All along the street people were running in and out of their houses. Everyone was doing something. People were digging long trenches away from their cellars and some were shoveling dirt and sand into big bags and throwing them up against their houses. I asked Brenda what this was for and she said it was to protect the houses from bombs she guessed. I told her someone had better do that to our house and she said all right come on and help. We left Keetje at the Baron's and went back and got shovels. Brenda and Betje and Grietje all worked with me to dig a trench from our cellar to the garden so that if a bomb hit our house we could get out of the cellar if we were there and couldn't get to the Baron's. We worked very hard for an hour and didn't get much done because people kept coming by and shouting things and a policeman came by with a paper for Father, but Brenda said Father was gone. Many soldiers came by. Then someone said the Queen was on the radio and we all stopped to listen. The Queen did not speak very long. I and my government will do our duty she said and she asked everyone not to get excited because of the Germans. She told the people that the Germans were wrong in coming into a peaceful country and that they would be driven out with God's help. We all felt better after hearing the Queen but the old men shook their heads. Pastor Opzoomer said we should go to the church and pray and that the bells in the Catholic Church were already ringing.

Just then Mijnheer van Helst ran in and said the Heinkels were coming again and it was true. The sirens started up and a little while later the bombs began to fall. We all stayed in the Baron's cellar. The noise was worse than it was before and nearer. I held Keetje's hand and she squeezed mine tight until it hurt. Once the cellar seemed to rock back and forth and the Baron said that was close. The people tried to talk but mostly they just waited. The bombing lasted an hour but it seemed longer. One small child vomited. When the sirens gave the all-clear signal we came outside and looked around. We knew what the signals meant because we have had practice drills many times. A little way away there was a big wreck where a bomb had torn down the house of a man named Schaepman. I wanted to run over to the house and so did Brenda and Betje but we didn't go very near because the policemen came on bicycles and put up ropes. Then the firemen came, for the house was burning slowly. Someone said that Mijnheer Schaepman had been killed and his daughter hurt. The ambulance had come and taken them away. There were bricks and boards thrown all over the street. Some of the house was still standing and we could see a table with dishes on it and pictures hanging sideways on the walls. Poor people.

Some of the people at the Baron's began to start for home but the Baron said they had better wait. The radio began again and everyone waited to hear reports. The reports were very, very sad. Almost all the country had been bombed. The Hague, Amsterdam at the large Schiphol airport, Sliedrecht, Haarlem, Maastricht, Arnhem, Hook of Holland, Delft—just about everywhere. The Germans had bombed Belgium and Luxembourg too. I wondered about Father and Mother and if they were all right. The Germans had crossed the Maas River in the Southeast. It was terrible. The announcer then told about the Germans coming in parachutes and for citizens to be on the lookout and to arm themselves. Pastor Opzoomer came in again and said come out and look. We went out and he pointed to the sky away toward Waalhaven airport. It was filled with white specks floating down. Parachutists he said. People began to get more excited and some of the women began to cry. Many people said we should pack up and flee into the country but Pastor Opzoomer said no.

But some people went away. The streets were filled with bicycles and cars stood in front of the houses as far as I could see and women and children were running in and out putting things into the cars. Brenda and Betje watched them and talked together excitedly. Mevrouw van der Heide should be here Brenda said. She was talking about Mother. I wished Mother would come too. Keetje stamped her foot and said the Germans were awful people to make all this noise and to kill people. They were naughty she said. Mevrouw van Helst hugged her and said never mind, never mind, Keetje. It won't last.

About 10 o'clock Mother called up from the hospital and the Baron called me to the telephone. Mother wanted to know if we were all right and I asked her if she was all right. She said yes but that she wouldn't be home for a while as they were taking the sick children out of the hospital and away to the country away from the bombing. She said she would be home when she could and that Uncle Pieter was coming out to our house if he could get there. There were no more bombings by lunch time but over Waalhaven we could still see the parachutists coming down and we counted 21 bombers and 17 more planes go over on their way to the airport. They were flying high and we could not tell if they were our planes or German ones. We could hear guns booming in the distance and the sound of smaller guns across the north side of the River Maas.

We live on the south side of Rotterdam where the airport factories, wharves, and ships are. I wanted to get on my bicycle and go over to Rotterdam to see what had happened but of course Brenda wouldn't let me. Brenda won't ever let me do anything. We all stayed by the radio which was going all the time giving instructions and reports. News came that Waalhaven airport was in the hands of the Germans and then a few minutes later we heard this wasn't true. Parachutists were supposed to be dropping down in Sliedrecht and Delft. Delft is only 12 1/2 miles from the capital. Pretty soon Haarlem, Geldermalsen and several other cities were talking about their bombing and parachutists. Military patrols, policemen, and citizens were warned that the parachutists might come down anywhere and to guard all roads and bridges and to shoot them. The Germans in parachutes wore Dutch uniforms and other things the radio said. South Holland reported that some had come down in the black robes and flat hats of Dutch priests. This news made Pastor Opzoomer shake with anger until his face was redder than ever. Everyone began to get more and more angry as the radio talked on about fires and bombings and all the terrible things the Germans were doing. Fifteen hundred people had been killed in Rotterdam since 3 A.M. the radio said. The bombing we thought had lasted hours had lasted 27 minutes.

Even Brenda became angry and she shook her fist at the sky several times when planes went over. The radio said several German soldiers and parachutists were lying dead in de Boompjes street under the elm trees. Thought of my teacher and the life of Erasmus which I was supposed to turn in today. I wrote it last night and now I might just as well not have. Teacher is young and will be fighting but perhaps not very long and he never forgets anything.

Had hardly any lunch. The Baron's cook who is very fat brought in some coffee and cakes and the older people had brandy but no one seemed hungry. Keetje ate quite well. She has always liked cakes. All afternoon we waited around not doing much but listening to the grown-ups talk and listening to the radio. People are all very kind to each other and friendly, even the ones who don't speak to each other usually. By five o'clock half of the fifty people at the Baron's house had gone home or run away in their cars to the country or somewhere. Anyway they were not around.

We got up a game with several other children playing soldiers and bombers. We took turns jumping off the high back steps holding umbrellas and pretending we were parachutists but we had to quit this because the grown-ups said it made them nervous. Just as it was getting dark the bombing started again. Mother came home on a bicycle which was not hers. She had taken the car in the morning but she said the roads were being barricaded and it was quicker to come by bicycle. We asked her many questions but she didn't talk much. She looked tired and white faced when she came into the air-shelter. The Baron and neighbors have brought in many cots and mattresses and a small electric stove on which coffee urns stand. It is damp and uncomfortable in the small shelter with so many people. It was all right this morning but it is not pleasant as time goes by. There are four old sick people near the stove but I don't know any of them though one is Mevrouw Klaes' mother I believe. The old sick people keep their eyes closed most of the time. Once in a while someone speaks to them and pulls the blankets up when they slip down. They are very silent and tired and dead looking.

Later

The air raid that came this time lasted 30 minutes. It was no better than the others but no worse. The Baron brought down a victrola and turned it on full blast to try to shut out the noise outside. Some of the music was German music, Mother said. How could it be from the same race who were attacking us she asked. The radio was off during the raid but it started up soon afterwards. The Premier of Holland, Dirk Jan de Geer, spoke and said for us to be confident because the Allies would help us and that hundreds of troops had been landed at Hoogezwaluwe, the big bridge which is between north and south Holland. When he finished, the radio said the landing field at Schiphol airdrome had been destroyed. Everyone was sad about this for it is our largest field. Had supper at the Baron's and settled down for the evening. All the lights have gone out upstairs and we are burning candles and lanterns down in the air-shelter.

Mother called the hospital after the last raid and Uncle Pieter but Uncle Pieter's hotel didn't answer. It is very hard to get anyone on the telephone. Everyone is calling everyone else after the raids are over to see if they are safe. The telephones are off during the raids. I hope Uncle Pieter is safe and Father too. Mother thinks Father has gone east to Maastricht and that's where the fighting is thickest the radio says though the bombing is bad everywhere.

Uncle Pieter came in after supper looking very sad. A big part of Coolsingle Street is gone he said. He came out on his bicycle and was stopped many times and made to show who he is. People who cannot prove who they are are being arrested. Uncle Pieter says the city of Rotterdam is damaged a great deal and that one German plane was shot down and landed in the streets. Many people have been killed and there is much sadness and many fires. Some people are frightened and some are very angry. Uncle Pieter says he saw parachute troops coming down by the hundreds and that the Germans are landing troops all the time at Waalhaven airport, just going back and forth like the trolley cars. The Baron said it sounded impossible and many other men argued with Uncle Pieter and he said he knew, he had seen it, hadn't he.

Old Mijnheer van Helst said I thought we were prepared. Where's our army? Where are our aviators and things? How about our dikes, trenches, pill-boxes, mined bridges and canals? He was very angry. Uncle Pieter said they were just where they were but no good against the Germans. He said there was fighting in the streets in Rotterdam and that Germans were there barricaded in houses. It is terrible, terrible beyond belief, Uncle Pieter said. Mother gave him a glass of gin and he drank it very quickly and began to smoke his cigar. We all sat around all evening talking about the war and going outside and looking up at the smoke in the sky over Rotterdam.

The sound of ambulances goes on all the time but no more have come down our street yet. The Baron says we three all have to stay in the shelter tonight but many people want to go home. Keetje looked tired and sleepy a little while ago and Mother put her in a cot. There is no bathroom, only two large basins in a little room off the shelter. There are not enough gas masks to go around and the grownups have given theirs to the children. The Baron has brought some coal in from a neighbor's house—the kind made out of cocoanut shells I think. This everyone is putting in wet bags, which is what the what-to-do instructions say. The wet bags are held up to the nose and this takes away gas they say. I don't know how. Our gas masks do not fit us very well and everyone hopes the Germans won't drop gas bombs. Not many people have bought gas masks yet. I put mine on and went to the mirror. I looked very funny in it and not at all like myself. Everything got very quiet after dark till nine o'clock. Keetje was asleep at last. Then the sirens sounded again and a new raid began. Several people went outside to watch it. Maybe they were not as frightened now. I went outside but was made to go back. I saw a little.

Young refugees fleeing the western front in early June 1940 pause until the threat of bombardment has passed.

The sky was streaked with lights from the searchlights looking for the Germans. We could hear the anti-aircraft fire and see red tracer bullets. The noise was worse than fireworks or thunder and went on all the time. It made my head ache and it made me a little sick to my stomach again. I wasn't frightened, but I felt a way I can't describe. Maybe I was frightened. The raid only lasted a few minutes this time. One bomb came down very near us and people all hurried back into the shelter. We heard the glass falling upstairs. Keetje sat up in her bed during the raid. She was neither all awake nor asleep but she was tired and her hair was stringy and her face pale and she wanted the noise stopped.

Finally it did stop, the sirens again saying come out. The Baron heard his cows mooing and his horses nickering in the stables. He took my hand and we walked down to the stone barn. We did not carry a lantern because the radio had been very strict in telling people to keep lights out after dark. The Baron called the horses by name and some of the cows. He told me the cows were so frightened by the bombing they could hardly be milked and that they had not given as much milk as usual at supper. They are good milk cows too according to Father who doctors them. Two of the horses were loose in their stalls. Their eyes looked frightened and wild when the Baron struck a match, and they kept on whinnying softly. They sounded like Keetje crying in her sleep. There are some pets, dogs and cats, in the air-shelter, and they are very upset when the bombing goes on. Mevrouw Klaes' Pekinese was the only dog whose hair didn't stand up. Dop's dog kept howling and walking back and forth all during the raid. He snapped at Dop when Dop tried to comfort him and Dop was very surprised and said he had never done anything like that before.

I am getting very sleepy but I hate to go to bed and miss anything. Mother says I must lie down now. People are still talking. The radio is not going any more tonight because it might direct the Germans. There goes an ambulance siren again. Uncle Pieter says the English and French will have to help us because we can't have another day like this one. I hope we don't. Mother looks so tired and worried. She is probably thinking about Father but she hasn't said anything except that we must be brave and not show we are frightened because of the other people.

Saturday, May 11, 1940

This was another bad day. The war didn't stop but got worse everywhere. Mother says the Germans have taken all of North Holland and she tried to telephone Grandfather and Grandmother Huyn but the telephone connections are gone now for good to that part of Friesland. Today was not like yesterday although the bombing and trouble are the same. It is now night and I am going to write what happened all day. We are in the air-shelter again. People are not talking as much as yesterday. Everyone is very tired from working. Yesterday no one knew what to do because the war had come so quickly but today we all worked, even the Baron and Uncle Pieter. The radio told citizens what to do to protect themselves. We have been piling sandbags around the houses and digging trenches away from cellars and laying in lots of food. Mother went to the bank this morning to get some money in case we had to leave but there was a long line and no one could take out more than two thousand guilders. There have been many air raids but we worked on outside during some of them. Soldiers are patrolling our little street, just going up and down which is patrolling. There are some soldiers on the housetops farther away. They are looking for parachutists and Dutch Nazis. A few people have tin or steel helmets like the soldiers but I wore a kettle over my head and so did many other people. We do this to keep from getting hit by shrapnel from the anti-aircraft guns and machine guns. People look very funny going around wearing kettles and pots over their heads and Keetje's keeps falling off all the time. The trolley cars have stopped running, to save electricity, the Baron says, and there is no drinking water in any of the houses in our section because the Germans blew up some of the water pipes yesterday. The telephone is not working either and all letters and telegrams have stopped coming. This is because of the traitors and parachutists. The radio says that no one is to go on the streets after 8:30 tonight unless he has the proper papers and not to go anyway unless it's absolutely necessary. There were seven air-raid alarms between this morning and supper. The radio says not to depend on sirens for warning because some of the traitors are giving false alarms. Uncle Pieter is furious about this and says he will shoot all traitors on sight and he has an army pistol to do it with too. He carries it inside his coat. There are not so many people here tonight because some of them were called out to fight fires and stand guard and help rescue and dig for people in fallen buildings. I wish I could do more.

This afternoon we saw our first parachutist. We were pasting strips of paper across the Baron's windows—the ones not broken—and across the windows of our own house so they won't break any more when the bombs come. About half of them were broken in all the houses around here yesterday. The parachutist came down at three o'clock. About fifty came down at once. This one was separated from the others. We saw the planes drop them but they seemed far away at first. Keetje was the first to see him because she was not doing much work. Mijnheer van Helst was near Keetje and when he saw the parachutist he called out to the women to go inside and then ran toward the man. The man came down behind the Baron's barn. We saw Mijnheer van Helst take out his pistol and aim and then he fired three times. He came back a moment later looking very sad and said the German was shot. The Baron and several others ran forward to see the German but Brenda kept me from going. Heintje Klaes went and came back and said the German was really dead and he was glad. Mijnheer van Helst didn't look glad and his hands were trembling. He is an old and very kind man and not used to shooting people the way regular soldiers do.

The parachutist, Heintje said, wore a one piece green suit like coveralls and his uniform was like a pair of ski pants. He had a flying eagle on his helmet which was of metal. The Baron brought back the helmet and he said someone could use this but no one wanted to put it on. Heintje got it later and is wearing it now. It is too big for him and he looks silly in it. Heintje is pretty silly looking anyway and his eyes stick out like tulip bulbs most of the time. Mijnvrouw Klaes went out to see the dead parachutist and came back very excited. She swore she knew him and that he was named Friedrich Buehler and had grown up in Holland after the other war. This caused a great deal of talk and excitement and Uncle Pieter said "the damned ungrateful swine. We took their war babies and fed them and this is what we get back." Some soldiers came and took the dead parachutist away.

Some more parachutists came down later in the afternoon. They landed nearer this time and right after they came down a squad of soldiers came running down our street toward the warehouses on the river. The Baron yelled at them but they did not stop. Later we heard firing and the warehouse was on fire. The soldiers came back and this time they stopped. The Germans had come down and run into an old deserted building on the wharf. They had set up their machine guns and our soldiers had driven them out with hand grenades and set the building on fire. They also caught a man on top of a house they said who was signaling to the parachutists. The soldiers said the Germans were doing this all over Holland, coming down and taking over houses and shooting from them at citizens or whoever passed. The soldiers looked very tired. They only stopped for a minute and then went on. Mother has been gone all day and Betje and Grietje and Brenda have been busy storing all the pictures and nice things of our house in the cellar and burying some of the silver where the Germans cannot get it if they come.

The Germans have been bombing all day and I have seen several bombs drop out of the planes. They look small so far away and are only big when they explode I guess. Some of our planes always go up to fight them and they make small puffs of smoke in the air when they fire at each other, and the planes dive around the sky at each other. None of the dive bombers have come very near but I have heard them coming down across the river and the sound is an awful roar. Some of the German planes dropped pieces of paper today and Max Blok brought one of the papers into our air-shelter. It said many things in Dutch and was written by the Germans. It said the Germans came as friends and they were sorry to be doing what they were doing but they had to protect us from the English and the French. This made everyone laugh at first and made them angry too. The paper also said that we should stop fighting for it was foolish and crazy for us to go on fighting when our country was almost completely beaten. Why did we want to fight against our friends the Germans, the paper asked. Our friends the Germans, Mijnheer van Helst said, spitting. He stuck the paper on the wall and ran his pencil through it.

The radio came on before supper and said that most of the west of Holland from the Zuider Zee down to the River Yssel and through the peat bogs had been flooded but the Germans were using rubber boats and still coming. The second water-line had been broken through by the Germans but the Dutch forces were fighting bravely and would go on. Several big important bridges had been captured by parachutists before they could be blown up the radio said but Dutch soldiers will get them back. Many soldiers are being killed on both sides and there is much trouble from bombing in Amsterdam. The Bethlehem hospital in Amsterdam has been all torn up. I was born in this hospital but of course I do not remember that. Mother pointed it out to me one time when we were in Amsterdam visiting the museum. The things the radio said are not very good. The Germans seem to be about everywhere. They have taken Waalhaven airport now and Schiphol and several others and are bringing troops back and forth. One plane was shot down with a horse in it which the radio said the German commander had brought for his victory parade. Citizens are warned to stay off the streets but to report any signs of shooting from private homes as some bad Dutch Nazis are helping the Germans.

Later, the same day

The worst air-raid of all has just come. About half the houses on our street are gone. One bomb landed on the lawn by our air-shelter and one side of the shelter is caved in but the Baron and others are repairing it now. Mevrouw Hartog broke down and cried during the air-raid and got everyone very nervous when she yelled. I think she almost went crazy.

Heintje Klaes was killed! He went outside to see the light from the big flares and incendiary bombs and didn't come back. He slipped out. Heintje was not afraid of anything but the bombs got him. The whole house rocked when the bombs came close. We put our fingers in our ears but it didn't help much. The fire wagons are working outside now and half the people in the air-shelter including Uncle Pieter have gone out. I went out for a while and they were taking dead people out of the bombed houses. Uncle Pieter sent me back to stay with Keetje. There is a funny smell in the air like burnt meat and a funny yellow light all over the country from the incendiary bombs. Three men were killed trying to get a bomb away that hadn't gone off yet. One of the men was our postmaster and I loved him very much. He gave me my first bicycle ride. It is awful to watch the people standing by their bombed houses. They don't do much. They just walk around and look at them and look sad and tired. I guess there isn't anything else they can do, but it seems awful.

Our house wasn't hit but the street in front of it between our house and the Baron's is just a great big hole and all the cobblestones are thrown up on our lawn and the Baron's until it doesn't look as if there ever was a street there. Mother is going to be surprised when she sees it. The street was just made over last year and was very smooth and nice.

At the end of our street the water is coming in where the canal locks were hit and I guess it will just keep running over the land until it is fixed. No one does anything about it because there are too many people to be helped and fires to fight. Twelve people on our street were killed and I knew every one of them but I knew Heintje best. Mevrouw Klaes has been crying ever since the bombing. Some people prayed all the time and some sang the national anthem and some just sat and stared. A woman who is very sick with a bad heart looked as if she might die. She was very pale when she came and still is. Jan Klaes is Mevrouw Klaes' other son and he is fighting somewhere like my father is. I said a prayer to myself for Father and I hope God heard it in spite of all the noise. I told Uncle Pieter I had prayed but he didn't say anything, just laid his hand on my shoulder. Uncle Pieter has gone off to the hospital to try to find Mother. It is getting late and he is worried I think. I know he will find her. Keetje has gone to sleep again but she talks in her sleep and wakes up all the time asking if the war is over and things like that.

Poor Keetje, she is so little and doesn't know what is happening. I think I do and it is worse than anything I ever heard about and worse than the worst fight in the cinema. The ambulances coming and going and so many dead people make it hard for me not to cry. I did cry some while the bombing was going on but so many other little children were that no one noticed me I think. I just got into bed with Keetje and hid my face. I was really frightened this time.

Later

Uncle Pieter came back. He didn't find Mother because she is dead. I can't believe it but Uncle Pieter wouldn't lie. We aren't going to tell Keetje yet. The ambulances are still screaming. I can't sleep or write any more now or anything.

17.

Churchill Takes Office

May 1940

Although Churchill had been the earliest and strongest advocate of British operations in Norway, it was, ironically, the costly and embarrassing failure of those operations that made him prime minister. Because the fiasco took place on Chamberlain's watch, Britons tended to blame him personally, and Parliament heeded their views. On May 7, during a contentious debate on Norway, Chamberlain made a

rather lackluster speech to the House of Commons defending his policy, after which he was rebuked not only by the opposition but also by several influential members of his own Conservative party. A vote of confidence was taken, and it revealed that Chamberlain's governing majority had dwindled from more than two hundred seats to merely eighty-one. Although the prime minister could still have remained in power, the defection of so many Conservatives meant that, as a practical matter, he would have to step down. He tendered his resignation on May 10, the day that the Germans invaded the Low Countries; and even though Churchill had been involved himself in the Norwegian bungling, the first lord of the admiralty nevertheless remained Chamberlain's obvious successor.

In Paris, meanwhile, the French were themselves undergoing similar leadership convulsions. When the Winter War broke out, there was considerable support among the French for aid to the Finns. However, Premier Edouard Daladier was understandably reluctant to incite a war with the Soviets when he already had one still to fight with the Germans. Even had the French been able to aid the Finns, which they weren't, the Finnish position was hardly tenable. Nevertheless, the French Parliament wanted Daladier's head and forced his resignation on March 20.

Daladier's successor, Paul Reynaud, was an independent thinker who had been an outspoken critic of French foreign and military policy before the war. Like Churchill, he had called for much more forceful containment of Germany and, as finance minister since 1938, had overseen a substantial increase in French arms production, especially the production of tanks. Unfortunately, Reynaud's maverick political style meant that he had a limited personal following, so he was forced to keep Daladier in his cabinet as war minister in order to ensure parliamentary support for his government. (For similar reasons, Churchill found it prudent to keep Chamberlain, still head of the Conservative party, in his new government as domestic policy chief.)

Winston Churchill leaves 10 Downing Street in mid-June 1940 to make a speech before Parliament announcing that Britain has more than 1.25 million men under arms in England and that it will fight on for years, if necessary, and alone, if necessary.

CHAMBERLAIN RESIGNS, CHURCHILL IS PREMIER

Coalition Assured; Labor Decides to Allow Leaders to Join New National Cabinet

By RAYMOND DANIELL

LONDON, May 10—In the gravest crisis Great Britain has faced since the World War, Winston Churchill became Prime Minister tonight as Allied armies raced across Belgium again for a death grapple with invading German armies.

Neville Chamberlain, who had headed the government since just after King George VI ascended the throne, resigned early in the evening after convincing himself that it was impossible to remain and give the country the truly national government that the people want.

A genuine coalition Cabinet was assured when the executive committee of the Labor party declared that it would accept a share in a government headed by a new Prime Minister who had the nation's confidence. This is expected also to result in the entry of Liberals into the government.

The German invasion of Belgium, the Netherlands and Luxembourg, which transformed the static conflict of the West into a total European if not yet World War, had been expected throughout the day to "freeze" Mr. Chamberlain in his job for a short time at least, despite the poor showing in Wednesday's division when the government's majority in the House of Commons was cut from 200 to eighty-one.

That Mr. Chamberlain would have to relinquish his high office became apparent last night when Clement H. Attlee and Arthur Greenwood, the Opposition Labor leaders, informed him to his face that they would not consent to serve in a Cabinet that he headed. Thus they provided the cue for the undecided Liberals and Conservatives who were critical of the government.

Without these dissidents, it was felt it would be impossible for the man who brought back "peace in our time" from Munich to establish a government satisfactory to the disturbed Members of Parliament and their worried constituents. These were too angry at the let-down to their hopes of the Allied withdrawal from Norway after the optimistic build-up their press had given them about the success of operations across the North Sea.

After the acrimonious debate that followed the Prime Minister's admission that the campaign in Central and Southern Norway was at an end, it was apparent that the country demanded a new administration in which the Opposition would share the responsibilities of leadership.

Early this evening Mr. Chamberlain drove to Buckingham Palace and told the King he thought the time had come for him to relinquish his seals of office. Soon afterward Mr. Churchill, who has been the nearest approach to a war leader this country has had since the conflict began, went to the Palace also and accepted an invitation to form a government.

This came as something of a surprise, for it was known that as late as last night, Mr. Chamberlain favored Foreign Secretary Viscount Halifax as his successor. A small crowd was waiting at Whitehall when the following announcement was issued from there:

"The Right Hon. Neville Chamberlain, M. P., resigned the office of Prime Minister and First Lord of the Treasury this evening, and the Right Hon. Winston Churchill, M. P., accepted His Majesty's invitation to fill the position.

British workers in early June 1940 remove road signs that might aid German invaders.

"The Prime Minister desires that all Ministers should remain at their posts and discharge their functions with full freedom and responsibility while the necessary arrangements for formation of a new administration are made."

It is expected that the former Prime Minister will accept a subordinate position in the Cabinet of the former First Lord of the Admiralty.

At the same time it was believed that Chancellor of the Exchequer Sir John Simon, Air Secretary Sir Samuel Hoare and possibly War Secretary Oliver Stanley, who shared with the Prime Minister the brunt of the Opposition attack, would be retired from the War Cabinet.

Mr. Churchill, who will move from Admiralty House to No. 10 Downing Street as soon as Mr. Chamberlain can move out, is expected to announce selection of his colleagues tomorrow or next day.

The German invasion of the Low Countries made it urgently necessary that the confused political situation here should be resolved immediately and a government that would have the united support of all elements in Parliament be established to lead the nation. That this could be accomplished only after Mr. Chamberlain's resignation became clear this morning after the meeting of the executive committee of the Parliamentary Labor party. From it Mr. Greenwood and Mr. Attlee sent this statement:

"The Labor party, in view of the latest series of abominable aggressions by Hitler, while firmly convinced that drastic reconstruction of the government is vital and urgent in order to win the war, reaffirms its determination to do its utmost to achieve victory. It calls on its members to devote all their energies to this end and stand firmly united through whatever trials and sacrifices lie ahead."

The Labor leaders then left to attend the party conference at Bournemouth, where the executive committee of the party issued the following statement:

"The national executive committee of the Labor party unanimously decided to take and share responsibility as a full partner in a new government under a new Prime Minister, who could command the confidence of the nation."

After the Labor declaration, events moved swiftly. Mr. Chamberlain called the War Cabinet and announced his decision to resign in the interest of national unity. Thirty minutes later all other Ministers of Cabinet rank were summoned to their last meeting with Mr. Chamberlain at the head of the table.

As his official family sat facing him, the 71-year-old former Lord Mayor Birmingham discussed the situation and said he could not carry on because a broader based government that would command the support of all parties was impossible under him. He thanked his listeners for the support they had given him.

Soon afterward the Ministers departed, their glum faces hinting at what was confirmed first by the grim, pale Prime Minister's visit to the Palace and the official statement issued soon after his return to his official home. A small crowd cheered him as he stepped into his car in Whitehall and women waved handkerchiefs. Mr. Churchill received louder cheers from a larger crowd when he returned from his visit to the Palace a little later.

Obviously nothing is known of Mr. Churchill's intentions, but it is generally accepted that Labor will have Mr. Attlee, Mr. Greenwood, Ernest Bevin, head of the Transport Workers Union, and possibly former First Lord of the Admiralty A. V. Alexander among its principal appointments, although all these will not be in the War Cabinet. Mr. Greenwood and Mr. Bevin, however, may win seats among the elect. The opposition Liberals naturally expect Sir Archibald Sinclair, their leader in the Commons, to be included and David Lloyd George, Britain's World War leader, is regarded as a possible though not a probable selection.

The rebels among government supporters, led by Leopold S. Amery, also can be expected to be found in Mr. Churchill's new Ministry.

There probably has been no more impersonal valedictory by a retiring Prime Minister than that made by Mr. Chamberlain tonight in a broadcast to the nation. His voice betrayed no sadness or bitterness at parting with his high office but rather grim determination to help Mr. Churchill wage war to the hilt.

When he reverted to the times when, as long as he believed there was a chance of preserving peace honorably, he strove to take it, he raised his voice as though challenging those who tried to misinterpret those efforts. The most dramatic passage of his speech was his final reference to Chancellor Hitler as a "wild beast which has sprung upon us from his lair."

Calling on the people to rally behind his successor for "the great battle just beginning," Mr. Chamberlain declared no other man in history had been responsible for such a "hideous total of human suffering and misery" as Herr Hitler.

"I have nothing to offer but blood, toil, tears and sweat."

Winston Churchill's speech to the House of Commons

Winston Churchill made this famous speech, his first as prime minister, to the House of Commons on May 13, 1940. He used it to introduce his request for a vote of confidence on the new union government. Subsequently, the Labor party voiced its strong approval, but the Conservatives, still yearning for Neville Chamberlain, responded more tepidly.

I beg to move,

That this House welcomes the formation of a Government representing the united and inflexible resolve of the nation to prosecute the war with Germany to a victorious conclusion.

On Friday evening last I received His Majesty's commission to form a new Administration. It was the evident wish and will of Parliament and the nation that this should be conceived on the broadest possible basis and that it should include all parties, both those who supported the late Government and also the parties of the Opposition. I have completed the most important part of this task. A War Cabinet has been formed of five Members, representing, with the Opposition Liberals, the unity of the nation. The three party Leaders have agreed to serve, either in the War Cabinet or in high executive office. The three Fighting Services have been filled. It was necessary that this should be done in one single day, on account of the extreme urgency and rigour of events. A number of other positions, key positions, were filled yesterday, and I am submitting a further list to His Majesty to-night. I hope to complete the appointment of the principal Ministers during to-morrow. The appointment of the other Ministers usually takes a little longer, but I trust that, when Parliament meets again, this part of my task will be completed, and that the administration will be complete in all respects.

I considered it in the public interest to suggest that the House should be summoned to meet today. Mr. Speaker agreed, and took the necessary steps, in accordance with the powers conferred upon him by the Resolution of the House. At the end of the proceedings today, the Adjournment of the House will be proposed until Tuesday, 21st May, with, of course, provision for earlier meeting, if need be. The business to be considered during that week will be notified to Members at the earliest opportunity. I now invite the House, by the Motion which stands in my name, to record its approval of the steps taken and to declare its confidence in the new Government.

To form an Administration of this scale and complexity is a serious undertaking in itself, but it must be remembered that we are in the preliminary stage of one of the greatest battles in history, that we are in action at many other points in Norway and in Holland, that we have to be prepared in the Mediterranean, that the air battle is continuous and that many preparations, such as have been indicated by my honorable Friend below the Gangway, have to be made here at home. In this crisis I hope I may be pardoned if I do not address the House at any length today. I hope that any of my friends and colleagues, or former colleagues, who are affected by the political reconstruction, will make allowance, all allowance, for any lack of ceremony with which it has been necessary to act. I would say to the House, as I said to those who have joined this government: "I have nothing to offer but blood, toil, tears and sweat."

We have before us an ordeal of the most grievous kind. We have before us many, many long months of struggle and of suffering. You ask, what is our policy? I can say: It is to wage war, by sea, land and air, with all our might and with all the strength that God can give us; to wage war against a monstrous tyranny, never surpassed in the dark, lamentable catalogue of human crime. That is our policy. You ask, what is our aim? I can answer in one word: It is victory, victory at all costs, victory in spite of all terror, victory, however long and hard the road may be; for without victory, there is no survival. Let that be realised; no survival for the British Empire, no survival for all that the British Empire has stood for, no survival for the urge and impulse of the ages, that mankind will move forward towards its goal. But I take up my task with buoyancy and hope. I feel sure that our cause will not be suffered to fail among men. At this time I feel entitled to claim the aid of all, and I say, "Come then, let us go forward together with our united strength."

18.

The Dunkirk Evacuation
May–June 1940

The Germans attacked the Low Countries with two army groups commanded by the same generals, Fedor von Bock and Gerd von Rundstedt, who had led the _Blitzkrieg_ against Poland. On May 10, Bock's Army Group B had moved into the Netherlands and northern Belgium, while Rundstedt's Army Group A, which included Guderian's Panzer corps, had attacked southern Belgium and northern France.

Gradually, the British and French troops fighting in Belgium found themselves forced into an ever-shrinking pocket between the two German army groups. On May 23, recognizing that the only hope for the British Expeditionary Force (BEF) lay in its evacuation, its commander, Field Marshal John Gort, ignored instructions to hold his positions and instead ordered all of his units to begin falling back to the English Channel.

As it turned out, Gort's order came just in time. After reaching the coast, Guderian's fast-moving tanks had turned north toward the BEF, hoping to seize the Channel ports of Boulogne, Calais, and Dunkirk before the main body of the BEF arrived. The first two cities were indeed surrounded, but on May 24 Rundstedt ordered Guderian to halt his advance fifteen miles short of Dunkirk, because Hitler had decided that Bock's infantry should have the prize instead.

Hitler and Rundstedt both considered a large-scale evacuation impractical and therefore believed they had plenty of time. They also

wanted to conserve Guderian's armor for the next phase of operations: the great push toward Paris. Even Churchill, who had been slow to recognize the danger and waited three days before affirming Gort's retreat, estimated initially that the Royal Navy would be able to save only 45,000 of the approximately 400,000 BEF troops. They were all mistaken.

The admiralty issued the order to commence Operation Dynamo, the code name given to the Dunkirk evacuation, at 7:57 P.M. London time on May 26. By the time the operation ended on June 4, the Royal Navy had demonstrated that, despite its difficulties in Norway, it was still a vastly superior force. The powerful guns of its destroyers shored up the BEF's defensive perimeter—granting hundreds of small civilian craft, recruited on a moment's notice, the time they needed to ferry British and French soldiers from the beaches to the large military and civilian transport ships waiting offshore. In all, about 340,000 Allied soldiers were saved, two-thirds of them British.

75% OF B.E.F. REPORTED SAFELY OUT OF FLANDERS

Britain Hails Men; Thousands More Arrive in Port to Receive a Frenzied Welcome

By HAROLD DENNY

LONDON, May 31—About three-quarters of the British Expeditionary Force thus far has been evacuated from Dunkerque and brought to England, it was estimated unofficially in well-informed quarters late tonight. Military authorities would not confirm or deny this estimate, the actual figures being kept secret.

[The United Press reported that it was estimated that 75 to 80 per cent of the British Expeditionary Force and some of its Allies trapped by the Germans in Flanders had been snatched from what had appeared to be the certain annihilation of more than 500,000 men. Original estimates of the strength of the B.E.F. ranged from 300,000 to 350,000.

["At least one Belgian army corps is still fighting side by side with the Allies," the British Broadcasting Corporation said early today in a news broadcast picked up in New York by the National Broadcasting Company. The corps was said to be under the command of the former commander of the Liège district who had refused to obey King Leopold's capitulation order.]

Ragged and battle-weary British and French soldiers who fought their way out of the shambles of Northern France and Belgium continued to stream into port during the day, still dazed but happy as they hurried inland for brief leaves at home.

They were greeted with almost delirious enthusiasm by the populace as they disembarked from the motley collection of large and small boats which had ferried them across the Channel and by cheering crowds all along the railway lines.

They were welcomed not sadly as a beaten army but proudly as the heroes in one of the bravest chapters in Great Britain's military annals.

Earlier this week high army officers had expressed the fear that almost the entire British Expeditionary Force would be lost. To date a far larger number has been returned safely to England than any one had dared to hope.

The primary reason for this result is said to have been the skillful coordination with the troops by the British Navy assisted by elements of the French Navy and by the Royal Air Force in conjunction with French aviators.

The behavior of the soldiers under a pounding by a vastly superior force such as no troops ever had had to withstand before is praised without measure by commanders returning with them, who have seen much of the war. These soldiers stood their ground and retired always in perfect order under admirable discipline. So these fine battalions, among them some of the best in the British Army, were not destroyed after all, but their survivors after a rest will be able to reform with additions and take the field again better than they were before, because now they are used to the most terrible engines the Germans can hurl against them.

Part of the B.E.F. and a considerable force of French still are holding a narrow strip of coast behind Dunkerque covering the withdrawal. This strip now is being called the "Corunna line" in memory of Sir John Moore's classic withdrawal from Spain in 1809, when his army had been placed in a similarly hopeless situation by the defection of the Spanish. French troops

Allied troops wade out from the beach at Dunkirk to board one of the warships taking part in the evacuation from Flanders.

are in this line with the British, while more are with General Rene Prioux among those who are fighting their way to the coast.

The part played by the British fleet is so brilliant that today's returning soldiers shouted to the crowds along the beach: "Thank God for the navy" and cheered sailors on shore whenever they sighted them. The French soldiers, also, wrung the sailors' hands and exclaimed: "Merci."

The navy has had two jobs in the evacuation. One has been to try to keep down the German fire on the British troops and to knock out tanks by fire from the warships lying out before Dunkerque. According to the returning soldiers, this strategy undoubtedly has done much to keep down the British and French casualties.

The warships have had to manoeuvre in shallow water against racing tides, in darkness and under a terrific German air bombardment, where the grounding of one ship, thus blocking

the channel, might have spelled doom to many soldiers. One of three destroyers whose loss was announced last night was sunk by an aerial bomb which performed the incredible feat of dropping straight down the ship's smokestack without touching its sides.

Another destroyer, one of four, was attacked by German dive bombers as she approached the French coast. Her crew brought down one plane with anti-aircraft fire. Further in toward the coast the same vessel was attacked by high bombers, but took on a full load of soldiers and set out for England. A transport departing at the same time came under a heavy air attack, but the destroyer crew put a blanket of fire on the German planes. These planes then turned their attention again to the destroyer and made twelve more attacks. The transport escaped unscathed, but a bomb struck the destroyer, breaking a steam pipe and causing some casualties, and forced the destroyer to halt. Another destroyer came to the assistance of the first and tried to tow her out, but as the German bombers again attacked the commander decided he was not justified in detaining the other ship and transferred his passengers to her.

It was an odd sight to see the fleet of transports, which, with destroyers and other naval craft, came steaming into these waters today crowded to the gunwales with cheering and smiling lads who a few days ago never had hoped to see the shores of England again. There were steamboats of all sizes, many of them had been pleasure boats in happier days, coastal tramp ships, dingy fishing boats and motor boats. A tug chugged in towing a string of five barges loaded with soldiers. One party of soldiers was brought by an officer—a yachtsman in civil life—in a sailboat he had "pinched" near Dunkerque when he could not find a transport.

The crews of these unorthodox transports were as varied as the boats—sturdy coastal seamen, fishermen and amateur yachtsmen. They have not hesitated to take their little ships to that thundering beach to bring back the soldiers.

The soldiers who arrived here were dog-tired and ravenously hungry. Many said they had snatched only a few hours' sleep in seventeen days of fighting and had little to eat but biscuits. Townswomen heaped oranges, apples, sandwiches and cups of tea on the barricade separating them from the troops, and one family contributed wedding cake baked for a ceremony tomorrow.

The soldiers' torn and stained clothing gave a hint of what they had been through. Most of them had lost all their kit except their rifles and had only the clothes they stood in. One man was in pajamas with a blanket draped over his shoulders. However, almost all of them were smiling and many remarked after a meal and a night's sleep that they would be ready for "another go at Jerry."

Most of them were too tired to talk, however, and many fell asleep the moment they sat down in the troop trains. Those who could tell of their adventures added to the tale of rushing on German tanks, of the incessant bombing and machine-gunning from the air, of the slaughter of refugees by German airplanes and tank crews.

Several insisted that "Fifth Column" activities behind the British lines had been marked. Wherever they moved, they said, the Germans seemed to know it and greeted them in their new positions with bombs. Whenever a headquarters moved also the Germans seemed to get instant word of it and however obscure the house, even if it was one of a long row, it was unerringly bombed.

"I now started to pack them on deck."

The Dunkirk evacuation from the viewpoint of a rescue-craft captain

The author of this account, retired naval commander C. H. Lightoller, was senior surviving officer of the *Titanic* and the principal witness at the inquiry into her sinking. His yacht, *Sundowner,* was one of more than six hundred civilian craft pressed into service by Vice Adm. Bertram Ramsay, who commanded Operation Dynamo. Ramsay requisitioned anything moored in southern England that could float and was over thirty feet long—from cabin cruisers to barges to fishing boats.

Halfway across we avoided a floating mine by a narrow margin, but having no firearms of any description—not even a tin hat—we had to leave its destruction to someone better equipped. A few minutes later we had our first introduction to enemy aircraft, three fighters flying high. Before they could be offensive, a British destroyer—*Worcester*, I think—overhauled us and drove them off. At 2.25 P.M. we sighted and closed the twenty-five-foot motor-cruiser *Westerly*; broken down and badly on fire. As the crew of two (plus three naval ratings she had picked up in Dunkirk) wished to abandon ship—and quickly—I went alongside and took them aboard, giving them the additional pleasure of again facing the hell they had only just left.

We made the fairway buoy to the Roads shortly after the sinking of a French transport with severe loss of life. Steaming slowly through the wreckage we entered the Roads. For some time now we had been subject to sporadic bombing and machine-gun fire, but as the *Sundowner* is exceptionally and extremely quick on the helm, by waiting till the last moment and putting the helm hard over—my son at the wheel—we easily avoided every attack, though sometimes near lifted out of the water.

It had been my intention to go right on to the beaches, where my second son, Second Lieutenant R. T. Lightoller, had been evacuated some forty-eight hours previously; but those of the *Westerly* informed me that the troops were all away, so I headed up for Dunkirk piers. By now dive-bombers seemed to be eternally dropping out of the cloud of enemy aircraft overhead. Within half a mile of the pierheads a two-funnelled grey-painted transport had overhauled and was just passing us to port when two salvos were dropped in quick succession right along her port side. For a few moments she was hid in smoke and I certainly thought they had got her. Then she reappeared, still gaily heading for the piers and entered just ahead of us.

The difficulty of taking troops on board from the quay high above us was obvious, so I went alongside a destroyer (*Worcester* again, I think) where they were already embarking. I got hold of her captain and told him I could take about a hundred (though the most I had ever had on board was twenty-one). He, after consultation with the military C.O., told me to carry on and get the troops aboard. I may say here that before leaving Cubitt's Yacht Basin, we had worked all night stripping her down of everything moveable, masts included, that would tend to lighten her and make for more room.

My son, as previously arranged, was to pack the men in and use every available inch of space—which I'll say he carried out to some purpose. On deck I detailed a naval rating to tally the troops aboard. At fifty I called below, "How are you getting on?," getting the cheery reply, "Oh, plenty of room yet." At seventy-five my son admitted they were getting pretty tight—all equipment and arms being left on deck.

I now started to pack them on deck, having passed word below for every man to lie down and keep down; the same applied on deck. By the time we had fifty on deck I could feel her getting distinctly tender, so took no more. Actually we had exactly a hundred and thirty on board, including three *Sundowner*s and five *Westerly*s.

During the whole embarkation we had quite a lot of attention from enemy planes, but derived an amazing degree of comfort from the fact that the *Worcester*'s A.A. guns kept up an everlasting bark overhead.

Casting off and backing out we entered the Roads again; there it was continuous and unmitigated hell. The troops were just splendid and of their own initiative detailed look-outs ahead, astern, and abeam for inquisitive planes, as my attention was pretty wholly occupied watching the steering and passing orders to Roger at the wheel. Any time an aircraft seemed inclined to try its hand on us, one of the look-outs would just call quietly, "Look out for this bloke, skipper," at the same time pointing. One bomber that had been particularly offensive, itself came under the notice of one of our fighters and suddenly plunged vertically into the sea just about fifty yards astern of us. It was the only time any man ever raised his voice above a conversational tone, but as that big black bomber hit the water they raised an echoing cheer.

Wounded members of the British Expeditionary Force arrive in England aboard a destroyer after their evacuation from Dunkirk.

My youngest son, Pilot Officer H. B. Lightoller (lost at the outbreak of war in the first raid on Wilhelmshaven), flew a Blenheim and had at different times given me a whole lot of useful information about attack, defence and evasive tactics (at which he was apparently particularly good) and I attribute, in a great measure, our success in getting across without a single casualty to his unwitting help.

On one occasion an enemy machine came up astern at about a hundred feet with the obvious intention of raking our decks. He was coming down in a gliding dive and I knew that he must elevate some ten to fifteen degrees before his guns would bear. Telling my son "Stand by," I waited till, as near as I could judge, he was just on the point of pulling up, and then "Hard a-port." (She turns a hundred and eighty degrees in exactly her own length.) This threw his aim completely off. He banked and tried again. Then "Hard a-starboard," with the same result. After a third attempt he gave it up in disgust. Had I had a machine-gun of any sort, he was a sitter—in fact, there were at least three that I am confident we could have accounted for during the trip.

Not the least of our difficulties was contending with the wash of fast craft, such as destroyers and transports. In every instance I had to stop completely, take the way off the ship and head the heavy wash. The M.C. being where it was, to have taken one of these seas on either the quarter or beam would have at once put paid to our otherwise successful cruise. The effect of the consequent plunging on the troops below, in a stinking atmosphere with all ports and skylights closed, can well be imagined. They were literally packed like the proverbial sardines, even one in the bath and another on the W.C., so that all the poor devils could do was sit and be sick. Added were the remnants of bully beef and biscuits. So that after discharging our cargo in Ramsgate at 10 P.M., there lay before the three of us a nice clearing-up job.

Arriving off the harbour I was at first told to "lie off." But when I informed them that I had a hundred and thirty on board, permission was at once given to "come in" (I don't think the authorities believed for a minute that I had a hundred and thirty), and I put her alongside a trawler lying at the quay. Whilst entering, the men started to get to their feet and she promptly went over to a terrific angle. I got them down again in time and told those below to remain below and lying down till I gave the word. The impression ashore was that the fifty-odd lying on deck plus the mass of equipment was my full load.

After I had got rid of those on deck I gave the order, "Come up from below," and the look on the official face was amusing to behold as troops vomited up through the forward companionway, the after companionway, and the doors either side of the wheelhouse. As a stoker P.O., helping them over the bulwarks, said, "God's truth, mate! Where did you put them?" He might well ask.

19.

The Fall of Paris

June 1940

Guderian's breakthrough at Sedan on May 13 seriously unnerved the French government. At 7:30 in the morning on May 15, Premier Paul Reynaud awoke Churchill with the desperate news, "We are beaten. We have lost the battle….The road to Paris is open." Reynaud then confessed that he was considering giving up the fight, but Churchill was able to calm him down, and the next day the British prime minister

flew to Paris to meet with Reynaud, Daladier (then defense minister), and Gen. Maurice Gamelin, the French commander in chief.

Gamelin had so badly underestimated the threat posed by Germany's Panzer divisions that two days after this meeting with Churchill, he was dismissed. Reynaud replaced him with Gen. Maxime Weygand, another aging hero of the First World War, and also brought into his government as vice premier eighty-four-year-old Philippe Pétain (so that the French might be inspired by the memory of Pétain's courageous defense of Verdun). However, neither Weygand nor Pétain believed that the German offensive could be stopped, and Pétain even used his new position to lobby quietly for a separate peace.

As best he could, Weygand established a new defensive line along the Somme and Aisne Rivers, but with only sixty-one weakened divisions, few tanks, and no permanent fortifications, it simply couldn't hold. On June 5, the Germans threw ninety-five divisions against the "Weygand line," which broke quickly, allowing German armor—flanked by hundreds of Stuka

dive-bombers—to speed south nearly at will. On June 10, Reynaud's government fled the French capital for Tours (and later Bordeaux), after which Paris was declared an open city so that it might be spared the torture suffered previously by Warsaw and Rotterdam. The Germans marched in on June 14.

In Bordeaux, Reynaud wanted to continue fighting from France's colonies in North Africa, but Pétain and Weygand—along with a majority of the cabinet—insisted on an armistice. Therefore, on June 16, Pétain replaced Reynaud and early the next morning sued for peace. On June 21, determined to humiliate the French, Hitler accepted their surrender in the same railway car near Compiègne—removed from a museum for the occasion—in which the Germans had capitulated at the end of World War I. The terms of the armistice, dictated by Hitler, provided for German occupation of the northern two-thirds of France, the remainder of the country to be governed by a new French authoritarian regime led personally by Pétain and headquartered in the southern spa city of Vichy.

A convoy of refugees in northern France halts in early June 1940 to allow the passage of American ambulances carrying wounded to the rear.

REICH TANKS CLANK IN CHAMPS-ELYSEES

Berlin Recounts Parade Into Paris—Third of Citizens Reported Remaining

BERLIN, June 14—German tanks today clanked across the Seine bridges, past the Arc de Triomphe and down the tree-lined Champs-Elysées into the heart of Paris at the head of the first cavalcade of invaders to enter the French capital in nearly seventy years.

Flanked by armored cars, the dust-stained tanks swung triumphantly into Paris from the northwest at the head of Nazi units occupying the "City of Light," German accounts of the event said.

It was the ninth recorded invasion of Paris and the first since Bismarck's legions trod the broad boulevards in 1871. The jubilant German press proclaimed the fall of Paris to be the "symbol of decision" in Chancellor Adolf Hitler's Western offensive.

[Berlin Nazis expected Adolf Hitler to visit Paris June 21, the twenty-first anniversary of Germany's acceptance of the Treaty of Versailles, an Associated Press dispatch said.]

The advance into Paris, through the suburbs of Argenteuil and Neuilly and into the aristocratic western part of the city, began early in the morning, the Germans said. It was exactly five weeks after the massive western offensive began with the German drive into the Netherlands and Belgium.

The tanks rumbled between thin lines of tense and silent Parisians, the Germans said. Reports from the French capital estimated that probably a third of the city's normal population of 2,800,000 had remained in Paris.

Behind the tanks rolled anti-tank units, still dusty and laden with evidence of the furious fighting in which they had taken part to the north.

As the long shadows of the early morning retreated, more and more Nazi contingents streamed into the capital, evacuated by French Armies hoping to save their beloved Paris from the fate of Warsaw.

Motorized infantry, riding in steel-shielded trucks mounting machine guns to command the broad streets, converged from the Seine bridges to the Place de l'Etoile.

In that hub from which radiate eleven streets stands the Arc de Triomphe and its tomb of the Unknown World War Soldier, where flickers the Eternal Flame.

German reports indicated that the parade through Paris swung around the Arc de Triomphe to move down the Champs-Elysées. Speculation had suggested that the honor of being the first to march beneath that historic arch might be reserved for Germany's self-styled first soldier, Adolf Hitler.

The great arch, started in the course of the Napoleonic triumphs, is a 160-foot pile of stones, each bearing the name of a victory or a hero in French military history.

Nazi officers at the head of the procession set their course for the headquarters of French officials still in the city, it was said, and formally took it over.

The French police, Fire Department, and other city departments were said to have placed themselves at the disposal of the Germans. They offered to maintain order and discipline during the occupation of the capital, the Germans stated.

Hitler on a sight-seeing tour of Paris with Albert Speer (on the Führer's left), June 23, 1940.

Negotiations with the French officials in Paris were said to have been conducted by German officers without benefit of intermediaries.

One of the first acts of the Germans in Paris was to take over the radio stations, over which the playing of German music began immediately.

[A London dispatch said that the No. 2 radio station of Paris began broadcasting in German at 12:10 P.M. (7 A.M. New York time). The station is the one that took over the wave length of Radio Luxembourg after the Germans occupied the Grand Duchy.]

The last refugees left Paris at midnight. By orders of the Prefecture of Police, the city gates were closed by policemen and civil guards. The French troops fell back on both sides of the city, flowing around it and not going through it.

The authorities, left here for the bitter duty of surrendering the city, refused permission for any more people to leave it, in order to avoid confusion or a clash.

The first Germans to approach were motor cycle machine-gunners. They established their posts outside the gates and awaited the orders of their High Command.

The capital was like a city of the dead—shops closed, iron shutters in windows, those people who remained mourning in their homes and wondering what was coming.

Police and civil guards patrolled the streets slowly, almost alone. They had handed in their rifles and pistols. They were now a completely civilian force.

"The cause of France is not lost."

Charles de Gaulle's broadcast from London

Tank commander Charles de Gaulle, who also served briefly as Reynaud's undersecretary of war, was the most prominent of the French who refused to accept Pétain's surrender. Instead, he escaped to Britain, where he organized a Free French government-in-exile and built up an army using colonial troops willing to accept his leadership. On June 18, he broadcast this famous appeal from London. Several weeks later, a military court set up by Pétain tried de Gaulle in absentia, found him guilty of treason, and sentenced him to death.

The leaders who, for many years past, have been at the head of the French armed forces, have set up a government.

Alleging the defeat of our armies, this government has entered into negotiations with the enemy with a view to bringing about a cessation of hostilities. It is quite true that we were, and still are, overwhelmed by enemy mechanized forces, both on the ground and in the air. It was the tanks, the planes, and the tactics of the Germans, far more than the fact that we were outnumbered, that forced our armies to retreat. It was the German tanks, planes, and tactics that provided the element of surprise which brought our leaders to their present plight.

But has the last word been said? Must we abandon all hope? Is our defeat final and irremediable? To those questions I answer—No!

Speaking in full knowledge of the facts, I ask you to believe me when I say that the cause of France is not lost. The very factors that brought about our defeat may one day lead us to victory.

For, remember this, France does not stand alone. She is not isolated. Behind her is a vast Empire, and she can make common cause with the British Empire, which commands the seas and is continuing the struggle. Like England, she can draw unreservedly on the immense industrial resources of the United States.

This war is not limited to our unfortunate country. The outcome of the struggle has not been decided by the Battle of France. This is a world war. Mistakes have been made, there have been delays and untold suffering, but the fact remains that there still exists in the world everything we need to crush our enemies some day. Today we are crushed by the sheer weight of mechanized force hurled against us, but we can still look to a future in which even greater mechanized force will bring us victory. The destiny of the world is at stake.

I, General de Gaulle, now in London, call on all French officers and men who are at present on British soil, or may be in the future, with or without their arms; I call on all engineers and skilled workmen from the armaments factories who are at present on British soil, or may be in the future, to get in touch with me.

Whatever happens, the flame of French resistance must not and shall not die.

20.

The Battle of Britain

August–September 1940

In all, Churchill made five trips to Paris to stiffen Reynaud's resolve during the battle for France, but he was never able to give Reynaud what the French leader most wanted: use of Britain's remaining fighter squadrons. Churchill knew that if Britain were to carry on alone after the fall of France, it would have to rely upon its navy and the Atlantic lifeline to America. Yet the Royal Navy couldn't possibly bear up

under such a strain unless the Royal Air Force (RAF) also competed effectively for control of the skies.

After France's defeat, a euphoric Hitler assumed that Britain, now isolated, would submit as well. Yet Churchill surprised the Führer by rebuffing several peace initiatives made through neutral countries, and Hitler instead went to work on a British invasion plan, code-named Operation Sea Lion.

The chief problem that the German planners encountered was that they couldn't transport large enough armies across the English Channel: The German navy had neither enough troopships to carry sufficient men and equipment, nor enough warships to protect such a fleet, even if one could be assembled. However, eager to shift the focus elsewhere, naval commander in chief Erich Raeder pointed out that, given any invasion scenario, air supremacy over the Channel would be vital. Therefore, while the naval planning continued, Hitler ordered Luftwaffe chief Hermann Göring to eliminate the RAF.

Göring accepted this task with his usual confidence, bordering on braggadocio. Wiping out the RAF's Fighter Command wouldn't be a problem, he told the Führer; in fact, Göring believed that his medium-range Heinkels, Dorniers, and Junkers could likely bomb the British into submission without any invasion. The first phase of his air operations over the Channel began on July 10, focusing primarily on British shipping lanes and thus rarely engaging the RAF. On August 8, however, the Luftwaffe began attacking the RAF's southern fighter bases in earnest, marking the start of the battle of Britain.

As the Germans soon learned, however, the British had several key technological advantages. The Hurricanes and Spitfires that they had been stockpiling since 1937, for example, could outperform most of the German fighters; and the new British radar, which had only recently become operational, now provided the RAF with reliable advanced warning of all incoming German planes. Thus the Luftwaffe could not use surprise, as it had in France, to destroy countless Allied aircraft on the ground.

NAZIS INTENSIFY AIR RAIDS ON BRITAIN AS 500 PLANES POUND AT STRONGHOLDS

Berlin Hails Gains; British Resistance Held Waning Under Blows to Vital Areas

By C. BROOKS PETERS

BERLIN, Aug. 12—For the second successive day, the German Air Force today carried out a carefully planned attack on the British Isles, this time against the naval base at Portsmouth. In air battles that ensued there, as well as in minor engagements elsewhere in the course of the day, the Germans claim to have shot down seventy-one British planes with a loss of seventeen of their own.

Thus the "pulverizing" process with which the Germans expect to reduce British resistance before dealing the final blow on land appears now to be in full swing. Unlike all the air raids on the British Isles since the beginning of the war, those yesterday and today each had a specific announced objective against which relatively large groups of bombers, protected by fighters, operated.

Although such concentrated attacks indicate the passage of the war into a new and more dynamic stage, they do not, the Germans emphatically emphasize, represent the "great attack" that the British still have to expect. It is interesting to observe that both yesterday's and today's attacks concentrated on the two most important Channel naval bases, Portland and Portsmouth.

Portland, as the Germans claim, is the most important British Channel base for light naval craft of all kinds, led by submarine chasers. Portsmouth, on the other hand, has repair facilities for the largest ships of the British Navy, including aircraft carriers. Informed quarters here think it significant that the activities of the German raiders have been concentrated between Dover and Portland—that is, along the sections of the British coast that are closest to the German-occupied French ports.

What particularly pleased the Germans, however, was their allegation that British fighter planes showed a disinclination to engage the Germans today. Instead of forming, as the Germans admit they did yesterday, an "impenetrable wall" along the English south coast, today, the Germans assert, the British kept at a safe distance and endeavored to fire upon the Nazi planes without coming too closely within range of the latter's guns.

This, the Germans assert, is the first sign of broken British resistance. It is therefore more remarkable, they add, that their fliers were able today to shoot down seventy-one British planes, for in most cases they had to be chased before they could be brought down.

The air raid on Portsmouth took place about 1 o'clock this afternoon, when some forty German bombers, protected by an undisclosed number of pursuit and destroyer planes, appeared over the harbor, coming from the south over Spithead. Because of the attitude of the British fliers today, the Germans declare, as well as the poor marksmanship of British anti-aircraft batteries, the Nazis were able to drop their cargoes of bombs virtually undisturbed.

As they approached Portsmouth, however, the German planes split into three groups, one of which bombed an ammunition dump, while another attacked docks of the naval base and the third concentrated on oil tanks. As a result of their bombing, the Germans declare, tremendous explosions were caused and fires started that were greater than any the German fliers had seen in the British Isles.

Although early German reports declared the British fliers were not inclined to fight today, later ones asserted that forty British planes had been shot down in the course of this engagement.

Earlier this morning, between 11 o'clock and noon, German dive-bombers attacked a British convoy near Margate, at the mouth of the Thames Estuary. The official news agency reported that four merchantmen, with an approximate total tonnage of 10,000, were set afire. Above the convoy, meanwhile, an air battle developed in the course of which, the Germans declare, their machines brought down three Hurricanes and two Spitfires, while all the dive-bombers returned to their bases safely.

German pursuit and destroyer planes also again attacked captive balloons on the southern coast of England. A number of these balloons, including four over Dover, were destroyed, the Germans claim. Small battles developed in the course of this action, it is added, during which five British pursuit planes and one German destroyer plane were shot down.

Also, British airdromes along the southern coast, particularly the Manston airport near Margate, were attacked by large numbers of German planes. The Manston field, the Germans claim, for example, looked as if it had been plowed up after the German fliers' visit.

Bombs of all calibers were dropped here, the Germans asserted, and barracks, hangars, and supply sheds were demolished, while four of a group of Hurricane pursuit planes, which tried

A gunner in a Dornier D-17 bomber fires at RAF fighters from his position atop the rear of the plane, August 16, 1940.

to take off to ward off the attackers, were destroyed before they were able to leave the ground. In the air battle that resulted from this action, the Germans claim, their fliers shot down three other British pursuit planes while the German squadron did not lose a single plane.

"If the Home Defence Force is drained away..."

The Dowding Letter on why fighter planes are critical

Much of the credit for the RAF's victory in the battle of Britain is often given to Fighter Command chief Hugh Dowding, whose relentless efforts to conserve his Hurricane and Spitfire squadrons prevented Churchill's war cabinet from wasting too many of them in France. This letter, written by Dowding to an undersecretary at the Air Ministry, persuasively summarized his views.

Headquarters Fighter Command,
Royal Air Force,
Bentley Priory,
Stanmore, Middlesex

16th May, 1940

Sir,

I have the honour to refer to the very serious calls which have recently been made upon the Home Defence Fighter Units in an attempt to stem the German invasion on the Continent.

2. I hope and believe that our Armies may yet be victorious in France and Belgium, but we have to face the possibility that they may be defeated.
3. In this case I presume that there is no-one who will deny that England should fight on, even though the remainder of the Continent of Europe is dominated by the Germans.
4. For this purpose it is necessary to retain some minimum fighter strength in this country and I must request that the Air Council will inform me what they consider this minimum strength to be, in order that I may make my dispositions accordingly.
5. I would remind the Air Council that the last estimate which they made as to the force necessary to defend this country was fifty-two squadrons, and my strength has now been reduced to the equivalent of thirty-six squadrons.
6. Once a decision has been reached as to the limit on which the Air Council and the Cabinet are prepared to stake the existence of the country, it should be made clear to the Allied commanders on the Continent that not a single aeroplane from Fighter Command beyond the limit will be sent across the Channel, no matter how desperate the situation may become.
7. It will, of course, be remembered that the estimate of fifty-two squadrons was based on the assumption that the attack would come from the eastwards except in so far as the defences might be outflanked in flight. We have now to face the possibility that attacks may come from Spain or even from the north coast of France. The result is that our line is very much extended at the same time as our resources are reduced.

8. I must point out that within the last few days the equivalent of ten squadrons have been sent to France, that the Hurricane Squadrons remaining in this country are seriously depleted, and that the more squadrons which are sent to France the higher will be the wastage and the more insistent the demands for reinforcements.

9. I must therefore request that as a matter of paramount urgency the Air Ministry will consider and decide what level of strength is to be left to the Fighter Command for the defences of this country, and will assure me that when this level has been reached, not one fighter will be sent across the Channel however urgent and insistent the appeals for help may be.

10. I believe that if an adequate fighter force is kept in this country, if the Fleet remains in being, and if Home Forces are suitably organized to resist invasion, we should be able to carry on the war single-handed for some time, if not indefinitely. But, if the Home Defence Force is drained away in desperate attempts to remedy the situation in France, defeat in France will involve the final, complete and irremediable defeat of this country.

> I have the honour to be
> Sir, Your obedient Servant,
> H. C. T. Dowding, Air Chief Marshal,
> Air Officer Commanding-in-Chief
> Fighter Command, Royal Air Force.

A British radar operator plots the movements of ships and plane within the range of his station.

21.

The Blitz

September 1940–May 1941

The London Blitz began on Saturday, September 7, 1940, when the Luftwaffe shifted its focus from the RAF airfields it had been attacking and began bombing civilian London instead. On September 4, in a major address at the Berlin Sportpalast, Hitler had excoriated the British for bombing Berlin and declared that the Germans would retaliate. "If the British air force drops 2,000, 3,000, or 4,000 kilograms of

bombs," the Führer told a wildly applauding crowd, "then we shall now in a single night drop 150,000, 180,000, 320,000 kilograms of bombs and more." Three days later, Hitler made good on his threat.

The Luftwaffe's September 7 raid began in the late afternoon with the dropping of incendiary bombs. These munitions lit fires that, in turn, gave directional guidance to the squadrons of Heinkel and Dornier bombers that followed and pounded London all night. The all-clear wasn't sounded until four-fifty the next morning.

Although British censors kept specific details of the bomb damage out of the press, the destruction was obviously extensive, especially in the East End, where most of London's port facilities were located. Many of the bombs fell on dockworkers' homes, killing several hundred. Nevertheless, this change in German strategy proved to be a costly mistake. Frustrated with the slow pace of the battle of Britain, Hitler and Luftwaffe chief Göring had concluded that savaging civilian targets would

pressure the British public into compelling their leaders to sue for peace. Instead, the terror bombing merely deepened British resolve and, far worse, gave something of a reprieve to the hard-pressed RAF, whose losses had been nearing a critical point.

Whether or not continued bombing of the RAF bases would have won the battle of Britain is a debatable matter; it quickly became clear, however, that the bombing of civilian targets—targets of questionable strategic value—wasn't going to win anything, at least not in the short term. Two heavy German raids on September 15, for example, resulted in such damaging losses for the Luftwaffe that Hitler and Göring decided that their efforts to destroy RAF Fighter Command had failed. Without air supremacy, of course, there could be no invasion, so on September 17, Hitler postponed Operation Sea Lion indefinitely. The bombing of London continued, however, and in November Göring extended the campaign to Coventry and other cities in the industrial Midlands.

An aircraft spotter stands on a London rooftop during the Blitz with the dome of St. Paul's Cathedral in the background. Although effective as a tactical force in support of army operations, the Luftwaffe was not designed for strategic missions and had difficulty carrying them out, despite Göring's confidence.

GERMANS POUND AT LONDON IN 8-HOUR ATTACK

London Is Harried; Night Invaders Resume Bombing After 4 Raids by Day Are Repelled

By RAYMOND DANIELL

LONDON, Wednesday, Sept. 11—As darkness fell last night a waxing moon rose above the smoldering embers of the previous night's great fires, which threatened for a time to destroy the beautiful St. Paul's Cathedral and St. Mary-le-Bow Church, whose sweet-toned chimes for generations have lulled the Cockney children to sleep. The German Air Force then returned in force to London to continue the attack that has made life in this capital a nightmare since Saturday.

The all clear was sounded at 4:39 this morning, after the raid had been in progress for eight hours and twenty-four minutes.

[Nazi bombers smashed at London with increasing violence early today, The Associated Press reported. Until early this morning, it was stated, the attack was much less ferocious than the previous three. Then the pace stepped up until four separate squadrons were wheeling about the capital at the same time at opposite points of the compass.]

The screams of their bombs, the earth-shaking crashes, the blazes that lit the sky, the clangor of fire engines and ambulances, the bark of anti-aircraft guns and nerve-racking hum of engines droning like a mosquito that does not bite, brought another sleepless and hideous night to 7,000,000 harried persons who are trying to carry on in the face of an attack that spares neither humble workmen's homes nor the homes of the nobility.

For nine hours last night explosive-laden planes roared overhead, dropping high explosive and incendiary bombs apparently whenever the spirit moved the man in charge of the bomb racks to press the button. They released death and destruction upon helpless civilians who shuddered each time the ground shook beneath them.

Two hospitals, one filled with ailing children and the other a maternity hospital, suffered heavy damage. It is not accurately known at present, while the raid is still going on, how many homes were wrecked or persons killed, for the rescue workers are still digging among the ruins.

It was estimated, however, that Sunday night's raid caused at least 286 deaths and sent 1,400 persons, including the lame, halt and blind, into hospitals, seriously injured.

But it is not the dead or the injured, or even the extensive property damage that really counts in this battle for London, which is a mere prelude to the Battle for Britain. It is what is happening to he city's life and the nerves of its people that matters the most.

They are standing up to the punishment that is being rained on them from the skies with a courage that makes the eyes of a neutral observer smart at times. There is no doubt about their bravery, but one cannot help but wonder how long any people's nerves can stand up under this kind of bombardment, in which every one knows that each breath may be the last one, and in which the suspense is awful.

That does not mean that a defeatist attitude is growing. Far from it. These people are getting madder by the minute.

Many homes are without gas and tea. Citizens are forced to undergo tremendous inconveniences in getting to and from the places where they earn their livelihood, and their

A Heinkel He 111 medium bomber flies over the Thames River and the London docks on September 7, 1940.

ingrained politeness to one another is becoming a little strained.

There is hardly any one who has not a friend who has been bombed out of his home or has had a narrow escape from death or injury.

Monday night bombs dropped on every section of London. Slum hovels, wealthy homes, warehouses and luxury apartments, all felt the indiscriminate blast of the German bombs. The central business district was scorched, too, by hot blasts from the skies.

The City of London, this capital's East End, West End and Northern environs suffered grievously. It was a general assault and so was last night's raid, wherein scattered German bombers turned the moonlit hours into a night of horror.

Tired folk who had spent wakeful hours below ground during Monday night's nine-hour attack straggled wearily to work yesterday, hitchhiking, walking and traveling round-about routes. Red-eyed and worn looking they tried to resume their regular tasks.

Recurrent raids made this difficult. Four times before the alarms screamed the night time warning that every one has learned to take seriously and treat with respect, the sirens had sounded. Once was at lunchtime, which many spent below ground in shelters. The next was at teatime.

The third and fourth came in rapid succession at the evening rush hour. Tired and hungry throngs were just preparing to assuage their hunger and thirst and then go home. The all clear after the fourth warning brought an outpouring from the shelters and a rush of home-goers that made most sections of London look like the section around the Yankee Stadium after a World Series game.

The lines of waiting travelers still stood waiting for buses and pouring into the Underground when, a little after 8 P.M., the fifth warning of the day announced that another night of terror had begun and that the paralyzing blight, which stills the city's life as though it had been abandoned, was upon it.

Life after dark has almost ceased, and tonight, even before whistles blew, there was little traffic moving. Most theatres have folded up and the cinemas have been urged to do so. Taxicab and bus drivers, aware of what has happened to their pals who defied the Blitzkrieg, are becoming steadily more eager for shelter and less eager for fares.

During one of the daylight raids yesterday a Messerschmitt cannon was heard barking in the skies while machine-gun bullets rattled on the roof-tops. Whether these latter came from raiders who were gunning the populace from high up or from the defending British fighters could not be told because it was impossible to see what was happening overhead among the clouds.

Last night, as every other night since the raids of horror began, the main mass of raiders was preceded by an advance guard of high-flying planes loaded with incendiary rather than explosive bombs. Their job is to light the fires that guide the night raiders.

Danger does not stop for London when the all clear sounds. First there are the constant interruptions of warning whistles, almost equally as disturbing as the all clear, but worst of all, in those periods when life is presumably peaceful, are the delayed-action bombs, planted the night before. Yesterday, in between warnings and the all clear, these delayed-action fuses set off explosives left behind by Monday night's raiders.

Bombs had fallen all over London. But even after the all clear sounded, as dawn broke, there was no surcease from those dull rumbling noises, which shook this steel and concrete building as they shook almost everything else.

The people of London are showing a remarkable facility in fitting themselves to the necessity of the moment. If it is necessary to sleep in their clothes underground, well, that is what they will do.

From Limehouse to Mayfair last night people were carrying pillows and blankets to the shelters at their normal bedtimes. They had had enough dashing back and forth to shelters each time the siren blew, and they had decided that it was easier to spend those nine hours sleeping on the floor of a shelter than sitting there wakefully awaiting an all clear signal.

A couple of days ago it became impossible to buy glass to repair broken window panes. It was almost impossible to buy sleeping bags, folding cots, thermos bottles and other paraphernalia that city dwellers usually associate with holidays. This was no holiday for which the people of this capital were preparing, but a whole winter in the new way of life that modern warfare had imposed upon them.

Three big sections of London were without gas and water last night. Thousands of men and women who had struggled to work after a sleepless night straggled homeward last night on foot. Truckloads of canned food were carried into one East London area to feed those who had no means of preparing their own dinners.

"This is London."

The radio broadcasts of Edward R. Murrow during the London Blitz

Edward R. Murrow headed CBS's European Bureau from 1937 until the end of the war. His dramatic and highly reliable reports from London marked, according to most scholars, the coming of age of American broadcast journalism.

September 9, 1940

I've spent the day visiting the bombed areas. The King did the same thing. These people may have been putting on a bold front for the King, but I saw them just as they were—men shoveling mounds of broken glass into trucks, hundreds of people being evacuated from the East End, all of them calm and quiet. In one street where eight or ten houses had been smashed a policeman stopped a motorist who had driven through a red light. The policeman's patience was obviously exhausted. As he made out the ticket and lectured the driver, everyone in the street gathered around to listen, paying no attention at all to the damaged houses; they were much more interested in the policeman.

These people are exceedingly brave, tough, and prudent. The East End, where disaster is always just around the corner, seems to take it better than the more fashionable districts in the West End.

The firemen have done magnificent work these last forty-eight hours. Early this morning I watched them fighting a fire which was obviously being used as a beacon by the German bombers. The bombs came down only a few blocks away, but the firemen just kept their hoses playing steadily at the base of the flame.

The Germans dropped some very big stuff last night. One bomb, which fell about a quarter of a mile from where I was standing on a rooftop, made the largest crater I've ever seen, and I thought I'd seen some big ones. The blast traveled down near-by streets, smashing windows five or six blocks away.

The British shot down three of the night bombers last night. I said a moment ago that Londoners were both brave and prudent. Tonight many theaters are closed. The managers decided the crowds just wouldn't come. Tonight the queues were outside the air-raid shelters, not the theaters. In my district, people carrying blankets and mattresses began going to the shelters before the siren sounded.

This night bombing is serious and sensational. It makes headlines, kills people, and smashes property; but it doesn't win wars. It may be safely presumed that the Germans know that, know that several days of terror bombing will not cause this country to collapse. Where then does this new phase of the air war fit? What happens next? The future must be viewed in relation to previous objectives; those objectives were the western ports and convoys, the Midlands, and Welsh industrial areas, and the southern airfields. And now we have the bombing of London. If this is the prelude to invasion, we must expect much heavier raids against London. After all, they only used about a hundred planes last night. And we must expect a sudden renewal of the attacks against fighter dromes near the coast, an effort to drive the fighters farther inland. If the Germans continue to hammer London for a few more nights and then sweep successfully to blasting airdromes with their dive bombers, it will probably be the signal for invasion. And the currently favored date for this invasion—and you will remember there have been others in the past—is sometime about September 18.

September 23, 1940

This is London, about ten minutes to four in the morning. Tonight's raid which started about eight is still in progress. The number of planes engaged is about the same as usual, perhaps a few more than last night. Barring lucky hits, both damage and casualties should be no greater than on previous nights. The next three hours may bring a change, but so far the raid appears to be routine, with the Germans flying perhaps a little lower than they did last night.

Often we wonder what you'd like to hear from London at four in the morning. There's seldom any spot news after midnight, so we just talk about the city and its people. Today I went to our district post office. There was a long line of people waiting for their mail. Their offices or homes had been bombed, and the mailman couldn't find them. There were no complaints. But that's not quite right. One woman said: "They've got to stop this; it can't go on." Her neighbor said: "Have you ever thought what would happen to you if we gave in?" And the lady replied, "Yes, I know, but have you seen what happened to Peter Robinson's?" Others in the queue—those who've been called by Mr. Churchill the more robust elements of the community—silenced the lady with well-modulated laughter.

To me one of the most impressive things about talking with Londoners these days is this—there's no mention of money. No one knows the dollar value of the damage done during these last sixteen days. But nobody talks about it. People who've had their homes or offices bombed will tell you about it, but they never think to tell you what the loss amounted to, whether it was so many tens or hundreds of pounds. The lead of any well-written news story dealing with fire, flood, or hurricane should tell something of the total damage done in terms of dollars, but here it's much more important that the bomb missed you; that there's still plenty of food to eat—and there is.

My own apartment is in one of the most heavily bombed areas of London, but the newspapers are on the doorstep each morning—so is the bottle of milk. When the light switch is pressed, there is light, and the gas stove still works, and they're still building that house across the street, still putting in big windowpanes. Today I saw shopwindows in Oxford Street, covered with plywood. In front of one there was a redheaded girl in a blue smock, painting a sign on the board covering the place where the window used to be. The sign read OPEN AS USUAL. A block away men were working an air hammer, breaking up huge blocks of masonry that had been blown into the streets, cracking those big lumps so that they might be carted away in trucks.

The people who have something to do with their hands are all right. Action seems to drive out fear. Those who have nothing to do would be better off outside London and there are signs that they will be encouraged to go. London comes to resemble a small town. There's something of a frontier atmosphere about the place. The other night I saw half a block evacuated. Time bombs plus incendiaries did it. In half an hour the people who had been turned out of their homes had been absorbed in near-by houses and apartments. Those who arranged for the influx of unexpected guests had, I think, been frightened when those bombs came down, but they were all right when there was something to do. Blankets to get out of closets, tea to be made, and all that sort of thing.

I've talked to firemen fighting a blaze that was being used as a beacon by German bomb aimers. They told me that the waiting about in fire stations was worst of all. They didn't mind the danger when there was something to do. Even my censor when I arrived in the studio tonight was sitting here underground composing music.

A half an hour before the King made his broadcast tonight the air-raid alarm sounded. At that moment a man with a deep voice was telling the children of Britain by radio how the wasps build their nests. He said, "Good night, children everywhere." There was a brief prayer for the children who went down in mid-Atlantic last week. There was a hymn well sung. After that a piano playing some nursery song, I didn't know its name. There was a moment of silence. Then the words, "This is London, His Majesty, the King." The King spoke for half a minute and then the welcome sound of the "all-clear," that high, steady note of the siren, came rolling through the open window. One almost expected His Majesty to pause and let the welcome sound come out through the loudspeaker, but he probably didn't hear it since he was speaking from an air-raid shelter under Buckingham Palace. The only news in the King's speech was the announcement of the two new medals, but his warning of grimmer days ahead must be taken as another indication of government policy—a warning that the full weight of German bombing is yet to be experienced.

Since the disastrous retreat from Norway, the government has been issuing few sunshine statements. Nearly every statement has been couched in subtle language, has contained a warning of worse things to come.

And now the King has added his warning to those of his ministers. He took the advice of his ministers, as he must, in speaking as he did, and his ministers judged, and rightly, that these people can stand up to that sort of warning. There has been much talk of terror bombings, but it is clear that London has not yet experienced anything like the full power of the Luftwaffe in these night raids. The atmosphere for full-scale terror bombing is not right. There is as yet no sizable portion of the population prepared to talk terms with the Nazis. You must remember that this war is being fought with political as well as military weapons. If the time comes when the Germans believe that mass night raids will break this government, then we may see German bombers quartering this night sky in an orgy of death and destruction such as no modern city has ever seen. There are no available official figures, but I have watched these planes night after night and do not believe that more than one hundred and fifty have been used in any single night. The Germans have more planes than that. Sometime they may use them. The people had to be warned about that. Therefore, the King spoke as he did.

WAR ON EVERY FRONT

Nazi and Japanese officers on an inspection tour of captured Maginot line fortifications near Schoeneburg, France. This photograph was taken on September 26, 1940, just after the announcement of the U.S. embargo on steel exports to Japan and just before the signing of the Tripartite Pact.

22.

The Tripartite Pact

September 1940

In 1940, Germany and Japan had much in common: Both were militaristic, totalitarian states; both were fighting regional wars of conquest; both were benefiting, at least temporarily, from Soviet neutrality; and both were eager to keep the United States out of the fighting as well. Thus motivated, the two governments eventually found common cause. Signed with great flourish on September 27, 1940, the Tripartite Pact obligated its signatories "to assist one another with all political, economic and military means when one of the three contracting Parties is attacked by a power at present not involved in the European War or in the Sino-Japanese Conflict." Because the Soviets were specifically exempted from this provision, its practical purpose was unmistakable: It was a direct threat to the United States. Should American troops be sent either to Europe or to Asia, the result would be a two-front war.

The third signatory to the Tripartite Pact was Italy, which had finally entered the European war on June 10. Mussolini had timed his move so that his troops could avoid the worst of the fighting yet still share in the spoils of victory. Unfortunately for the Italians, France's unexpectedly swift capitulation prevented them from seizing very much, and Mussolini was left wanting more. Jealous of Hitler's successes and eager for his own measure of military glory, the Duce looked around and finally settled on neutral Greece. Making an issue of the port and airfield access that Greek dictator Ioannis Metaxas had been granting British forces in the Mediterranean, Mussolini demanded similar privileges for his own troops. When Metaxas—a fascist, but a patriot first—refused, the Italians invaded. More than 150,000 troops poured into northern Greece from Italian-controlled Albania at dawn on October 28, but they proved so inept that by mid-January 1941 the Greek army had not only kicked them out of Greece but also taken from them a quarter of Albania.

From the start, Hitler had opposed Mussolini's aspirations in the Balkans because (although he didn't share this information with the Duce) his own intention to invade the Soviet Union in the summer of 1941 required stability farther south. Thus, as he watched with disgust the Italians flounder in Greece, he began making his own plans to impose German discipline on the situation come spring. He also strengthened his position in the Balkans by meanwhile pressuring Hungary, Rumania, Bulgaria, and Yugoslavia into signing the Tripartite Pact.

JAPAN JOINS AXIS ALLIANCE SEEN AIMED AT U.S.; ROOSEVELT ORDERS STUDY OF THE PACT'S EFFECT

Russia Reassured; Accord Viewed as Threat to Soviet, in Spite of Safeguard Clause

By GUIDO ENDERIS

BERLIN, Sept. 27—By another of those bold forays into the realm of "Blitz diplomacy" with which the world has now become familiar, the Reich's Chancellery at noon today became the birthplace of a tripartite military alliance linking Germany, Italy and Japan. Its implications seem designed to have a profound effect not only on the further course of Europe's war but more directly on the world situation in general.

It is expressly specified that the commitments assumed today shall not affect the political status existing between each of the three signatories and Soviet Russia.

Opinion in neutral diplomatic quarters tonight appears to concur on two points, one being by implication that the pact contains a veiled threat to Russia, while that to the United States is decidedly less obscure.

On the latter point advance press comment leaves no doubt, and opinions gathered in informed quarters also frankly suggest that the pact may be interpreted as being directed against "certain groups in the United States who are trying to disrupt relations between peoples and nations."

In a highly ceremonial setting in the Chancellery's reception chamber, the German and Italian Foreign Ministers and the Japanese Ambassador pledged their respective countries for ten years to cooperation in the interest of lasting peace and to "the creation of the preconditions necessary to that new order that will promote the welfare and prosperity of their peoples."

The signing formalities occupied just about two minutes, after which Chancellor Hitler joined the scene, entering the chamber through a door opening from his private working apartments. It was the same chamber in which the German-Italian military pact was signed in 1939, but today's audience did not include the diplomatic corps. Those who witnessed the formalities comprised government officials, Nazi party leaders and representatives of the German and foreign press.

The pact negotiated today consists of a brief preamble and six articles. By its terms Japan recognizes Germany's and Italy's leadership in constituting "a new order in Europe." The Axis powers, for their part, recognize and respect Japan's priority rights in the establishment of "a new order in Eastern Asia." It was authoritatively stated that the Russian Government had been duly apprised of the impending conclusion of the three-power pact and informed that the signatory powers were in accord on this point.

On the basis of these premises, the partners to the pact agree to support one another in fulfillment of their tasks and to throw their complete political, economic and military resources into the defense of any of the partners who may be attacked by any power not at present involved in the European war or in the Chinese-Japanese conflict

In pronouncing his benediction on the pact after signing formalities were concluded, Foreign Minister Joachim von Ribbentrop declared: "Organized warmongers in the Jewish capitalistic

Signing the Tripartite Pact in Berlin are, seated from left to right, Ciano, Ribbentrop, and Japanese ambassador Kurusu Saburo.

democracies have succeeded in plunging Europe into a new war which was not wanted by Germany. Our fight is not directed against other peoples, but against the existence of international plotters who once before succeeded in plunging Europe into a sanguinary war."

The German Foreign Minister then added this significant warning:

"Any State that attempts to interfere in the closing phase of the wars which seek a solution of European problems or those of Eastern Asia will run afoul of the combined determined forces of 250,000,000 people. To this extent this pact is destined to serve the cause of restoring world peace."

Count Ciano and Saburo Kurusu, Japanese Ambassador to Berlin, struck the same note in their addresses, but it was noted that all three speeches studiously sought to allay Russian apprehensions, if any exist, that the new alliance was hostile to the Soviet Union.

There were considerable conflicting reports current tonight as to the nature and scope of the mandate accorded to Japan under the three-power pact and what exactly constituted the "Greater East Asia" that she is to rule unmolested. If it comprises all the areas east of India, it would nominally include French Indo-China, the Netherlands Indies and the Philippines, not to mention various British possessions.

In a political sense, Japan, with the consent of the Axis powers, would also be installed as final arbiter of what constitutes "the open door" in China.

Upon one point neutral commentators here were in complete accord: that the pact, if backed up, will measurably buttress Japan's political and economic prestige in the Far East, unless the geographic delineations of her mandate are severely curtailed after the early enthusiasm has cooled off.

Official quarters tonight point out that the presence of Chancellor Hitler at today's ceremonies must be accepted as an indication that the pact is viewed as something more than a diplomatic gesture. Berlin, Rome and Tokyo, it is suggested, regard the pact as constituting a bloc that is resolved to assume responsibility for achieving "a new order in Europe and Greater East Asia" and is determined to accomplish this without compromise and, if necessary, with the aid of arms, should any power alien to those sections attempt to interfere.

"This pact," says an inspired comment, "constitutes an effective counterweight to London attempts to prolong the war by invoking continuation of the principles of the Berlin-Rome Axis, by restricting the spread of the war and by affording military security against such machinations."

For the first time, it is emphasized, "Greater Asia has found a place in an international treaty."

It was only a few hours before the formalities were concluded that the nature of today's diplomatic developments was revealed. Conservation of official secretiveness probably never reached the efficiency attained today, as it was only when phalanxes of school children were under way to the Chancellery to welcome Count Ciano that the mystery was solved. Each youngster carried three paper flags—German, Italian and Japanese.

It was then that the red herring that had been pulled over the trail of mystery surrounding Count Ciano's visit was lifted and that it became known that today's events were not concerned with a project identifying Spain with the Axis powers and the war. That legend was so cleverly maintained that even veteran press observers failed to suspect that something more obvious was in the making.

Count Ciano arrived by plane from Munich, where he left his train from Rome. He went directly to the Chancellery, where he found the Japanese delegation led by Mr. Kurusu awaiting him.

The reception chamber rapidly filled up with the governmental party, military dignitaries and correspondents, and the ceremonies got under way promptly, lasting less than an hour.

There was a large sprinkling of Spaniards present but Ramon Serrano Suñer, the minister of government, who has been conferring with Herr von Ribbentrop, was not among them. One Spanish spokesman unofficially summed up his sentiments thus: "Spain wants peace and dreads becoming involved in foreign complications."

Italian quarters, however, divulged that Count Ciano took advantage of Señor Serrano Suñer's presence here to exchange views. "An extended conversation" took place between the two following the signing of the pact, it is learned.

To Japan's Foreign Minister, Yosuke Matsuoka, and Ambassador Kurusu, Chancellor Hitler awarded the Great Cross of the Order of the German Eagle on the occasion of today's historic agreement. Congratulatory telegrams were sent by Herr Hitler to King Victor Emmanuel and Premier Mussolini of Italy and to Emperor Hirohito of Japan. In a two-way radio broadcast with Herr von Ribbentrop, Count Ciano and Mr. Matsuoka participating the German Foreign Minister extended an invitation to his Japanese colleague to visit Berlin and Rome, expressing his hope that this would soon be possible. Mr. Matsuoka replied that he would "gladly accept this invitation" and would visit both Axis capitals "at the earliest opportunity."

"Hitler always wanted to have good relations with the U.S.A."

Excerpt from the Nuremberg testimony of Joachim von Ribbentrop

German foreign minister Joachim von Ribbentrop was one of twenty-four defendants prosecuted for war crimes before the International Military Tribunal sitting at Nuremberg. He gave this testimony under cross-examination on March 30, 1946. Eight months later, he was found guilty and hanged.

March 30, 1946

Q. What were the causes which precipitated the conflict with Russia?

A. In the winter of 1940–41 the Fuehrer was confronted with the following situation. I think it is most important to make this clear.

England was not prepared to make peace. The respective attitudes of the United States of America and of Russia were therefore of decisive importance to the Fuehrer. He told me the following (I had a very lengthy discussion with him on the subject and asked him to give me clearly defined diplomatic directives).

He said, "Japan's attitude is not absolutely in favour of Germany. Although we have concluded the Tripartite Pact, there are strong elements at work against us in Japan and we do not know what position she will take up. Italy proved to be a very weak ally in the Greek campaign. Germany might, therefore, have to stand entirely alone."

After that, he spoke of the American attitude. He said that he had always wanted to have good relations with the U.S.A., but that in spite of extreme caution the U.S.A. had grown steadily more hostile to Germany. The Tripartite Pact had been concluded with a view to keeping the U.S.A. out of the war, as it was our wish and our belief that in this way those circles in the U.S.A. which were working for peace and for good relations with Germany could be strengthened. We were not successful in this, however, as the attitude of the U.S.A. was not favourable to Germany after the conclusion of the Tripartite Pact. The Fuehrer's main idea—and mine—namely, that if the U.S.A. did enter the war, she would have to reckon with a war on two fronts and therefore would prefer not to intervene, was not realised. Now the further question of Russia's attitude came up and in this connection the Fuehrer made the following statement: "We have a friendship pact with Russia. Russia has assumed the attitude which we have just been discussing and which causes me a certain amount of concern. We do not know, therefore, what to expect from that side."

More and more troop movements were reported; he had himself taken military countermeasures, the exact nature of which was—and still is—unknown to me. However, his great anxiety was that Russia on the one hand and the U.S.A. and Britain on the other might proceed against Germany. On the one hand, therefore, he had to reckon with an attack by Russia and on the other hand with a joint attack by the U.S.A. and England—that is to say, with large-scale landings in the West. These considerations caused the Fuehrer to take preventive measures by starting a preventive war against Russia of his own accord.

Q. What political reasons were there for the Tripartite Pact?

A. The Tripartite Pact was concluded, I believe, in September 1940. The situation was as I have just described it—that is to say, the Fuehrer was alarmed that the U.S.A. might sooner or later enter the war. For this reason I wanted to do all I could, through diplomatic channels, to strengthen Germany's position. I thought we had Italy as an ally, but Italy showed herself to be a weak ally.

As we could not win France over to our side, the only friend we could count on outside the Balkans was Japan.

In the summer of 1940 we tried to achieve closer ties with Japan. Japan was trying to do the same with us, and that led to the signing of the pact. The aim, or substance, of this pact was a political, military and economic alliance. There is no doubt, however, that it was intended as a defensive alliance; and we considered it as such from the start. By that I mean that it was intended in the first place to keep the U.S.A. out of the war; and I hoped that a combination of this kind might enable us to make peace with England after all.

The pact itself was not based on any plan for aggression or world domination, as has often been said. That is not true; our purpose was, as I have just said, to form a combination which would enable Germany to introduce a new order in Europe and which would also allow Japan to reach a solution acceptable to her in East Asia—especially in regard to the Chinese problem.

That was what I had in mind when I negotiated and signed the pact. The situation was not unfavourable. The pact might keep the U.S.A. neutral, and isolate England so that she would have to compromise on peace terms, a possibility of which we never lost sight during the whole course of the war, and for which we worked steadily.

23.

The Arsenal of Democracy

December 1940

Revision of the neutrality law in November 1939 allowed Great Britain to purchase armaments in the United States. Beyond this, however, Anglo-American cooperation languished. Although President Roosevelt had made numerous private assurances to the British, he continued to defer publicly to the isolationists and wavered for a year as to which course he should pursue.

To some extent, Roosevelt's caginess can be attributed to the ongoing 1940 presidential campaign. Running for an unprecedented third term, he faced strong opposition from Republican Wendell L. Willkie, who charged that FDR had made secret deals to lead the nation into war. When polls showed support for Willkie building, Roosevelt made corresponding adjustments in his own position, promising American mothers, "Your boys are not going to be sent to foreign wars."

The president won the election handily, but three weeks later a new complication arose: On November 23, returning from a brief trip to London, British ambassador Lord Lothian told reporters gathered at the airport, "Well, boys, Britain's broke. It's your money we want." The cost of the war had apparently exhausted Britain's dollar reserves, thus threatening her ability to purchase desperately needed arms on the cash-and-carry basis required by the neutrality law. In fact, according to hurried calculations made by Henry Morgenthau's Treasury Department, the British could barely afford to pay for orders already placed. This was a situation intolerable to Roosevelt, who—now politically secure—finally decided to act.

The president's "all methods short of war" strategy depended on Britain's ability to act as a bulwark against Hitler—which it could not do unless well armed. Therefore, Roosevelt set out to change the public's mind about the neutrality law. During a December 17 press conference, for example, he revealed that he would ask Congress to liberalize the terms under which Great Britain purchased U.S. arms. To explain his reasoning, he used a memorable parable: If your neighbor's house is on fire, and he asks you for your garden hose to put it out, you don't haggle with him over price. You simply loan him the hose until the fire is out, at which time he'll surely return it to you. "I think you all get it," FDR told the reporters gathered around his desk. Twelve days later, he made the same point directly to the American public in a fireside chat that became famous for Roosevelt's use of the phrase "arsenal of democracy."

ROOSEVELT CONFERS ON BRITISH AID, MAY ALSO HELP GREECE AND CHINA

President to Act; He Considers Concrete Steps to Speed and Increase Help to Britain

By TURNER CATLEDGE

WASHINGTON, Dec. 30—Encouraged by country-wide favorable reaction to his "fireside" plea that America make herself "the arsenal of democracy," President Roosevelt today turned attention to practical steps to speed up the flow of material aid to the countries at war with the totalitarian Axis.

He conferred for more than an hour at luncheon with Arthur B. Purvis, head of the British Purchasing Mission, and with him and Secretary Morgenthau went over aid proposals which he expects to lay before the new Congress soon after it convenes. High among these was understood to be the scheme which the President recently outlined of lending or leasing vital equipment and supplies to England as a means for obviating the depletion of that nation's gold and American resources which the British have said will soon result under the "cash-and-carry plan" of purchases being followed at present.

Meanwhile, there were indications that the President might follow up his pledge of "all-out" aid to foes of the Berlin-Rome-Tokyo Axis by extending this same lend-lease plan to such countries as Greece and China, as well as to Britain. Most important of these signs came from Secretary Morgenthau, who said that his own understanding of the plan was that it "might apply to anybody"—"anybody" meaning any nation at war with one or more of the Axis nations.

A Chinese military mission, headed by Major Gen. Fan Chu-mow, conferred with Administration officials during the day in an attempt to obtain release of a number of fighting planes to China. This government has delayed action on China's request for planes on the ground that Britain's immediate need was the greater and must be filled first from limited production. China would like to purchase from 100 to 400 pursuit planes and several heavy bombers, it was said.

Secretary Morgenthau declined to discuss the question of division of production when asked about it at his press conference this afternoon. But he indicated that the Administration was concerned in the matter of aiding China, just as it was in aiding Britain.

"There are simply not enough planes to go around at present," the Secretary said.

Officials throughout the government stressed the idea that the next step in aid to the British, and other non-Axis powers, is now a matter for Congress. This was the view expressed, too, by Mr. Purvis, the British purchasing agent, as he left the President's office.

"I await the opinion of Congress," Mr. Purvis said, as he characterized the President's lend-lease plan as a "new chapter" in the program of American aid for Britain.

Mr. Purvis said he and Mr. Roosevelt had a "general discussion" of the war supply problem but that he had presented no new list of British needs. He termed Mr. Roosevelt's fireside chat last night "one of the most thrilling things I have ever listened to."

Asked specifically if there had been any talk at the luncheon of possible convoys by American naval vessels for British merchant ships, Mr. Purvis replied:

"I have a great respect for your laws, which I understood prohibit that, and there was no discussion of it."

He also said they did not discuss the suggestion that the United States requisition for the British a large number of foreign ships laid up in American waters to escape the war.

The ship-seizure matter is, however, under serious consideration by this government, and a decision one way or the other may be expected in the next few days. The question may be put up to Congress by the President in his annual message, or he may act on his own responsibility. Studies of the legality of the move have been made, and discussion of the diplomatic course has taken place. All things considered, the Administration is known to lean heavily toward the idea of commandeering the ships and either turning them directly over to the British or transferring to the British a comparable amount of our own shipping and using the seized vessels for replacements in the American merchant fleet.

Mr. Morgenthau refused flatly to discuss the possibility of ship seizure at his press conference and disclaimed knowledge of reports that the Coast Guard already had inspected the ships to be taken over.

President Roosevelt was represented as being "tremendously pleased" at the response to his fireside chat. Stephen Early, White House secretary, said that within forty minutes after Mr. Roosevelt had concluded his address last night 600 messages were received and they ran 100

to 1 in favor of the general tenor of his remarks.

The President was said to have been particularly pleased by the favorable messages and comment received from Republicans. All in all, it was the greatest response that Mr. Roosevelt has ever had to any speech, Mr. Early said.

Indications mounted today, as evidenced by both public and private reaction to the President's virtual defiance of the Axis, that he will have his way on war and preparedness measures with Congress, at least in the earlier part of the new session. There was, however, a definite showing of opposition as reflected in a nationally broadcast speech by Senator Wheeler tonight, and as seen in a meeting of several "non-interventionist" Senators today with Verne Marshall, Cedar Rapids (Iowa) editor and chairman of the "No Foreign War Committee."

After a luncheon meeting with a group, Mr. Marshall repeated the suggestion that the United States offer itself as a mediator to bring peace out of the present war. This was the suggestion that Mr. Roosevelt ruled out so definitely in his talk last night.

Senator Holt charged on the Senate floor this afternoon that the Roosevelt Administration did not want peace, but was trying to provoke the Axis powers to declare war upon us.

"Let's be truthful," Mr. Holt said. "The strategy today is to provoke the Axis powers to declare war upon us. It is the first time in American history that we have sacrificed honor to get into a war."

Mr. Holt declared he would continue "to expose war-mongers," whether he is a Senator or not. His term expires at noon on Friday.

"We must be the great arsenal of democracy."

Franklin Roosevelt's fireside chat on the danger to the nation

Franklin Roosevelt delivered his December 29, 1940, fireside chat from the White House's diplomatic reception room. Among the guests were Roosevelt's mother; members of his cabinet (led by Secretary of State Cordell Hull); a collection of his personal staff; and, incongruously, film stars Clark Gable and Carole Lombard.

This is not a fireside chat on war. It is a talk on national security; because the nub of the whole purpose of your President is to keep you now, and your children later, and your grandchildren much later, out of a last-ditch war for the preservation of American independence and all of the things that American independence means to you and to me and to ours.

Tonight, in the presence of a world crisis, my mind goes back eight years ago to a night in the midst of a domestic crisis. It was a time when the wheels of American industry were grinding to a full stop, when the whole banking system of our country had ceased to function.

I well remember that while I sat in my study in the White House, preparing to talk with the people of the United States, I had before my eyes the picture of all those Americans with whom I was talking. I saw the workmen in the mills, the mines, the factories; the girl behind the counter; the small shopkeeper; the farmer doing his spring plowing; the widows and the old men wondering about their life's savings.

I tried to convey to the great mass of American people what the banking crisis meant to them in their daily lives.

Tonight, I want to do the same thing, with the same people, in this new crisis which faces America.

We met the issue of 1933 with courage and realism.

We face this new crisis—this new threat to the security of our Nation—with the same courage and realism.

Never before since Jamestown and Plymouth Rock has our American civilization been in such danger as now.

For, on September 27, 1940, by an agreement signed in Berlin, three powerful nations, two in Europe and one in Asia, joined themselves together in the threat that if the United States interfered with or blocked the expansion program of these three nations—a program aimed at world control—they would unite in ultimate action against the United States.

The Nazi masters of Germany have made it clear that they intend not only to dominate all life and thought in their own country, but also to enslave the whole of Europe, and then to use the resources of Europe to dominate the rest of the world.

Three weeks ago their leader stated, "There are two worlds that stand opposed to each other." Then in defiant reply to his opponents, he said this: "Others are correct when they say: 'With this world we cannot ever reconcile ourselves.'...I can beat any other power in the world." So said the leader of the Nazis.

A line of hastily constructed Liberty cargo ships at the outfitting docks of the California Shipbuilding Corporation in Los Angeles.

In other words, the Axis not merely admits but proclaims that there can be no ultimate peace between their philosophy of government and our philosophy of government.

In view of the nature of this undeniable threat, it can be asserted, properly and categorically, that the United States has no right or reason to encourage talk of peace until the day shall come when there is a clear intention on the part of the aggressor nations to abandon all thought of dominating or conquering the world.

At this moment, the forces of the states that are leagued against all peoples who live in freedom are being held away from our shores. The Germans and Italians are being blocked on the other side of the Atlantic by the British, and by the Greeks, and by thousands of soldiers and sailors who were able to escape from subjugated countries. The Japanese are being engaged in Asia by the Chinese in another great defense.

In the Pacific is our fleet.

Some of our people like to believe that wars in Europe and in Asia are of no concern to us. But it is a matter of most vital concern to us that European and Asiatic war-makers should not gain control of the oceans which lead to this hemisphere.

One hundred and seventeen years ago the Monroe Doctrine was conceived by our Government as a measure of defense in the face of a threat against this hemisphere by an alliance in continental Europe. Thereafter, we stood on guard in the Atlantic, with the British as neighbors. There was no treaty. There was no "unwritten agreement."

Yet, there was the feeling, proven correct by history, that we as neighbors could settle any disputes in peaceful fashion. The fact is that during the whole of this time the Western Hemisphere has remained free from aggression from Europe or from Asia.

Does anyone seriously believe that we need to fear attack while a free Britain remains our most powerful naval neighbor in the Atlantic? Does anyone seriously believe, on the other hand, that we could rest easy if the Axis powers were our neighbor there?

If Great Britain goes down, the Axis powers will control the continents of Europe, Asia, Africa, Australia, and the high seas—and they will be in a position to bring enormous military and naval resources against this hemisphere. It is no exaggeration to say that all of us in the Americas would be living at the point of a gun—a gun loaded with explosive bullets, economic as well as military.

We should enter upon a new and terrible era in which the whole world, our hemisphere included, would be run by threats of brute force. To survive in such a world, we would have to convert ourselves permanently into a militaristic power on the basis of war economy.

Some of us like to believe that even if Great Britain falls, we are still safe, because of the broad expanse of the Atlantic and of the Pacific.

But the width of these oceans is not what it was in the days of clipper ships. At one point between Africa and Brazil the distance is less than from Washington to Denver—five hours for the latest type of bomber. And at the north end of the Pacific Ocean, America and Asia almost touch each other.

Even today we have planes which could fly from the British Isles to New England and back without refueling. And the range of the modern bomber is ever being increased.

During the past week many people in all parts of the Nation have told me what they wanted me to say tonight. Almost all of them expressed a courageous desire to hear the plain truth about the gravity of the situation. One telegram, however, expressed the attitude of the small minority who want to see no evil and hear no evil, even though they know in their hearts that evil exists. That telegram begged me not to tell again of the ease with which our American cities could be bombed by any hostile power which had gained bases in this Western Hemisphere. The gist of that telegram was: "Please, Mr. President, don't frighten us by telling us the facts."

Frankly and definitely there is danger ahead—danger against which we must prepare. But we well know that we cannot escape danger, or the fear of it, by crawling into bed and pulling the covers over our heads.

Some nations of Europe were bound by solemn non-intervention pacts with Germany. Other nations were assured by Germany that they need never fear invasion. Non-intervention pact or not, the fact remains that they were attacked, overrun, and thrown into the modern form of slavery at an hour's notice or even without any notice at all. As an exiled leader of one of these nations said to me the other day: "The notice was a minus quantity. It was given to my government two hours after German troops had poured into my country in a hundred places."

The fate of these nations tells us what it means to live at the point of a Nazi gun.

The Nazis have justified such actions by various pious frauds. One of these frauds is the claim that they are occupying a nation for the purpose of "restoring order." Another is that they are occupying or controlling a nation on the excuse that they are "protecting it" against the aggression of somebody else.

For example, Germany has said that she was occupying Belgium to save the Belgians from the British. Would she hesitate to say to any South American country, "We are occupying you to protect you from aggression by the United States"?

Belgium today is being used as an invasion base against Britain, now fighting for its life. Any South American country, in Nazi hands, would always constitute a jumping-off place for German attack on any one of the other republics of this hemisphere.

Analyze for yourselves the future of two other places even nearer to Germany if the Nazis won. Could Ireland hold out? Would Irish freedom be permitted as an amazing exception in an unfree world? Or the islands of the Azores which still fly the flag of Portugal after five centuries? We think of Hawaii as an outpost of defense in the Pacific. Yet, the Azores are closer to our shores in the Atlantic than Hawaii is on the other side.

There are those who say that the Axis powers would never have any desire to attack the Western Hemisphere. This is the same dangerous form of wishful thinking which has destroyed the powers of resistance of so many conquered peoples. The plain facts are that the Nazis have proclaimed, time and again, that all other races are their inferiors and therefore subject to their orders. And most important of all, the vast resources and wealth of this hemisphere constitute the most tempting loot in all the world.

Let us no longer blind ourselves to the undeniable fact that the evil forces which have crushed and undermined and corrupted so many others are already within our own gates. Your Government knows much about them and every day is ferreting them out.

Their secret emissaries are active in our own and neighboring countries. They seek to stir up suspicion and dissension to cause internal strife. They try to turn capital against labor and vice versa. They try to reawaken long slumbering racial and religious enmities which should have no place in this country. They are active in every group that promotes intolerance. They exploit for their own ends our natural abhorrence of war. These trouble-breeders have but one purpose. It is to divide our people into hostile groups and to destroy our unity and shatter our will to defend ourselves.

There are also American citizens, many of them in high places, who, unwittingly in most cases, are aiding and abetting the work of these agents. I do not charge these American citizens with being foreign agents. But I do charge them with doing exactly the kind of work that the dictators want done in the United States.

These people not only believe that we can save our own skins by shutting our eyes to the fate of other nations. Some of them go much further than that. They say that we can and should become the friends and even the partners of the Axis powers. Some of them even suggest that we should imitate the methods of the dictatorships. Americans never can and never will do that.

The experience of the past two years has proven beyond doubt that no nation can appease the Nazis. No man can tame a tiger into a kitten by stroking it. There can be no appeasement with ruthlessness. There can be no reasoning with an incendiary bomb. We know now that a nation can have peace with the Nazis only at the price of total surrender.

Even the people of Italy have been forced to become accomplices of the Nazis; but at this moment they do not know how soon they will be embraced to death by their allies.

The American appeasers ignore the warning to be found in the fate of Austria, Czechoslovakia, Poland, Norway, Belgium, the Netherlands, Denmark, and France. They tell you that the Axis powers are going to win anyway; that all this bloodshed in the world could be saved; and that the United States might just as well throw its influence into the scale of a dictated peace, and get the best out of it that we can.

They call it a "negotiated peace." Nonsense! Is it a negotiated peace if a gang of outlaws surrounds your community and on threat of extermination makes you pay tribute to save your own skins?

Such a dictated peace would be no peace at all. It would be only another armistice, leading to the most gigantic armament race and the most devastating trade wars in history. And in these contests the Americas would offer the only real resistance to the Axis powers.

With all their vaunted efficiency and parade of pious purpose in this war, there are still in their background the concentration camp and the servants of God in chains.

The history of recent years proves that shootings and chains and concentration camps are not simply the transient tools but the very altars of modern dictatorships. They may talk of a "new order" in the world, but what they have in mind is but a revival of the oldest and the worst tyranny. In that there is no liberty, no religion, no hope.

The proposed "new order" is the very opposite of a United States of Europe or a United States of Asia. It is not a government based upon the consent of the governed. It is not a union of ordinary, self-respecting men and women to protect themselves and their freedom and their dignity from oppression. It is an unholy alliance of power and pelf to dominate and enslave the human race.

The British people are conducting an active war against this unholy alliance. Our own future security is greatly dependent on the outcome of that fight. Our ability to "keep out of war" is going to be affected by that outcome.

Thinking in terms of today and tomorrow, I make the direct statement to the American people that there is far less chance of the United States getting into war if we do all we can now to support the nations defending themselves against attack by the Axis than if we acquiesce in their defeat, submit tamely to an Axis victory, and wait our turn to be the object of attack in another war later on.

If we are to be completely honest with ourselves, we must admit there is risk in *any* course we may take. But I deeply believe that the great majority of our people agree that the course that I advocate involves the least risk now and the greatest hope for world peace in the future.

The people of Europe who are defending themselves do not ask us to do their fighting. They ask us for the implements of war, the planes, the tanks, the guns, the freighters, which will enable them to fight for their liberty and our security. Emphatically we must get these weapons to them in sufficient volume and quickly enough, so that we and our children will be saved the agony and suffering of war which others have had to endure.

Let not defeatists tell us that it is too late. It will never be earlier. Tomorrow will be later than today.

Certain facts are self-evident.

In a military sense Great Britain and the British Empire are today the spearhead of resistance to world conquest. They are putting up a fight which will live forever in the story of human gallantry.

There is no demand for sending an American Expeditionary Force outside our own borders. There is no intention by any member of your Government to send such a force. You can, therefore, nail any talk about sending armies to Europe as deliberate untruth.

Our national policy is not directed toward war. Its sole purpose is to keep war away from our country and our people.

Democracy's fight against world conquest is being greatly aided, and must be more greatly aided, by the rearmament of the United States and by sending every ounce and every ton of munitions and supplies that we can possibly spare to help the defenders who are in the front lines. It is no more unneutral for us to do that than it is for Sweden, Russia, and other nations near Germany to send steel and ore and oil and other war materials into Germany every day.

We are planning our own defense with the utmost urgency; and in its vast scale we must integrate the war needs of Britain and the other free nations resisting aggression.

This is not a matter of sentiment or of controversial personal opinion. It is a matter of realistic military policy, based on the advice of our military experts who are in close touch with existing warfare.

Secretary of War Henry L. Stimson is blindfolded prior to selecting the first capsule in the new draft lottery, October 29, 1940.

These military and naval experts and the members of the Congress and the administration have a single-minded purpose—the defense of the United States.

This Nation is making a great effort to produce everything that is necessary in this emergency and with all possible speed. This great effort requires great sacrifice.

I would ask no one to defend a democracy which in turn would not defend everyone in the Nation against want and privation. The strength of this Nation shall not be diluted by the failure of the Government to protect the economic well-being of all citizens.

If our capacity to produce is limited by machines, it must ever be remembered that these machines are operated by the skill and the stamina of the workers. As the Government is determined to protect the rights of workers, so the Nation has a right to expect that the men who man the machines will discharge their full responsibilities to the urgent needs of defense.

The worker possesses the same human dignity and is entitled to the same security of position as the engineer or manager or owner. For the workers provide the human power that turns out the destroyers, the airplanes, and the tanks.

The Nation expects our defense industries to continue operation without interruption by strikes or lock-outs. It expects and insists that management and workers will reconcile their differences by voluntary or legal means, to continue to produce the supplies that are so sorely needed.

And on the economic side of our great defense program, we are, as you know, bending every effort to maintain stability of prices and with that the stability of the cost of living.

Nine days ago I announced the setting up of a more effective organization to direct our gigantic efforts to increase the production of munitions. The appropriation of vast sums of money and a well-coordinated executive direction of our defense efforts are not in themselves enough. Guns, planes, and ships have to be built in the factories and arsenals of America. They have to be produced by workers and managers and engineers with the aid of machines, which in turn have to be built by hundreds of thousands of workers throughout the land.

In this great work there has been splendid cooperation between the Government and industry and labor.

American industrial genius, unmatched throughout the world in the solution of production problems, has been called upon to bring its resources and talents into action. Manufacturers of watches, of farm implements, linotypes, cash registers, automobiles, sewing machines, lawn mowers, and locomotives are now making fuses, bomb-packing crates, telescope mounts, shells, pistols, and tanks.

But all our present efforts are not enough. We must have more ships, more guns, more planes—more of everything. This can only be accomplished if we discard the notion of "business as usual." This job cannot be done merely by superimposing on the existing productive facilities the added requirements for defense.

Our defense efforts must not be blocked by those who fear the future consequences of surplus plant capacity. The possible consequences of failure of our defense efforts now are much more to be feared.

After the present needs of our defense are past, a proper handling of the country's peacetime needs will require all of the new productive capacity—if not more.

No pessimistic policy about the future of America shall delay the immediate expansion of those industries essential to defense.

I want to make it clear that it is the purpose of the Nation to build now with all possible speed every machine and arsenal and factory that we need to manufacture our defense material. We have the men, the skill, the wealth, and above all, the will.

I am confident that if and when production of consumer or luxury goods in certain industries requires the use of machines and raw materials essential for defense purposes, then such production must yield to our primary and compelling purpose.

I appeal to the owners of plants, to the managers, to the workers, to our own Government employees, to put every ounce of effort into producing these munitions swiftly and without stint. And with this appeal I give you the pledge that all of us who are officers of your Government will devote ourselves to the same whole-hearted extent to the great task which lies ahead.

As planes and ships and guns and shells are produced, your Government, with its defense experts, can then determine how best to use them to defend this hemisphere. The decision as to how much shall be sent abroad and how much shall remain at home must be made on the basis of our over-all military necessities.

We must be the great arsenal of democracy. For us this is an emergency as serious as war itself. We must apply ourselves to our task with the same resolution, the same sense of urgency, the same spirit of patriotism and sacrifice, as we would show were we at war.

We have furnished the British great material support and we will furnish far more in the future.

There will be no "bottlenecks" in our determination to aid Great Britain. No dictator, no combination of dictators, will weaken that determination by threats of how they will construe that determination.

The British have recieved invaluable military support from the heroic Greek Army and from the forces of all the governments in exile. Their strength is growing. It is a strength of men and women who value their freedom more highly than they value their lives.

I believe that the Axis powers are not going to win this war. I base that belief on the latest and best information.

We have no excuse for defeatism. We have every good reason for hope—hope for peace, hope for the defense of our civilization and for the building of a better civilization in the future.

I have the profound conviction that the American people are now determined to put forth a mightier effort than they have ever yet made to increase our production of all the implements of defense, to meet the threat to democratic faith.

As President of the United states I call for that national effort. I call for it in the name of this Nation which we love and honor and which we are privileged and proud to serve. I call upon our people with absolute confidence that our common cause will greatly succeed.

Two members of the British Auxiliary Territorial Service stockpile armfuls of Winchester rifles recently arrived from the United States under the Lend-Lease program.

24.

Lend-Lease

March 1941

Until President Roosevelt formally proposed the Allied aid program known as Lend-Lease, he had been conducting his pro-British foreign policy primarily through executive action. On September 2, for instance, he had signed an executive order presenting fifty surplus U.S. destroyers to the British in exchange for the use of military bases in Newfoundland and the Caribbean. With Lend-Lease, however,

the president made his intentions much more plain. "We don't want to fool the public," he told his treasury secretary, Henry Morgenthau; "we want to do this thing right out and out."

The president unveiled the Lend-Lease bill on January 6, 1941, in his annual message to Congress, which also contained the first enunciation of the "four essential human freedoms" that Roosevelt said his policies were designed to secure. (These Four Freedoms, which became the subject of pervasive propaganda, were the freedom of speech, the freedom of religion, the freedom from want, and the freedom from fear.) Four days later, congressional committees began debating whether or not to appropriate the seven billion dollars that Roosevelt wanted. Meanwhile, the president sent his close aide Harry Hopkins to Churchill to advise the prime minister on the politics of passing Lend-Lease. The result was a disingenuous speech, treacly even by Churchillian standards, that asked Americans merely for arms, not men, and ended, "Give us the tools, and we will finish the job."

The isolationists were not so easily fooled. They understood perfectly well that financing the British war effort would make the United States a co-belligerent, and, once this happened, a shooting war would likely follow (a judgment in which they were proved essentially correct). Nevertheless, outside the staunchly Republican Midwest, most Americans found themselves persuaded of the worthiness of the British cause, and the bill passed in March by wide margins.

Another reason for the success of the Lend-Lease policy was the distinction that Roosevelt continued to make between the United States as an arsenal and America as a combatant. When asked at a press conference in late January whether he anticipated any need for American warships to "convoy" (that is, escort) merchantmen across the North Atlantic, the president replied that such escorts might lead to shooting "and shooting comes awfully close to war, doesn't it? That is about the last thing we have in our minds."

BILL GIVES PRESIDENT UNLIMITED POWER TO LEND WAR EQUIPMENT AND RESOURCES

Goes to Congress; Measure Would Allow British Naval Repair in Our Ports

By TURNER CATLEDGE

WASHINGTON, Jan. 10—A bill to confer upon President Roosevelt practically unlimited personal power to place American war equipment, new and old, at the disposal of foreign nations in the interest of the defense of the United States was introduced in Congress today amid signs of a brewing legislative storm.

Presented as an Administration proposal by the majority leader in each house, and intended solely to implement the policy of "all out" aid to the non-Axis powers now under attack, the bill carries one of the greatest grants of authority ever extended by Congress to the President, either in peace or war.

As interpreted by authorities, including some who helped frame the measure, the President would be empowered, under its terms, to transfer the whole or any part of the Navy or Army equipment to other countries and place new defense production at their disposal—all upon such terms and under such conditions as he himself might determine. The sole limitation would be that the transfer of materials should be deemed by the President to be in the interest of American defense.

Administration spokesmen scouted as "ridiculous" any suggestion that the President would use the bill's powers to these possible limits. The whole purpose, they said, was to do the job of aid-to-the-Allies which the country seems to be demanding and "do it right."

The President himself urged the quickest possible action on the bill, saying at his press conference that speed was the most vital element in translating the Allied-aid policy into action. He had no personal desire to have the vast powers conferred by the measure, he said, but they were needed to avoid delays.

The Capitol appeared somewhat surprised by the nature and extent of the bill, although its terms had been discounted by advance publication. Administration leaders laid plans immediately for pushing it through Congress as rapidly as possible, with hearings to start next week before the Senate and House committees dealing with foreign affairs. They want to rush it through ahead of any possible reactions which might make more bitter the fight they expect.

The extent of opposition can hardly be gauged at this time. Enough was seen today to indicate that the measure will have a stormy legislative course whatever the result. Signs of disapproval came not alone from the "noninterventionist" group which would have fought any Allied-aid proposal, but from some others who, although they were unwilling to speak out because of the peculiar nature of the subject and the times, were nonplussed at the magnitude of executive authority proposed in the bill.

Resistance to additional grants of executive powers has been mounting steadily over the last few years, but how much it has been softened under the urgency of the foreign situation with repeated underscorings by the President and other advocates of aid to the Allies is something yet to be seen.

The bill was introduced by Senator Barkley in the Senate and Representative McCormack of

A community kitchen serves some of the first Lend-Lease food aid to arrive in Britain, September 1941.

Massachusetts in the House. No drama attended its presentation in either body.

Shortly before introducing it the two leaders issued a joint statement explaining its terms. The major purpose was simply to translate into legislative form the policy of making this country "the arsenal of democracy," the leaders said, and to carry out President Roosevelt's pledge to send to beleaguered democracies "in ever-increasing numbers, ships, planes, tanks, guns." They explained the bill in detail, which, briefly, provides the following:

The President is empowered, "notwithstanding the provisions of any other law," when he deems it in the interest of national defense, to authorize the Secretary of War, the Secretary of the Navy, or the head of any other department or agency of the government, to manufacture in government arsenals, factories, shipyards, etc., or otherwise procure any defense article for the government of any country whose defense the President deems vital to the United States.

He is authorized to order these officials to sell, transfer, exchange, lease, lend "or otherwise dispose of" such defense article to any such government.

This means, Messrs. Barkley and McCormack explained, that the President can dispose of new material as well as equipment now in the hands of our Army and Navy, according to our own needs "as he (the President) sees them." A certificate from our Chief of Staff or the Chief of Naval Operations to the effect that transfers of materials would not impair American defense, would no longer be needed, these leaders said.

The President would be authorized to instruct his defense subordinates to test, inspect, prove, repair, outfit, recondition or otherwise place in good working order any defense article for any such government. This could mean, for example, that the British battle cruiser Renown could be repaired in the Brooklyn Navy Yard if the President considered it to be in the interest of our national defense to do so. The provision is broad enough, Messrs. Barkley and McCormack said, to permit the use of any of our military, naval, or air bases to outfit and repair the weapons of countries whose defense is deemed by the President to be vital to the defense of the United States.

The President would be authorized, moreover, to communicate to foreign governments defense information, pertaining to any defense article furnished by the United States. This means that the President, in his discretion, could make available to foreign governments designs, blueprints, and other information for using particular equipment. The transfer and use of the secret American bomb-sight was said to have figured in the discussions preceding the writing of this section.

The bill leaves the matter of remuneration and financing strictly up to the President. Terms and conditions would be those the President deemed satisfactory and the benefits to the United States may be payment or repayment in kind or property or any other direct or "indirect" benefit the President elects.

Senator George of Georgia, chairman of the Foreign Relations Committee, said the bill would come before that body next Wednesday when procedure as to its consideration would be decided. He disclosed that he had asked Senator Barkley to introduce the measure because it raised the question of jurisdiction, as three committees conceivably could have handled it. It was sent to Mr. George's group, however.

An inter-committee dispute sprang up in the House over the bill after it had been referred to the Foreign Affairs Committee, headed by Representative Bloom of New York. Representative May of Kentucky, chairman of the Military Affairs Committee, insisted it should go there, and intimated he would seek to take it over.

"Are you for the bill?" Mr. May was asked.

"Yes, sir, and yes, ma'am," he replied.

The first adverse reaction came from the Republican side immediately upon introduction of the bill. The complaint was not lodged against the merits of the bill necessarily, but on the ground that the Administration apparently was making it a party matter. Representative Martin of Massachusetts, minority leader, demanded to know if the measure was to be considered from a partisan standpoint. Majority Leader McCormack replied that Secretaries Stimson and Knox both participated in the drafting of the bill and that they were Republicans.

The general impression in Washington tonight was that the bill would pass both Houses in substantially the form introduced, with perhaps a few and not very consequential limitations. This conclusion was based primarily upon an analysis of the practical political situation in Congress in which, to overturn the Administration, a coalition ordinarily has to develop out of a relatively solid Republican corps and dissident Democrats. The Republicans hitherto have been divided several ways on foreign issues and may be expected to be so again. Furthermore, in past anti–New Deal coalitions, much of the Democratic strength has been furnished from a conservative Southern bloc which, on the war issue, is intensely pro-Administration.

The question likely will be fought out as much, if not more, on the issue of confidence in President Roosevelt as upon the merits or demerits of aid to the Allies.

The Democratic stalwarts who rushed to the defense of the bill today indicated that the Administration would not be lacking in skillful leadership. Senators Byrnes and Harrison, two of the most successful legislators in the Senate, each expressed wholehearted approval of the proposal and showed they would join Senator Barkley in helping to drive it through the Senate, where it is expected to encounter the most dramatic opposition on account of the liberality of the rules governing debate.

"Our boys will be returned in caskets."

Attack on Lend-Lease in the U.S. Senate

Democratic senator Burton K. Wheeler of Montana was an ardent supporter of Roosevelt's New Deal until the two men split over foreign policy. Wheeler made the remarks reprinted here during a January 12, 1941, Senate debate on Lend-Lease. Roosevelt later called Wheeler's attack "the rottenest thing that has been said in public life in my generation."

The lend-lease policy translated into legislative form, stunned a Congress and a nation wholly sympathetic to the cause of Great Britain. The Kaiser's blank check to Austria-Hungary in the First World War was a piker compared to the Roosevelt blank check of World War II. It warranted my worst fears for the future of America, and it definitely stamps the President as war-minded.

The lend-lease-give program is the New Deal's triple-A foreign policy; it will plow under every fourth American boy. Never before have the American people been asked or compelled to give so bounteously and so completely of their tax dollars to any foreign nation. Never before has the Congress of the United States been asked by any President to violate international law. Never before has this nation resorted to duplicity in the conduct of its foreign affairs. Never before has the United States given to one man the power to strip this nation of its defenses. Never before has a Congress coldly and flatly been asked to abdicate.

If the American people want a dictatorship—if they want a totalitarian form of government and if they want war—this bill should be steam-rollered through Congress, as is the wont of President Roosevelt.

Approval of this legislation means war, open and complete warfare. I, therefore, ask the American people before they supinely accept it—Was the last World War worthwhile?

If it were, then we should lend and lease war materials. If it were, then we should lend and lease American boys. President Roosevelt has said we would be repaid by England. We will be. We will be repaid, just as England repaid her war debts of the First World War—repaid those dollars wrung from the sweat of labor and the toil of farmers with cries of "Uncle Shylock." Our boys will be returned— returned in caskets, maybe; returned with bodies maimed; returned with minds warped and twisted by sights of horrors and the scream and shriek of high-powered shells.

25.

Fortress America

September 1940–December 1941

The America First Committee (AFC), established in September 1940 following the destroyers-for-bases deal, quickly became the leading voice for isolationism. The group had four guiding principles: First and foremost, AFC members believed that the United States needed to rearm as quickly and extensively as possible. Against the war but far from pacifists, they demanded an impregnable defense for the

United States—a strategy they called Fortress America. Second, they were certain that no foreign power, or group of powers, could ever successfully invade a prepared United States. Third, they believed that American democracy could not withstand U.S. entry into the European war and that an American dictatorship might result. Fourth, they contended that the president's "all methods short of war" policy weakened American defense by diverting essential armaments overseas and making U.S. involvement in the European war more likely.

Paying close attention, however, one could also detect a fifth element in AFC ideology: anti-Semitism. Many of the committee's leading members displayed severe prejudice against Jews, and in some cities, notably Boston, the committee's core membership was rabidly anti-Semitic. "From its inception," Roosevelt biographer Kenneth S. Davis has written, "America First was attractive to people who sympathized with Hitler's 'solution' to the 'Jewish prob-

lem'—people who believed or professed to believe that Jews, dominating the financial community, had inveigled this country into World War I for profit-making reasons and were now engaged in the same nefarious enterprise during World War II." Such AFC members advocated a "negotiated peace," Davis continues, precisely because they knew such a settlement would have to be concluded on Hitler's terms.

Of course, there were also many people who joined America First—an organization of some eight hundred thousand members—simply because they believed sincerely that Britain's cause was lost and that American entry into World War II would "preserve democracy" about as effectively as U.S. participation in World War I had. They failed to block Lend-Lease aid and, later, the use of navy escorts in the North Atlantic, but the public pressure they brought undeniably reduced the amount of assistance that Roosevelt would have otherwise sent to Great Britain.

This 1940 cartoon ridicules Charles Lindbergh for advocating isolationism. Lindbergh had moved his family to England in 1935 following the kidnapping and murder of his infant son. While living abroad, he attended the 1936 Summer Olympics in Berlin and enjoyed Luftwaffe chief Göring's hospitality.

BRITISH SEEK ANOTHER A.E.F., LINDBERGH TELLS 10,000 HERE

London Misinformed Allies on Strength, He Says at America First Rally; 35,000 Jam Streets at Manhattan Center

Colonel Charles A. Lindbergh declared at a mass meeting of the America First Committee here last night that "the British Government have one last desperate plan remaining; they hope that they may be able to persuade us to send another American Expeditionary Force to Europe, and to share with England militarily, as well as financially, the fiasco of this war."

The address marked Colonel Lindbergh's first appearance here as a leader of organized opinion through the America First Committee, which he joined in Chicago last Thursday. Heretofore, he has expressed himself as an individual.

"A crisis is here," he explained to an audience of some 10,000 persons in the auditorium and overflow hall as well as around loudspeakers in the street outside Manhattan Center, 311 West Thirty-fourth Street.

He asked them and his radio listeners to join with him in the America First Committee, because "we have been led toward war by a minority of our people; this minority has power; it has influence; it has a loud voice, but it does not represent the American people."

The applause that constantly punctuated Colonel Lindbergh's address served to diagram the likes and dislikes of the audience. He was interrupted by wild cheers when he said, "It is obvious that England is losing the war," and again when he said, "England has misinformed us."

He got a double-barreled cheer when he said, "We in this country have a right to think of the welfare of America first, just as the people in England thought first of their own country when they encouraged the smaller nations of Europe to fight against hopeless odds."

There were hisses when he asserted, "Our air force is deplorably lacking in modern fighting planes, because most of them have been sent to Europe." The audience cheered and stamped when he declared, "The policy of the interventionists has led to the defeat of every country that followed their advice since this war began."

Plainly there was much more interest in Colonel Lindbergh's criticism of intervention in Europe and of propaganda in that direction than in his proposed hemisphere defense or his analysis of the geographic safety of the United States.

A detail of 100 policemen, including fifteen mounted men, kept order inside and outside the hall. Police officials estimated that during the evening the detail handled 35,000 persons. Detectives were scattered throughout the auditorium to keep heckling in check. The doors were closed at 7:30 o'clock, when the building was filled to capacity.

Plans for picketing the meeting as "a Nazi transmission belt," which had been announced in advance by the Friends of Democracy, Inc., in connection with the Youth Committee of the Federal Union and the Student Defenders of Democracy, in conjunction with members of various A.F. of L. and C.I.O. unions, caused the police to forbid picketing directly in front of Manhattan Center and to double the previously ordered police details.

Deputy Chief Inspector John J. DeMartino and Inspector John J. Sullivan directed

A crowd estimated by police at ten to fifteen thousand jams the street outside the Manhattan Center as Charles Lindbergh speaks.

mounted police to clear the sidewalk in front of the building, and ruled that if any anti-Nazi pickets appeared they would have to remain across the way on the south side of Thirty-fourth Street.

That section of the street was jammed with the larger part of a crowd of several thousand persons who stood outside. Many of these persons had tickets for the meeting, but had been unable to get in. German accents were numerous among the holders of both the white tickets, which had been sent out as invitations, and the blue tickets, which had been sold at the box office for $1 each.

Holders of white tickets refused to tell where they had got them or to what organizations they belonged when questioned about rumors that tickets had been sent to Nazi organizations.

The crowd started to gather before 6 o'clock, and caused such congestion that all traffic except

mail trucks was stopped on Thirty-fourth Street between Eighth and Ninth Avenues. A line extended around the corner on Ninth Avenue.

A man with a German accent complained to the police that when he yelled "Down with the British," another man in a sailor's hat had punched him in the face, breaking his glasses. The attacker disappeared, and the police advised the complainant to do likewise when he said he intended to go back into the crowd and yell "Down with the British" again.

Hawkers peddled "Social Justice," the Coughlinite magazine, in the crowd. Competing with them were representatives of the Nonsectarian Anti-Nazi League to Champion Human Rights, who distributed copies of a circular entitled "What One Hitler Medal Can Do."

At 8:10 o'clock, when the hall was packed to its limits and huge crowds stood outside in the streets listening to the speeches through amplifiers, a disturbance took place at Eighth Avenue and Thirty-fourth Street.

Nearly 100 persons, identified as members of the Friends of Democracy, the Youth Committee of the Federal Union and the Student Defenders of Democracy, marched down Eighth Avenue and attempted to cross Thirty-fourth Street from north to south. The vanguard consisted of ten pickets with a girl leader, all carrying placards that read, "Maintain the British Blockade," "Aid to France Will Help Hitler Now," and the like.

Several hundred persons from the crowd first booed and then attacked the parade, knocking down the pickets, tearing up their placards, and breaking the wooden staffs to which the placards had been fixed. In a few minutes the parade had been dispersed and its members had disappeared.

Herman Levine of 216 Bay Thirty-fourth Street, Brooklyn, a metal worker, told reporters he had seen a short, stocky man hit the girl picket leader in the face and knock her down. M. Barkan of 243 East Fifty-ninth Street, an agent for the Metropolitan Life Insurance Company, said he had seen several pickets beaten and kicked. They had yelled for help, he added, but the police had failed to respond.

The police explained that only two policemen had been in the vicinity of the trouble. One turned on the siren of a radio car, but the crowd was packed together so tightly that by the time the police arrived in force the disturbance was over. Friends took the beaten pickets away in taxicabs. No arrests were made and no one was hurt badly enough to require the police to summon medical aid.

During the disturbance pro-Nazi members of the crowd shouted, "Get out of here or we'll kill you" at the pickets, and anti-Nazi elements yelled accusations that the crowd included "Joe McWilliams's gang," referring to Joseph McWilliams, self-proclaimed anti-Semitic fuehrer of the Christian Mobilizers, who was reported to have postponed his regular weekly meeting and instructed his followers to attend the Lindbergh rally.

George Wythe, chairman of the Youth Committee of the Federal Union, complained that the police had failed to afford protection to the pickets, although "Inspector Brown" of the police yesterday afternoon gave permission for six pickets to march and for others to distribute leaflets. He asserted that Inspector DeMartino at the scene refused to allow any picketing. When it was decided to picket anyway, he went on, the picket line operated only for a minute and one-half before "a mob" broke it up. Only then did the police take action to hold back the mob and allow the pickets to get away, he went on.

At 8:30 o'clock the police estimated that the street crowd had increased to 15,000 or 20,000 in Thirty-fourth Street alone, which was then solidly blocked except for a square in front of the hall that the police kept open. A smaller crowd milled around in West Thirty-fifth Street, where holders of $25 box tickets, reserved seats, platform and press tickets were admitted through the stage door.

Rain that started about 9:45 o'clock drove a large part of the crowd away, but several thousand remained in the street, seeking shelter under the marquee of the hall, in doorways and elsewhere.

The meeting started turbulently at 8:20 o'clock, with a three-minute ovation when Colonel Lindbergh appeared on the platform. Small American flags waved in almost every hand. Excited voices cried, "We want Lindy."

Eventually the meeting started with the singing of "The Star-Spangled Banner" and an invocation by the Rev. Edward L. Hunt, founder of the American Good-Will Union, who asked God to "help the President resist the efforts to make him betray the promises he made to keep us out of war."

John T. Flynn, chairman of the New York Chapter of the America First Committee, presided. He was introduced by Mrs. John P. Marquand, wife of the novelist.

Mr. Flynn was applauded when he declared: "We have distinguished speakers on this platform and we need no other speakers. We don't want any questions, and we want no heckling. To those on our side and those on the other side—and I hope there are many on the other side—I hope we will have no boos. If you don't like anything you hear, hold a meeting some place else."

"Further," he continued, "literature is to be found in the lobby presenting aspects of these arguments. It is there with the permission of the America First Committee. We are not responsible, however, for what takes place outside this theatre. Anybody can give away any kind of literature he wants in the streets. It may be passed out by Bundists, Fascists, Communists, or by foreign agents working in themselves or through American citizens to involve this country in war."

After the disavowal of anti-democratic organizations by the temporary chairman, and the prohibition of heckling and boos from any of the varied schools of opinion present, the meeting proceeded only with vociferous bursts of applause through the speech of Senator David I. Walsh of Massachusetts, one of the leaders of the Senate non-interventionists.

The greatest outburst greeted the Senator's references to the "damnation, vilification and abuse to which this great man, Colonel Lindbergh, has been subjected in this country, where free speech should be respected."

Senator Walsh reviewed at length the "propaganda" that began by urging "steps short of war" and now "tells us we are at war and should recognize it." He read extracts from letters he had received from citizens asking him to keep this country out of war.

The Senator closed with a denunciation of the current proposal to convoy the lend-lease supplies to Britain that are now being sunk.

"We should resist those propaganda and pressure groups," he said. "When we go into the zone of actual combat through the convoy route, there is no turning back. Convoys mean war. Do we want convoys?"

"No," roared the audience.

In his speech Colonel Lindbergh laid down the considerations that moved him to undertake this campaign for the America First Committee, substantially as expressed in his first speech for them in Chicago, but with heightened emphasis here.

"I do not believe," he said, "that our American ideals, and our way of life will gain through an unsuccessful war.

"I do not blame England for asking for our assistance. But we now know that she declared a war under circumstances which led to the defeat of every nation that sided with her from Poland to Greece. We know that in the desperation of war, England promised to all those nations armed assistance that she could not send.

"We know that she misinformed them, as she has misinformed us, concerning her state of preparation, her military strength, and the progress of the war."

Colonel Lindbergh advocated as the proper policy of the United States "the policy advocated by Washington and incorporated in the Monroe Doctrine. It recommends the maintenance of armed forces sufficient to defend this hemisphere from attack by any combination of foreign powers. This is the policy of the America First Committee today. It is a policy not of isolation, but of independence; not of defeat, but of courage."

He declared in his closing paragraphs that he was addressing himself to "the people who must do the paying, and the fighting, and the dying, if this country enters the war."

Colonel Lindbergh was preceded by Kathleen Norris, novelist, who came by plane from Hollywood to address the meeting.

"Every nation in Europe has quarreled with every other nation," she said. "They speak to us now of defending democracy and defending a certain type of living. There is no democracy there. And their sort of living never has been ours, and never will be ours.

"Therefore we are justified in feeling that, although a cruel and unbalanced dictator has arisen in Europe to spread panic and to assume a temporary puppet government in neighboring States, this state of affairs will last no longer than it has lasted in the past, when Peter the Great, Louis XIV, Cromwell, Philip of Spain and Napoleon have all caused them panic in turn. And, as we can point to no historical instance in which an invader has remained in the invaded country in Europe, we may hope that, within a few years, these despots will disappear, and these peoples will return to normality and to the sanity that we saw in them a short while ago. Because we know that the hearts of those peoples are not in a great ruinous war, any more than is our own.

"Our first line of defense is, and will always be, our own border. The only navy that will ever protect us is our own navy. The only army upon which we may rely, and which is an army unbeaten as yet in history, is our own army. These we will support, these we will maintain, and in these we will put our confidence. For America, if she is to continue America, there can be no other course."

Mr. Flynn explained that the meeting had been offered to the three major broadcasting chains, but that they found it impossible to make space for it among their commercial broadcasts. The only station carrying it, he said, was WMCA.

An announcement was made later by WMCA that it would carry a reply to Colonel Lindbergh to be made at 10 o'clock tonight at a rally of the Fight for Freedom Committee with Rex Stout and James P. Warburg as speakers.

Because of the crush outside, the police admitted only 1,500 persons to the overflow auditorium on the seventh floor of the building.

But these listeners displayed the same enthusiastic temper, even though there was dinned lustily into their ears all evening the air of "Tipperary" rendered by 300 members of the British Great War Veterans Association who were holding their monthly social on the floor below.

The British veterans gained access to their meeting with the greatest difficulty. Three hundred of them, in fact, were unable to get into the building at all. The band that was to have played for them and a detachment of British sailors, who were to have been the guests of honor at their social, likewise were stopped outside.

In front of the building the crowds stood in the rain behind a line established in the middle of the street listening to the speeches as they came over the loudspeakers.

Persons active in nearly all the organizations opposing United States intervention in the war or aid to Britain were noted in the crowd, but they were present as private individuals and members of the America First Committee emphasized that they had no official connection with the rally.

United States flags were hung about the walls and balconies inside the hall and patriotic emblems were on sale. Nearly everybody carried a small American flag.

One of the early arrivals inside the hall was J. F. Condon, the "Jafsie" of the Lindbergh kidnapping case, who was Invited to sit on the platform.

Among the more than seventy-five persons on the platform were Mrs. Lindbergh, Amos Pinchot, former Representative Bruce Barton, Mrs. Marquand, Dr. Hunt and Miss Katherine Lewis, daughter of John L. Lewis.

"We cannot win this war for England."

Charles Lindbergh's prediction of defeat at an isolatinist rally

Charles A. Lindbergh helped organize the America First Committee, served on its national board of directors, and became its most popular spokesperson. He was quite familiar with the Nazi leadership, having visited Germany several times, and tended to see the European war in fratricidal terms rather than as a conflict between right and wrong. He made these remarks on April 23, 1941, at an America First Committee rally.

There are many viewpoints from which the issues of this war can be argued. Some are primarily idealistic. Some are primarily practical. One should, I believe, strive for a balance of both. But, since the issues that can be covered in a single address are limited, tonight I shall discuss the war from a viewpoint which is primarily practical. It is not that I believe ideals are unimportant, even among the realities of war; but if a nation is to survive in a hostile world, its ideals must be backed by the hard logic of military practicability. If the outcome of war depended upon ideals alone, this would be a different world than it is today.

I know I will be severely criticized by the interventionists in America when I say we should not enter a war unless we have a reasonable chance of winning. That, they will claim, is far too materialistic a standpoint. They will advance again the same arguments that were used to persuade France to declare war against Germany in 1939. But I do not believe that our American ideals, and our way of life, will gain through an unsuccessful war. And I know that the United States is not prepared to wage war in Europe successfully at this time. We are no better prepared today than France was when the interventionists in Europe persuaded her to attack the Siegfried Line.

I have said before, and I will say again, that I believe it will be a tragedy to the entire world if the British Empire collapses. That is one of the main reasons why I opposed this war before it was declared, and why I have constantly advocated a negotiated peace. I did not feel that England and France had a reasonable chance of winning. France has now been defeated; and, despite the propaganda and confusion of recent months, it is now obvious that England is losing the war. I believe this is realized even by the British Government. But they have one last desperate plan remaining: They hope that they may be able to persuade us to send another American Expeditionary Force to Europe and to share with England militarily, as well as financially, the fiasco of this war.

I do not blame England for this hope, or for asking for our assistance. But we now know that she declared a war under circumstances which led to the defeat of every nation that sided with her, from Poland to Greece. We know that in the desperation of war, England promised to all these nations armed assistance that she could not send. We know that she misinformed them, as she has misinformed us, concerning her state of preparation, her military strength, and the progress of the war.

In time of war, truth is always replaced by propaganda. I do not believe we should be too quick to criticize the actions of a belligerent nation. There is always the question whether we, ourselves, would do better under similar circumstances. But we in this country have a right to think of the welfare of

America first, just as the people in England thought first of their own country when they encouraged the smaller nations of Europe to fight against hopeless odds. When England asks us to enter this war, she is considering her own future, and that of her empire. In making our reply, I believe we should consider the future of the United States and that of the Western Hemisphere.

It is not only our right, but it is our obligation as American citizens to look at this war objectively, and to weigh our chances for success if we should enter it. I have attempted to do this, especially from the standpoint of aviation; and I have been forced to the conclusion that we cannot win this war for England, regardless of how much assistance we send.

I ask you to look at the map of Europe today and see if you can suggest any way in which we could win this war if we entered it. Suppose we had a large Army in America, trained and equipped. Where would we send it to fight? The campaigns of the war show only too clearly how difficult it is to force a landing, or to maintain an Army, on a hostile coast.

Suppose we took our Navy from the Pacific, and used it to convoy British shipping. That would not win the war for England. It would, at best, permit her to exist under the constant bombing of the German air fleet. Suppose we had an Air Force that we could send to Europe. Where could it operate? Some of our squadrons might be based in the British Isles; but it is physically impossible to base enough aircraft in the British Isles alone to equal in strength the aircraft that can be based on the Continent of Europe.

I have asked these questions on the supposition that we had in existence an Army and an Air Force large enough and well enough equipped to send to Europe; and that we would dare to remove our Navy

Göring entertains Charles and Anne Morrow Lindbergh in July 1936. The photograph is from Göring's personal collection.

from the Pacific. Even on this basis, I do not see how we could invade the Continent of Europe successfully as long as all of that Continent and most of Asia is under Axis domination. But the fact is that none of these suppositions are correct. We have only a one-ocean Navy. Our Army is still untrained and inadequately equipped for foreign war. Our Air Force is deplorably lacking in modern fighting planes, because most of them have already been sent to Europe.

When these facts are cited, the interventionists shout that we are defeatists, that we are undermining the principles of democracy, and that we are giving comfort to Germany by talking about our military weakness. But everything I mention here has been published in our newspapers, and in the reports of congressional hearings in Washington. Our military position is well known to the governments of Europe and Asia. Why, then, should it not be brought to the attention of our own people?

I say it is the interventionist in America, as it was in England, and in France, who gives comfort to the enemy. I say it is they who are undermining the principles of democracy when they demand that we take a course to which more than 80 percent of our citizens are opposed. I charge them with being the real defeatists, for their policy has led to the defeat of every country that followed their advice since this war began. There is no better way to give comfort to an enemy than to divide the people of a nation over the issue of foreign war. There is no shorter road to defeat than by entering a war with inadequate preparation. Every nation that has adopted the interventionist policy of depending on someone else for its own defense has met with nothing but defeat and failure.

When history is written, the responsibility for the downfall of the democracies of Europe will rest squarely upon the shoulders of the interventionists who led their nations into war uninformed and unprepared. With their shouts of defeatism, and their disdain of reality, they have already sent countless thousands of young men to death in Europe. From the campaign of Poland to that of Greece, their prophecies have been false and their policies have failed. Yet these are the people who are calling us defeatists in America today. And they have led this country, too, to the verge of war.

There are many such interventionists in America, but there are more people among us of a different type. That is why you and I are assembled here tonight. There is a policy open to this nation that will lead to success—a policy that leaves us free to follow our own way of life, and to develop our own civilization. It is not a new and untried idea. It was advocated by Washington. It was incorporated in the Monroe Doctrine. Under its guidance, the United States has become the greatest nation in the world.

It is based upon the belief that the security of a nation lies in the strength and character of its own people. It recommends the maintenance of armed forces sufficient to defend this hemisphere from attack by any combination of foreign powers. It demands faith in an independent American destiny. This is the policy of the America First Committee today. It is a policy not of isolation, but of independence; not of defeat, but of courage. It is a policy that led this nation to success during the most trying years of our history, and it is a policy that will lead us to success again.

We have weakened ourselves for many months, and still worse, we have divided our own people by this dabbling in Europe's wars. While we should have been concentrating on American defense, we have been forced to argue over foreign quarrels. We must turn our eyes and our faith back to our own country before it is too late. And when we do this, a different vista opens before us. Practically every difficulty we would face in invading Europe becomes an asset to us in defending America. Our enemy, and not we, would then have the problem of transporting millions of troops across the ocean and landing them on a hostile shore. They, and not we, would have to furnish the convoys to transport guns and trucks and munitions and fuel across three thousand miles of water. Our battleships and submarines would then be fighting close to their home bases. We would then do the bombing from the air and the torpedoing at sea. And if any part of an enemy convoy should ever pass our Navy and our Air Force, they would still be faced with the guns of our coast artillery and behind them the divisions of our Army.

The United States is better situated from a military standpoint than any other nation in the world. Even in our present condition of unpreparedness, no foreign power is in a position to invade us today. If we concentrate on our own defenses and build the strength that this nation should maintain, no foreign army will ever attempt to land on American shores.

War is not inevitable for this country. Such a claim is defeatism in the true sense. No one can make us fight abroad unless we ourselves are willing to do so. No one will attempt to fight us here if we arm ourselves as a great nation should be armed. Over a hundred million people in this nation are opposed to entering the war. If the principles of democracy mean anything at all, that is reason enough for us to stay out. If we are forced into a war against the wishes of an overwhelming majority of our people, we will have proved democracy such a failure at home that there will be little use fighting for it abroad.

The time has come when those of us who believe in an independent American destiny must band together and organize for strength. We have been led toward war by a minority of our people. This minority has power. It has influence. It has a loud voice. But it does not represent the American people.

During the last several years I have traveled over this country from one end to the other. I have talked to many hundreds of men and women, and I have letters from tens of thousands more, who feel the same way as you and I.

Most of these people have no influence or power. Most of them have no means of expressing their convictions, except by their vote which has always been against this war. They are the citizens who have had to work too hard at their daily jobs to organize political meetings. Hitherto, they have relied upon their vote to express their feelings, but now they find that it is hardly remembered except in the oratory of a political campaign. These people—the majority of hardworking American citizens—are with us. They are the true strength of our country. And they are beginning to realize, as you and I, that there are times when we must sacrifice our normal interests in life in order to insure the safety and the welfare of our nation.

Such a time has come. Such a crisis is here. That is why the America First Committee has been formed—to give voice to the people who have no newspaper, or newsreel, or radio station at their command, to give voice to the people who must do the paying, and the fighting, and the dying if this country enters the war.

Whether or not we do enter the war rests upon the shoulders of you in this audience, upon us here on this platform, upon meetings of this kind that are being held by Americans in every section of the United States today. It depends upon the action we take, and the courage we show at this time. If you believe in an independent destiny for America, if you believe that this country should not enter the war in Europe, we ask you to join the America First Committee in its stand. We ask you to share our faith in the ability of this nation to defend itself, to develop its own civilization, and to contribute to the progress of mankind in a more constructive and intelligent way than has yet been found by the warring nations of Europe. We need your support, and we need it now. The time to act is here. I thank you.

26.

Operation Barbarossa

June 1941

The Nazi-Soviet Nonaggression Pact of 1939 was widely seen as a delaying tactic by Hitler. The German dictator's long-standing antipathy for Bolshevism and his insatiable longing for *Lebensraum* in the East meant that, sooner or later, he would attack the Soviet Union. Hitler also mistrusted Stalin deeply and feared that German industry had become too dependent on Soviet raw

materials, which made up a quarter of all German imports.

Stalin mistrusted Hitler as well and had no illusions about the stability of their relationship. Even so, he couldn't change the fact that the Soviet Union wasn't yet ready for war and wouldn't be until at least 1942. Therefore, he had no immediate plans to invade Germany and, like the British, considered a longer war to be in his favor. Hitler could afford no such patience and. Getting nowhere on the western front, he decided that the key to defeating the British was removing their hope that the Soviets would one day come to their aid. The Führer certainly recognized the risks inherent in creating a two-front war but discounted them because he had such contempt for the fighting ability of the Red Army.

Code-named Operation Barbarossa, the German invasion of the Soviet Union was originally scheduled to begin on May 15, 1941, but an unanticipated anti-Nazi coup in Yugoslavia

required German attention there and pushed the invasion date back to June 22. Even so, the German High Command expected a quick and easy victory. Hitler himself estimated that the operation would take no longer than eight to ten weeks. Given that pace, even at the outside, the Germans would reach Moscow well before the onset of Russia's notoriously harsh winter weather.

In fact, historians now agree that Germany's only chance lay in such a speedy triumph. Otherwise, the Soviets simply had too many resources in manpower, territory, and industrial capacity for the Germans to overcome. With the benefit of hindsight, military historians have since pointed out many turning points in the Barbarossa campaign that "lost" the war for Hitler—beginning with the delay caused by Germany's spring 1941 campaign in the Balkans. All such speculation, however, misses the point that Hitler's mistake was grasping for the Soviet ring at all. It was simply beyond his reach.

HITLER BEGINS WAR ON RUSSIA, WITH ARMIES ON MARCH FROM ARCTIC TO THE BLACK SEA

Bad Faith Charged; Goebbels Reads Attack on Soviet—Ribbentrop Announces War

By C. BROOKS PETERS

BERLIN, Sunday, June 22—As dawn broke over Europe today the legions of National Socialist Germany began their long-rumored invasion of Communist Soviet Russia. The non-aggression and amity pact between the two countries, signed in August, 1939, forgotten, the German attack began along a tremendous front, extending from the Arctic regions to the Black Sea. Marching with the forces of Germany are also the troops of Finland and Rumania.

Adolf Hitler, in a proclamation to the German people read over a national hook-up by Propaganda Minister Dr. Joseph Goebbels at 5:30 this morning, termed the military action begun this morning the largest in the history of the world. It was necessary, he added, because in spite of his unceasing efforts to preserve peace in this area it had definitely been proved that Russia was in a coalition with England to ruin Germany by prolonging the war.

Herr Hitler, in his proclamation as reported here, made one vitally interesting statement, namely, that the supreme German military command did not feel itself able to force a decisive victory in the West—apparently on the British Isles—when large Russian troop concentrations were on the Reich's borders in the East.

The Russian troop concentrations in the East began in August, 1940, Herr Hitler asserted. "Thus, there occurred the effect intended by the Soviet-British cooperation," he added, "namely, the binding of such powerful German forces in the East that a radical conclu-

sion of the war in the West, particularly as regards aircraft, could no longer be vouched for by the German High Command."

[The German radio announced early today that documentary proof would shortly be given of a secret British-Russian alliance, made behind Germany's back.]

The German action, Herr Hitler explained to his fellow National Socialists, is designed to save the Reich and with it all Europe from the machinations of the Jewish Anglo-Saxon warmongers.

The German Foreign Minister, Joachim von Ribbentrop, followed Dr. Goebbels on the air with a declaration of the Reich Government read before the foreign correspondents in the Foreign Office. Herr von Ribbentrop said he received V. G. Dekanosoff, the Russian Ambassador, this morning and informed him that in spite of the Russian-German non-aggression pact of Aug. 23, 1939, and an amity pact of Sept. 28, 1939, Russia had betrayed the trust that the Reich had placed in her.

"Contrary to all engagements which they had undertaken and in absolute contradition to their solemn declarations, the Soviet Union had turned against Germany," the Reich note asserted. "They have first not only continued, but even since the outbreak of war intensified their subversive activities against Germany in Europe. They have second, in a continually increasing measure, developed their foreign policy in a tendency hostile to Germany, and they have third massed their entire forces on the German frontier ready for action."

Soldiers of the Wehrmacht undertake the invasion of the Soviet Union.

The Soviet Government, it was charged, had violated its treaties and broken its agreements with Germany. This was characterized as evidence that Moscow's "hatred of National Socialism was stronger than its political wisdom." Recalling the enmity between bolshevism and nazism, it was asserted that Bolshevist Moscow was "about to stab National Socialist Germany in the back" while the latter was "engaged in a struggle for existence."

"Germany has no intention of remaining inactive in the face of this grave threat to her Eastern frontier," it was proclaimed. "The Fuehrer has therefore ordered the German forces to oppose this menace with all the might at their disposal. In the coming struggle the German people are fully aware that they are called upon not only to defend their native land but to save the entire civilized world from the deadly dangers of bolshevism and clear the way for true social progress in Europe."

Continuing his allegations, Herr von Ribbentrop declared that the German High Command had repeatedly directed the attention of the German Foreign Office to the steadily increasing menace of the Russian Army to Germany. These communications from the High Command will be published in detail, it was declared.

All doubts of the aggressive intention of the Russian concentration were dispelled, it was declared, by the news that the Russian general mobilization was complete and that 160 divisions were concentrated facing Germany.

This apprehension was heightened, it was stated, by news from England concerning the negotiations of Sir Stafford Cripps with a view to establishing closer collaboration between Britain and the Soviet Union and the appeal of Lord Beaverbrook to support Russia in her forthcoming conflict.

The announcements made in Berlin were heard here by short-wave listening stations of both the Columbia and National Broadcasting Systems.

Adolf Hitler's proclamation was followed by a statement containing a formal declaration of war by the Nazi Foreign Minister, Joachim von Ribbentrop.

Berlin announced that the German Army was on the march, and that "German troops all along the Russian border from the Baltic to the Balkans are moving into their last-minute positions."

A London broadcast by the British Broadcasting Corporation, however, formally denied that report.

"It can be definitely stated," said the BBC, "that no actual troop movements on the part of either Germany or Russia have as yet taken place."

The only word from Moscow, received several hours after the German announcement, was a London report of a statement issued in the Russian capital declaring that the Soviet and Great Britain were now "in full accord" on the international situation.

Herr Hitler's proclamation, read by Dr. Goebbels at 5:30 A.M., Berlin time, included a vicious attack on the Reich's former associate in European policy, and a charge that Russia had acted in concert with Britain and the United States to "throttle" the Reich.

Finland and Rumania were hailed in the Hitler proclamation as German allies and clear intimation was given that invasion of Russia already might have begun.

"In this very moment," said Herr Hitler's statement, addressed "to the German people," "a marching of German armies is taking place which has no precedent."

Charging against Russia a whole series of border violations, the Hitler proclamation asserted that Soviet planes "again and again" had crossed the Reich's frontiers.

He added that the German people could no longer look peacefully upon these developments.

"I have therefore today decided to give the fate of the German people and the Reich and of Europe into the hands of our soldiers," the announcement from Herr Hitler continued.

The statement indicated that Rumania, in association with Germany, might stand ready to attempt the recapture of Bessarabia, seized by Stalin's legions earlier in the war.

Herr Hitler declared that German and Rumanian soldiers united under Premier Ion Antonescu, stood ready "from the river of the Danube to the shores of the Black Sea."

"The task is to safeguard Europe and thus to save all," the proclamation set forth.

The phrase was seen as a return by Herr Hitler to his assertion, frequently made in earlier years, that Germany stood as Europe's bulwark against bolshevism.

Heavy concentrations of Nazi troops have been reported for several weeks along the borders of partitioned Poland, in apparent readiness for such a stroke. Finland, now referred to as an associate by Herr Hitler's proclamation, recently announced advanced degrees of army mobilization.

Herr Hitler's proclamation denounced the Russian occupation of the Baltic State of Lithuania, annexed to the Soviet Union with Estonia and Latvia after Mr. Stalin's troops had been permitted to occupy bases there.

Germany, he said, never intended to occupy that Baltic country—an intimation that the Soviet Union had made a pretext of such a desire on the part of the Reich as a basis for action.

"Russia," he said, "always put out the lying statement that she was protecting these [the Baltic] countries."

Herr Hitler's proclamation gave an official German version of British relations with Russia, designed, he charged, to prevent the realization of European peace, which he, himself, desired.

Foreign Minister von Ribbentrop's statement declared that Germany, at the time of the announcement, already was taking what he called "military measures of defense" in the Russian situation and that he had so informed the Russian Ambassador in Berlin.

The phrase used recalled that German description of the preliminary phases of the attack on Poland—"counter-attack with pursuit."

Neither Dr. Goebbels's reading of Herr Hitler's proclamation nor the formal statement by Herr von Ribbentrop, which immediately followed on the German radio, gave details of demands reported to have been made on Russia by the Reich.

Included in these, it had been reported earlier, were claims on the Ukraine and the Caucasus for wheat and oil. Since the demands were launched, Russia had been reported organizing elaborate "war games" in these southern areas.

Herr Hitler last night asserted that, in these, the Soviet had mobilized 160 divisions.

He blamed Russia also for causing Germany the necessity of intervention in the Near East, charging that the Soviet "organized the putsch" in Yugoslavia—after the Yugoslav Government had agreed to Axis terms.

In addition, Herr Hitler's proclamation, according to an unofficial translation made here, blamed Russian "penetration" into Rumania, as well as the British guarantee of Greece, for placing "new large areas in the war."

"I again feel spiritually free."

Der Führer's letter to il Duce

Never one to reveal his plans unnecessarily, Hitler waited until the last moment before informing Mussolini of his intention to attack the Soviets.

June 21, 1941

Duce!

I am writing this letter to you at a moment when months of anxious deliberation and continuous nerve-racking waiting are ending in the hardest decision of my life. I believe—after seeing the latest Russian situation map and after appraisal of numerous other reports—that I cannot take the responsibility for waiting longer, and, above all, I believe that there is no other way of obviating this danger—unless it be further waiting, which, however, would necessarily lead to disaster in this or the next year at the latest.

The situation: England has lost this war. With the right of the drowning person, she grasps at every straw which, in her imagination, might serve as a sheet anchor. Nevertheless, some of her hopes are naturally not without a certain logic. England has thus far always conducted her wars with help from the Continent. The destruction of France—in fact, the elimination of all west-European positions—is directing the glances of the British warmongers continually to the place from which they tried to start the war: to Soviet Russia.

Both countries, Soviet Russia and England, are equally interested in a Europe fallen into ruin, rendered prostrate by a long war. Behind these two countries stands the North American Union goading them on and watchfully waiting. Since the liquidation of Poland, there is evident in Soviet Russia a consistent trend, which, even if cleverly and cautiously, is nevertheless reverting firmly to the old Bolshevist tendency to expansion of the Soviet State. The prolongation of the war necessary for this purpose is to be achieved by tying up German forces in the East, so that—particularly in the air—the German Command can no longer vouch for a large-scale attack in the West. I declared to you only recently, Duce, that it was precisely the success of the experiment in Crete that demonstrated how necessary it is to make use of every single airplane in the much greater project against England. It may well happen that in this decisive battle we would win with a superiority of only a few squadrons. I shall not hesitate a moment to undertake such a responsibility if, aside from all other conditions, I at least possess the one certainty that I will not then suddenly be attacked or even threatened from the East. The concentration of Russian forces—I had General Jodl submit the most recent map to your Attaché here, General Maras—is tremendous. Really, all available Russian forces are at our border. Moreover, since the approach of warm weather, work has been proceeding on numerous defenses. If circumstances should give me cause to employ the German air force against England, there is danger that

Russia will then begin its strategy of extortion in the South and North, to which I would have to yield in silence, simply from a feeling of air inferiority. It would, above all, not then be possible for me, without adequate support from an air force, to attack the Russian fortifications with the divisions stationed in the East. If I do not wish to expose myself to this danger, then perhaps the whole year of 1941 will go by without any change in the general situation. On the contrary. England will be all the less ready for peace for it will be able to pin its hopes on the Russian partner. Indeed, this hope must naturally even grow with the progress in preparedness of the Russian armed forces. And behind this is the mass delivery of war material from America which they hope to get in 1942.

Aside from this, Duce, it is not even certain whether we shall have this time, for with so gigantic a concentration of forces on both sides—for I also was compelled to place more and more armored units on the eastern border, and also to call Finland's and Rumania's attention to the danger—there is the possibility that the shooting will start spontaneously at any moment. A withdrawal on my part would, however, entail a serious loss of prestige for us. This would be particularly unpleasant in its possible effect on Japan. I have, therefore, after constantly racking my brains, finally reached the decision to cut the noose before it can be drawn tight. I believe, Duce, that I am hereby rendering probably the best possible service to our joint conduct of the war this year. For my over-all view is now as follows:

1) *France* is, as ever, not to be trusted. Absolute surety that North Africa will not suddenly desert does not exist.

2) *North Africa* itself, insofar as your colonies, Duce, are concerned, is probably out of danger until fall. I assume that the British, in their last attack, wanted to relieve Tobruk. I do not believe they will soon be in a position to repeat this.

3) *Spain* is irresolute and—I am afraid—will take sides only when the outcome of the war is decided.

4) In *Syria*, French resistance can hardly be maintained permanently either with or without our help.

5) An attack on *Egypt* before autumn is out of the question altogether. I consider it necessary, however, taking into account the whole situation, to give thought to the development of an operational unit in Tripoli itself which can, if necessary, also be launched against the West. Of course, Duce, the strictest silence must be maintained with regard to these ideas, for otherwise we cannot expect France to continue to grant permission to use its ports for the transportation of arms and munitions.

6) Whether or not *America* enters the war is a matter of indifference, inasmuch as she supports our opponent with all the power she is able to mobilize.

7) The situation in England itself is bad; the provision of food and raw materials is growing steadily more difficult. The martial spirit to make war, after all, lives only on hopes. These hopes are based solely on two assumptions: Russia and America. We have no chance of eliminating America. But it does lie in our power to exclude Russia. The elimination of Russia means, at the same time, a tremendous relief for Japan in East Asia, and thereby the possibility of a much stronger threat to American activities through Japanese intervention.

I have decided under these circumstances, as I already mentioned, to put an end to the hypocritical performance in the Kremlin. I assume—that is to say, I am convinced—that Finland, and likewise Rumania, will forthwith take part in this conflict, which will ultimately free Europe, for the future also, of a great danger. General Maras informed us that you, Duce, wish also to make available at least one corps. If you have that intention, Duce—which I naturally accept with a heart filled with gratitude—the time for carrying it out will still be sufficiently long, for in this immense theater of war the troops cannot be assembled at all points at the same time anyway. You, Duce, can give the decisive aid, however, by strengthening your forces in North Africa, also, if possible, looking from Tripoli toward the West; by proceeding further to build up a group which, though it be small at first, can march into France in case of a French violation of the treaty; and finally, by carrying the air war and, so far as it is possible, the submarine war, in intensified degree, into the Mediterranean.

So far as the security of the territories in the West is concerned, from Norway to and including France, we are strong enough there—so far as army troops are concerned—to meet any eventuality with lightning speed. So far as the air war on England is concerned, we shall, for a time, remain on the defensive—but this does not mean that we might be incapable of countering British attacks on Germany; on the contrary, we shall, if necessary, be in a position to start ruthless bombing attacks on British home territory. Our fighter defense, too, will be adequate. It consists of the best squadrons that we have.

As far as the war in the East is concerned, Duce, it will surely be difficult, but I do not entertain a second's doubt as to its great success. I hope, above all, that it will then be possible for us to secure a common food-supply base in the Ukraine for some time to come, which will furnish us such additional supplies as we may need in the future. I may state at this point, however, that, as far as we can tell now, this year's German harvest promises to be a very good one. It is conceivable that Russia will try to destroy the Rumanian oil region. We have built up a defense that will—or so I think—prevent the worst. Moreover, it is the duty of our armies to eliminate this threat as rapidly as possible.

If I waited until this moment, Duce, to send you this information, it is because the final decision itself will not be made until 7 o'clock tonight. I earnestly beg you, therefore, to refrain, above all, from making any explanation to your Ambassador at Moscow, for there is no absolute guarantee that our coded reports cannot be decoded. I, too, shall wait until the last moment to have my own Ambassador informed of the decisions reached.

The material that I now contemplate publishing gradually is so exhaustive that the world will have more occasion to wonder at our forbearance than at our decision, except for that part of the world which opposes us on principle and for which, therefore, arguments are of no use.

Whatever may now come, Duce, our situation cannot become worse as a result of this step; it can only improve. Even if I should be obliged at the end of this year to leave 60 or 70 divisions in Russia, that is only a fraction of the forces that I am now continually using on the eastern front. Should England nevertheless not draw any conclusions from the hard facts that present themselves, then we can, with our rear secured, apply ourselves with increased strength to the dispatching of our opponent. I can promise you, Duce, that what lies in our German power will be done.

Any desires, suggestions, and assistance of which you, Duce, wish to inform me in the contingency before us, I would request that you either communicate to me personally or have them agreed upon directly by our military authorities.

In conclusion, let me say one more thing, Duce. Since I struggled through to this decision, I again feel spiritually free. The partnership with the Soviet Union, in spite of the complete sincerity of the efforts to bring about a final conciliation, was nevertheless often very irksome to me, for in some way or other it seemed to me to be a break with my whole origin, my concepts, and my former obligations. I am happy now to be relieved of these mental agonies.

With hearty and comradely greetings,
Your
Adolf Hitler

27.

Roosevelt Embargoes Japan

July 1941

According to Joseph Grew, who served as U.S. ambassador to Japan from 1932 until Pearl Harbor, the news of Hitler's impressive military victories in Europe went to the heads of the Japanese leaders "like strong wine." Immediately, they began pressuring the Dutch East Indies government-in-exile and the Vichy French, who had inherited Indochina, for a variety of concessions. The most important concerned

increased exports of Dutch East Indian oil and the closure of Chinese supply routes through Indochina. (Even the British were at this time moved to appease the Japanese by closing the Burma Road, then Chiang's principal lifeline.)

Alarmed by these developments, President Roosevelt acted on July 26, 1940, to embargo shipments to Japan of high-grade scrap iron and steel as well as high-octane aviation gasoline. He did so with the full knowledge of what might result. "If we once start sanctions," Grew had warned, "we must see them through to the end, and the end may conceivably be war." If the United States cut off fuel shipments, Grew predicted, Japan would "in all probability send her fleets down to take the Dutch East Indies." Such sanctions could not be forsworn, however, because Japan was especially vulnerable to them. The Japanese, for instance, imported 88 percent of their oil—80 percent from the United States alone.

Yet economic sanctions did little to deter the Japanese, who in mid-September compelled the Vichy French to accept Japanese troops in

northern Indochina and later that month signed the Tripartite Pact. In response, President Roosevelt extended the U.S. trade embargo to include all grades of scrap iron and steel, and so began a series of ratcheting escalations that continued for months.

The next cinching of the noose came in July 1941 after Japanese troops occupied southern Indochina—an obvious precursor to attacks on British Malaya (the world's leading source of rubber and tin) and the Dutch East Indies. Roosevelt retaliated on July 26 by freezing all Japanese assets in the United States and creating a board of overseers to review future exports. He considered such a step moderate because the board was empowered to clear certain Japanese purchases and release funds as necessary to pay for them. What happened, however, was that the president immediately left Washington for several diplomatic missions; and while he was gone, truculent bureaucrats rejected every Japanese export request, thus transforming FDR's measured response into an unforeseen total embargo.

TWO-THIRDS CUT DUE IN OIL SALES

Washington Will Restrict Its Permits for Shipments of Petroleum to Japan

By HALLETT ABEND

WASHINGTON, July 26—Although the Department of State was entirely noncommittal concerning the possibilities of an embargo on sales of oil and gasoline to Japan, responsible government circles believe that such sales will be sharply curtailed under the new licensing system that went into effect last night simultaneously with the freezing of Japanese credits in this country.

When asked this morning whether petroleum sales to Japan would be discontinued, Under-Secretary of State Sumner Welles replied guardedly that, as had already been announced, every individual transaction with Japan would be considered on its own merits before a license was granted or refused. He added after a moment that this system afforded complete flexibility and control. Mr. Welles declined to comment on Japan's order "freezing" American assets in that country on the grounds that he had not seen the official text.

If Japan continues to attempt to buy petroleum and petroleum products in the United States it is considered likely that licenses may be granted at the rate of one out of every three applications. Such a system would show Japan how seriously a complete embargo would affect her industries and her military forces and might, it is thought, restrain her from further aggressive projects. Licenses may be refused with the excuse that a shortage exists in the United States and that domestic needs take precedence.

In view of President Roosevelt's statement of last Thursday to the effect that if a complete embargo on oil sales to Japan had been instituted "then you would have war," it is doubted if sales will be entirely prohibited.

Japan, under her agreement with the Netherlands Indies, can still purchase about 4,000,000 tons of oil a year if the Netherland authorities decide to license such purchases. It is believed Indies sales of oil to Japan will not be sharply curtailed, lest such curtailment result in an immediate attempt by the Japanese Army and Navy to conquer the rich archipelago.

Even if Netherland plans to ruin the wells in case of a Japanese invasion are entirely disregarded, the geography of the region and the location of the richest wells present a serious problem to Japan.

The Borneo wells now produce only about one-third of their former flow. The Netherlanders, more than twenty years ago, spent more than 150,000,000 guilders on their huge refining plants at Balik Papan, on the eastern shore of Borneo. Today the production of the Borneo wells has decreased to such an extent that a large fleet of tankers is hauling oil from new Sumatra wells to Balik Papan for refining. So even a quick conquest of Borneo by the Japanese would not profit much, even though Borneo is closest to Indo-China and to Japan.

The difficulty lies in the fact that the major production of Indies oil comes from Sumatra, and that Sumatra lies just west of Singapore. Singapore and Sumatra would have to be seized before Japanese tankers could carry oil from Sumatra with any degree of safety.

Sales of petroleum and petroleum products by the United States to Japan totaled $54,600,000 in value in 1940, and have averaged about $4,000,000 a month this year. In 1939 our petroleum exports to Japan totaled only $45,285,000.

Opposing a boycott of Japanese silk sponsored by Washington debutantes, three hundred hosiery workers march up Constitution Avenue.

"it took a nipponized bit of the old sixth avenue el"

E. E. Cummings's "plato told"

E. E. Cummings published his poem "plato told" in *1 x 1* (1944). "The war was very much on his mind," critic Charles Norman has written, "and many of the poems in that book reflect his preoccupation with the world's ills which, as he foresaw, the war would not resolve."

XIII

plato told

him:he couldn't
believe it(jesus

told him;he
wouldn't believe
it)lao

tsze
certainly told
him,and general
(yes

mam)
sherman;
and even
(believe it

or

not)you
told him:i told
him;we told him
(he didn't believe it,no

sir)it took
a nipponized bit of
the old sixth

avenue
el;in the top his head:to tell

him

28.

The Atlantic Charter

August 1941

The first face-to-face meeting between Roosevelt and Churchill in their respective roles as president and prime minister took place in August 1941 aboard the U.S. cruiser *Augusta,* anchored off Newfoundland. The two leaders had originally intended to meet months earlier, but the vagaries of war had delayed their conference several times. Finally, in mid-July, Roosevelt sent Harry Hopkins to London to suggest

that the meeting be held during the second week of August on Placentia Bay, where the United States was building a new naval base at Argentia, a defunct silver-mining town on Newfoundland's southern coast. The site was symbolic because the Argentia base had been part of the September 1940 destroyers-for-bases deal.

About nine in the morning on August 9, lookouts on the *Augusta* spotted through the mist on the bay the gun turrets of the British battleship *Prince of Wales*, aboard which Prime Minister Churchill had traveled to the meeting. Two hours later, the British leader, wearing a plain blue naval uniform, made his way up the gangplank of the *Augusta* to the strains of "God Save the King." Roosevelt, for his part, wore a light brown tropical-weight suit and stood to greet Churchill, supported by his son Elliot and the deck rail.

During their first working session, Roosevelt brought up the idea of making a joint declaration at the end of the conference stating several gen-

eral principles regarding the conduct of the war and the making of the peace. Operation Barbarossa had only recently transformed the Soviet Union into an ally, and the president wanted to make a statement that would allay domestic fears that a wartime alliance with the Soviets would degrade U.S. war aims. Churchill himself was eager for any statement that would demonstrate how very close the war-worn British and the "neutral" Americans had become. The result was the Atlantic Charter, for which the Argentia Conference is chiefly remembered.

Meanwhile, Churchill pressured Roosevelt for an American declaration of war, which Roosevelt continued to resist. However, the president did indicate a willingness to begin providing U.S. Navy escorts to British merchantmen as far east as Iceland. According to Churchill's subsequent report to his war cabinet, Roosevelt "said he would wage war, but not declare it, and that he would become more and more provocative."

ROOSEVELT DECLARES U.S. IS NO NEARER WAR; REVEALS FULL ACCORD ON WORLD CONFLICT

President Debarks; He Refuses to Disclose Meeting Place as He Lands in Maine

By JOHN H. CRIDER

ROCKLAND, Me., Aug. 16—President Roosevelt said upon coming ashore here this afternoon from his historic meeting at sea with Winston Churchill that he and the British Prime Minister had reached a complete understanding on all aspects of the war situation.

Although stating in answer to a question that the United States was no nearer to war than when he departed, the President left no doubt that his return signalized the opening of a new era of anti-Axis collaboration to achieve the "final destruction of the Nazi tyranny" which he and Mr. Churchill proclaimed as their objective in their joint statement on Thursday.

Tanned and refreshed after his thirteen days at sea, the President jovially received newspaper men in the ward room of the Presidential yacht, Potomac, a few minutes after her arrival here at about 3:15 P.M., Eastern daylight time.

He laughed when a reporter asked whether Mr. Churchill had any intentions of coming to the United States, replying that so far as he knew the Prime Minister had no more of such intentions than he had of going to Britain—at least, for a while.

His mood changed to one of deep solemnity when he said that something that both the statement (presumably the Roosevelt-Churchill statement) and the comment upon it had overlooked was the need for exchange of views on what is happening in the world under a Nazi regime as applied to other nations.

The more one discussed and looked into it, he added, the more terrible the thought became of having those influences at work in occupied or affiliated nations. It was a thing, the President said, that the peoples of the democracies needed to have driven home more and more.

Sitting in the white-walled room, pleasantly decorated with soft green window drapes, the President sat with cigarette holder in hand, discussing impressions of the Churchill meeting but refusing, for what he said were obvious reasons, to give the dates of the conferences aboard the United States cruiser Augusta and the British battleship Prince of Wales, or the position of the ships when the conferences occurred.

Apropos of the reason for secrecy, the President said he felt like slaying Bill Hassett (William D. Hassett, press secretary), for having disclosed last night that he would arrive at Rockland this afternoon. But, the President added, the weather was foggy and as far as could be determined no submarines launched any torpedoes in their direction.

Clad in a pepperish tweed suit, blue shirt and tie, the President sat a few feet from a corner of the ward room in which Harry L. Hopkins, Lend-Lease Administrator, reclined in a big chair.

When asked about the meetings at sea, the President said he would give the impressions that stood out in his mind.

The first thing, he said, was the very remarkable religious service held on the quarter-deck of the British battleship Prince of Wales on Sunday

Roosevelt and Churchill during one of the shipboard meetings that produced the Atlantic Charter.

morning. The whole complement of the ship was present with some two or three hundred American Marines mingled in the congregation with British tars and marines.

The services were conducted by English and American chaplains, but the lesson was read by the captain of the British battleship, in accordance with naval custom.

All but one of his conferences with the Prime Minister were held aboard the Augusta on account of the difficulty he had in getting aboard the British man-o-war, the President said.

The President named the following as attending the conferences for the United States: General George C. Marshall, Chief of Staff; Major Gen. Henry H. Arnold, Assistant Chief of Staff in Charge of Air; General James H. Burns, of the lend-lease staff; Colonel Charles W. Bundy of the Army's war plans section; Admiral Harold R. Stark, Chief of Naval Operations; Rear Admiral

Ernest J. King, Commander of the Atlantic Fleet; Rear Admiral Richard K. Turner of the Navy's war plans section; Captain Forest P. Sherman of the Office of Naval Operations; Mr. Hopkins; W. Averill Harriman, lend-lease executive in London; Major Gen. E. M. Watson, the President's secretary and military aide; Captain John R. Beardall, his naval aide; and Dr. Ross T. McIntire, his physician.

When asked about the presence at the conference of his sons, Captain Elliott Roosevelt and Ensign Franklin D. Roosevelt Jr., the President replied that this was pure luck, that the party had happened to catch them after having got there.

The President said that he had been with Mr. Churchill for more than a day—he would be no more specific than that—and that at one time or another they had discussed the situation on every continent. Every continent you ever heard of, he added facetiously. There wasn't a single section of a single continent that hadn't been discussed, he said.

He said the idea of the conference had been jointly that of Mr. Churchill and himself, that it had been talked about since February, but because of the Greek and Crete campaigns had been delayed for three months beyond the intended date.

The President was reminded by a reporter that the eight peace aims jointly announced on Thursday said nothing about how the "Nazi tyranny" was to be destroyed.

The President replied that this was a narrow way to look at it. The conferences, he said, were primarily an interchange of views on the present and future—a swapping of information that was imminently successful.

Mr. Roosevelt was asked whether it could be assumed that he and Mr. Churchill had reached a complete understanding with regard to all aspects of the war situation. He replied: Yes, he thought so.

Some one asked: "Are we any closer to entering the war?"

The President replied that he should say no. He declined, however, to permit direct quotation of this answer when a reporter asked whether it might be enclosed in quotation marks.

On how the Churchill conferences would be implemented, the President would only say that there would be further exchanges of ideas.

"Will Russia be asked to subscribe to the eight points?" the President was asked.

He replied that no one had suggested it until the reporter asked the question.

The President added, however, that the confer-

ees had discussed fitting Russian needs into the existing production program. These needs, he said, could be divided in two ways: (1) The things most immediately available that could reach there before Winter, and (2) the materials that could be sent for the opening of the Spring campaign.

Asked whether he had any doubts about the Russians holding out, the President replied that he believed there was an assumption that they would not hold out in what he had already said.

The President said he was not up on the latest developments in France and the Far East but would confer with Secretary of State Cordell Hull upon his return to Washington tomorrow.

When newspaper men asked whether there were any American writers at the Churchill conferences to record the event for history, Mr. Roosevelt replied that there were not.

It was learned from White House sources that the two "British journalists" with the conferences at sea did not attend any of the conferences.

The Potomac was first sighted beyond the $1,000,000 Rockland seawall at about 3 P.M. Eastern daylight time.

The boatswain piped the President off at 4 P.M. He went across the gangplank to a point where his car was waiting.

Mayor Edward R. Veazie of Rockland welcomed the President when he had entered his car.

To the solid line of spectators who crowded the way for the mile drive to the Rockland depot the President smiled broadly and waved a brown fedora hat. Several hundred persons crowded the station plaza and cheered unlike Maine Republicans for a Democratic President as he boarded the train at 4:10 P.M.

"Their countries seek no aggrandizement."

The Atlantic Charter communiqué

This "joint declaration" was released to the press by the State Department on August 14, 1941, two days after the conclusion of the Argentia Conference, while both the president and the prime minister were still at sea.

The President of the United States and the Prime Minister, Mr. Churchill, representing His Majesty's Government in the United Kingdom, have met at sea.

They have been accompanied by officials of their two Governments, including high-ranking officers of their Military, Naval, and Air Services.

The whole problem of the supply of munitions of war, as provided by the Lease-Lend Act, for the armed forces of the United States and for those countries actively engaged in resisting aggression has been further examined.

Lord Beaverbrook, the Minister of Supply of the British Government, has joined in these conferences. He is going to proceed to Washington to discuss further details with appropriate officials of the United States Government. These conferences will also cover the supply problems of the Soviet Union.

The President and the Prime Minister have had several conferences. They have considered the dangers to world civilization arising from the policies of military domination by conquest upon which the Hitlerite government of Germany and other governments associated therewith have embarked, and have made clear the stress which their countries are respectively taking for their safety in the face of these dangers.

They have agreed upon the following joint declaration:

Joint declaration of the President of the United States of America and the Prime Minister, Mr. Churchill, representing His Majesty's Government in the United Kingdom, being met together, deem it right to make known certain common principles in the national policies of their respective countries on which they base their hopes for a better future for the world.

First, their countries seek no aggrandizement, territorial or other;

Second, they desire to see no territorial changes that do not accord with the freely expressed wishes of the peoples concerned;

Third, they respect the right of all peoples to choose the form of government under which they will live; and they wish to see sovereign rights and self-government restored to those who have been forcibly deprived of them;

Fourth, they will endeavor, with due respect for their existing obligations, to further the enjoyment by all States, great or small, victor or vanquished, of access, on equal terms, to the trade and to the raw materials of the world which are needed for their economic prosperity;

Fifth, they desire to bring about the fullest collaboration between all nations in the economic field with the object of securing, for all, improved labor standards, economic advancement, and social security;

Sixth, after the final destruction of the Nazi tyranny, they hope to see established a peace which will afford to all nations the means of dwelling in safety within their own boundaries, and which will afford assurance that all the men in all the lands may live out their lives in freedom from fear and want;

Seventh, such a peace should enable all men to traverse the high seas and oceans without hindrance;

Eighth, they believe that all of the nations of the world, for realistic as well as spiritual reasons, must come to the abandonment of the use of force. Since no future peace can be maintained if land, sea, or air armaments continue to be employed by nations which threaten, or may threaten, aggression outside of their frontiers, they believe, pending the establishment of a wider and permanent system of general security, that the disarmament of such nations is essential. They will likewise aid and encourage all other practicable measures which will lighten for peace-loving peoples the crushing burden of armaments.

Franklin D. Roosevelt
Winston S. Churchill

Prime Minister Churchill aboard the HMS Prince of Wales *during the Argentia Conference.*

29.

The Siege of Leningrad
August 1941–January 1944

Even after the triumph of *Blitzkrieg* in Poland, Hitler and his generals were reluctant to let their tank commanders race too far ahead of the infantry. In France, for example, they had ordered Guderian to halt several times in his dash to the coast so that the infantry could catch up. Once the results of the Case Yellow campaign were analyzed, however, the magnitude of the Panzers' success became

apparent, and all doubts concerning the effectiveness of *Blitzkrieg* vanished from the minds of the German High Command.

Therefore, Operation Barbarossa was drawn up to follow the Case Yellow model; in fact, its army groups were led by the same three generals—Bock, Rundstedt, and Wilhelm Ritter von Leeb, who had commanded the forces before the Maginot line. Now Leeb was placed in charge of Army Group North, whose twenty-seven infantry and three Panzer divisions punched through the Baltic states to attack Leningrad. Meanwhile, Bock's Army Group Center, the largest of the three groups with forty-two infantry and nine armored divisions, moved through Soviet-occupied Poland toward Moscow. Finally, Rundstedt's Army Group South, composed of thirty-eight infantry and five Panzer divisions, was detailed to capture the Ukraine.

At first, the German forces made impressive gains, plunging hundreds of miles into Soviet territory in just the first week. "In seven short days," the German propaganda ministry announced, "the Führer's offensive has smashed the Red Army to splinters....The eastern continent lies, like a limp virgin, in the mighty arms of the German Mars." However, because the campaign involved such vast areas, logistical problems developed. Important contributing factors were bad Russian roads and the Soviet rail system, which had a wider gauge than Western European track, thus making German resupply by rail highly problematic.

As a result, Operation Barbarossa began to slow in August and stall in October, yet Hitler insisted that the Wehrmacht press on. The last major German offensive began on November 15, by which time the temperature was already dropping as low as forty degrees below zero. Two weeks later, the German push ended with limited gains, still fifty miles from Moscow. Lacking adequate winter clothing, the Wehrmacht was now losing more soldiers to frostbite than to the Soviets. Nevertheless, Hitler ordered his troops to "hold fast" at their advance supply points and fight on—which they did, even in the face of the strong Soviet counterattacks that began on December 5.

LENINGRAD SIEGE BITTER, SAY NAZIS

Russians Reported Hurling Great Masses of Men Into Fight to Ease Pressure

By C. BROOKS PETERS

BERLIN, Sept. 25—Leningrad is still being shelled unremittingly by guns of many calibers from German field positions. Reich land forces are reported by the official news agency, D. N. B., to have tightened the noose about that beleaguered metropolis.

There is, however, no indication in authoritative quarters that the Germans count capture of the city imminent. Russian resistance has definitely not yet been broken. From various points in the Leningrad area D. N. B. reports furious Soviet counter-attacks, carried out with artillery and tank support.

[The Russians were throwing "great masses" of troops against German positions west of Moscow, apparently in a futile attempt to relieve pressure on Leningrad, according to an Associated Press dispatch from Berlin quoting D. N. B.]

Long-range German artillery apparently engaged in duels with Soviet warships in Leningrad harbor. In the course of these exchanges a Russian merchantman of 10,000 tons is reported to have been sunk.

German naval units whose task is to keep the Russian Baltic fleet bottled up in Kronstadt Bay—chiefly, it would appear, through mine-laying activities—every now and then engage small Soviet vessels. Yesterday a German patrol boat and ten Russian torpedo boats are reported by D. N. B. to have engaged each other. One Russian speedboat was destroyed by gunfire, the news agency adds.

In the same waters a Russian submarine is reported to have run upon a German mine field and been destroyed.

A German soldier war correspondent's dispatch in today's Essener National Zeitung declares that the Soviet strategy is based upon mass and terror. Thus, he adds, "The Bolshevist potentates have without doubt accomplished one thing: The bloodiest campaign in the world's history."

Officially, except for the statement that Moscow and the rifle manufacturing city of Tula had been bombed by its air force last night, the German High Command today revealed nothing further relative to the progress of the operations on other sectors of the Russian front. This silence extended also to informed quarters, who suggested only that when the time was ripe the world would again be treated to a series of special communiqués from Reichsfuehrer Hitler's field headquarters.

The remnants of four Russian armies said by the Germans to be trapped east of Kiev since Sept. 13 face imminent destruction, it was asserted here today. Desperate last minute efforts of the Russian forces to break through the cordon the Germans have drawn around them were repulsed, it is reported. The Soviet losses in these operations are especially declared to have been high.

Elsewhere in the Ukrainian sector, the Germans reported, they had trapped other Soviet divisions. Two of the latter were said to have tried vainly to pierce the main German lines yesterday morning.

Other Reich units in their eastward drive are reported to have engaged in numerous skirmishes, in the course of which the Germans claim to have captured 600 horses and destroyed twelve tanks.

A Red Army sniper credited with killing 181 Germans peers through binoculars on the Leningrad front in 1942.

The Russian Commander in Chief on the Kiev front, Colonel General Mikhail Petrovitch Kirponos, is officially reported by the Germans to have fallen on the battlefield during one of the attempts of his troops to escape from a pocket east of Kiev. One of the young Russian generals, he distinguished himself as commander of the Leningrad district in 1940 during the war with Finland. Since last May he had commanded the Kiev district. Both General Kirponos's staff and the staff of the Soviet Fifth and Twenty-first Armies are officially declared to have been "annihilated" in these operations.

The Russians are using land mines "in quantities surpassing those used in any other war or campaign and in a manner that can be envisaged only by brutal minds, long trained to insidious methods of warfare," a German soldier-reporter writes in an article released to the press today.

"In the battle for the town of Luga alone," he declares, "our engineers cleared away more than 26,000 mines. Still today over broad acres of the battlefield one can see white chalked boundary lines that indicate these areas have not yet been cleared of all mines.

"In the first three days of the battle for the outermost defense girdle of Leningrad alone, 10,000 mines had to be cleared away. The sign painted with a death's head and the words 'Beware of mines!' has become a familiar sight in the east.

"Inside the town of Luga alone our engineers removed 2,007 mines, but this is but a fraction of the number that was planted. Large sections of the town are still barricaded.

"More than 150 of those removed contained explosive charges of from six ounces to fifty pounds. The local Communist party headquarters contained fifty such mines."

"Practically every basement had its machine-gun nest."

An excerpt from Alexander Fadeyev's *Leningrad in the Days of the Blockade*

The Germans never intended to storm Leningrad but planned instead to besiege the city and starve it into submission. That first winter, the strategy seemed to be working. Between November 1941 and January 1942, more than two hundred thousand residents died either of starvation or from disease brought on by malnutrition. The only supplies that reached Leningrad during those months came across frozen Lake Ladoga, through whose treacherous ice many supply trucks disappeared. Alexander Fadeyev published this account of life in the city in 1944.

All my life I shall preserve the memory of that evening towards the end of April, 1942, when our plane, escorted by fighters, flew very low over Lake Ladoga and beneath us, on the ice, which was cracked and fissured, with surging tides of water in between, stretched the road, the only road, which throughout the winter had linked Leningrad with the rest of the country. The people of Leningrad called it The Road of Life. It had already been torn to shreds—virtually obliterated—and in places was a mere flood of water. The plane flew straight towards the misty, crimson, diffuse globe of the sun, which caught the tops of the pines and firs along the entire length of the lakeshore behind us in the tender glow of spring.

"Leningrad! How shall I find it? What is it like after all the hardships of the first winter of war? What do its streets and houses look like? What have its people thought and felt during all this time? And how are they now, those people?"

Such were the thoughts and feelings that filled my being. From the information given in the Soviet Press and from the stories of eyewitnesses I knew how cruel the winter of 1941–42 had been for the people of Leningrad. At the most difficult phase the bread ration for factory workers had fallen to 200 grammes, while for office employees and non-working members of the family it was 125 grammes. The ration of other foodstuffs was exiguous in the extreme and scarcely sufficed to maintain life. People starved and died of starvation. There was barely enough food to keep the most important industrial plants going or to supply the largest hospitals and the most essential public offices. The whole city was in darkness and no trains were running. The water supply and the sewage system did not function. The streets grew an icy crust about a yard thick and were heaped with snow and refuse.

The sight of somebody—man, woman or child—dragging a child's sledge on which lay a dead body wrapped up in a blanket or a bit of canvas became a daily commonplace of the winter Leningrad landscape. The spectacle of somebody dying of hunger in a snow-covered street was by no means rare. Pedestrians passed by, removed their caps and muttered a word or two in sympathy, or sometimes did not even stop, since there was no help they could offer.

During the autumn of 1941 Leningrad was subjected to violent bombing from the air. This was renewed in the spring. Throughout the autumn and winter Leningrad had been under systematic artillery bombardment.

All the world knows that notwithstanding these incredible hardships and privations the people of Leningrad not only held out, not only repulsed the onslaught of the heavily armed Hitlerite forces, but inflicted on the enemy enormous losses in both men and material and laid a road across the ice of Lake Ladoga, thanks to which they freed themselves from blockade and starvation.

How was this miracle of history accomplished? Where did the people of Leningrad find the strength for all this?

My companion in the plane was the poet Nikolai Tikhonov, an old resident of Leningrad. That hard winter, as also during the winter of the war with Finland in 1939–40, he stayed in Leningrad, in the service of the army. For a brief space he was summoned to Moscow by the Union of Writers in order to carry out certain tasks of a literary character and he was now returning to the city of his birth as the recipient of a Stalin literary prize for 1941. He had received a Stalin prize for his poem *Kirov is with Us* and for his verses celebrating the war of the Soviet peoples' Fatherland against German Fascism. A whole group of writers who were Stalin prize-winners, Tikhonov among them, had handed over the full amount of their prize for the purpose of building more tanks. My dear friend Tikhonov was somewhat apprehensive because he was not sure whether the amount would run to a really big tank or whether the tank would fall into the hands of a really experienced commander.

It was already well into the night and almost freezing, with a cold and penetrating wind blowing and bringing to us the distant sound of occasional gunfire, when we were driven in a truck into the city.

And in the misty, diffuse light the majestic and beautiful vistas of Leningrad opened up before us: the Neva, its cold waters flowing in tranquil grandeur; the embankment, the canals, the palaces; the vast St. Isaac's Cathedral, the Admiralty and the Peter and Paul fortress raising their slender spires to the night sky.

In some places, exhibiting dark, gaping holes for windows or with their ruined interiors wholly exposed, stood houses which had been demolished by high-explosive bombs or wrecked by shellfire. But these evidences of destruction—here only occasional, there more frequent—could not change the face of the city of the great architects. It lay stretched out before me now just as it had been, just as I had many times seen it before the war. In its graceful vistas, its harmonious ensembles, in its severity and spaciousness there was something infinitely beautiful....

The Leningrad crowd of that first day of my stay in the city was not the normal street crowd of a bright spring day. In spite of the sun, it was still cool, and more than that it was plain that the people of Leningrad still had a lively memory of the cold of winter; the cold had lodged in their bones. People walked about in autumn coats, and many, more particularly among the old, were still in winter fur coats and caps.

The children's share in the animation of the street scene was specially touching. They had been brought out into the sun from their kindergartens. Twittering like birds, they played in the squares, or bowled along the pavement on their tricycles, or busied themselves with their toys on the sunny side of the street. Some—those who were still weak—sat quietly in the sun, looking very serious in their white hoods. They had only just thawed out, as it were, only just returned to themselves.

Since the time of the civil war Leningrad has preserved the custom of displaying copies of newspapers in the streets, both the local newspapers and those of Moscow. The Moscow papers were delivered to Leningrad in matrix form and printed here. The *Leningrad Pravda* now came out in a double sheet. I approached a group of people gathered round a new issue of *Leningrad Pravda*. The first page carried a report of the results of two mass enemy air raids upon Leningrad. The enemy had launched the first of these two attacks at the beginning of April, the other had occurred the night before we had flown to Leningrad. He had tried to repeat what he had done with impunity during the autumn. But he had evidently had no idea that Leningrad now possessed a formidable air defence. During those two attacks the enemy had succeeded in dropping a certain number of bombs on the city, but he had sustained a severe defeat in the air. Our aircraft and anti-aircraft artillery had brought down dozens of planes. The people of Leningrad now commented in lively fashion on the report.

"Well, let's see what Comrade Andreyenko has to say," a middle-aged citizen said gaily and significantly, elbowing his way towards the newspaper.

I ran my eyes over the sheet, looking for an article under the signature of Andreyenko. But there was no such article. Then I followed the direction of the man's eyes and saw that he was reading the announcement of the Trading Department of the Leningrad Soviet. It was signed by the head of the department, Comrade Andreyenko.

It announced a special distribution of provisions to every category among the population for the forthcoming celebration of the First of May. There were to be increased rations of meat, millet, dried peas, herring, sugar. In addition it announced that, on this holiday occasion, vodka and beer would be on sale. This, I realized, explained the presence of large numbers of women in the streets equipped with shopping bags of one kind or another and also the eager look that I read on every face.

Strolling through the streets I looked at the bakers' shops and the provision stores. Neither on that first day nor on any that followed did I see queues anywhere; there were adequate supplies for the entire population. Queues formed at the newspaper kiosks, at the shops where soya milk for children was issued, and at the special-dietary public restaurants. These public restaurants had to serve in relays, at comparatively short intervals, the most enfeebled part of the population of Leningrad. Naturally there was not a sufficient number of properly equipped premises for the purpose in the city.

When I turned from the Karl Liebknecht Prospect towards the Tuchkov Bridge I heard the whine of a shell—it burst somewhere on Vasilievsky Island. There followed a second and yet a third. The shells fell behind the houses on the other side of the bridge. Pillars of smoke could be seen suddenly rising above the houses.

Nobody seemed to take any notice of this artillery bombardment. A vast crowd of people waiting at the tram stop at Tuchkov Bridge continued to wait, and so also did the winding queue on the pavement for the special-dietary public restaurant at the corner. Pedestrians, crossing the Tuchkov Bridge from the Petrograd side to Vasilievsky Island, continued on their way, although they were going in the direction of the falling shells. Trams still came from Vasilievsky Island and still went towards it. The city's life was not in the smallest degree disturbed.

I crossed Tuchkov Bridge and got out on the First Line at the corner of Proletarian Victory Prospect. I saw that the shells had fallen in the depth of the Prospect, not in the street itself but somewhere in the neighbourhood of the Eleventh Line and deeper still—towards the Thirteenth, Fifteenth, Seventeenth Lines and so on. Something was burning thereabouts, and black smoke was rising to the sky. Along the Prospect movement had ceased. But the people had not hidden themselves; they simply stood against the walls of the houses or under porches or in gateways, waiting until the gunfire should cease.

From the gate of one of the nearby buildings came a group of girls in white overalls and kerchiefs, carrying bags marked with a red cross. Two of them bore an empty stretcher. I went along with the girls.

We passed fresh traces of destruction. One shell had fallen on the Prospect itself in the district of the Eleventh Line, shattering the pavement. Shell fragments had burst the windows and struck the wall of a building on one side of the Prospect, but since there were no signs of activity inside the building or close by it must have been empty.

We went on a little farther, and at the back of the Fourteenth Line, on the side towards the Neva, we saw a group of people clustered round something on the pavement. The girls ran in that direction, and I ran after them. A heavy-calibre shell had fallen here, shattering the pavement and the lower part of a building. The pavement was strewn with fragments of stone and brick and mortar.

A shell fragment gleamed amidst a pile of rubble. I picked it up; it was still warm.

On the pavement lay an elderly, gaunt woman. Her hand grasped very tightly a string bag in which a loaf of bread, the tail of a herring protruding from a piece of newspaper, and some white paper bags were visible. There were bloodstains on her coat near the hip and shoulder. But she had been killed by a fragment of shell which struck her in the head. A crimson pool of blood, dazzling in the sunlight, had formed on the asphalt.

"There's nothing we can do here that's any good," one of the first-aid girls said quickly.

"All the same we'll have to take her away," said the senior girl there.

She quickly bent over the woman and, taking care not to get stained with blood, began to examine the pockets of the woman's coat.

"Here's her passport and money. Zina, find her address and take the food there and tell the people in the house....Where are her ration cards?" she said to herself. She unbuttoned the woman's blouse, slipped a finger into the bodice and drew out a soiled bread card and a provisions card. "Well, here they are, thank heaven. We'll return the cards. Just imagine how dreadful it would be if the family had to go without their ration cards."...

This still from the Soviet film Leningrad in Struggle *shows a hospital set on fire by enemy bombs in July 1942.*

At the union of writers I met a political instructor, a young sunburned fellow in an air pilot's cap and very dusty boots. He had evidently come from a long distance away and was in a great hurry. Sweat poured down his face in little streams, and dark stains showed under the armpits and on the front of his winter tunic. His eyes indicated extreme exhaustion; the lids were heavy and dark from lack of sleep.

He was surrounded by a group of young writers, whose names he was writing down on a piece of paper.

"Where are you off to?" I asked, greeting my comrades, whom I had not seen since the spring of 1941.

"Come along with us. This is the political instructor of a tank-destroyer unit. We're due to pay them a visit to-day."

"Whereabouts are you?" I asked the political instructor.

"I'll write your name down at once so that you can get a pass from the Political Administration and come and see us at the front," he replied.

"This is very sudden. I shall have to go and pack."

"Why do you need to pack? We'll get on a tram—and we'll be there. You'll be back to-morrow morning."

Less than half an hour later we were riding in the tram towards one of the sectors of the Leningrad front. We passed through one of the historic outer districts of Leningrad. Here the destruction caused by the daily artillery bombardment was more noticeable. Both the streets and the houses bore the marks of more frequent hits. The streets were ringed round by a network of barricades. At various points, at cross-roads and at bridges, timber and timber-and-earth pillboxes had been constructed. Practically every basement dwelling had its machine-gun nest and loopholes for firing.

But life went on in this district just as it did in the rest of the city. The population had nowhere else to go and did not in any case want to leave its own district. So the shops, the bakeries, the special-dietary public restaurants carried on. The streets were hung with the same newspapers, proclamations, posters; the children played in the same way. And the tram was full of people returning home from work. There was not a vacant seat. Our political instructor almost fell asleep on his feet.

"Are you tired?" I asked him.

"Yes, I haven't been able to get much sleep. The men of our unit are rather scattered all over the front. I work as the head of a club. Political-educational work has to be carried out both in sections stationed in the forward area and at our principal base, where the staff are and where we train reserves. Every twenty-four hours one has to do perhaps a dozen kilometres on foot."

"But you like your work?"

"I should say so! There's a lot of satisfaction in ministering to the troops. Lecturers, reporters, writers and artists come to us from the city. You'll see how pleased the troops will be to see you."

We reached the tram terminus and got out. There was a military post here, where our papers were examined. But this was still not the end of the inhabited zone. We went on for another two kilometres through inhabited streets—the people living here were provided with regular permits. But this district, or this part of it, was different from all the others: there were army units everywhere and there were in fact more people in uniform than civilians. The district had been heavily fortified and was enclosed by a network of anti-tank obstacles of various kinds.

We passed still more military posts, where our papers were again examined, and eventually we approached the last post almost beyond the city. Here there was no longer a single civilian. We had reached the rear echelons of one of the sectors of the front.

It was already twilight. There was some activity in the forward zone, the prelude to night operations. Machine-gun and rifle fire was heard, now dying down, now bursting out again with redoubled violence. Somewhere on the right flank an artillery duel was developing.

The unit among which we found ourselves was an original and versatile school for tank destroyers. The founder of the school was the unit commander, Major Zavodchikov, an old officer of the regular army and a veteran of the civil war—broad-natured, racy, truly Russian in his hospitality, a hunter, a breeder of dogs, a lover of nature.

Night fell as our literary party was in progress. Heavy firing started up on different sectors in the forward zone. Our artillery and the enemy's artillery both got busy, and towards the end it became difficult to hear the authors who were reading from their own work.

Major Zavodchikov, the commissar of the unit and I retired to a hut in the middle of a little wood. We put out the light and opened the window. The night was clear, the stars shone in the sky. The guns were firing so close that it seemed as if the hut would fall to pieces at any moment.

We were not sleepy. Major Zavodchikov kept on asking questions about writers whom he knew or had read. He was very fond of Prishvin as a lover of nature and connoisseur of hunting; also of Charushin, who wrote such simple and attractive stories for children about nature and animals, although he had never in his life gone hunting.

I always love these conversations at night at the front, when people open their hearts simply and naturally and reveal the best sides of their nature to one another.

"Yes, I was quite a young fellow when I fought here, in these parts," said Major Zavodchikov. "They're my native heath, I've hunted here a good many times....We fought here, in 1918, against Yudenich. It was civil war, it went on all over the country, and there was nothing very strange in our fighting against the White Guards just here. If we could have thought then that the Germans...The Germans!" he exclaimed suddenly, hatred flaring up in his voice. "If we had thought that they would ever be at the gates of Leningrad, would trample our native fields, destroy our memorials, our sacred things...Have you seen what they've made of Pushkino, Pavlovsk, Gachina, Peterhof?...The swine, the swine!..."

"THERE IS NO DANGER TO THIS COUNTRY FROM WITHOUT"—CHARLES A. LINDBERGH.

Clifford Berryman published this editorial cartoon in the Washington Evening Star *on November 1, 1941.*

30.

The Sinking of the *Reuben James*

October 1941

As the isolationists had predicted, the passage of Lend-Lease soon begged the question of U.S. naval escorts. The chain of events was simple: Roosevelt's announcement of Lend-Lease had caused Hitler to reconsider Germany's western strategy and change its focus from strategic bombing to attacks on British shipping. Specifically, on March 25, the Führer extended the German naval combat zone to forty

degrees west longitude (approximately the eastern coast of Greenland) and began producing new long-range Type IX submarines at the brisk pace of four a month. Thereafter, sinkings increased so rapidly that many Americans began to wonder, What was the point of spending seven billion dollars on aid to Britain when so much of it ended up on the ocean bottom?

In April 1941 alone, the British lost 650,000 tons of merchant shipping, most of it to U-boats (*Unterseebooten*). These German submarines belonged to a fleet of more than two hundred vessels run by Karl Dönitz out of Brittany. With so many submarines at his disposal, Dönitz was able to deploy them in large, effective groups known as "wolf packs."

"The decision for 1941 lies upon the seas," Churchill warned FDR pointedly that spring, yet the president found himself shackled both legally and politically. The remnants of the old neutrality law still kept U.S. cargo ships out of the war zone, and reversing himself so quickly

on escorts for British ships would, FDR believed, cost him too much politically. The president did, however, quietly extend America's "coastal" security zone to twenty-five degrees west longitude, thus overlapping the western third of the German combat zone. U.S. patrols still wouldn't engage U-boats, but they could (and did) provide helpful reconnaissance to the Royal Navy and the RAF.

Of course, the mere presence of U.S. warships in a combat zone meant that, sooner or later, shots would be fired. On September 4, 1941, U-652 mistook the USS *Greer* for a British destroyer and fired at her. The torpedo missed, but Roosevelt used this incident as a pretext to begin naval escorts. Six weeks later, on October 17, U-568 fired a torpedo into the USS *Kearny* that failed to sink her but killed eleven sailors, the first American casualties of the war. Two weeks after that, U-552 sent a torpedo into the midship ammunition magazine of the USS *Reuben James*, causing her to split apart and sink almost immediately.

U.S. DESTROYER SUNK, 44 OF 120 CREW RESCUED; PRESIDENT SEES NO CHANGE IN FOREIGN POLICY

Reuben James Hit; First American Warship Lost in War Torpedoed West of Iceland

By CHARLES HURD

WASHINGTON, Oct. 31—The United States lost its first warship in the Battle of the Atlantic when the destroyer Reuben James was torpedoed and sunk last night west of Iceland while on convoy duty, the Navy Department announced today.

The Navy later announced that forty-four members of the crew had been rescued. It was without word, however, as to the fate of the other members of the crew of 120 officers and men which made up her complement.

The text of the Navy's second announcement read:

"The Navy Department has received a report that forty-four members of the crew of the U.S.S. Reuben James have been rescued. The survivors who have been accounted for are all enlisted men.

"The Navy Department has no further information at this time, but additional details will be released when received."

The Navy Department made public the names of the seven officers on the ship. They were:

Lieut. Comdr. Heywood L. Edwards, 35, commanding officer, of San Saba, Texas.

Lieutenant Benjamin Ghetzler, 34, Annapolis, Md.

Lieutenant (Junior Grade) Dewey G. Johnston, 31, El Cajon, Calif.

Lieutenant (J. G.) John J. Daub, 30, Saltsburg, Pa.

Lieutenant James M. Belden, 30, Naval Reserve, Syracuse, N. Y.

Ensign Craig Spowers, 24, East Orange, N. J.

Ensign Howard V. Wade, Naval Reserve, 22, Glen Ridge, N. J.

The meager reports on the sinking were believed to be due to the fact that radio silence for all but the moat urgent messages is an inviolate rule of ships serving on the Atlantic patrol. The flashing of detailed messages by wireless serves in effect as a beacon to notify other enemy vessels where to find the ships which sent them out.

News of the sinking of the Reuben James created an immediate stir in Washington, on Capitol Hill particularly, but President Roosevelt sounded a conservative note in a press conference when he stated that the sinking did not change any aspect of the international position of the United States.

The sinking of the Reuben James represented only the result which might have attended torpedo attacks on two other destroyers which recently have engaged German submarines. The destroyer Greer, first to figure in such an incident, escaped without being hit. The destroyer Kearny was hit by one of three torpedoes launched simultaneously and survived, but with the loss of eleven members of her crew.

The Kearny was a new destroyer, which proved the strength of its type in surviving a torpedo hit. The Reuben James, twenty-one-year-old member of the "tin-can" fleet, met the fate that all sailors long have agreed a destroyer faced if hit by a torpedo.

The Reuben James is believed to have gone down in the area where the other American destroyers were attacked.

The Navy's first announcement of the sinking was as follows:

"The Navy Department announced that the United States destroyer Reuben James was sunk by a torpedo during the night of Oct. 30–31 while convoying in the North Atlantic, west of Iceland.

"The commanding officer is Lieut. Comdr. H. L. Edwards, United States Navy.

"No further details are available at this time, but will be released when received."

If the engagement which cost the Reuben James occurred in the place where the previous attacks were made the vessel or vessels which witnessed and reported its sinking presumably would be some hundreds of miles from land, whether Iceland or Newfoundland, and perhaps a day or more would elapse before they could fully determine who survived and reach a safe place from which to relay further news.

It seemed probable to informed persons here acquainted with fleet operations and with the destroyer itself (in the absence of official comment) that the Reuben James probably was sunk in a general engagement rather than in single combat with a submarine.

American destroyers, like the British ones, are equipped with various devices which make it virtually impossible for a single submarine to catch a destroyer unawares and approach within torpedoing distance. It appeared probable, therefore, that a "pack" of submarines was involved in this attack. By the same token, in view of the system of naval operation, it is probable that other destroyers were on the scene in addition to the Reuben James and there is at least an even chance that the submarine which won this victory did not long survive it.

This correspondent last Summer traversed the route along which the Reuben James presumably was sunk while cruising with a Task Force of the Atlantic Fleet, convoying a group of transports to Iceland.

The Reuben James was one of a squadron of destroyers which did out-ranging patrol as a screen for the transports and larger ships making up the convoy.

On the Summer cruise the days in the Northern Atlantic were twenty hours long. Now they are proportionately short, and the long dark hours make the work of submarines easier and that of convoy escorts proportionately difficult.

The Reuben James was a low-lying, four-stack destroyer of the long-familiar type, identical in design with the fifty destroyers traded to Great Britain under the lease-lend program. Like her sister ships, the tall stacks shown in photographs had been cut down to stubs, so that it presented racy lines in profile as it and the other destroyers zig-zagged along the predetermined course.

There was more than sufficient life-saving equipment aboard the destroyer if its complement survived to use it. This included two boats, each with a capacity of twenty-four people, and at least six large balsa rafts, to each of which twenty-five men could cling. But the water in that region is very cold.

The Reuben James was commissioned Sept. 24, 1920. It was 314 feet long and had a maximum width of 30 feet. It displaced 1,190 tons and was armed with four 4-inch naval rifles and a battery of anti-aircraft guns. To this original equipment had been added the modern secret detectors developed in the last two years.

"Did you have a friend on the good *Reuben James*?"

Woody Guthrie's ballad "The Sinking of the *Reuben James*"

When Woody Guthrie read about the sinking of the *Reuben James* in *The New York Times,* he decided to write a song to memorialize the incident. Initially, he thought that the best way to humanize the tragedy was to list the names of the men who had died: "There's Harold Hammer Beasley, a first-rate man at sea/From Hinton, West Virginia, he had his first degree/There's Jim Franklin Benson, a good machinist's mate/Come up from North Carolina to sail the *Reuben James.*" A week or so later, Guthrie brought his work-in-progress to a meeting of his group, the Almanac Singers. The other members liked the idea but not the list of names. Pete Seeger advised him to describe the sinking of the destroyer instead and add a rousing chorus, which Seeger himself helped to write.

The Sinking of the *Reuben James*

Have you heard of a ship called the good *Reuben James*
Manned by hard fighting men both of honor and fame?
She flew the Stars and Stripes of the land of the free
But tonight she's in her grave at the bottom of the sea.

Chorus
Tell me what were their names, tell me what were their names,
Did you have a friend on the good *Reuben James*?

One hundred men were drowned in that dark watery grave
When that good ship went down only forty-four were saved.
'Twas the last day of October we saved the forty-four
From the cold icy waters off that cold Iceland shore.

It was there in the dark of that uncertain night
That we watched for the U-boats and waited for a fight.
Then a whine and a rock and a great explosion roared
And they laid the *Reuben James* on that cold ocean floor.

Now tonight there are lights in our country so bright
In the farms and in the cities they're telling of the fight.
And now our mighty battleships will steam the bounding main
And remember the name of that good *Reuben James*.

31.

The Night and Fog Decree

December 1941

Under the terms of the June 1940 armistice agreed to by Pétain, his Vichy government technically retained administrative control over all of France. In practice, however, the Wehrmacht never relinquished its grip on the northern "occupied" zone, which included Paris—until, that is, the Allies liberated France in August 1944. (The Wehrmacht did, however, face constant challenges to its jurisdiction

from the SS and the Nazi party's rabid economic and cultural agencies, especially with regard to the pleasures of Paris.)

Although the fabled French resistance movement known as the Maquis (French for "underbrush") didn't become particularly widespread until the Germans expanded their forced-labor program in 1943, there were nevertheless significant numbers of resisters operating in concert with de Gaulle's Free French as early as 1941. Attacks against the German occupation forces had always been punishable by death; yet once Operation Barbarossa began on the eastern front in June 1941, underground activity increased considerably and became enough of a problem for the Germans that Wilhelm Keitel, chief of the German High Command, was moved to take additional—and dramatic—action.

Following Hitler's specific instructions, Keitel issued on December 7, 1941, a secret order concerning "the prosecution of offenses against the Reich or against the occupation authorities in

the occupied territories." The purpose of the order, Keitel wrote, was "intimidation." Henceforth, German military courts would be empowered to impose the death penalty without the unanimous verdict previously required. The process would also be speeded up: All trials and sentences would now have to be carried out within eight days. Furthermore, all persons suspected of resistance activity were to be arrested under the cover of "night and fog," their cases never to be discussed and their fates never to be revealed. Those condemned to die were to be executed immediately; all others were to be sent to concentration camps in the Reich.

It's not known how many "persons endangering German security" were quietly executed under the authority granted by the Night and Fog Decree, but twenty-four thousand prisoners remained in the system, still awaiting trial, when Nazi minister of justice Otto Thierack transferred them all to the custody of the Gestapo (the Nazi political police) in September 1944.

100 HOSTAGES SHOT BY NAZIS IN FRANCE

Billion-Franc Fine Levied on Jews—Deportation of Dissidents Ordered

BERNE, Switzerland, Dec. 13—Charging that attacks on German soldiers of the occupying forces in Paris and elsewhere in France were the work of an organized "Jewish, anarchist and Anglo-Saxon" plot to ruin France, General Otto von Stuelpnagel, Commander in Chief of the Nazi military forces in France, late this afternoon announced in a special bulletin pasted up all over Paris that 100 "Jews, Communists and, anarchists who have for certain had relations with authors of these attacks on our troops" would be immediately executed.

[According to United Press reports received here last night, Vichy officially announced the new executions and the beginning of large-scale deportations to Eastern Europe for hard labor.]

He also announced the imposition of a billion-franc fine to be paid exclusively by the Jews in Occupied France and finally the deportation of a large number of Frenchmen to the Eastern area.

His order read:

During the last few weeks attacks by dynamite and revolver have been carried out against the members of the German Army. The authors of these acts, sometimes youths, are in the pay of the Anglo-Saxons, Jews and Bolshevists and obey the infamous orders of these elements. The attacked German soldiers were wounded or killed from behind, and in no case has the assassin been apprehended.

To strike at the real authors of these cowardly attacks I have ordered the immediate carrying out of the following orders:

1. A fine of 1,000,000,000 francs to be imposed on the Jews inhabiting the occupied territory.

2. A large number of criminal Judeo-Bolsheviki elements will be deported to hard labor in the eastern territories [probably Poland]. Other deportations of still greater numbers will follow immediately should there be any further attacks, and this independently of other measures which may be taken.

3. One hundred Jews, Communists and anarchists who have definite relations with the authors of these previous attacks will be immediately executed.

These measures do not strike at France but merely at those individuals who, in the pay of the enemies of the Reich, wish to precipitate France's decline and sabotage the reconciliation of France and Germany.

Signed: von Stuelpnagel, Commandant of the Occupation Troops in France.

As additional proof that this measure was expected to "liquidate" the "outstanding differences" between Frenchmen and their occupying conquerers, he further announced that the curfew restrictions imposed on the Paris region on Dec. 7 had been rescinded as from tonight.

That his final statement and the lifting of the curfew might not suffice to preserve the peace he wishes to maintain, however, was indicated in several bulletins over clandestine radio stations in France throughout the evening warning the

Reinhard Heydrich (center), the Reich protector of Bohemia and Moravia, visits Paris in May 1942.

population against precipitate action and promising it that the executions would only be carried out at "terrible cost to the cowardly brutes" who planned them.

Notable among these appeals for patience were that of the Chevaliers du Coup de Bala, whose broadcasts over a powerful mobile station have long been a thorn in the flesh of the occupying authorities. They promised the occupying authorities in a "special broadcast"—given at their regular hour during the evening—that if these executions were carried out a "certain number of hostages" at present in their hands would also be executed and warned General von Stuelpnagel to cease leaving the Crillon Hotel in Paris by the side door which is directly across the Rue Boissy d'Anglas from the American Embassy building. The hint was obvious; whether they would or could implement it, of course, only time will tell.

"They came in the night, men in boots and brown shirts."

Wendell L. Willkie's speech to the people of Lidice, Illinois

Although Wendell L. Willkie based his 1940 presidential campaign on isolationist rhetoric, he was, in actuality, a rabid internationalist and after Pearl Harbor became a close ally of President Roosevelt and a leading advocate of Wilsonian universalism. Beginning in 1942, Willkie's semiofficial duties included the delivery of patriotic speeches across the country in support of the war effort. He gave the most memorable of these on July 12, 1942, at a small town in Illinois. Its residents had recently voted to change the name of their town from Stern Park Gardens to Lidice in honor of a Czechoslovakian village burned to the ground a month earlier because of its alleged connection to the Czech resistance movement.

Fellow Citizens and all who love freedom everywhere:

Let me tell you a story. Ten miles west of Prague, in Czechoslovakia, there was a little village called Lidice, spelled L I D I C E. It was a mining village, a mile off the main highway, with some lovely old inns, a blacksmith or two, a shoemaker, a wheelwright, a tailor. The village had been there for over six hundred years.

Above the ninety roofs of the town rose the spire of St. Margaret's Church, built in 1736, the home of the faith of the community. This town was remote, peaceful, almost like a village in a fairy tale. But it was not a village in a fairy tale, for its people had tasted the bread and wine of freedom. In this village one of the main streets was named Wilson Street, after an American who had a vision and wanted to share it with the world. And the people of Lidice dreamed the same dream, saw the same vision.

But the Nazis came, and with them, misery and hardship. The altar of St. Margaret's Church was no longer open to the people as it had been for over two hundred years. Men had to watch their words and in their actions, they could no longer be free. But in their hearts, the hearts of the inn-keeper, and the tailor, and the farmer, and the miner, and the priest, was the stubborn independence of their fathers.

Not far from Lidice ran a winding road. On this road, on May 27th, six weeks ago, at 10:30 in the morning, a motor car was passing, carrying Hitler's governor of Czechoslovakia, "Hangman" Heydrich, for his cruelties the most hated man in all Europe. The car was held up by two unknown men. Bullets burrowed into the spine of Reinhard Heydrich. The two patriots disappeared, and one of them, it is said, is now safe in London.

I do not wish to speak of the reign of terror that thereupon swept over all Czechoslovakia. I wish to speak today only of Lidice, and I will give you only the facts. This is not my version of the facts. This is not a version of the facts issued by any of the United Nations as propaganda. These are the facts as officially attested by the German government. They are facts of which the Nazis are proud. They are facts they wish the world to know. They are facts they believe will frighten you and me, and turn our hearts and our knees to water, and make us cry "Truce!"

For Heydrich the Hangman died in agony, just as he had caused thousands of innocent people to die. No proof from that day to this has ever been adduced to show that any of the inhabitants of

Lidice had anything to do with the assassination. But the Nazis made their own proof. They were afraid not to, for Heydrich was one of their great men. "One of the best Nazis," Hitler called him, and that, no doubt, is true.

On June 10th an official German statement was issued, not for domestic consumption, but for the world to hear. I quote from it: "It is officially announced that in the course of the search for the murderers of General Heydrich, it has been ascertained that the population of the village of Lidice supported and assisted the perpetrators who came into question....Because the inhabitants, by their support of the perpetrators, have flagrantly violated the law, all men of the village have been shot. The women have been deported to a concentration camp, and the children sent to appropriate centers of education. All buildings of the village were leveled to the ground, and the name of the village was immediately abolished."

That is the official Nazi report.

They came in the night, men in boots and brown shirts, and they took from their homes the bewildered miners and farmers, the tailor and the priest, the boy of seventeen and the old man of seventy, more than two hundred in all, and they shot them, because they could think of no other way to avenge the death of Heydrich. Fifty-six women they took also and killed, and proudly listed their names. The rest of the women they drove into what they called concentration camps; and these women the world will never see again. They herded the pale, terror-stricken children into trucks and carried them off to correction schools where they would be taught that they must honor the murderers of their fathers

Massacred inhabitants of Lidice, Czechoslovakia, killed by the Germans in retaliation for the murder of Heydrich, June 10, 1942.

and the brutalizers of their mothers. The ninety homes, they burned to the ground, the church of St. Margaret they stamped into the earth. And the name of the little town of Lidice, through which ran the street called after a President of the United States, they rubbed out, they thought, from history.

Why did they do this deed, more terrible than anything that has happened since the Dark Ages, a deed not of passion, but of cold, premeditated, systematic murder and rapine? Why? They did it because they are afraid. They are afraid because the free spirit in men has refused to be conquered. Theirs is a system of force and terror and Lidice is the terrible symbol of that system.

But it is not the only one. Of the five hundred thousand men, women and children who have been shot in Europe by the Nazis, at least twenty-five thousand have perished in mass massacres. Poland, Norway, Belgium, Yugoslavia, all have their Lidices. But this one—a symbol of all we have sworn to remember, if only because the Nazis themselves demand that we forget it. Once more, they have misjudged the human spirit.

Because a hangman was killed, Lidice lives. Because a hangman was killed, Wilson Street must once again be part of a little Bohemian town. Because the lanterns of Lidice have been blacked out, a flame has been lit which can never be extinguished. Each of the wounds of those two hundred men and fifty-six women is a mouth that cries out that other free men and free women must not suffer a like fate. Everywhere, but particularly in our own country, the wave of stubborn, stern resolve rises. Lidice lives. She lives again, thirty-five hundred miles from Wilson Street and St. Margaret's Church, in this little village in Illinois.

I look about me here, and I can see in the distance the black smoke of steel factories, swarming with American workers of all bloods and races. No contrast could be greater than the peaceful Lidice the Nazis thought they had destroyed, and this Illinois country, alive with factories in which the arms of victory are being forged. But I tell you that the two are related. For while such deeds as Lidice are done in another country, we cannot rest until we are sure that they will never be done in our own.

Let us here highly resolve that the memory of this little village of Bohemia, now resurrected by the people of a little village in Illinois, will fire us, now and until the battle is over, with the iron resolution that the madness of tyrants must perish from the earth, so that the earth may return to the people to whom it belongs, and be their village, their home, forever.

AMERICA JOINS THE WAR

This captured Japanese propaganda photograph was captioned: "The moment at which the Hawaii surprise attack force is about to take off from the carrier....On the faces of those who go forth to conquer and those who send them off there floats only that beautiful smile which transcends death."

32.

The Attack on Pearl Harbor

December 1941

The Japanese government coveted the oil, rubber, and tin resources of the Dutch East Indies and British Malaya; yet, in order to conquer and hold those territories, it would have to establish long supply lines through the South China Sea, which would be vulnerable to American B-17s flying out of the Philippines. Therefore, any offensive war plan developed by the Japanese would have to take into

account operations against the U.S. forces on Luzon.

Having spent many years in the United States, first as a student and later as a naval attaché, Adm. Yamamoto Isoroku, commander in chief of the imperial navy, understood better than most that his country's only chance to survive a war with the United States was to punish it so severely at the outset that enough time could be gained to set up an impenetrable ring of defenses in the western Pacific. To deliver such a blow, however, conquest of the Philippines was insufficient; nothing less than the devastation of the U.S. Pacific Fleet at Pearl Harbor would do. Once this became apparent, Yamamoto began planning a surprise attack—because without surprise, he concluded, there could be no victory.

Yamamoto's plan, code-named Operation Z, called for a strike force of six aircraft carriers under Adm. Nagumo Chuichi to leave Japanese waters and sail in a wide arc through the nearly deserted North Pacific. Then, at a point 500

miles north of Hawaii, the fleet would turn sharply south and close to within 220 miles of Oahu before launching its first wave of planes. Sunday morning, December 7, was chosen as the time for the attack because, despite the dangerous international situation, most U.S. military personnel were still being given the weekend off. The ships of the Pacific Fleet, therefore, would likely be in port—sitting ducks for Nagumo's planes—and many servicemen would probably still be sleeping off Saturday-night hangovers.

Because of the ongoing negotiations in Washington, Admiral Nagumo was told to wait for a final radioed command before preparing his attack. If the talks with the Americans went well (an eventuality not considered likely), he was to hold his fleet in the North Pacific and await further orders. Instead, on December 2, his flagship received the message "Climb Mount Niitakayama" (the highest peak on Taiwan). This was the "go" code, irrevocably ordering the attack.

JAPAN WARS ON U.S. AND BRITAIN; MAKES SUDDEN ATTACK ON HAWAII; HEAVY FIGHTING AT SEA REPORTED

Guam Bombed; Army Ship Is Sunk

By FRANK L. KLUCKHOHN

WASHINGTON, Monday, Dec. 8—Sudden and unexpected attacks on Pearl Harbor, Honolulu, and other United States possessions in the Pacific early yesterday by the Japanese air force and navy plunged the United States and Japan into active war.

The initial attack in Hawaii, apparently launched by torpedo-carrying bombers and submarines, caused widespread damage and death. It was quickly followed by others. There were unconfirmed reports that German raiders participated in the attacks.

Guam also was assaulted from the air, as were Davao, on the island of Mindanao, and Camp John Hay, in Northern Luzon, both in the Philippines. Lieut. Gen. Douglas MacArthur, commanding the United States Army of the Far East, reported there was little damage, however.

[Japanese parachute troops had been landed in the Philippines and native Japanese had seized some communities, Royal Arch Gunnison said in a broadcast from Manila today to WOR-Mutual. He reported without detail that "in the naval war the ABCD fleets under American command appeared to be successful" against Japanese invasions.]

Japanese submarines, ranging out over the Pacific, sank an American transport carrying lumber 1,300 miles from San Francisco, and distress signals were heard from a freighter 700 miles from that city.

The War Department reported that 104 soldiers died and 300 were wounded as a result of the attack on Hickam Field, Hawaii. The National Broadcasting Company reported from Honolulu that the battleship Oklahoma was afire. [Domei, the Japanese news agency, reported the Oklahoma sunk.]

The news of these surprise attacks fell like a bombshell on Washington. President Roosevelt immediately ordered the country and the Army and Navy onto a full war footing. He arranged at a White House conference last night to address a joint session of Congress at noon today, presumably to ask for declaration of a formal state of war.

This was disclosed after a long special Cabinet meeting, which was joined later by Congressional leaders. These leaders predicted "action" within a day.

After leaving the White House conference Attorney General Francis Biddle said that "a resolution" would be introduced in Congress tomorrow. He would not amplify or affirm that it would be for a declaration of war.

Congress probably will "act" within the day, and he will call the Senate Foreign Relations Committee for this purpose, Chairman Tom Connally announced.

[A United Press dispatch from London this morning said that Prime Minister Churchill had notified Japan that a state of war existed.]

As the reports of heavy fighting flashed into the White House, London reported semi-officially that the British Empire would carry out

The USS Arizona *burns after the Japanese attack on Pearl Harbor.*

Prime Minister Winston Churchill's pledge to give the United States full support in case of hostilities with Japan. The President and Mr. Churchill talked by transatlantic telephone.

This was followed by a statement in London from the Netherland Government in Exile that it considered a state of war to exist between the Netherlands and Japan. Canada, Australia and Costa Rica took similar action.

A Singapore communiqué disclosed that Japanese troops had landed in Northern Malaya and that Singapore had been bombed.

The President told those at last night's White House meeting that "doubtless very heavy losses" were sustained by the Navy and also by the Army on the island of Oahu [Honolulu]. It was impossible to obtain confirmation or denial of reports that the battleships Oklahoma and West Virginia had been damaged or sunk at Pearl Harbor, together with six or seven destroyers,

and that 350 United States airplanes had been caught on the ground.

The White House took over control of the bulletins, and the Navy Department, therefore, said it could not discuss the matter or answer any questions about how the Japanese were able to penetrate the Hawaiian defenses or appear without previous knowledge of their presence in those waters.

Administration circles forecast that the United States soon might be involved in a worldwide war, with Germany supporting Japan, an Axis partner. The German official radio tonight attacked the United States and supported Japan.

Axis diplomats here expressed complete surprise that the Japanese had attacked. But the impression gained from their attitude was that they believed it represented a victory for the Nazi attempt to divert lease-lend aid from Britain, which has been a Berlin objective ever since the legislation was passed and began to be implemented.

Secretary of the Treasury Henry Morgenthau Jr. announced that his department had invoked the Trading With the Enemy Act, placing an absolute United States embargo on Japan.

Robert P. Patterson, Under-Secretary of War, called on the nation to put production on a twenty-four-hour basis.

A nation-wide round-up of Japanese nationals was ordered by Attorney General Biddlle through cooperation by the FBI and local police forces.

Action was taken to protect defense plants, especially in California, where Japanese are particularly numerous. Orders were issued by the Civil Aeronautics Authority to ground most private aircraft except those on scheduled lines.

The Navy last night swept out to sea from its bombed base at Pearl Harbor after Secretary of State Cordell Hull, following a final conference with Japanese "peace envoys" here, asserted that Japan's had been a "treacherous" attack. Neither the War nor the Navy Department had been able to communicate with its commanders in Manila.

Secretary of War Henry L. Stimson ordered the entire United States Army to be in uniform by today. Secretary Frank Knox followed suit for the Navy. They did so after President Roosevelt had instructed the Navy and Army to expect all previously prepared orders for defense immediately.

United States naval craft are expected to operate out of Singapore as soon as possible in protecting the vital rubber and tin shipments necessary to our national defense program.

Despite these preliminary defense moves, however, it was clear that further detailed discussions would soon take place between officials of the United States, Great Britain, China, the Netherlands and Australia to devise a total scheme of limiting the activities of the Japanese Fleet.

Immediate steps will be taken also to meet the increased menace to China's lifeline, the Burma Road. Reliable information indicates that the Japanese are preparing a large-scale assault on the road in the hope of cutting off American supplies before the Allies can transport sufficient forces into defensive positions.

Censorship was established on all messages leaving the United States by cable and radio.

In Tokyo United States Ambassador Joseph C. Grew obtained a reply to Secretary Hull's early message, according to dispatches from the Japanese capital.

The attack on Pearl Harbor and Honolulu began "at dawn," according to Stephen Early, Presidential secretary. Because of time difference, the first news of the bombing was released in Washington at 2:22 P.M. Subsequently it was announced at the White House that another wave of bombers and dive bombers had come over Oahu Island, on which Honolulu is situated, to be met by anti-aircraft fire again.

An attack on Guam, the tiny island outpost, subsequently was announced. The White House at first said that Manila also had been attacked but, after failure to reach Army and Navy commanders there, President Roosevelt expressed the "hope" that no such attack had occurred. Broadcasts from Manila bore out this hope.

The Japanese took over the Shanghai Bund. Japanese airplanes patrolling over the city dropped some bombs, reportedly sinking the British gunboat Peterel.

Reports from Hawaii indicated that Honolulu had no warning of the attack. Japanese bombers, with the red circle of the Rising Sun of Japan on their wings, suddenly appeared, escorted by fighters. Flying high, they suddenly dive-bombed, attacking Pearl Harbor, the great Navy base, the Army's Hickam Field and Ford Island. At least one torpedo plane was seen to launch a torpedo at warships in Pearl Harbor.

A report from Admiral C. C. Bloch, commander of the naval district at Hawaii, expressed the belief that "there has been heavy damage done in Hawaii and there has been heavy loss of life."

This was subsequently confirmed by Governor Joseph B. Poindexter of Hawaii in a telephone conversation with President Roosevelt. The Governor also said that there were heavy casualties in the city of Honolulu.

At the White House it was officially said that the sinking of the Army transport carrying lumber and the distress signal from another Army ship "indicate Japanese submarines are strung out over that area." Heavy smoke was seen from Ford Island near Honolulu.

In the raids on Hawaii Japanese planes were shot down, one bomber hitting and bursting into flames just behind a post office on the Island of Oahu. It was reported without confirmation that six Japanese planes and four submarines were destroyed.

The second attack on Honolulu and its surrounding bases occurred just as President Roosevelt was talking to Governor Poindexter at 6 o'clock last evening.

There was no official confirmation of United Press reports from Honolulu that parachute troops had been sighted off Pearl Harbor.

Many Japanese and former Japanese who are now American citizens are in residence in Hawaii.

Saburo Kurusu, the special Japanese envoy who has been conducting "peace" negotiations while Japan was preparing for this attack, and Ambassador Kichisaburo Nomura called at the State Department at 2:05 P.M. after asking for the appointment at 1 P.M. They arrived shortly before Secretary Hull had received news Japan had started a war without warning. Mrs. Roosevelt revealed in her broadcast last night that the Japanese Ambassador was with the President when word of the attacks was received.

The two envoys handed a document to Mr. Hull, who kept them waiting about fifteen minutes. Upon reading it, he turned to his visitors to exclaim that it was "crowded with infamous falsehoods and distortions."

President Roosevelt ordered war bulletins released at the White House as rapidly as they were received. A sentence or two was added to the story of the surprise attack every few minutes for several hours.

Cabinet members arrived promptly at 8:30 last evening for their meeting in the White House Oval Room. President Roosevelt had been closeted with Harry L. Hopkins in the Oval Room since receiving the first news. He had conferred with Secretaries Stimson and Knox by telephone and also with General George C. Marshall, Chief of Staff. Admiral Harold H. Stark, Chief of Naval Operations, was too busy to talk to the President even by telephone.

The first to arrive was Secretary of Commerce Jesse H. Jones. Secretary Knox came last. Secretary Hull was accompanied by two bodyguards.

Congressional leaders joining the Cabinet in the Oval Room at 9 P.M. included Senator Hiram Johnson of California, hitherto an isolationist and for long the ranking minority member of the Senate Foreign Relations Committee.

Others present were Speaker Rayburn; Representative Jere Cooper of Tennessee, representing Representative John W. McCormack, the House Majority Leader, who was not able to reach Washington in time for the conference; Chairman Sol Bloom of the House Foreign Affairs Committee and Representative Charles A. Eaton, ranking minority member; Vice President Wallace, who flew here from New York; Senator Alben W. Barkley, majority leader; Senator McNary; and Senator Warren R. Austin, ranking minority member of the Foreign Relations Committee.

Cheering crowds lined Pennsylvania Avenue to see them arrive, another evidence of the national determination to defeat Japan and her Axis allies which every official is confident will dominate the country from this moment forth.

Senator W. Lee O'Daniel of Texas, of hillbilly band and hot biscuits fame, added a touch of inadvertent comedy to the scene when he arrived uninvited. He said he had come to "try to learn a few things" and "to make sure Texas is represented at this conference," thus ignoring the presence of Senator Connally.

Senator Barkley, who arrived in Washington by automobile about 7 P.M., said he did not find out about the Japanese attack until nearly 6 o'clock.

The formal positions of the United States and Japanese Governments toward the war were officially set forth by the release at the White House of the text of President Roosevelt's message of yesterday to Emperor Hirohito and by the Japanese document handed Ambassador Grew in Tokyo.

The President's message expressed a "fervent hope for peace" and outlined the dangers of the situation.

"We have hoped that a peace of the Pacific could be consummated in such a way that the nationalities of many diverse peoples may exist side by side without fear of invasion," the President told the Emperor.

The President, recalling that the United States had been directly responsible for bringing Japan into contact with the outside world, said that in seeking peace in the Pacific "I am certain that it will be clear to Your Majesty, as it is to me, that both Japan and the United States should agree to eliminate any form of military threat."

The Japanese document, despite the obviously carefully prepared attack on American bases, insisted that:

"On the other hand, the American Government, always holding fast to theories in disregard of realities and refusing to yield an inch on its impractical principles, caused undue delay in the [peace] negotiations."

Late last night, the United States Government announced that all American republics had

Wreckage at Naval Air Station, Pearl Harbor. A third of U.S. planes were destroyed and nearly all the rest damaged.

been informed of the "treacherous attack" by Japan. It was stated that "very heartening messages of support" were being received in return.

The State Department statement on this matter said:

"All the American republics have been informed by the Government of the United States of the treacherous attack by Japan upon the United States. Immediately upon receipt of word of the attacks on Hawaii and other American territory, wires were dispatched to the American diplomatic missions, instructing them to inform the Foreign Offices at once. This government is receiving very heartening messages of support from the other American republics."

Senator Connally, as head of the powerful Foreign Relations Committee, predicted that world-wide war involving this nation probably depended on European developments within the next few days, according to The United Press.

As Roland Young, committee clerk, took to Senator Connally's apartment drafts of the war declaration of April 2, 1917, Mr. Connally said:

"Professing a desire for peace and under the pretext that she coveted amicable relations with us, Japan stealthily concealed under her robe a dagger of assassination and villainy. She attacked us when the two nations were legally at peace.

"With rare and tolerant patience our government has striven to adjust our differences with Japan.

"Japan has now declared war upon the United States and on Great Britain. We shall resist this cruel and unjustifiable assault with naval power and all the resources of our country. We shall wreak the vengeance of justice on these violators of peace, these assassins who attack without warning and these betrayers of treaty obligations and responsibilities of international law.

"Let the Japanese Ambassador go back to his masters and tell them that the United States answers Japan's challenge with steel-throated cannon and a sharp sword of retribution. We shall repay this dastardly treachery with multiplied bombs from the air and heaviest and accurate shells from the sea."

Late last night American officers at the Mexican border were detaining all Japanese attempting to enter or leave the United States, according to a United Press dispatch from San Diego.

New York City, Chicago and other police forces acted to control Japanese nationals and with regard to consulates.

James L. Fly, chairman of the Federal Communications Commission and the Defense Communications Board, said further activity by amateur radio stations would be permitted only upon special governmental authorization.

He said he has been in constant touch with heads of all important communications companies with relation to execution of preexisting plans for cooperation during any emergency.

"It is clear that a continuance of the situation is unthinkable."

The diplomatic exchange between the U.S. and Japanese governments on the eve of the attack on Pearl Harbor

Although the Japanese sent veteran diplomat Kurusu Saburo to Washington in mid-November 1941 to revive bilateral talks with the Americans, little was expected. With the European war having thoroughly discredited appeasement as a response to aggression, the Roosevelt administration was holding fast to its demand that the Japanese withdraw from both Indochina and China. U.S. resolve was further stiffened by the "Magic" intercepts, which showed that Japan was prepared to go to war should negotiations with the United States fail. (Magic was the code name given to naval intelligence's breaking of the Japanese diplomatic code.) Reprinted here are the final texts of that negotiation: The first is the diplomatic note passed on by Japanese ambassador Nomura Kichisaburo on December 5; the second is the message sent by President Roosevelt to Emperor Hirohito the following day; and the last is the text of the final Japanese communication, intended to be delivered just before the first bombs fell on Pearl Harbor but delayed by slow transcription. It wasn't delivered to Secretary of State Hull until an hour after the attack on Battleship Row began.

December 5
Statement of the Japanese Ambassador

Reference is made to your inquiry about the intention of the Japanese Government with regard to the reported movements of Japanese troops in French Indo-China. Under instructions from Tokyo, I wish to inform you as follows:

As Chinese troops have recently shown frequent signs of movements along the northern frontier of French Indo-China bordering on China, Japanese troops, with the object of mainly taking precautionary measures, have been reinforced to a certain extent in the northern part of French Indo-China. As a natural sequence of this step, certain movements have been made among the troops stationed in the southern part of the said territory. It seems that an exaggerated report has been made of these movements. It should be added that no measure has been taken on the part of the Japanese Government that may transgress the stipulations of the Protocol of Joint Defense between Japan and France.

◆　◆　◆

December 6
Message from the President

Almost a century ago the President of the United States addressed to the Emperor of Japan a message extending an offer of friendship of the people of the United States to the people of Japan. That offer was accepted, and in the long period of unbroken peace and friendship which has followed, our respective nations, through the virtues of their peoples and the wisdom of their rulers, have prospered and have substantially helped humanity.

Only in situations of extraordinary importance to our two countries need I address to Your Majesty messages on matters of state. I feel I should now so address you because of the deep and far-reaching emergency which appears to be in formation.

Developments are occurring in the Pacific area which threaten to deprive each of our nations and all humanity of the beneficial influence of the long peace between our two countries. Those developments contain tragic possibilities.

The people of the United States, believing in peace and in the right of nations to live and let live, have eagerly watched the conversations between our two Governments during these past months. We have hoped for a termination of the present conflict between Japan and China. We have hoped that a peace of the Pacific could be consummated in such a way that nationalities of many diverse peoples could exist side by side without fear of invasion; that unbearable burdens of armaments could be lifted for them all; and that all peoples would resume commerce without discrimination against or in favor of any nation.

I am certain that it will be clear to Your Majesty, as it is to me, that in seeking these great objectives both Japan and the United States should agree to eliminate any form of military threat. This seemed essential to the attainment of the high objectives.

More than a year ago Your Majesty's Government concluded an agreement with the Vichy Government by which five or six thousand Japanese troops were permitted to enter into Northern French Indo-China for the protection of Japanese troops which were operating against China further north. And this Spring and Summer the Vichy Government permitted further Japanese military forces to enter into Southern French Indo-China for the common defense of French Indo-China. I think I am correct in saying that no attack has been made upon Indo-China, nor that any has been contemplated.

During the past few weeks it has become clear to the world that Japanese military, naval and air forces have been sent to Southern Indo-China in such large numbers as to create a reasonable doubt on the part of other nations that this continuing concentration in Indo-China is not defensive in its character.

Because these continuing concentrations in Indo-China have reached such large proportions and because they extend now to the southeast and the southwest corners of that Peninsula, it is only reasonable that the people of the Philippines, of the hundreds of Islands of the East Indies, of Malaya and of Thailand itself are asking themselves whether these forces of Japan are preparing or intending to make attack in one or more of these many directions.

I am sure that Your Majesty will understand that the fear of all these peoples is a legitimate fear inasmuch as it involves their peace and their national existence. I am sure that Your Majesty will understand why the people of the United States in such large numbers look askance at the establishment of military, naval and air bases manned and equipped so greatly as to constitute armed forces capable of measures of offense.

It is clear that a continuance of such a situation is unthinkable.

None of the peoples whom I have spoken of above can sit either indefinitely or permanently on a keg of dynamite.

There is absolutely no thought on the part of the United States of invading Indo-China if every Japanese soldier or sailor were to be withdrawn therefrom.

I think that we can obtain the same assurance from the Governments of the East Indies, the Governments of Malaya and the Government of Thailand. I would even undertake to ask for the same assurance on the part of the Government of China. Thus a withdrawal of the Japanese forces from Indo-China would result in the assurance of peace throughout the whole of the South Pacific area.

I address myself to Your Majesty at this moment in the fervent hope that Your Majesty may, as I am doing, give thought in this definite emergency to ways of dispelling the dark clouds. I am confident that both of us, for the sake of the peoples not only of our own great countries but for the sake of humanity in neighboring territories, have a sacred duty to restore traditional amity and prevent further death and destruction in the world.

◆　◆　◆

December 7
Memorandum from the Government of Japan

1. The Government of Japan, prompted by a genuine desire to come to an amicable understanding with the Government of the United States in order that the two countries by their joint efforts may secure the peace of the Pacific Area and thereby contribute toward the realization of world peace, has continued negotiations with the utmost sincerity since April last with the Government of the United States regarding the adjustment and advancement of Japanese-American relations and the stabilization of the Pacific Area.

The Japanese Government has the honor to state frankly its views concerning the claims the American Government has persistently maintained as well as the measures the United States and Great Britain have taken toward Japan during these eight months.

2. It is the immutable policy of the Japanese Government to insure the stability of East Asia and to promote world peace and thereby to enable all nations to find each its proper place in the world.

Ever since the China Affair broke out owing to the failure on the part of China to comprehend Japan's true intentions, the Japanese Government has striven for the restoration of peace and it has consistently exerted its best efforts to prevent the extension of war-like disturbances. It was also to that end that in September last year Japan concluded the Tripartite Pact with Germany and Italy.

However, both the United States and Great Britain have resorted to every possible measure to assist the Chungking régime so as to obstruct the establishment of a general peace between Japan and China, interfering with Japan's constructive endeavours toward the stabilization of East Asia. Exerting pressure on the Netherlands East Indies, or menacing French Indo-China, they have attempted to frustrate Japan's aspiration to the ideal of common prosperity in cooperation with these regions. Furthermore, when Japan in accordance with its protocol with France took measures of joint defence of French Indo-China, both the American and British Governments, willfully misinterpreting it as a threat to their own possessions and inducing the Netherlands Government to follow suit, enforced the assets-freezing order, thus severing economic relations with Japan. While manifesting thus an obviously hostile attitude, these countries have strengthened their military preparations perfecting an encirclement of Japan, and have brought about a situation which endangers the very existence of the Empire.

Nevertheless, to facilitate a speedy settlement, the Premier of Japan proposed, in August last, to meet the President of the United States for a discussion of important problems between the two countries covering the entire Pacific area. However, the American Government, while accepting in principle the Japanese proposal, insisted that the meeting should take place after an agreement of view had been reached on fundamental and essential questions.

3. Subsequently, on September 25th the Japanese Government submitted a proposal based on the formula proposed by the American Government, taking fully into consideration past American claims and also incorporating Japanese views. Repeated discussions proved of no avail in producing readily an agreement of view. The present cabinet, therefore, submitted a revised proposal, moderating still further the Japanese claims regarding the principal points of difficulty in the negotiation and endeavoured strenuously to reach a settlement. But the American Government, adhering steadfastly to its original assertions, failed to display in the slightest degree a spirit of conciliation. The negotiation made no progress.

Therefore, the Japanese Government, with a view to doing its utmost for averting a crisis in Japanese-American relations, submitted on November 20th still another proposal in order to arrive at an equitable solution of the more essential and urgent questions which, simplifying its previous proposal, stipulated the following points:

(1) The Governments of Japan and the United States undertake not to dispatch armed forces into any of the regions, excepting French Indo-China, in the Southeastern Asia and the Southern Pacific area.

Japanese envoys Nomura Kichisaburo (left) and Kurusu Saburo greet reporters in Washington.

(2) Both Governments shall cooperate with the view to securing the acquisition in the Netherlands East Indies of those goods and commodities of which the two countries are in need.

(3) Both Governments mutually undertake to restore commercial relations to those prevailing prior to the freezing of assets.
The Government of the United States shall supply Japan the required quantity of oil.

(4) The Government of the United States undertakes not to resort to measures and actions prejudicial to the endeavours for the restoration of general peace between Japan and China.

(5) The Japanese Government undertakes to withdraw troops now stationed in French Indo-China upon either the restoration of peace between Japan and China or the establishment of an equitable peace in the Pacific Area; and it is prepared to remove the Japanese troops in the southern part of French Indo-China to the northern part upon the conclusion of the present agreement.

As regards China, the Japanese Government, while expressing its readiness to accept the offer of the President of the United States to act as 'introducer' of peace between Japan and China as was previously suggested, asked for an undertaking on the part of the United States to do nothing prejudicial to the restoration of Sino-Japanese peace when the two parties have commenced direct negotiations.

The American Government not only rejected the above-mentioned new proposal, but made known its intention to continue its aid to Chiang Kai-shek; and in spite of its suggestion mentioned above, withdrew the offer of the President to act as so-called 'introducer' of peace between Japan and China, pleading that time was not yet ripe for it. Finally on November 26th, in an attitude to impose upon the Japanese Government those principles it has persistently maintained, the American Government made a proposal totally ignoring Japanese claims, which is a source of profound regret to the Japanese Government.

4. From the beginning of the present negotiation the Japanese Government has always maintained an attitude of fairness and moderation, and did its best to reach a settlement, for which it made all possible concessions often in spite of great difficulties. As for the China question which constitutes an important subject of the negotiation, the Japanese Government showed a most conciliatory attitude. As for the principle of non-discrimination in international commerce, advocated by the American Government, the Japanese Government expressed its desire to see the said principle applied throughout the world, and declared that along with the actual practice of this principle in the world, the Japanese Government would endeavour to apply the same in the Pacific area, including China, and made it clear that Japan had no intention of excluding from China economic activities of third powers pursued on an equitable basis. Furthermore, as regards the question of withdrawing troops from French Indo-China, the Japanese Government even volunteered, as mentioned above, to carry out an immediate evacuation of troops from Southern French Indo-China as a measure of easing the situation.

It is presumed that the spirit of conciliation exhibited to the utmost degree by the Japanese Government in all these matters is fully appreciated by the American Government.

On the other hand, the American Government, always holding fast to theories in disregard of realities, and refusing to yield an inch on its impractical principles, caused undue delay in the negotiation. It is difficult to understand this attitude of the American Government and the Japanese Government desires to call the attention of the American Government especially to the following points:

(1) The American Government advocates in the name of world peace those principles favorable to it and urges upon the Japanese Government the acceptance thereof. The peace of the world may be brought about only by discovering a mutually acceptable formula through recognition of the reality of the situation and mutual appreciation of one another's position. An attitude such as ignores realities and imposes one's selfish views upon others will scarcely serve the purpose of facilitating the consummation of negotiations.

Of the various principles put forward by the American Government as a basis of the Japanese-American Agreement, there are some which the Japanese Government is ready to accept in principle, but in view of the world's actual condition it seems only a utopian ideal on the part of the American Government to attempt to force their immediate adoption.

Again, the proposal to conclude a multilateral non-aggression pact between Japan, the United States, Great Britain, China, the Soviet Union, the Netherlands and Thailand, which is patterned after the old concept of collective security, is far removed from the realities of East Asia.

(2) The American proposal contained a stipulation which states—"Both Governments will agree that no agreement, which either has concluded with any third power or powers, shall be interpreted by it in such a way as to conflict with the fundamental purpose of this agreement, the establishment and preservation of peace throughout the Pacific area." It is presumed that the above provision has been proposed with a view to restrain Japan from fulfilling its obligations under the Tripartite Pact when the United States participates in the war in Europe, and, as such, it cannot be accepted by the Japanese Government.

The American Government, obsessed with its own views and opinions, may be said to be scheming for the extension of the war. While it seeks, on the one hand, to secure its rear by stabilizing the Pacific Area, it is engaged, on the other hand, in aiding Great Britain and preparing to attack, in the name of self-defense, Germany and Italy, two Powers that are striving to establish a new order in Europe. Such a policy is totally at variance with the many principles upon which the American Government proposes to found the stability of the Pacific Area through peaceful means.

(3) Whereas the American Government, under the principles it rigidly upholds, objects to settle international issues through military pressure, it is exercising in conjunction with Great Britain and other nations pressure by economic power. Recourse to such pressure as a means of dealing with international relations should be condemned as it is at times more inhumane than military pressure.

(4) It is impossible not to reach the conclusion that the American Government desires to maintain and strengthen, in coalition with Great Britain and other Powers, the dominant position it has hitherto occupied not only in China but in other areas of East Asia. It is a fact of history that the countries of East Asia for the past hundred years or more have been compelled to observe the *status quo* under the Anglo-American policy of imperialistic exploitation and to sacrifice themselves to the prosperity of the two nations. The Japanese Government cannot tolerate

the perpetuation of such a situation since it directly runs counter to Japan's fundamental policy to enable all nations to enjoy each its proper place in the world.

The stipulation proposed by the American Government relative to French Indo-China is a good exemplification of the above-mentioned American policy. Thus the six countries—Japan, the United States, Great Britain, the Netherlands, China, and Thailand—excepting France, should undertake among themselves to respect the territorial integrity and sovereignty of French Indo-China and equality of treatment in trade and commerce would be tantamount to placing that territory under the joint guarantee of the Governments of those six countries. Apart from the fact that such a proposal totally ignores the position of France, it is unacceptable to the Japanese Government in that such an arrangement cannot but be considered as an extension to French Indo-China of a system similar to the Nine Power Treaty structure which is the chief factor responsible for the present predicament of East Asia.

(5) All the items demanded of Japan by the American Government regarding China such as wholesale evacuation of troops or unconditional application of the principle of non-discrimination in international commerce ignore the actual conditions of China, and are calculated to destroy Japan's position as the stabilizing factor of East Asia. The attitude of the American Government in demanding Japan not to support militarily, politically or economically any régime other than the régime at Chungking, disregarding thereby the existence of the Nanking Government, shatters the very basis of the present negotiation. This demand of the American Government falling, as it does, in line with its above-mentioned refusal to cease from aiding the Chungking régime, demonstrates clearly the intention of the American Government to obstruct the restoration of normal relations between Japan and China and the return of peace to East Asia.

5. In brief, the American proposal contains certain acceptable items such as those concerning commerce, including the conclusion of a trade agreement, mutual removal of the freezing restrictions, and stabilization of yen and dollar exchange, or the abolition of extra-territorial rights in China. On the other hand, however, the proposal in question ignores Japan's sacrifices in the four years of the China Affair, menaces the Empire's existence itself and disparages its honour and prestige. Therefore, viewed in its entirety, the Japanese Government regrets that it cannot accept the proposal as a basis of negotiation.

6. The Japanese Government, in its desire for an early conclusion of the negotiation, proposed simultaneously with the conclusion of the Japanese-American negotiation, agreements to be signed with Great Britain and other interested countries. The proposal was accepted by the American Government. However, since the American Government has made the proposal of November 26th as a result of frequent consultation with Great Britain, Australia, the Netherlands and Chungking, and presumably by catering to the wishes of the Chungking régime in the questions of China, it must be concluded that all these countries are at one with the United States in ignoring Japan's position.

7. Obviously it is the intention of the American Government to conspire with Great Britain and other countries to obstruct Japan's efforts toward the establishment of peace through the creation of a new order in East Asia, and especially to preserve Anglo-American rights and interests by keeping Japan and China at war. This intention has been revealed clearly during the course of the present negotiation. Thus, the earnest hope of the Japanese Government to adjust Japanese-American rela-

The White House on the night of December 7, 1941. Inside, the president confers with his cabinet and congressional leaders.

tions and to preserve and promote the peace of the Pacific through cooperation with the American Government has finally been lost.

The Japanese Government regrets to have to notify hereby the American Government that in view of the attitude of the American Government it cannot but consider that it is impossible to reach an agreement through further negotiations.

33.

War Declared on Japan

December 1941

Shortly before noon in Washington, as Admiral Nagumo ordered his carriers into the wind, U.S. Army chief of staff George C. Marshall read the decoded text of Tokyo's latest message to Ambassador Nomura, which instructed Nomura to break off negotiations "at 1:00 P.M. on the 7th, your time." Marshall immediately ordered that a warning be radioed to army commanders in the Philippines, Hawaii, Panama,

and San Francisco. "Japanese are presenting at one P.M. Eastern Standard Time what amounts to an ultimatum....Just what significance the hour set may have we do not know but be on the alert accordingly. Inform naval authorities of this communication." Unfortunately, atmospheric static blocked the channel to Honolulu, so the signal officer on duty used the next fastest method: the Western Union cable. His telegram reached Honolulu sixteen minutes later, at 7:33 A.M. local time. A Western Union motorcycle messenger was immediately dispatched to carry the urgent telegram to Fort Shafter, several miles away. The messenger was en route when the attack began.

Flight Comdr Fuchida Mitsuo led the first wave of 183 attack planes. As he approached Pearl Harbor, he could see the battleships moored off Ford Island in the same position described by intelligence reports provided by the Japanese consulate in Honolulu. At 7:53, he broke radio silence to shout into his mouthpiece, *"Tora! Tora! Tora!"* The Japanese word for "tiger" signaled to Admiral Nagumo on his flag-

ship that complete surprise had been achieved. The high-level bombers attacked first—at Wheeler and Hickam Fields, where the army air force planes sat clustered together like sheep in a pen. Then the dive-bombers and torpedo bombers hit Battleship Row.

In Washington, Secretary of State Hull was waiting at his desk for ambassadors Kurusu and Nomura when his phone rang at 2:05 P.M., just as the Japanese diplomats arrived. It was the president calling to tell him that Pearl Harbor had been attacked. After finishing the call, Hull had the ambassadors brought into his office, where they handed him the same document he'd read two hours earlier. Nevertheless, Hull read it again so that the Japanese wouldn't know their code had been broken. Then he told Nomura and Kurusu, "In all my fifty years of public service, I have never seen a document that was more crowded with infamous falsehoods and distortions—infamous falsehoods and distortions on a scale so huge that I never imagined that any government on this planet was capable of uttering them."

President Roosevelt asks a joint session of Congress to declare war on Japan, calling December 7 a "day of infamy." Directly behind FDR are Vice Pres. Henry A. Wallace and Speaker of the House Sam Rayburn. To the president's left is his son James, a marine captain.

U.S. DECLARES WAR, PACIFIC BATTLE WIDENS; MANILA AREA BOMBED; 1,500 DEAD IN HAWAII

Unity in Congress; Only One Negative Vote as President Calls to War and Victory

By FRANK L. KLUCKHOHN

WASHINGTON, Dec. 8—The United States today formally declared war on Japan. Congress, with only one dissenting vote, approved the resolution in the record time of 33 minutes after President Roosevelt denounced Japanese aggression in ringing tones. He personally delivered his message to a joint session of the Senate and House. At 4:10 P.M. he affixed his signature to the resolution.

There was no debate like that between April 2, 1917, when President Wilson requested war against Germany, and April 6, when a declaration of war was approved by Congress.

President Roosevelt spoke only 6 minutes and 30 seconds today compared with Woodrow Wilson's 29 minutes and 34 seconds.

The vote today against Japan was 82 to 0 in the Senate and 388 to 1 in the House. The lone vote against the resolution in the House was that of Miss Jeanette Rankin, Republican, of Montana. Her "No" was greeted with boos and hisses. In 1917 she voted against the resolution for war against Germany.

The President did not mention either Germany or Italy in his request. Early this evening a statement was issued at the White House, however, accusing Germany of doing everything possible to push Japan into the war. The objective, the official statement proclaimed, was to cut off American lend-lease aid to Germany's European enemies, and a pledge was made that this aid would continue "100 per cent."

President Roosevelt's brief and decisive words were addressed to the assembled representatives of the basic organizations of American democracy—the Senate, the House, the Cabinet and the Supreme Court.

"America was suddenly and deliberately attacked by naval and air forces of the Empire of Japan," he said. "We will gain the inevitable triumph, so help us God."

Thunderous cheers greeted the Chief Executive and Commander in Chief throughout the address. This was particularly pronounced when he declared that Americans "will remember the character of the onslaught against us," a day, he remarked, which will live in infamy.

"This form of treachery shall never endanger us again," he declared amid cheers. "The American people in their righteous might will win through to absolute victory." Then, to the accompaniment of a great roar of cheering, he asked for war against Japan.

The President officially informed Congress that in the dastardly attack by Japan, delivered while the Imperial Japanese Government was expressing hope for continued peace, "very many American lives have been lost" and American ships reportedly have been "torpedoed on the high seas between San Francisco and Honolulu."

Mentioning one by one in staccato phrases the Japanese attacks on the Philippines, American Midway, Wake and Guam Islands, British Hong Kong and Malaya, he bluntly informed the people by radio and their representatives directly:

President Roosevelt signs on December 8 the U.S. declaration of war against Japan passed by Congress earlier in the day.

"Hostilities exist. There is no blinking at the fact that our people, our territory and our interests are in grave danger. The people of the United States have already formed their opinions and well understand the implications to the very life and safety of our nation."

It may take a long time, Mr. Roosevelt warned, "to overcome this premeditated invasion," but of the unbounding determination of the American people and confidence in our armed forces neither he nor they had any doubt. Then he said:

"I ask that the Congress declare that since the unprovoked and dastardly attack by Japan on Sunday, Dec. 7, a state of war has existed between the United States and the Japanese Empire."

It was to a solemn Congress and to grim galleries that the President mentioned the casualties in Hawaii—officially estimated at 1,500 dead and 1,500 wounded.

Before him, on his left was the Supreme Court, its members clad in black robes. On the right in the front row sat the Cabinet, with Secretary Hull in the ranking position on the aisle. Behind the Cabinet were the Senators and then the members of the House.

Mr. Roosevelt spoke concisely, clearly and to the point to an already convinced audience already stirred to belligerency by the wantonness of the Japanese attack.

Extraordinary precautions were taken by the Secret Service to guard the President during his short trip over the indirect mile and a quarter route from the Executive Mansion to the Capitol and back to the White House.

Crowds, solemn but determined, greeted the Chief Executive with cheers from the time he was driven out of the East Gate of the White House until he reached the rear entrance of the House after passing through crowded Capitol Plaza. The same crowds stood silently by as he returned.

The two houses split up immediately after the address and passed the war resolution separately without debate, the time consumed being accountable to having the resolution officially introduced and in the physical problem involved.

Stephen T. Early, Presidential secretary, said that nothing official had been received by this government tonight on European reports that Germany and Italy were contemplating declaration of war against the United States. Germany, however, was widely expected to carry out its treaty commitments arranged by Hitler with Japan and to declare war on the United States with her Italian satellite following suit.

Since the Constitution provides that Congress alone can declare war, there was some doubt here as to whether the United States was officially at war with Japan from the time the House adopted the war resolution at 1:10 P.M., ten minutes after the Senate, or from the time the President signed the resolution at 4:10 P.M. Most attorneys consulted inclined to the belief the latter time marked the historic step.

It was just forty-seven minutes, at any rate, after Vice President Wallace affixed his signature at the Capitol until the President affixed his signature without great ceremony in the presence of Senate and House leaders.

The President shook hands with his guests, signed the document with an ordinary pen and promised the pen to Chairman Bloom of the House Foreign Affairs Committee. Besides officials, only an exceptionally large number of news reel and other photographers, including one in Army uniform, saw the ceremony.

Present at the ceremony in the Executive office were the following Congressional leaders: Vice President Wallace, Senators Barkley, Austin, McNary, Connally and Glass; Speaker Rayburn and Representatives McCormack, Martin, Bloom, Eaton and Luther A. Johnson of Texas.

The President went to the Capitol cheered by telegrams and messages in tremendous quantity all of which were said by Mr. Early to express "horror at this attack and full loyalty to the President and the government."

The messages came from Governors, Mayors, religious leaders, heads of civic movements, newspaper editors and radio broadcasters, many offering their personal services.

A Washington taxicab driver named Smith telephoned to the White House late last night, saying he had just finished paying for his cab, but that he offered it to the government and offered, further, to drive free of charge any government official needing transportation.

Alfred M. Landon, Republican Presidential candidate in 1936, telegraphed to the White House:

"The Japanese leave no choice. Nothing must be permitted to interfere with our victory over a foreign foe."

A committee to escort President Roosevelt into the House chamber was appointed by Speaker Rayburn. It consisted of Representative McCormack, House majority leader; Joseph W. Martin, House minority leader; Chairman Doughton of the House Ways and Means Committee; Senate Majority Leader Barkley, Senate Minority Leader McNary and Senator Glass of Virginia.

The President went from his automobile to the Speaker's room where he remained until he addressed the joint session at 12:30 P.M.

"A date which will live in infamy."

Franklin D. Roosevelt's speech to Congress requesting a declaration of war on Japan

On December 8, a grim-faced president went before Congress, meeting in joint session.

Yesterday, December 7, 1941—a date which will live in infamy—the United States of America was suddenly and deliberately attacked by naval and air forces of the Empire of Japan.

The United States was at peace with that Nation and, at the solicitation of Japan, was still in conversation with its Government and its Emperor looking toward the maintenance of peace in the Pacific. Indeed, one hour after Japanese air squadrons had commenced bombing in Oahu, the Japanese Ambassador to the United States and his colleague delivered to the Secretary of State a formal reply to a recent American message. While this reply stated that it seemed useless to continue the existing diplomatic negotiations, it contained no threat or hint of war or armed attack.

It will be recorded that the distance of Hawaii from Japan makes it obvious that the attack was deliberately planned many days or even weeks ago. During the intervening time the Japanese Government has deliberately sought to deceive the United States by false statements and expressions of hope for continued peace.

The attack yesterday on the Hawaiian Islands has caused severe damage to American naval and military forces. Very many American lives have been lost. In addition American ships have been reported torpedoed on the high seas between San Francisco and Honolulu.

Yesterday the Japanese Government also launched an attack against Malaya.

Last night Japanese forces attacked Hong Kong.

Last night Japanese forces attacked Guam.

Last night Japanese forces attacked the Philippine Islands.

Last night the Japanese attacked Wake Island.

This morning the Japanese attacked Midway Island.

Japan has, therefore, undertaken a surprise offensive extending throughout the Pacific area. The facts of yesterday speak for themselves. The people of the United States have already formed their opinions and well understand the implications to the very life and safety of our Nation.

As Commander in Chief of the Army and Navy I have directed that all measures be taken for our defense.

Always will we remember the character of the onslaught against us.

No matter how long it may take us to overcome this premeditated invasion, the American people in their righteous might will win through to absolute victory.

I believe I interpret the will of the Congress and of the people when I assert that we will not only defend ourselves to the uttermost but will make very certain that this form of treachery shall never endanger us again.

Hostilities exist. There is no blinking at the fact that our people, our territory, and our interests are in grave danger.

With confidence in our armed forces—with the unbounded determination of our people —we will gain the inevitable triumph—so help us God.

I ask that the Congress declare that since the unprovoked and dastardly attack by Japan on Sunday, December seventh, a state of war has existed between the United States and the Japanese Empire.

34.

Germany and Italy Declare War

December 1941

Appearances notwithstanding, the September 4, 1941, German attack on the USS *Greer* was an ambiguous event. After making sonar contact with U-652, the destroyer had assumed a bow-on, narrow-target orientation to the submarine and trailed it for three hours, relaying its position to an RAF plane circling overhead. Finally, the plane, running low on fuel, dropped four depth charges before flying off.

The U-652 commander responded by firing at the *Greer*, which he mistook for one of the American destroyers transferred to the Royal Navy in the destroyers-for-bases deal. President Roosevelt likely knew all of this when he announced on September 11, "These Nazi submarines and raiders are the rattlesnakes of the Atlantic....In the waters which we deem necessary for our defense, American naval vessels and American planes will no longer wait until Axis submarines lurking under the water, or Axis raiders on the surface of the sea, strike their deadly blow—first....From now on, if German or Italian vessels enter the waters, the protection of which is necessary for American defense, they do so at their own peril."

Roosevelt later described this policy as "shoot on sight," which sounded very much like war. Yet, even after the sinking of the *Reuben James*, he refused to seek a declaration of war against Germany because, like Hitler, he wanted more time. To Roosevelt, this meant more time to retool America's factories for defense; to

Hitler, it meant more time to complete Operation Barbarossa. The Japanese attack on Pearl Harbor, however, created an unexpected wrinkle in German-American relations.

It remains an open question whether the United States would have declared war on Germany had Hitler not declared war first. What would have been the pretext? How could the Japanese attack on Pearl Harbor have provided sufficient justification when the German sinking of the *Reuben James* had not? Furthermore, Hitler was under no treaty obligation to join Japan's war because Japan had been the aggressor. In fact, as Churchill feared, all manner of mischief might have resulted from the Japanese attack had Hitler not declared war on December 11. For instance, the American public would have surely demanded that munitions allocated to Britain be redirected to support America's only declared war—the one against Japan. Fortunately for Roosevelt's, Hitler's rather impetuous move meant that he wouldn't have to face such choices.

U.S. NOW AT WAR WITH GERMANY AND ITALY

War Opened on Us; Congress Acts Quickly as President Meets Hitler Challenge

By FRANK L. KLUCKHOHN

WASHINGTON, Dec. 11—The United States declared war today on Germany and Italy, Japan's Axis partners. This nation acted swiftly after Germany formally declared war on us and Italy followed the German lead. Thus, President Roosevelt told Congress in his message, the long-known and the long-expected has taken place.

"The forces endeavoring to enslave the entire world now are moving toward this hemisphere," he said.

"Never before has there been a greater challenge to life, liberty and civilization."

Delay, the President said, invites great danger. But he added:

"Rapid and united effort by all of the peoples of the world who are determined to remain free will insure a world victory of the forces of justice and righteousness over the forces of savagery and barbarism."

For the first time in its history the United States finds itself at war against powers in both the Atlantic and the Pacific.

Congress acted not only rapidly but without a dissenting vote to meet the Axis challenge. Within two and three-quarters hours after the reading of Mr. Roosevelt's message was started in the Senate and House at 12:26 P.M., the President had signed the declarations against Germany and Italy. Seventy-two hours previously the Japanese attack on Hawaii had brought about the declaration of war against the other Axis partner.

Congress also quickly completed legislation to allow selectees and National Guardsmen to serve outside the Western Hemisphere and set the term of service in the nation's forces until six months after the termination of the war.

In the Senate the vote was 88 to 0 for war against Germany and 90 to 0 for war against Italy. The vote in the House was 393 to 0 for war against Germany and 399 to 0 for war against Italy. The larger Congressional vote against Italy was attributable to the fact that some members reached the floor too late to vote on the declaration against Germany.

In the House, Miss Jeannette Rankin, Republican, of Montana, who cast the lone dissenting vote on Monday against declaring war on Japan, today voted a non-committal "present" with regard to Germany and Italy.

Ignoring Hitler's declarations before the Reichstag today regarding American policy, and Mussolini's to a crowd before the Palazzo di Venezia in Rome, Congress adopted identical resolutions against Germany and Italy. It merely noted that their governments had thrust war upon the United States.

Congress acted in a grim mood, but without excitement. Not only on the floors of the Senate and House, but in the galleries the grim mood prevailed. President Roosevelt, busy at the White House directing the battle and production effort as Commander in Chief, did not appear to read his message, as he did when war was declared upon Japan.

There was a deeply solemn undernote as the members assembled at noon. Senator Walsh, chairman of the Senate Naval Affairs Committee, had announced that the naval casualty lists resulting from the Japanese bombing of Pearl

Harbor Sunday had arrived, and that families would be notified by the Navy Department as soon as possible.

Tonight the State Department called newspaper offices to announce that the Hungarian Government had broken off diplomatic relations with the United States. Notice was given to the United States Minister to Budapest at 8 P.M., Budapest time [2 P.M. Eastern standard time], by the Hungarian Prime Minister. The State Department's announcement said:

> "The Hungarian Prime Minister at 8 P.M. informed the American Minister that in view of the solidarity of the Central European States, which he compared with the solidarity of the States of the Western Hemisphere, Hungary was obliged to break diplomatic relations with the United States. He said this was not with the intention of declaring war on this country."

The declarations against Germany and Italy pledged all the resources of United States manpower, material and production "to bring the conflict to a successful termination." After signing that against Germany at 3:05 P.M., and that against Italy at 3:06 P.M., before the same group of congressional leaders who on Monday saw him sign the declaration against Japan, President Roosevelt remarked:

"I've always heard things came in threes. Here they are."

Senator Glass of Virginia, who was Secretary of the Treasury in the last World War, told Mr. Roosevelt that "some men in the Senate Foreign Relations Committee wanted to soften the resolutions so as not to hurt the feelings of civilians in the Axis countries.

"I said, 'Hell, we not only want to hurt their feelings but we want to kill them,'" the Virginian remarked.

As a result of the ending of peace between Germany and the United States, which has

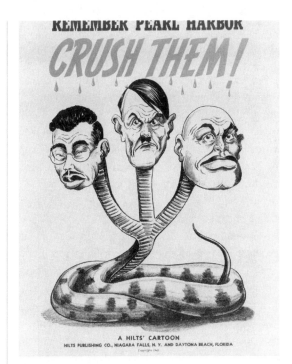

This 1942 poster uses the images of a three-headed hydra (with the visages of Hirohito, Hitler, and Mussolini) to remind Americans of the threat posed by the Axis.

existed, at least formally, for twenty-three years, the United States is at war with Germany, Italy, Japan and Manchukuo, and Hungary has suspended diplomatic relations.

Among the countries at war with one or all of the Axis powers are Great Britain, Canada, Australia, New Zealand, South Africa, the Soviet Union, China, the Netherands Government and its East Indies possessions; the refugee governments of France, Belgium, Poland, Greece, Yugoslavia, Czechoslovakia and Norway; and these others in the Western Hemisphere: Panama, Nicaragua, El Salvador, Honduras, Haiti, the Dominican Republic, Cuba and Guatemala.

Announcement was made early in the day that the President would send a message to Congress. This was soon after Hans Thomsen, German chargé d'affaires, delivered the Nazi dictator's declaration of war to the State Department at 8:15 A.M. and after the Italian declaration was delivered to George Wadsworth, American chargé d'affaires in Rome.

Stephen Early, Presidential secretary, told reporters that "as expected," Germany had declared war and "Italy had goose-stepped along, apparently following orders."

After the declaration against Germany was voted the commotion in the House gallery was so great that Speaker Rayburn suspended proceedings until all the visitors who wished to depart had done so. About three-quarters of those in the galleries then left.

Viscount Halifax, the British Ambassador, sat in the front row of the Senate diplomatic gallery with Lady Halifax, Dr. A. Loudon, the Netherlands Minister, and Henrik de Kaufmann, the Danish Minister.

They saw the Senate vote the resolution for war against Germany in five minutes after the start of the President's message, time taken up largely with recording the vote. The House, with a larger roll-call, took twelve minutes to record its unanimous vote. Both houses acted in more leisurely fashion with regard to Italy. The Senate took another thirteen minutes, and the House completed action in another twenty minutes.

The signing ceremony was equally simple and rapid. Congressional leaders did not reach the White House until a minute after 3 P.M. Those present were Vice President Wallace, Senate Majority Leader Barkley, Chairman Connally of the Senate Foreign Relations Committee, Senate Minority Leader McNary and Senators Austin and Glass. From the House came Speaker Rayburn, Majority Leader McCormick, Chairman Bloom of the Foreign Affairs Committee, Minority Leader Martin and Representatives Eaton of New Jersey and Luther Johnson of Texas.

Earlier in the day the President sent telegrams to Representative Martin, as chairman of the Republican National Committee, and to Edward J. Flynn, chairman of the Democratic National Committee, thanking them for the patriotic action of both major parties in eschewing partisan politics and thus promoting unity.

"The powers behind Roosevelt were those I had fought."

Excerpt from Hitler's speech to the Reichstag declaring war on the United States

Hitler's announcement was typically long and turgid. This excerpt represents somewhat less than half of the full speech; the rest Hitler devoted primarily to praising Germany and recounting its many recent military triumphs.

And now permit me to define my attitude to that other world, which has its representative in that man, who, while our soldiers are fighting in snow and ice, very tactfully likes to make his chats from the fireside, the man who is the main culprit of this war. When in 1939 the conditions of our national interest in the then Polish State became more and more intolerable, I tried at first to eliminate those intolerable conditions by way of a peaceful settlement. For some time it seemed as though the Polish Government itself had seriously considered to agree to a sensible settlement. I may add that in German proposals nothing was demanded that had not been German property in former times. On the contrary, we renounced very much of what, before the World War, had been German property. You will recall the dramatic development of that time, in which the sufferings of German nationals increased continuously. You, my deputies, are in the best position to gauge the extent of the blood sacrifice, if you compare it to the casualties of the present war. The campaign in the East has so far cost the German armed forces about 160,000 killed; but in the midst of peace more than 62,000 Germans were killed during those months, some under the most cruel tortures. It could hardly be contested that the German Reich had a right to object to such conditions on its Frontiers and to demand that they should cease to exist and that it was entitled to think of its own safety; this could hardly be contested at a time when other countries were seeking elements of their safety even on foreign continents. The problems which had to be overcome were of no territorial significance. Mainly they concerned Danzig and the union with the Reich of the torn-off province, East Prussia. More difficult were the cruel persecutions the Germans were exposed to, in Poland particularly. The other minorities, incidentally, had to suffer a fate hardly less bitter.

When in August the attitude of Poland—thanks to the *carte blanche* guarantee received from England—became still stiffer, the Government of the Reich found it necessary to submit, for the last time, a proposal on the basis of which we were willing to enter into negotiations with Poland—negotiations of which we fully and completely apprised the then British Ambassador. I may recall these proposals today: "Proposal for the settlement of the problem of the Danzig Corridor and of the question of the German-Polish minorities. The situation between the German Reich and Poland has become so strained that any further incident may lead to a clash between the Armed Forces assembled on both sides. Any peaceful settlement must be so arranged that the events mainly responsible for the existing situation cannot occur again—a situation which has caused a state of tension, not only in Eastern Europe, but also in other regions. The cause of this situation lies in the impossible Frontiers laid down by the Versailles dictate and the inhuman treatment of the German minorities in Poland." I am now going to read the proposals in question.

[Hitler then proceeded to read the first twelve points of these proposals.] The same goes for the proposals for safeguarding the minorities. This is the offer of an agreement such as could not have been made in a more loyal and magnanimous form by any government other than the National Socialist Government of the German Reich.

The Polish Government at that period refused even as much as to consider this proposal. The question then arises: how could such an unimportant State dare simply to refuse an offer of this nature and, furthermore, not only indulge in further atrocities to its German inhabitants who had given that country the whole of its culture, but even order mobilization? Perusal of documents of the Foreign Office in Warsaw has given us later some surprising explanations. There was one man who, with devilish lack of conscience, used all his influence to further the warlike intentions of Poland and to eliminate all possibilities of understanding. The reports which the then Polish Ambassador in Washington, Count Potocki, sent to his Government are documents from which it may be seen with a terrifying clearness to what an extent one man alone and the forces driving him are responsible for the second World War. The question next arises, how could this man fall into such fanatical enmity toward a country which in the whole of its history has never done the least harm either to America or to him personally?

So far as Germany's attitude towards America is concerned, I have to state: (i) Germany is perhaps the only great power which has never had a colony either in North or South America, or otherwise displayed there any political activity, unless mention be made of the emigration of many millions of Germans and of their work, which, however, has only been to the benefit of the American Continent and of the U.S.A. (ii) In the whole history of the coming into being and of the existence of the U.S.A. the German Reich has never adopted a politically unfriendly, let alone hostile attitude, but, on the contrary with the blood of many of its sons, it helped to defend the U.S.A. The German Reich never took part in any war against the U.S.A. It itself had war imposed upon it by the U.S.A. in 1917, and then for reasons which have been thoroughly revealed by an investigation committee set up by President Roosevelt himself. There are no other differences between the German and the American people, either territorial or political, which could possibly touch the interests let alone the existence of the U.S.A. There was always a difference of constitution, but that cannot be a reason for hostilities so long as the one state does not try to interfere with the other. America is a Republic, a Democracy, and today is a Republic under strong authoritative leadership. The ocean lies between the two States. The divergences between Capitalist America and Bolshevik Russia, if such conceptions had any truth in them, would be much greater than between America led by a President and Germany led by a Führer.

But it is a fact that the two conflicts between Germany and the U.S.A. were inspired by the same force and caused by two men in the U.S.A.—Wilson and Roosevelt. History has already passed its verdict on Wilson; his name stands for one of the basest breaches of the given word, that led to disruption not only among the so-called vanquished, but also among the victors. This breach of his word alone made possible the Dictate of Versailles. We know today that a group of interested financiers stood behind Wilson and made use of this paralytic professor because they hoped for increased business. The German people have had to pay for having believed this man with the collapse of their political and economic existence.

But why is there now another President of the U.S.A. who regards it as his only task to intensify anti-German feeling to the pitch of war? National Socialism came to power in Germany in the same year as Roosevelt was elected President. I understand only too well that a world-wide distance separates Roosevelt's ideas and my ideas. Roosevelt comes from a rich family and belongs to the class whose path is smoothed in the Democracies. I am only the child of a small, poor family and had to fight my way by work and industry. When the Great War came, Roosevelt occupied a position where he got to know only its pleasant consequences, enjoyed by those who do business while others bleed. I was only one of those who carry out orders, as an ordinary soldier, and naturally returned from the war just as poor as I was in Autumn 1914. I shared the fate of millions, and Franklin Roosevelt only the fate of the so-called Upper Ten Thousand.

After the war Roosevelt tried his hand at financial speculation: he made profits out of the inflation, out of the misery of others, while I, together with many hundreds of thousands more, lay in hospital. When Roosevelt finally stepped on the political stage with all the advantages of his class, I was unknown and fought for the resurrection of my people. When Roosevelt took his place at the head of the U.S.A., he was the candidate of a Capitalist Party which made use of him; when I became Chancel-lor of the German Reich, I was the Führer of the popular movement I had created. The powers behind Roosevelt were those powers I had fought at home. The Brain Trust was composed of people such as we have fought against in Germany as parasites and removed from public life.

And yet there is something in common between us. Roosevelt took over a State in a very poor economic condition, and I took over a Reich faced with complete ruin, also thanks to Democracy. In the U.S.A. there were 13,000,000 unemployed, and in Germany 7,000,000 part-time workers. The finances of both States were in a bad way, and ordinary economic life could scarcely be maintained. A development then started in the U.S.A. and in the German Reich which will make it easy for posterity to pass a verdict on the correctness of the theories.

While an unprecedented revival of economic life, culture and art took place in Germany under National Socialist leadership within the space of a few years, President Roosevelt did not succeed in bringing about even the slightest improvements in his own country. And yet this work must have been much easier in the U.S.A. where there live scarcely 15 persons on a square kilometer, as against 140 in Germany. If such a country does not succeed in assuring economic prosperity, this must be a result either of the bad faith of its leaders in power, or of a total inefficiency on the part of the leading men. In scarcely five years, economic problems had been solved in

A third grader at the Lincoln School of Teachers' College, Columbia University, acts the part of Hitler in a 1942 theatrical produced by his class.

Germany and unemployment had been overcome. During the same period, President Roosevelt had increased the State Debt of his country to an enormous extent, had decreased the value of the dollar, had brought about a further disintegration of economic life, without diminishing the unemployment figures. All this is not surprising if one bears in mind that the men he had called to support him, or rather, the men who had called him, belonged to the Jewish element, whose interests are all for disintegration and never for order. While speculation was being fought in National Socialist Germany, it thrived astoundingly under the Roosevelt regime.

Roosevelt's New Deal legislation was all wrong: it was actually the biggest failure ever experienced by one man. There can be no doubt that a continuation of this economic policy would have done in this President in peace time, in spite of all his dialectical skill. In a European State he would surely have come eventually before a State Court on a charge of deliberate waste of the national wealth; and he would have scarcely escaped at the hands of a Civil Court, on a charge of criminal business methods.

This fact was realized and fully appreciated also by many Americans including some of high standing. A threatening opposition was gathering over the head of this man. He guessed that the only salvation for him lay in diverting public attention from home to foreign policy. It is interesting to study in this connection the reports of the Polish Envoy in Washington, Potocki. He repeatedly points out that Roosevelt was fully aware of the danger threatening the card castle of his economic system with collapse, and that he was therefore urgently in need of a diversion in foreign policy. He was strengthened in this resolve by the Jews around him. Their Old Testament thirst for revenge thought to see in the U.S.A. an instrument for preparing a second "Purim" for the European nations which were becoming increasingly anti-Semitic. The full diabolical meanness of Jewry rallied round this man, and he stretched out his hands.

Thus began the increasing efforts of the American President to create conflicts, to do everything to prevent conflicts from being peacefully solved. For years this man harboured one desire—that a conflict should break out somewhere in the world. The most convenient place would be in Europe, where the American economy could be committed to the cause of one of the belligerents in such a way that a political interconnection of interests would arise calculated slowly to bring America nearer such a conflict. This would thereby divert public interest from bankrupt economic policy at home towards foreign problems.

His attitude to the German Reich in this spirit was particularly sharp. In 1937, Roosevelt made a number of speeches, including a particularly mean one pronounced in Chicago on 5th October, 1937. Systematically he began to incite American public opinion against Germany. He threatened to establish a kind of Quarantine against the so-called Authoritarian States. While making these increasingly spiteful and inflammatory speeches, President Roosevelt summoned the American Ambassador to Washington to report to him. This event followed some further declarations of an insulting character; and ever since, the two countries have been connected with each other only through Chargés d'Affaires.

From November 1938 onwards, his systematic efforts were directed towards sabotaging any possibility of an appeasement policy in Europe. In public, he was hypocritically pretending to be for peace; but at the same time he was threatening any country ready to pursue a policy of peaceful understanding with the freezing of assets, with economic reprisals, with demands for the repayment of loans, etc. Staggering information to this effect can be derived from the reports of Polish Ambassadors in Washington, London, Paris and Brussels.

In January, 1939, this man began to strengthen his campaign of incitement and threatened to take all possible Congressional measures against the Authoritarian States, with the exception of war, while

alleging that other countries were trying to interfere in American affairs and insisting on the maintenance of the Monroe Doctrine; he himself began, from March 1939 onwards, to meddle in European
affairs which were no concern at all of the President of the U.S.A., since he does not understand those
problems, and even if he did understand them and the historic background behind them, he would
have just as little right to worry about the central European area as the German Reich has to judge
conditions in a U.S. State and to take an attitude towards them.

But Mr. Roosevelt went even farther. In contradiction to all the tenets of international law, he
declared that he would not recognize certain Governments which did not suit him, would not accept
readjustments, would maintain Legations of States dissolved long before or actually set them up as
legal Governments. He even went so far as to conclude agreements with such Envoys, and thus to
acquire a right simply to occupy foreign territories.

On 5th April, 1939, came Roosevelt's famous appeal to myself and the Duce. It was a clumsy combination of geographical and political ignorance and of the arrogance of the millionaire circles around
him. It asked us to give undertakings to conclude non-aggression Pacts indiscriminately with any
country, including mostly countries which were not even free, since Mr. Roosevelt's allies had annexed
them or changed them into Protectorates. You will remember, my Deputies, that I then gave a polite
and clear reply to this meddling gentleman. For some months at least, this stopped the flow of elo-
quence from this honest warmonger. But his place was taken by his honourable spouse. She declined to
live with her sons in a world such as the one we have worked out. And quite right, for this is a world of
labour and not of cheating and trafficking.

After a little rest, the husband of that woman came back on the scene and on the 4th November,
1939, engineered the reversion of the Neutrality Law so as to suspend the ban on the export of arms,
in favor of a one-sided delivery of arms to Germany's opponents. He then begins, somewhat as in Asia
and in China, by the roundabout way of an economic infiltration to establish a community of interests
destined to become operative sooner or later. In the same month, he recognizes, as a so-called Government in exile, a gang of Polish emigrants, whose only political foundation was a few million gold coins
taken with them from Warsaw. On the 9th of April he goes on and he orders the blocking of Norwegian
and Danish assets under the lying pretext of placing them beyond the German reach, although he
knows perfectly well that the Danish Government in its financial administration is not in any way
being interfered with, let alone controlled, by Germany. To the various exiled Governments recognized by him, the Norwegian is now added. On the 15th May, 1940, he recognizes the Dutch and Belgian emigre Governments. This is followed by blocking Dutch and Belgian assets. His true mentality
then comes clearly to light in a telegram of 15th June to the French Prime Minister, Reynaud. He
advises him that the American government will double its help to France, provided that France continues the war against Germany. So as to give still greater expression to this, his wish for a continuation of the war, he issues a, declaration that the American Government will not recognize the results
of the conquest of territories—i.e., the restoration to Germany of lands which had been stolen from
her. I don't need to assure you, Members of the Reichstag, that it is a matter of complete indifference
to every German Government whether the President of the U.S.A. recognizes the frontiers of Europe
or no, and that this indifference will likewise continue, in the future. I merely quote this to illustrate
the methodical incitement which has come from this man who speaks hypocritically of peace, but
always urges to war.

But now he is seized with fear that if peace is brought about in Europe, his squandering of billions
of money on armaments will be looked upon as plain fraud, since nobody will attack America—and he

then himself must provoke this attack upon his country. On the 17th July, 1940, the American President orders the blocking of French assets with a view, as he puts it, to placing them beyond German reach, but really in order to transfer the French gold from Casablanca to America with the assistance of an American cruiser. In July 1940 he tries by enlisting American citizens in the British Air Force and by training British airmen in the U.S.A. to pave ever better the way to war. In August 1940, a military programme is jointly drawn up between the U.S.A. and Canada. To make the establishment of a Canadian-U.S. Defence Committee plausible—plausible at least to the biggest fools—he invents from time to time crises, by means of which he pretends that America is being threatened with aggression....

I will pass over the insulting attacks made by this so-called President against me. That he calls me a gangster is uninteresting. After all, this expression was not coined in Europe but in America, no doubt because such gangsters are lacking here. Apart from this, I cannot be insulted by Roosevelt for I consider him mad just as Wilson was. I don't need to mention what this man has done for years in the same way against Japan. First he incites war then falsifies the causes, then odiously wraps himself in a cloak of Christian hypocrisy and slowly but surely leads mankind to war, not without calling God to witness the honesty of his attack—in the approved manner of an old Freemason. I think you have all found it a relief that now, at last, one State has been the first to take the step of protest against his historically unique and shameless ill-treatment of truth, and of right—which protest this man has desired and about which he cannot complain. The fact that the Japanese Government, which has been negotiating for years with this man, has at last become tired of being mocked by him in such an unworthy way, fills us all, the German people, and I think, all other decent people in the world, with deep satisfaction.

We have seen what the Jews have done in Soviet Russia. We have made the acquaintance of the Jewish Paradise on earth. Millions of German soldiers have been able to see this country where the international Jews have destroyed people and property. The President of the U.S.A. ought finally to understand—I say this only because of his limited intellect—that we know that the aim of this struggle is to destroy one State after another. But the present German Reich has nothing more in common with the old Germany. And we, for our part, will now do what this provocateur has been trying to do so much for years. Not only because we are the ally of Japan, but also because Germany and Italy have enough insight and strength to comprehend that, in these historic times, the existence or non-existence of the nations is being decided perhaps for ever. We clearly see the intention of the rest of the world towards us. They reduced Democratic Germany to hunger. They would exterminate our social things of today. When Churchill and Roosevelt state that they want to build up a new social order, later on, it is like a hairdresser with a bald head recommending an unfortunate hair-restorer. These men, who live in the most socially backward states, have misery and distress enough in their own countries to occupy themselves with the distribution of foodstuffs.

As for the German nation, it needs charity neither from Mr. Churchill nor from Mr. Roosevelt, let alone from Mr. Eden. It wants only its rights! It will secure for itself this right to life even if thousands of Churchills and Roosevelts conspire against it.

In the whole history of the German nation, of nearly 2,000 years, it has never been so united as today and, thanks to National Socialism, it will remain united in the future. Probably it has never seen so clearly, and rarely been so conscious of its honour. I have therefore arranged for his passports to be handed to the American Chargé d'Affaires today, and the following...[drowned in applause].

As a consequence of the further extension of President Roosevelt's policy, which is aimed at unrestricted world domination and dictatorship, the U.S.A. together with England have not hesitated from using any means to dispute the rights of the German, Italian and Japanese nations to the basis of their natural existence. The Governments of the U.S.A. and of England have therefore resisted, not only now but also for all time, every just understanding meant to bring about a better New Order in the world. Since the beginning of the war the American President, Roosevelt, has been guilty of a series of the worst crimes against international law; illegal seizure of ships and other property of German and Italian nationals were coupled with the threat to, and looting of, those who were deprived of their liberty by being interned. Roosevelt's ever-increasing attacks finally went so far that he ordered the American Navy to attack everywhere ships under the German and Italian flags, and to sink them—this in gross violation of international law. American ministers boasted of having destroyed German submarines in this criminal way. German and Italian merchantships were attacked by American cruisers, captured and their crews imprisoned. With no attempt at an official denial there has now been revealed in America President Roosevelt's plan by which, at the latest in 1943, Germany and Italy were to be attacked in Europe by military means. In this way the sincere efforts of Germany and Italy to prevent an extension of the war and to maintain relations with the U.S.A. in spite of the unbearable provocations which have been carried on for years by President Roosevelt, have been frustrated. Germany and Italy have been finally compelled, in view of this, and in loyalty to the Tri-Partite Pact, to carry on the struggle against the U.S.A. and England jointly and side by side with Japan for the defense and thus for the maintenance of the liberty and independence of their nations and empires.

35

The Internment of Japanese Americans
February 1942

Whites on the West Coast had long distrusted and persecuted the region's Asian minorities. Therefore, it came as no surprise when, not long after Pearl Harbor, public pressure built for the government to take action against the "threat" posed by allegedly disloyal Japanese Americans. Californians became particularly hysterical when a federal report issued in late January 1942 asserted that Japan's Hawaii-

based agents had included American citizens of Japanese descent.

Ironically, FBI director J. Edgar Hoover was not among those pressing for evacuation of the Japanese from the West Coast. Government surveillance operations, begun during the mid-1930s, had identified about two thousand suspected Japanese subversives, all of whom were taken into custody during late 1941—along with fourteen thousand German and Italian security risks. These detentions satisfied Hoover that the sabotage threat had been contained. Yet they didn't satisfy Lt. Gen. John L. De Witt, head of the army's Western Defense Command, who recommended to Secretary of War Henry L. Stimson that all Japanese, whether citizens or not, be completely evacuated from the Pacific Coast military zone. "A Jap's a Jap," De Witt said. "...I don't want any of them."

Mindful of his constitutional responsibilities, Attorney General Francis Biddle initially opposed De Witt's position, but when Stimson pressured Biddle strongly on February 17, the attorney general relented. Two days later, with little discussion, President Roosevelt signed Executive Order 9066, directing the War Department to "prescribe military areas...from which any and all persons may be excluded." This order provided all the legal basis deemed necessary for the evacuation and subsequent internment of the Japanese (whom it never mentioned specifically).

During the next month, fifteen thousand Japanese voluntarily left the West Coast to stay with friends and family in the East and Midwest. (Japanese outside De Witt's jurisdiction were never subjected to internment.) On March 27, however, De Witt issued a "freeze order" that prevented any further voluntary resettlement. Instead, he directed all of the remaining Japanese in the Pacific Coast military zone to report to "assembly centers," from which they were later transferred inland to more permanent "relocation centers" in the parched, barren shadow of the Sierra Nevada. Within weeks, more than a hundred thousand people, most of them American citizens, were forced to uproot themselves for what would be an unspecified period. Furthermore, they were given precious little time to make arrangements for their houses and businesses, creating quite a buyer's market.

This May 1942 photograph by Dorothea Lange shows Japanese Americans waiting for the special bus that will take them to the Tanforan Assembly Center. The father of this small family can be seen in the background, attending to their luggage and bedrolls.

ENEMY ALIENS BAFFLE WEST COAST AUTHORITY

Restrictions Prove Hard to Enforce and Problems Are Many and Varied

By LAWRENCE E. DAVIES

SAN FRANCISCO, Feb. 14—Many a habitation—a squalid shack, quarters in a boarding-house or a well-kept seven-room dwelling—was being vacated this week as enemy aliens in "prohibited" areas of the West Coast began to find new homes in line with a steadily developing program of the War and Justice Departments aimed at solving a highly perplexing wartime problem.

All of these things were happening because of what happened at Pearl Harbor. Realization of the part played in the Japanese attack there by the Fifth Column in Hawaii aroused the Pacific Coast and Federal officials in Washington to an awareness of what might happen here unless early, and extensive, precautionary steps were taken.

People began asking what 18,000 Japanese aliens in this State, and several thousand in Oregon and Washington, might do to sabotage defense plants or to aid invaders if they were permitted to live and travel without restriction with short-wave radio sets, powerful searchlights and other signaling devices, rifles and ammunition. California possessed at the same time an estimated 52,000 Italian aliens and 19,000 Germans.

Here, then, on Dec. 7 was a potential West Coast Fifth Column army of perhaps 120,000 members and the Japanese problem was heightened by the "dual citizenship" held by an unknown number of American-born Japanese. How many of these second-generation Japanese could be trusted?

Step by step, but far too slowly to suit many critics, the Department of Justice has sought to cope with the problems presented. It made such things as radio sets, arms and flashlights contraband when held by nationals of Japan, Germany and Italy, and ordered their surrender. It made travel by enemy aliens vastly more difficult and, in many cases, impossible. At the recommendation of the War Department, which had conducted its own West Coast survey and in turn had received suggestions from the Navy, Attorney General Biddle began plotting a new way of life for thousands of Coast aliens.

He established well over 100 restricted areas near vital defense plants and military installations in Oregon, Washington and California, in some of which after next Monday and Feb. 24, respectively, no enemy alien may set foot under penalty of internment. And a great section of the California coast, from thirty to 150 miles inland and extending from the Oregon border southward more than 500 miles, he made a "curfew" zone in which enemy aliens must remain at home from 9 P.M. to 6 A.M.

Meanwhile the Federal Bureau of Investigation was raiding Shinto and Buddhist temples, arresting in one instance a "priest" identified as a former police officer in Japan, and finding contraband materials as well as "dangerous" aliens in Japanese colonies in far-separated cities of the Coast. The "boss man"—known in the community as "the emperor"—of a farm colony of Japanese in the Salinas Valley, many of whom did not speak English, was one of the prisoners.

Along with the closing of foreign language schools, which have been widely regarded as Fascist propaganda centers, these represent the chief steps taken to date by Federal agencies, amid continued agitation for more vigorous action. Much of this agitation falls about the ears of a mild-mannered Texan named Thomas C. Clark, who temporarily has quit "trust busting" for Thurman Arnold to labor under the title of Coordinator of Enemy Control for the Western Defense Command. He has heard growing demands for the declaration of at least a modified martial law, so that American-born Japanese suspected of disloyalty might be moved out of vital areas along with the aliens.

The California personnel board, in spite of an opinion of Earl Warren, State Attorney General, that its action was discriminatory and illegal, prepared to circulate a questionnaire among all Japanese-Americans in the State's employ and on its civil service–eligible list to try to determine who were "dual citizens" or "disloyal Americans" preparatory to initiating ouster proceedings.

What do the Japanese-Americans think of the situation? According to their more rabid critics, it is impossible to ascertain what they think. But leaders of the Japanese-American Citizens League, with a membership of 20,000, have told this correspondent that they have "great faith" in the Federal Government, which they think has been "very fair." One of them expressed it this way:

"Many of us are confronted with questions of investments, our homes, our businesses and we don't want to give them up. But if the Federal Government decided definitely that, in the interest of national defense, martial law ought to be declared and the citizens as well as the Japanese aliens should be told to get out, why, then, we are ready to follow orders. But if it's dangerous for second-generation Japanese to remain, what of second-generation Italians and Germans? Discrimination like that is what we would object to."

Another speaks of the "resentment" shown by Japanese adolescents in the country over Pearl Harbor.

"Resentment against whom?" one is asked.

"Against Japan," is the reply.

This Japanese-American grocery store in Oakland was closed following the evacuation order. Its owner had put up the I AM AN AMERICAN sign the day after the attack on Pearl Harbor.

In the same vein are stories told the writer by public school teachers. After the first blackout of San Francisco a six-year-old American-born Japanese said to his teacher: "I couldn't sleep during the blackout; I was afraid the Japanese would come."

There is a pretty definite feeling, among officials as well as aliens, that the greatest need is immediate, positive, vigorous action, so that everybody will know just where he stands. Let this statement be applied, for purposes of illustration, to the agricultural situation. The Japanese, through long training, have developed a very specialized technique in tomato culture, with the result that a substantial part of the tomato plants produced for transplanting in California are raised by Japanese. Any dislocation in the present status of Japanese farm labor therefore would result in some curtailment of the tomato acreage, according to agricultural experts.

This is one of the factors to be carefully weighed before a final answer will be given to this most serious and complex question.

"Can this be the same America we left a few weeks ago?"

Description of life in an internment camp

This article appeared in the June 15, 1942, issue of *The New Republic*. Its author, Ted Nakashima, was thirty years old when the government ordered him to take his family to Camp Harmony, an assembly center located at the Puyallup, Washington, fairgrounds. The Nakashimas were later transferred to a relocation center in Idaho. After the war, Nakashima worked as a chicken farmer in Spokane before spending his later years as a director of facilities planning for two Washington school districts.

Concentration Camp: U.S. Style

Unfortunately in this land of liberty, I was born of Japanese parents, born in Seattle of a mother and father who have been in this country since 1901. Fine parents, who brought up their children in the best American way of life. My mother served with the Volunteer Red Cross Service in the last war—my father, an editor, has spoken and written Americanism for forty years.

Our family is almost typical of the other unfortunates here at the camp. The oldest son, a licensed architect, was educated at the University of Washington, has a master's degree from the Massachusetts Institute of Technology and is a scholarship graduate of the American School of Fine Arts in Fontainebleau, France. He is now in camp in Oregon with his wife and three-months-old child. He had just completed designing a much-needed defense housing project at Vancouver, Washington.

The second son is an M.D. He served his internship in a New York hospital, is married and has two fine sons. The folks banked on him, because he was the smartest of us three boys. The army took him a month after he opened his office. He is now a lieutenant in the Medical Corps, somewhere in the South.

I am the third son, the dumbest of the lot, but still smart enough to hold down a job as an architectural draftsman. I have just finished building a new home and had lived in it three weeks. My desk was just cleared of work done for the Army Engineers, [and] another stack of 391 defense houses was waiting (a rush job), when the order came to pack up and leave for this resettlement center called "Camp Harmony."

Mary, the only girl in the family, and her year-old son, "Butch," are with our parents—interned in the stables of the Livestock Exposition Buildings in Portland.

Now that you can picture our thoroughly American background, let me describe our new home.

The resettlement center is actually a penitentiary—armed guards in towers with spotlights and deadly tommy guns, fifteen feet of barbed-wire fences, everyone confined to quarters at nine, lights out at ten o'clock. The guards are ordered to shoot anyone who approaches within twenty feet of the fences. No one is allowed to take the two-block-long hike to the latrines after nine, under any circumstances.

The apartments, as the army calls them, are two-block-long stables, with windows on one side. Floors are shiplaps on two-by-fours laid directly on the mud, which is everywhere. The stalls are about eighteen by twenty-one feet; some contain families of six or seven persons. Partitions are seven feet high, leaving a four-foot opening above. The rooms aren't too bad, almost fit to live in for a short while.

The food and sanitation problems are the worst. We have had absolutely no fresh meat, vegetables or butter since we came here. Mealtime queues extend for blocks: standing in a rainswept line, feet in the mud, waiting for the scant portions of canned wieners and boiled potatoes, hash for breakfast or canned wieners and beans for dinner. Milk only for the kids. Coffee or tea dosed with saltpeter and stale bread are the adults' staples. Dirty, unwiped dishes, greasy silver, a starchy diet, no butter, no milk, bawling kids, mud, wet mud that stinks when it dries, no vegetables—a sad thing for the people who raised them in such abundance. Memories of a crisp head of lettuce with our special olive oil, vinegar, garlic and cheese dressing.

Today one of the surface sewage-disposal pipes broke and the sewage flowed down the streets. Kids play in the water. Shower baths without hot water. Stinking mud and slops everywhere.

Can this be the same America we left a few weeks ago?

As I write, I can remember our little bathroom—light coral walls. My wife painting them, and the spilled paint in her hair. The open towel shelving and the pretty shower curtains which we put up the day before we left. How sanitary and clean we left it for the airlines pilot and his young wife who are now enjoying the fruits of our labor.

It all seems so futile, struggling, trying to live our old lives under this useless, regimented life. The senselessness of all the inactive manpower. Electricians, plumbers, draftsmen, mechanics, carpenters, painters, farmers—every trade—men who are able and willing to do all they can to lick the Axis. Thousands of men and women in these camps. Energetic, quick, alert, eager for hard, constructive work, waiting for the army to do something for us, an army that won't give us butter.

I can't take it! I have 391 defense houses to be drawn. I left a fine American home which we built with our own hands. I left a life, highballs with our American friends on weekends, a carpenter, laundry-truck driver, architect, airlines pilot—good friends, friends who would swear by us. I don't have enough of that Japanese heritage *"ga-man"*—a code of silent suffering and ability to stand pain.

Oddly enough I still have a bit of faith in army promises of good treatment and Mrs. Roosevelt's pledge of a future worthy of good American citizens. I'm banking another $67 of income tax on the future. Sometimes I want to spend the money I have set aside for income tax on a bit of butter or ice cream or something good that I might have smuggled through the gates, but I can't do it when I think that every dollar I can put into "the fight to lick the Japs," the sooner I will be home again. I must forget my stomach.

What really hurts most is the constant reference to us evacues as "Japs." "Japs" are the guys we are fighting. We're on this side and we want to help.

Why won't America let us?

ACTION IN THE PACIFIC

36.

The Surrender of Bataan

April 1942

With the U.S. Pacific Fleet temporarily sidelined, Japan had about six months, Yamamoto predicted, to do as it pleased in Southeast Asia. The Japanese navy quickly isolated Hong Kong, which fell on Christmas Day, 1941. Meanwhile, in Malaya, the Japanese army humiliated the defending British colonial forces, who fell back onto Singapore before surrendering on February 15, 1942. Elsewhere, Japanese

soldiers moved through Thailand to attack the British troops in Burma, while the Japanese navy occupied itself conquering the Dutch East Indies.

The Japanese attack on the Philippines, then a U.S. commonwealth, began at noon local time on December 8. Nine hours earlier, Lt. Gen. Douglas MacArthur, commander of the U.S. Army's forces in the Far East, had been informed of the surprise attack on Hawaii. In that message, he was also told to expect a similar raid on Clark Field, the principal U.S. air base in the Far East, located on the main Philippine island of Luzon. Inexplicably, MacArthur took little action, and when the fog-delayed Japanese bombers finally arrived at midday, they found MacArthur's planes lined up in neat rows on the ground, just as the aircraft on Oahu had been. The Japanese were thus able to destroy 105 planes, or a third of the entire U.S. Far East command, while losing only seven planes of their own.

MacArthur never recovered. On December 22, Lt. Gen. Homma Masaharu landed the bulk

of his invasion force on the western coast of Luzon and began driving toward Manila. Two days later, MacArthur finally ordered implementation of Orange 3, a long-laid defense plan calling for the withdrawal of all American and Filipino forces onto the Bataan Peninsula, which jutted out into Manila Bay west of the Philippine capital.

U.S. military planners had estimated that, from this consolidated position, American forces could hold out for up to six months, until relief from the United States could arrive. However, MacArthur's inability to protect his air support and his failure (in his haste) to bring along adequate supplies of food significantly undermined the fighting ability of his troops. By mid-March, the situation on Bataan had become so perilous that President Roosevelt ordered MacArthur to leave the Philippines for Australia in order to avoid capture. Three weeks later, Homma's reinforced army broke through the final defensive line on Bataan and accepted the surrender of seventy-six thousand American and Filipino soldiers.

This captured Japanese photograph shows imperial troops celebrating on Bataan after the surrender of the American forces there.

JAPANESE CAPTURE BATAAN AND 36,000 TROOPS

Defense Crushed; Stimson Reveals Defeat Followed Failure to Get in More Food

By CHARLES HURD

WASHINGTON, April 9—An overwhelming Japanese Army, aided by the allies of hunger, fatigue and disease, today crushed the small mixed force that had held Bataan Peninsula since December.

Japanese forces, heretofore estimated at 200,000 men, including fresh assault troops, and supported by tanks, artillery, bombers and attack planes in profusion, enveloped an exhausted defending army of 36,853 men, as counted officially yesterday afternoon.

The defeat of the American and Filipino forces was officially announced as a "probability" in a War Department communiqué issued as of 5:15 A.M. today. A few hours later Secretary of War Henry L. Stimson announced the defeat at his regularly scheduled weekly press conference. He already had carried the word to President Roosevelt.

When Secretary Stimson met reporters in his conference room he paid the highest praise to the spirit of the defenders in a fight recognized as hopeless from the beginning and pledged that the Philippines would be reconquered. In the same talk he described extraordinary efforts made to provision the garrison, saying that "several shiploads of supplies" were sent into the Philippines, "but for every ship that arrived safely we lost nearly two."

As far as was known here today the rocky fortress of Corregidor Island still held its own astride the entrance to Manila Bay and other troops held adjacent fortified islands. The decision as to whether they should continue fighting was laid squarely on Lieut. Gen. Jonathan M.

Wainwright, to whom President Roosevelt dispatched yesterday a message giving him absolute authority to continue the fight or make terms, as he might see fit.

This responsibility is a heavy one for General Wainwright, for it is assumed here that he lacks transport to take more than a handful of the Bataan forces across the four miles of water that separates Bataan Peninsula from Corregidor. Even so his food is desperately short, Secretary Stimson having said this morning that every man in Bataan had been on short rations since Jan. 11. This was a primary reason for the collapse of the defense after five days of savage hand-to-hand fighting.

The long-expected defeat, which by its deferment wrote an epic in American military history, was officially indicated in War Department Communiqué 183, which read as follows:

"A message from General Wainwright at Fort Mills just received at the War Department states that the Japanese attack on Bataan Peninsula succeeded in enveloping the east flank of our lines, in the position held by the II Corps. An attack by the I Corps, ordered to relieve the situation, failed due to complete physical exhaustion of the troops. Full details are not available, but this situation indicates the probability that the defenses on Bataan have been overcome."

It appeared probable that American forces made up about half of the effective strength of the defenders in the last hours of the battle. These included the Thirty-first Regiment of Infantry, the permanent garrison of the islands; some 5,000 men originally attached to the oblit-

American prisoners of war during the May 1942 Death March from the Bataan Peninsula to the Cabana Tuan prison camp.

erated air force, of whom 2,000 had been equipped and trained as infantrymen during the siege; a force of Marines; and more than 1,000 sailors, who formerly operated the Cavite Naval Base. In addition, there were originally 10,000 Philippine Scouts or Filipinos enlisted in the Regular Army, and contingents of the Philippine National Army.

With these military forces were 18,000 to 20,000 civilians evacuated from other parts of Luzon, who, Secretary Stimson said, had been protected and maintained with the same allotments of food as were given to the troops, and about 6,000 Filipinos hired as laborers.

Secretary Stimson, himself a former Governor General of the Philippines, spoke with deep emotion at his press conference.

"Our troops," he said, "were outnumbered and worn down by successive attacks as well as lack of food and the diseases peculiar to the tropics. Their lines were finally broken. I don't know what happened, but it is evident that Bataan has been overthrown. Corregidor is still fighting.

"It was a long and gallant defense. We have nothing but praise for these men. I believe it to be a temporary loss. This country, in fulfillment of its pledge, will ultimately drive out the invaders. During the long defense we have heard from Generals MacArthur and Wainwright nothing but praise for the Filipinos who have been fighting side by side with our soldiers in that battle. The Philippines now have been united with us in battle as well as linked by the cooperation between the United States and the Philippines during the last forty years."

Secretary Stimson said he regretted that he could not read to correspondents the message that President Roosevelt sent yesterday to General Wainwright.

"He expressed his full appreciation of the enormous difficulties," Mr. Stimson said, "and told him that he had nothing but praise for the method in which he had been conducting his defense, and that the result was due to matters over which he had no control. He left to General Wainwright the decision as to what to do."

The War Secretary made public the actual figures of persons on Bataan, he said, in anticipation of Japanese claims with greatly exaggerated totals. For his part, he declined to estimate the size of the Japanese attacking forces.

He then went on to tell for the first time of desperate efforts to supply the troops on Bataan. These efforts were begun, Secretary Stimson said, in the first week in January, when the main body of defenders had been forced to retire to positions in Bataan. The work was started before Singapore fell and before the invasion of the Netherlands Indies.

"As soon as General MacArthur had taken his position in Bataan," Mr. Stimson said, "we began efforts to make his stay as long as possible. We have made every effort to get food and ammunition to the forces there. That work was started before Jan. 7.

"By Jan. 17, Army officers were arriving in Australia to organize a base. Part of their duties were to try and break the blockade [of the China Sea]. In order to make sure of special efforts, General Patrick Hurley, the former Secretary of War and Minister to New Zealand, was detached from his duties as Minister and directed to take every step to supply food and ammunition. Very large sums of money were placed to his credit, and also to General MacArthur's, for the purchase of supplies locally.

"General Hurley was very successful in his part of the work and sent several shiploads of supplies which got into the Philippines, and part of which were transported to Corregidor and Bataan. But for every ship that arrived safely we lost nearly two.

"I am glad to say the men have never been short of ammunition. They have had plenty of all types. But they have been on short rations ever since Jan. 11. That long strain has been an important factor in wearing down the troops, and it put them in a position where they could not rebound to counter-attack."

Mr. Stimson ascribed the defeat largely to the lack of air support for the ground forces, echoing a view held here by experts in modern warfare. He said "there has been no air support of a substantial character" at any time, and a very great number of planes were lost on the first day of the war when the Japanese made a surprise attack.

The last word of air operations by the defenders came several weeks ago when General MacArthur, then still in the Philippines, reported that four patched-up P-40's laden with bombs sank five Japanese vessels in Subic Bay. That attack, incidentally, was believed to have put off by its success a grand Japanese offensive planned for a month ago. It was followed within a few days by the suicide of Lieut. Gen. Masaharu Homma, the first Japanese commander, and his replacement by Lieut. Gen. Tomoyuki Yamashita, conqueror of Malaya and Singapore.

"Through the dust clouds and blistering heat, we marched."

A survivor's account of the Bataan Death March

Combat pilot Ed Dyess arrived with his squadron in the Philippines just eighteen days before the Japanese attack. After the surrender of Bataan on April 9, 1942, he took part in—and survived—what has become known as the Bataan Death March. Dyess remained a prisoner for nearly a year until he escaped into the jungle with eleven other American and Filipino prisoners on April 3, 1943. They successfully evaded pursuing Japanese troops and four days later joined a guerrilla unit. Dyess served four months with the 110th Guerrilla Division before being evacuated to Australia, where he was debriefed and gave this account of the Death March. He was then sent home to regain his health but died on December 22, 1943, in a P-38 crash while preparing to return to duty in the Pacific.

A Japanese soldier took my canteen, gave the water to a horse, and threw the canteen away. We passed a Filipino prisoner of war who had been bayoneted. Men recently killed were lying along the roadside; many had been run over and flattened by Japanese trucks. Many American prisoners were forced to act as porters for military equipment. Such treatment caused the death of a sergeant in my squadron, the 21st Pursuit. Patients bombed out of a nearby hospital, half dazed and wandering about in pajamas and slippers, were thrown into our marching column of prisoners. What their fate was I do not know. At 10 o'clock that night, we were forced to retrace our march for two hours, for no apparent reason.

At midnight we were crowded into an enclosure too narrow to lie down. An officer asked permission to get water and a Japanese guard beat him with a rifle butt. Finally, a Japanese officer permitted us to drink water from a nearby carabao wallow.

Before daylight the next morning, the 11th, we were awakened and marched down the road. Japanese trucks sped by. A Japanese soldier swung his rifle from one of them in passing, and knocked an American prisoner unconscious beside the road.

Through the dust clouds and blistering heat, we marched that entire day without food. We were allowed to drink dirty water from a roadside stream at noon. Some time later three officers were taken from our marching column, thrown into an automobile and driven off. I never learned what became of them. They never arrived at any of the prison camps.

Our guards repeatedly promised us food, but never produced it. The night of the 11th, we again were searched and then the march resumed. Totally done in, American and Filipino prisoners fell out frequently, and threw themselves moaning beside the roadside. The stronger were not permitted to help the weaker. We then would hear shots behind us.

At 3 o'clock on the morning of April 12th, we were introduced to a form of torture which came to be known as the "sun treatment." We were made to sit in the boiling sun all day long without cover. We had very little water; our thirst was intense. Many of us went crazy and several died. The Japanese dragged out the sick and delirious. Three Filipino and three American soldiers were buried while still alive.

On the 13th, each of those who survived was given a mess kit of rice. We were given another full day of the sun treatment. At nightfall, we were forced to resume our march. We marched without water until dawn of April 14, with one two-hour interval when we were permitted to sit beside the roadside. The very pace of our march itself was a torture. Sometimes we had to go very fast, with the Japanese pacing us on bicycles. At other times, we were forced to shuffle along very slowly. The muscles of my legs began to draw and each step was an agony.

Filipino civilians tried to help both Filipino and American soldiers by tossing us food and cigarettes from windows or from behind houses. Those who were caught were beaten. The Japanese had food stores along the roadside. A United States Army colonel pointed to some of the cans of salmon and asked for food for his men. A Japanese officer picked up a can and hit the colonel in the face with it, cutting his cheek wide open. Another colonel and a brave Filipino picked up three American soldiers who had collapsed before the Japs could get to them. They placed them on a cart and started down the road toward San Fernando. The Japanese seized them as well as the soldiers, who were in a coma, and horsewhipped them fiercely.

Along the road in the province of Pampanga, there are many wells. Half-crazed with thirst, six Filipino soldiers made a dash for one of the wells. All six were killed. As we passed Lubao we marched by a Filipino soldier, gutted and hanging over a barbed-wire fence. Late that night of the 14th, we were jammed into another bull pen at San Fernando with again no room to lie down. During the night, Japanese soldiers with fixed bayonets charged into the compound to terrorize the prisoners.

Before daylight on April 15, we were marched out and 115 of us were packed into a small, narrow-gauge box car. The doors were closed and locked. Movement was impossible. Many of the prisoners were suffering from diarrhea and dysentery. The heat and stench were unbearable. We all wondered if we would get out of the box car alive. At Capas, Tarlac, we were taken out and given the sun treatment for three hours. Then we were marched to Camp O'Donnell, a prison camp under construction, surrounded with barbed wire and high towers, with separate inner compounds of wire. On this last leg of the journey the Japanese permitted the stronger to carry the weaker.

I made that march of about 85 miles in six days on one mess kit of rice. Other Americans made "The March of Death" in 12 days, without any food whatever. Much of the time, of course, they were given the sun treatment along the way.

37

The Doolittle Raid

April 1942

Before the war, one of the primary concerns of Japanese military planners was the possibility that, in wartime, enemy planes might bomb Japan's cherished home islands. By April 1942, that fear had receded. The sea approaches to Japan were so well guarded that no U.S. carriers could slip close enough to launch their short-range naval bombers, and the Japanese army had so far extended the

empire's defensive perimeter on land that no Allied air bases remained within striking distance. Even long-range army bombers stationed in unoccupied China couldn't manage the round trip. Nevertheless, on April 18, sixteen American B-25s bombed Tokyo and three other Japanese cities. Where had they come from? "Shangri-la," President Roosevelt told the press and the world.

Actually, the bombers, modified to hold extra fuel tanks, had come from the aircraft carrier *Hornet*. According to the top-secret plan developed by Lt. Col. James H. Doolittle in January 1942, the *Hornet* would carry the B-25s to a point about four hundred miles from the coast of Japan. The bombers would then take off, fly on to Japan, drop their payloads, and continue flying west to land in Nationalist-controlled China.

At first, the mission went smoothly. The newly outfitted *Hornet* rendezvoused with Vice Adm. William F. "Bull" Halsey's Task Force 16 north of Midway Island on April 13 and proceeded westward through empty, if turbulent,

seas. On the morning of April 18, however, the task force encountered a small Japanese patrol boat, quickly sunk by the cruiser *Nashville*, but not before it got off a hasty radio message. Fearing that this warning may have gotten through, Halsey ordered the immediate launch of Doolittle's raiders, even though the *Hornet* was still more than two hundred miles short of the anticipated launch point.

As it turned out, the Japanese defenses weren't alerted, and the B-25s easily reached their targets. Their bombs caused some minor physical damage, but the more important effects were psychological. Badly in need of a morale boost, the American public rejoiced at the news that Tokyo had been hit, while Japan's military elite experienced the raid as deeply humiliating. They immediately began looking for a way to retaliate and found one in a plan being pushed by Yamamoto, thus far without much support, to lure the remnants of the U.S. Pacific Fleet into a showdown battle at Midway.

JAPAN REPORTS TOKYO, YOKOHAMA BOMBED BY ENEMY PLANES IN DAYLIGHT; CLAIMS 9

Damage Is 'Light'; Japanese Say Raiders Hit Schools, Hospitals, Not War Objectives

SAN FRANCISCO, April 17—The Tokyo radio announced tonight that "enemy bombers" had attacked Tokyo, the Columbia Broadcasting System's listening station reported. The Tokyo broadcast said:

"Enemy bombers appeared over Tokyo for the first time in the current war, inflicting damage on schools and hospitals. The raid occurred shortly past noon on Saturday [Tokyo time].

"Invading planes failed to cause any damage on military establishments, although casualties in the schools and hospitals were as yet unknown.

"This inhuman attack on these cultural establishments and on residential districts is causing widespread indignation among the populace."

"It is confirmed that three enemy aircraft were shot down when hostile planes attacked the Tokyo-Tosame region this afternoon for the first time since the war [started]," said a communiqué issued by Japanese Imperial Headquarters. "The enemy planes approached from several directions." Later another Tokyo radio broadcast reported that nine of the raiders had been shot down.

This later broadcast said that none of the hostile planes had penetrated to the heart of the city. It was said that they had released "a few bombs on the outskirts" and that "Japanese interceptor planes immediately took chase."

The Columbia Broadcasting System said the first announcement of the bombing was in an English-language broadcast. The announcement was repeated a few minutes later in a Japanese-language broadcast, which injected a new angle that "the enemy planes did not attempt to hit military establishments."

The Japanese-language broadcast said:

"Just after noon on the 18th the first enemy planes appeared over the city of Tokyo. A number of bombs were dropped. The enemy planes did not attempt to hit military establishments and only inflicted damage on grammar schools, hospitals and cultural establishments.

"These planes were repulsed by a heavy barrage from our defense guns.

"The previous training of the Tokyo populace for air raid defense was put into immediate practice. I wish to reveal that our losses were exceedingly light."

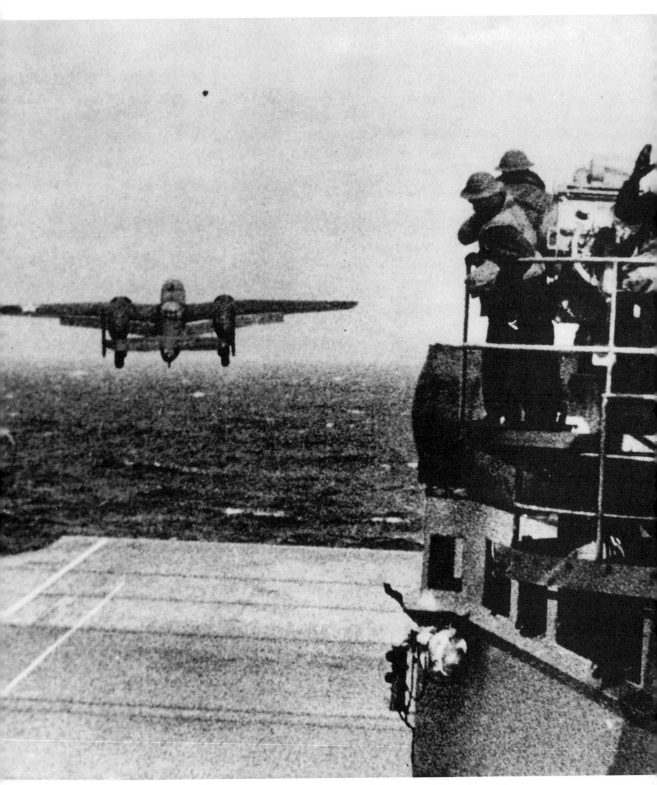

One of the B-25s that took part in the Doolittle Raid takes off from the deck of the USS Hornet *on its way to Japan.*

"TOKYO SUCCESSFULLY BOMBED."

James H. Doolittle's preliminary report from China

Because bad weather and nightfall over China made precise navigation impossible, nearly all of Doolittle's men were forced to bail out as their B-25s ran low on fuel. Amazingly, sixty-two of the seventy-five fliers who jumped landed in unoccupied territory, found friendly Chinese units, and survived the war. Doolittle himself was among their number, and he wrote this terse preliminary report while still in China. Those with decidedly less fortunate outcomes included one man who died while bailing out, four who drowned, and eight who were captured by the Japanese (three of these were executed and another died in a prisoner-of-war camp). Curiously, the one flight crew that did land its plane, at a Soviet air base near Vladivostok, was also arrested—by the Soviets, who were still neutral with regard to the Pacific war.

Took off at 8:20 A.M. ship time. Take-off was easy. Night take-off would have been possible and practicable.

Circled carrier to get exact heading and check compass. Wind was from around 300 degrees.

About a half hour after take-off, was joined by A/C 40-2292, Lt. Hoover, pilot, the second plane to take off. About an hour out passed a Japanese camouflaged naval surface vessel of about 6,000 tons. Took it to be a light cruiser. About two hours out passed a multi-motored land plane headed directly for our flotilla and flying at about 3,000 ft.—2 miles away. Passed and endeavored to avoid various civil and naval craft until landfall was made north of Inubo Shuma.

Was somewhat north of desired course but decided to take advantage of error and approach from a northerly direction, thus avoiding anticipated strong opposition to the west. Many flying fields and the air full of planes north of Tokyo. Mostly small biplanes apparently primary or basic trainers.

Encountered nine fighters in three flights of three. This was about ten miles north of the outskirts of Tokyo proper. All this time had been flying as low as the terrain would permit. Continued low flying due south over the outskirts of and toward the east center of Tokyo.

Pulled up to 1,200 ft., changed course to the southwest and incendiary-bombed highly inflammable section. Dropped first bomb at 1:30 (ship time).

Anti-aircraft very active but only one near hit. Lowered away to housetops and slid over western outskirts into low haze and smoke. Turned south and out to sea. Fewer airports on west side but many army posts. Passed over small aircraft factory with a dozen or more newly completed planes on the line. No bombs left. Decided not to machine gun for reasons of personal security. Had seen five barrage balloons over east central Tokyo and what appeared to be more in the distance.

Passed on out to sea flying low. Was soon joined by Hoover who followed us to the Chinese coast. Navigator plotted perfect course to pass north of Yaki Shima. Saw three large naval vessels just before passing west end of Japan. One was flatter than the others and may have been a converted carrier. Passed innumerable fishing and small patrol boats.

Made landfall somewhat north of course on China coast. Tried to reach Chuchow on 4495 (kilocycles) but could not raise.

It had been clear over Tokyo but became overcast before reaching Yaki Shima. Ceiling lowered on coast until low islands and hills were in it at about 600 feet. Just getting dark and couldn't live under overcast so pulled up to 6,000 feet and then 8,000 feet in it. On instruments from then on though occasionally saw dim lights on ground through almost solid overcast. These lights seemed more often on our right and pulled us still farther off course.

Directed rear gunner to go aft and secure films from camera.

(Unfortunately, they were jerked out of his shirt front where he had put them when his chute opened.)

Decided to abandon ship. Sgt. Braemer, Lt. Potter, Sgt. Leonard and Lt. Cole jumped in order. Left ship on A.F.C.E. (automatic pilot), shut off both gas cocks and I left. Should have put flaps down. This would have slowed down landing speed, reduced impact and shortened glide.

Left airplane about 9:30 P.M. (ship time) after 13 hours in the air. Still had enough gas left for half hour flight but right front tank was showing empty. Had transferred once as right engine used more fuel. Had covered about 2,250 miles, mostly at low speed, cruising but about an hour at moderate high speed which more than doubled the consumption for this time.

All hands collected and ship located by late afternoon of 19th. Requested General Ho Yang Ling, Director of the Branch Government of Western Chekiang Province, to have a lookout kept along the seacoast from Hang Chow Bay to Wen Chow Bay and also have all sampans and junks along the coast keep a lookout for planes that went down at sea, or just reached shore.

Early morning of 20th, four planes and crews, in addition to ours, had been located and I wired General Arnold, through the Embassy at Chungking: TOKYO SUCCESSFULLY BOMBED. DUE BAD WEATHER ON CHINA COAST BELIEVE ALL AIRPLANES WRECKED. FIVE CREWS FOUND SAFE IN CHINA SO FAR. Wired again on the 27th giving more details.

Discussed possibility of purchasing three prisoners on the seacoast from Puppet Government and endeavoring to take out the three in the lake area by force. Believe this desire was made clear to General Ku Cho-tung (who spoke little English) and know it was made clear to English-speaking members of his staff. This was at Shangjao. They agreed to try to purchase of three but recommended against force due to large Japanese concentration.

Bad luck:
(1) Early take-off due to naval contact with surface and air craft.
(2) Clear over Tokyo.
(3) Foul over China.

Good luck:
(1) A 25 mph tail wind over most of the last 1,200 miles.

Take-off should have been made three hours before daylight, but we didn't know how easy it would be and the Navy didn't want to light up. Dawn take-off, closer in, would have been better as things turned out. However, due to the bad weather it is questionable if even daylight landing could have been made at Chuchow without radio aid.

Still feel that original plan of having one plane take off three hours before dusk and others just at dusk was best all-around plan for average conditions.

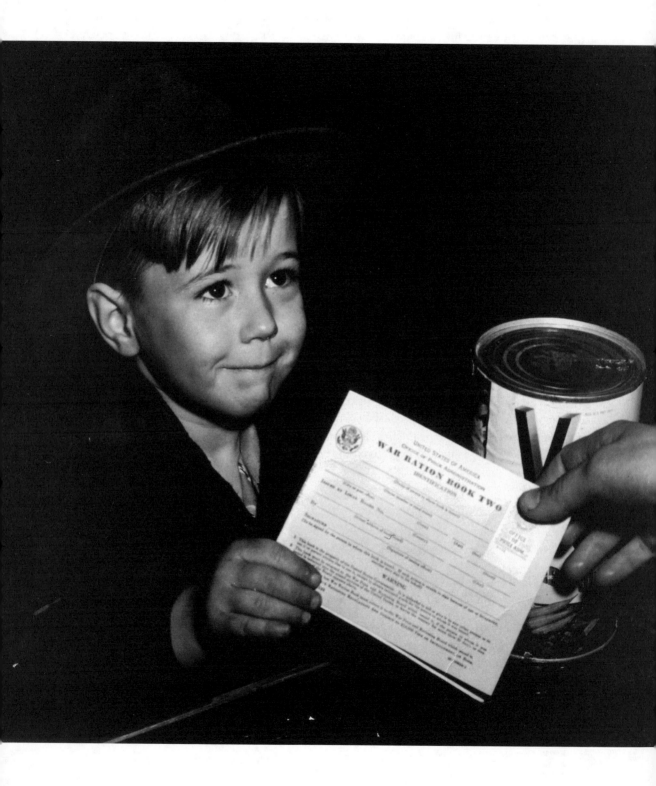

38

The Imposition of Price Controls

April 1942

Once the European war broke out in September 1939, Great Britain and France began deluging U.S. factories with orders for both military and civilian goods. All this economic activity put more money into the hands of American workers, who used it to boost domestic demand as well. Under normal circumstances, this would certainly have caused immediate runaway inflation. But so many U.S.

factories still lay idle as a result of the Great Depression that nearly eighteen months passed before foreign and domestic demand finally outstripped the available supply of goods.

President Roosevelt's first attempt to control the cost-of-living surge that occurred in February 1941 was an executive order creating the Office of Price Administration (OPA). This agency's mandate was to stabilize the prices being charged for a wide range of commodities, goods, and services; but the president's existing authority proved inadequate. So Roosevelt sent a special message to Congress on July 30 asking for enactment of more extensive price-control legislation.

Emphasizing the socially harmful aspects of unrestrained inflation, Roosevelt pointed out that higher prices wouldn't increase the supply of scarce goods but merely determine who would be able to buy them—that is, the wealthiest Americans, who could afford to pay the most. "The consequences of inflation are well known," the president continued, warning that producers might become unwilling to enter into contracts because they wouldn't be able to esti-

mate with confidence their likely costs. At the same time, speculators, anticipating the same price increases, would begin withholding essential raw materials from the marketplace in order to reap greater profits later. Both would be disastrous for the defense effort.

After six months of wrangling, Congress finally passed the Emergency Price Control Act of January 1942, which empowered the OPA to set enforceable price ceilings. Meanwhile, the agency also gained the authority to ration scarce goods and commodities, which it did using a variety of methods. The most common were coupon rationing and point rationing. Under the coupon system, the OPA distributed books of coupons that allowed consumers to purchase, at controlled prices, the commodity named on the face of each coupon. Under the point system, introduced in early 1943, some coupons were replaced with stamps of varying point values. These entitled consumers to make purchases from within a range of commodities—thus allowing individuals to buy all beef and no pork, or vice versa, instead of predetermined quantities of each.

A schoolboy makes use of the newly issued War Ration Book Two in February 1943. With so many parents employed in war-related work during the day, children had to take care of many families' marketing needs and therefore had to learn point rationing.

SALES PRICES, RENTS, SERVICE CHARGES FROZEN

March Prices Top; Practically Every Item in Cost of Living Put Under OPA Curb

By CHARLES E. EGAN

WASHINGTON, April 28—Prices of every major item affecting living costs were ordered frozen today by the Office of Price Administration.

Acting to halt inflationary spiralling which had carried the cost of living 15 per cent above pre-war levels, the OPA called upon retailers, wholesalers and manufacturers of all essential products to freeze their selling prices at March levels. In companion regulations the Federal agency fixed a ceiling on rents.

A licensing system under which retailers and wholesalers who violate terms of the orders can be deprived of the right to do business was set up to enforce compliance with the ceiling levels. Powers granted to the Price Administrator under the Emergency Price Control Act of 1942 were held sufficient to compel compliance with the rental order.

The price control measures, together with an expansion of rationing, will assure families in the low- and middle-income brackets of an equal opportunity with those of greater income to buy available goods, Leon Henderson, the Federal Price Administrator, said in announcing the orders.

At a press conference where he outlined the inflationary influences which compelled aggressive action by the government, Mr. Henderson admitted that the orders are more comprehensive than many had expected.

"They are of such magnitude," he said, "that even we who have been busy framing them for the last few weeks, cannot fully visualize their ramifications."

Under the order on retail prices, stores are called upon, beginning May 18, to hold prices for goods they sell at the highest levels they charged during March. Beginning May 11, wholesalers and manufacturers prices likewise are frozen at the "highs" of last month.

Service industries, such as laundries, garages and so forth, come within the scope of the order and go under price ceilings July 1, with maximum prices fixed at the highest point reached in March.

The order on rents applies to 301 newly defined rental areas including all of metropolitan New York. It brings to 323 the number of defense rental areas now covered by OPA orders. Landlords in most of the areas are forbidden to advance rates beyond those charged on March 1, thus wiping out any increases which may have been made during the Spring moving and leasing period.

"This universal control of prices is the keystone of the Administration's attack upon inflation," Mr. Henderson said. "It serves as a setting for companion steps in savings, profits and fiscal policy."

There will be many casualties among retailers, wholesalers and landlords complying with the spirit and letter of today's orders, he added, but he called upon them to make the sacrifices necessary to see that costs are stabilized.

"This is a war against inflation, and retailers and others are in the front lines," he continued. "I am sure that they will see the situation in that light and cooperate willingly."

Prices on literally millions of articles of all descriptions are automatically controlled by the regulations. A few exemptions, mainly among food commodities, are provided by the order.

Among the items on which fixed prices are imposed are almost all processed food commodities, including bread, cake and bakery products; beef, pork and their products; sugar, fluid milk and cream sold at retail; ice cream; canned meats, soups, canned fruits and vegetables; canned fish and other canned seafoods; cereals; lard and shortening; coffee, tea, salt and spices.

Ceilings also apply to all clothing, shoes, dry goods and yard goods, soap in all forms; every kind of common fuel (including even firewood); pipes, cigars and cigarettes and prepared smoking and chewing tobacco; drugs, toiletries and sundries; furniture and furnishings, appliances and equipment and hardware and miscellaneous agricultural supplies.

Retailers are called upon to display publicly their ceiling prices and to keep available a complete file of their ceiling prices which customers are privileged to consult upon demand.

It was emphasized that nothing in the order prevents sales below the established level but on the contrary such procedure is encouraged.

Commodities not covered by the regulation comprise three general classifications:

1. Those which are exempt because of the Emergency Price Control Act of 1942, including such things as advertising, newspapers, books, magazines, motion pictures, wages, common carrier and public utility rates, insurance, real estate and professional services, all of which do not fall into a definition of "commodity." Also those agricultural products for which parity provisions call for special treatment under the terms of the act.

2. Commodities which do not have organized markets and for which it would be almost impossible to determine maximum prices either on the basis of previous sales or prices for comparable articles. Examples cited were highly seasonal fresh vegetables, fresh fish and game, objects of art and collectors' items.

3. Primary raw materials, such as timber and mineral ores, all prices for which are substantially controlled by ceilings already in effect.

A junked auto arrives at a salvage yard in North Arlington, New Jersey, where the scrap metal it contains will be extracted and repurposed for munitions.

Among the items specifically excepted are unprocessed agricultural commodities, except bananas. In general, prices for such commodities are fixed at the stage of first processing under existing ceilings.

Others on the "excepted" list are eggs and poultry; all milk products including butter, cheese, condensed and evaporated milk (but not fluid milk sold at retail, cream sold at retail and ice cream); flour; mutton and lamb; dried prunes; dry edible beans; leaf tobacco (whether dried or green); nuts (except peanuts); linseed oil cake and meal; mixed feed for animals; manure; living animals, wild or domesticated; stumpage, logs and pulpwood; stamps and coins; precious stones; antiques; knotted oriental rugs; paintings and etchings and other art objects; used autos; wood and gum for naval stores; and notes, stocks and bonds, commonly known as securities.

Special exemptions are provided for hotels, restaurants, soda fountains, bars, cafes and similar establishments selling food or beverages for consumption on the premises.

Also exempt are sales of used personal or household effects by the owner, bona fide auction sales of used personal or household effects and sales by farmers of goods grown and processed on their farms including smoked hams, bacon, maple syrup and etc., if the total of such sales or deliveries does not exceed $75 in any one month.

Personal services not connected with commodities and professional services likewise are excluded from terms of the order. Thus rates charged by automobile repair shops, garages, tailors, laundries, dry cleaners, shoe repair establishments and etc., are covered by the regulations effective July 1, while the prices set by barbers and beauty shops (services to the person) and the fees of doctors, dentists, lawyers (professional services) are not.

Donald Gordon, chairman of Canada's Wartime Prices and Trade Board, accompanied Mr. Henderson to the press conference, and was an interested spectator throughout the session.

"The price ceiling we are announcing today," Mr. Henderson explained, in introducing the Canadian, "was inspired in large measure by Canada's success with a somewhat similar regulation and we have had continued and close exchanges of experience since this matter was first taken up in a serious way here."

Asked if it were not true that Canada's price ceiling also covered wages, Mr. Henderson refused to be drawn into a discussion of a wage ceiling here.

Emphasizing the necessity for prompt control of prices he added that, including an estimated 1 1/2 per cent rise this month in the cost of living, costs are now up about 15 per cent since September, 1939.

"This country is heading rapidly toward a living standard comparable to that which prevailed in 1932," he continued. "By that I mean that by 1943 the amount of goods available for the public to buy will be as limited as it was ten years ago. The difference, however, will be that there will be billions of dollars of spending power poured into workers' hands from armament jobs, and pressing to be spent.

"The natural result of such a situation would be the greatest inflation this country has ever witnessed. It is to prevent such a development, with all the terrible after-effects which would follow, that we are setting up a universal price ceiling."

The order, he said, is only part of a broad plan in which taxes, savings, consumer credit restrictions, expansion of social security classifications and other means will be used to siphon off as much spending power as possible.

"This price control and the rationing which will be a necessary part of the activity," he continued, "will assure those of low income a fair share of the goods available for sale."

He declined to speculate as to the items likely to be brought under the rationing expansion which he said will be necessary.

"I have maintained over a long period," he said, "that you can't have complete price control unless you have rationing on important and essential commodities, particularly on those products on which you have a continuing supply."

Because of recent price increases, Mr. Henderson continued, the country is now spending almost exactly the same amount of money it did in the "peak" civilian sales month of last August, for 7 to 8 per cent less goods than were available then.

"In other words," he continued, "while the supply of goods has been falling off, prices have been rising so rapidly that sellers are getting the same return in dollars that they got last August."

He emphasized that the price ceiling attempts to cover cost-of-living items which are most significant in the budgets of low- and middle-income family groups.

"My dear Mr. Griffen, is this where you ration everything?"

Observations on the workings of a local rationing board

Brendan Gill began contributing to *The New Yorker* in 1936, writing mostly about film and the theater. During World War II, he covered the American home front for the magazine. This article appeared in its June 13, 1942, issue.

X, B, and Chiefly A

Tuesday afternoon last week, I saw one of the country's eight thousand ration boards at work. This particular board, which has jurisdiction over sugar, gas, new tires, and the recapping of old ones, is in White Plains, but it is unquestionably a good deal like the board in Rye or Greenwich or New Rochelle. Last week it was occupied almost entirely with listening to gas-rationing appeals. Its behavior struck me as peculiarly American and somehow cheering, and perhaps worth telling about. The White Plains ration board occupies two dusty rooms on the second floor of an old high-school building on Main Street. According to a sign tacked on a door at the head of the stairs, the board meets every afternoon from two to four, Monday through Friday. It was shortly before two when I arrived, and the door was locked. I rapped, and a good-looking young woman opened it. It seemed to me that she glanced rather apprehensively up and down the empty corridor. When I introduced myself she smiled in relief. "Come along in," she said. "I'm Mrs. Christenson. I guess you'd call me a sort of secretary to the board. When I heard your knock I was afraid the rush was beginning already. Yesterday we had to handle a couple of hundred people. In two hours!"

I told Mrs. Christenson I was sorry to bother her, but she invited me to sit down. Shoving the white stacks of paper covering her desk to one side, she said, "Say, I'm glad to forget about this for a while. I never did any bookkeeping before in my life—just legal typing—and it isn't so easy to keep things straight. You see, some of our reports have to be sent to county headquarters, some to Albany, others to Washington. All reports have to be typed in duplicate, triplicate, or quadruplicate, and they all have to be kept on file here. That's the catch. So far we've only got two little files for the whole job. Two files, one typewriter, and one telephone."

I asked her how she had happened to take on the job.

"I volunteered," she answered. "I hadn't worked since I got married, but I wanted to help."

"You mean you're handling this job without pay?" I asked.

"Of course," she said. "Just like the members of the board. Lately we've been allowed one salaried clerk to help us, but he's only paid about twenty-five a week."

Mrs. Christenson typed a few reports while I wandered about waiting for the board to convene. In the first room there were only Mrs. Christenson's desk and chair, a long table and three chairs for the board, and two long wooden benches against the walls. There was nothing in the other room but some loosely piled pamphlets, sugar-ration books, and gas-ration cards. It wasn't long before the members of the board began to arrive, and Mrs. Christenson introduced me as they came in. The chairman is Mr. Chauncey Griffen, a prominent real-estate man and a former mayor of White Plains. Mr. Griffen is white-haired and handsome and talks with a pleasant, country-club accent. The two other members of the board are Edward Schirmer, a director of several banks, and Thomas Holden, a lawyer. At two o'clock sharp, the board clerk, a former bakery salesman named Mr. Miller, arrived and Mrs. Christenson opened the hall door. As a queue of men and women moved timidly forward, I assured Mr. Griffen that I would not mention the names of all those appearing before the board.

The three members of the board, who sat only a couple of feet apart at the same table, heard cases individually, so there was a certain amount of confusion. The first appeal to which I listened was that of a middle-aged man who was in a state of great excitement. He appeared before Mr. Griffen. "My God," he said, leaning over Mr. Griffen's desk, "it would buy two bonds! It would help win the war! And I got to give it to the railroad." He spread his hands, palms up. "Where's the sense in that?"

"Now, now," Mr. Griffen said. "What would buy two bonds?"

"The price of the railroad tickets. My wife and I, if we want to go down to Maine to see her family, we always hop in the car. It costs five dollars, maybe, to get there by car. Now they give us an A card and say, 'Listen, you go by train.' But by train it costs us up to forty dollars. Thirty-five dollars wasted. That's practically two bonds!"

Mr. Griffen shook his head and said, "I'm sorry, but you go by train." The man began to argue, and Mr. Griffen, looking beyond him, said, "You might just remember that it takes fifty gallons of gas to warm up a bomber. And we need a lot of bombers. Next, please."

The next petitioner was a White Plains man who had come up by train from Florida, where he had found a war job for himself, in order to sell his house in White Plains and drive his car back to Florida. His car, however, had not yet been registered for 1942. Mr. Griffen pointed out to him that he would have to register his car before a gas-ration card could be issued to him. Then he would be given a B-3 card entitling him to fifty-seven gallons of gas, which would be enough, probably, to carry him over halfway to Florida. He would have to stop in some town along the route when his gas ran low and apply to the ration board there for another B-3 card to carry him the rest of the way.

The man thanked Mr. Griffen, and a woman took his place before the desk. She said, rather archly, "My dear Mr. Griffen, is this where you ration everything?"

"Everything but the ladies, Madam," Mr. Griffen said gallantly. "The government hasn't let us do that yet."

The woman fluttered her eyelids. Evidently everything was going to be just as she had hoped it would be. "Well, I've an A card," she said, "but I think I deserve better. You see, my dear mother's eighty, and she's had a stroke. The only real pleasure she gets out of life is a little ride every evening in the fine summer weather. And I'm afraid we won't be able to take our little rides unless you give me a B-3 card, or perhaps an X."

His air of gallantry still intact, Mr. Griffen said, "I happen to have a mother, too, who's over eighty and has had a stroke. She likes to go out riding whenever she can, too. But she'll have to make a certain number of sacrifices, just like the rest of us. She'll have to manage on an A card."

The woman stopped smiling. "But, of course, an A card isn't enough," she said. "It may be the death of my poor mother."

"All right," Mr. Griffen said, standing up as a hint that the interview was about over. "You go out and get an affidavit from your mother's physician swearing that unless she can ride a minimum of forty or fifty miles a week, every week, she'll die. Then you can come back here and get more gas."

A New York City grocer voluntarily limits the purchase of canned foods to prevent hoarding before the start of rationing in February 1943.

I walked over to Mr. Schirmer's place at the table. He was apparently having some difficulty with an Italian workman. Behind me I could hear Mrs. Christenson dealing with an old man who was asking for thirty-three pounds of sugar for a church supper, and in another part of the room the clerk, who wandered around because he had no place to sit down, was filling out an application for a set of recaps for a man who scraped floors. The room was filled with people by now, most of them looking amiable enough but a few staring at one another in mutual suspicion. I overheard one man ask, of no one in particular, "Well, did you think we'd ever come to this in the good old U.S.A.?"

Mr. Schirmer was saying to the Italian, "Take it easy. One step at a time. You say you work for the New York Central?"

"That's it. That's right."

"You make repairs along the tracks from White Plains to Crestwood? That means you spend the day riding back and forth on the different trains, doesn't it? You just get off wherever there's a length of track that needs repairing?"

"Sure. But at night, after midnight, is no trains. And suppose it rains, suppose I got to get up, emergency, I got to fix the tracks. Then I need a gas for my car."

"But you told me you lived a mile from the White Plains Station. You can't drive your car up and down the tracks. An A card ought to get you back and forth to work as often as you like." The two men had begun to sweat. Mr. Schirmer called to a well-dressed man he evidently knew, who was seated, waiting his turn, on one of the long wooden benches against the wall. The man came up and asked the workman one or two questions in Italian, then exploded into what sounded like a series of unforgivable insults. The workman's head lowered and his hands dropped to his sides. Then he got up and walked quietly out of the room.

"What was that about?" Mr. Schirmer asked the man who had helped him out.

"He was just trying to get away with murder," the man said. "He'd heard about somebody else on the road who got a B-3, so he wanted one. I asked him what kind of a country he thought this was. I asked how he'd like it back in Posilipo."

Just then a short, thin man with a waxed mustache—a dentist, it turned out—hurried into the room and threw down a salmon-pink card on Mr. Schirmer's desk. "I never asked for that X card," the man said, almost fiercely. "I don't want it. I won't touch it. For God's sake, tear it up."

Mr. Schirmer wiped his forehead and said, "Take it easy. One step at a time. How did you happen to get this card?"

"I went over to the nearest school the night they started handing them out. And one of the teachers said to me, 'Why, you deserve an X card, Doctor, if anybody does.' And she made me take it. I tell you, she forced it on me."

Mr. Schirmer smiled. "Cheer up," he said. "You're not the only one. A lot of dentists and a lot of nurses and a whole pack of cops and other city employees got X cards they weren't entitled to." He patted a thick envelope on the table. "We've been calling them in, and over fifty have been turned back voluntarily so far. What kind of a card do you think you ought to have?"

The dentist hesitated. Mr. Schirmer said, "I guess we'd better make it an A card, hadn't we?"

"Yes, sir," the dentist said. "I guess maybe we had."

Mr. Schirmer picked up an A card. "Say, Shine," he called over to Mr. Griffen, who was obviously known to his colleagues as Shine, "what the devil have you done with my pen?"

Mr. Griffen raised his eyebrows. "Why, Eddie, I don't know what you mean," he said, in a tone of mock injury. "I wouldn't borrow that cheap little pen on a bet."

Apparently this was an old and familiar argument, for Mrs. Christenson walked over and searched the drifts of paper on Mr. Griffen's desk until she found a pen under a corner of the blotter. In a stage whisper, she said to me, "Imagine, only one pen among the three of them! They're just like three kids."

Leaving Mr. Schirmer shaking his head in self-pity and filling out an A card for the dentist, I moved over to Mr. Holden. A small, middle-aged woman wearing silver-framed pince-nez was speaking rapidly and, I thought, a trifle desperately into Mr. Holden's ear. Mr. Holden was nodding, his eyes nearly closed. "In the first place, you see," I heard the woman say, "my two children and I have just driven North to spend the summer in Rhode Island. Yesterday I left the children with some relatives out in Quogue, Long Island, while I did some necessary business here in White Plains. Now I have to drive back to Quogue, pick up the children, and drive on to Rhode Island. That'll be over three hundred and fifty miles in two days, and all I have is an A card. My tank has about half a gallon left in it now. At least, the needle's been shivering over zero for miles and miles."

Mr. Holden nodded gently. "There's nothing to worry about, young lady," he said. "We'll see that you get what gas you need." Mr. Holden made this sound like a sort of divine benefaction. "Won't we, Eddie?" Mr. Holden asked, turning to the other members of the board. "Won't we, Shine?" Mr. Schirmer and Mr. Griffen nodded. "You'll just have to sign a statement explaining why you need the gas," Mr. Holden went on. "When you reach Rhode Island we'd like you to mail back to us the supplemental B-3 card I'm going to give you." He fingered the pocket of his coat. "I seem to have left my pen at home. Eddie, would it be too much trouble—"

The woman took off her pince-nez and smiled. She opened her purse. "I think I have a pen," she said. "You can use mine if you like."

When I returned to Mr. Griffen, he had just called up a young man who had been nervously pacing the room. "I'm a manufacturer's salesman," the young man said. "My territory's Connecticut, eastern New York, and New Jersey. I've built up a pretty good business in the last four or five years. I'm married. I got two kids."

Mr. Griffen played with a paper clip. "No reason you can't get as much gas as you need to carry on your business," he said. "I suppose you've used up most of your first B-3 card with a territory as big as that."

"Yes, sir. A boy and a girl," the young man answered excitedly. "We've just bought a house. On the FHA. We have to pay for it by the month."

Mr. Griffen looked as if he thought the young man might break down. "Listen!" he said. "There's nothing for you to worry about. Our ruling, straight from the OPA, is that all you have to do to get another B-3 card is to get your boss to write us a letter. Have him sign his name to what you've told me and you're all set."

"Yes, sir," the young man said. "That's what I told my boss, but he won't listen to me. He's made a ruling of his own that we must sell our stuff by phone or not at all. That's not so bad for the other salesmen, because I'm the only one working outside New York City. My boss says he won't ask any favors for me. He says he loves his country. He says I ought to learn to be a patriot."

Mr. Griffen said, "Well, we have a ruling and we're supposed to stick to it. No letter, no gas." He threw the paper clip on the floor and picked up Mr. Shirmer's pen. "By God," he said, "you just give me your boss's name, and I'll write him a letter! I may not be acting altogether according to Hoyle, but I think you can stop worrying."

As the young man, having given the name, grinned and left, I said to Mr. Griffen, "Isn't it odd that no commuters have bothered you today? I expected them to make more trouble than anyone else."

"Commuters aren't so bad," Mr. Griffen said. "You see, most of them fought it out with the teachers when they got their cards. They're reconciled by now to buses and walking and doubling up. They grouse, but they don't ask the impossible. That's been our experience and the experience of all the other boards in the county, though we've heard of a couple of odd cases. There's a lawyer who practices not only in New York but also in the town where he has his country home. He's elderly, a widower, and has no one to take care of him but his staff of servants. He claims he needs his car to drive himself and the staff back and forth from town every week, that he'd go bankrupt if he had to send the servants by train. At his age it's obvious that he can't just picnic out. And he's working in both places, you see. It's a risky decision, but I guess he deserves a B-3 card. I heard of a case, too, where a man managed to get B-3 cards for three of his cars and only A cards for the remaining two. And he practically tore his ration board apart!" Mr. Griffen tossed me a letter. "We get a few of these every day, but not as many as you might think."

Dear Mr. Griffen:

I am delighted to know that a man of your integrity and high standing in this community should be chairman of our ration board. It is certainly a lucky thing for all of us that a man of your calibre is willing to serve. I am writing to explain that I'm afraid our A card isn't quite suitable for us. I must take Evangeline to school each morning...

Mr. Griffen made a face. Handing me another letter, he said, "And we also get a few like this." It read:

Dear Mr. Griffen:

I hope you will check up on all drivers. While our boys are fighting and dying all over the world, I can't see why anyone should knowingly waste a fraction of an inch of rubber or a single gallon of gas.

The letter was signed: "Brokenhearted."

Mr. Griffen looked apologetic as I finished reading the letter. "Sort of emotional, of course," he said. "Some soldier's mother, I suppose."

He leaned forward over his desk toward the remaining petitioners on the benches. "Next complaint," he said, a bit severely.

39.

The Fall of Corregidor

May 1942

Until Bataan surrendered on April 9, 1942, most Americans had chosen to ignore the hopelessness of the army's position in the Philippines. So many things had gone wrong in the Pacific during the winter of 1941–1942 that Americans at home were desperate for positive news. Therefore, as one British colony fell after another, public attention focused increasingly on the fighting in the

Philippines—if only because it hadn't ended yet.

The troops holding out on Bataan—and especially their commander, Douglas MacArthur—became prominent symbols of the heroic resistance that all Americans wished to emulate. The reality of the situation, however, was not quite so inspiring. Both MacArthur and Maj. Gen. Jonathan M. Wainwright, who succeeded MacArthur on March 11, knew that the Japanese would win sooner or later. Plan Orange 3 had assumed the arrival of a U.S. relief expedition within six months. However, the Japanese conquest of the South Pacific had been so thorough that relief would now take years rather than months to arrive. MacArthur withheld this information from his troops on Bataan and Corregidor (the island fortress at Bataan's southern tip where MacArthur had made his headquarters), but the grunts realized their situation soon enough.

After the surrender of Bataan on April 9, the Japanese army moved its heaviest siege guns onto the peninsula and began shelling Corregi-

dor for hours at a time. Of the fifteen thousand men that Wainwright had with him on the island, about half were battle-hardened marines stationed in caves or bunkers along the beaches; the rest, however, were mostly administrative personnel assigned to the Malinta Tunnel headquarters complex.

When the Japanese finally landed troops just before midnight on May 5, the marines put up a strong resistance, but it wasn't enough. By midmorning on May 6, Japanese advance units had already reached the Malinta Tunnel and were bouncing machine-gun bullets off its gates. At this point, Wainwright informed the president that he intended to surrender: "With broken heart and head bowed in sadness but not in shame I report to Your Excellency that today I must arrange terms for the surrender of the fortified islands of Manila Bay....There is a limit to human endurance and that limit has long since been passed. Without prospect of relief I feel it is my duty to my country and to my gallant troops to end this useless effusion of blood."

SILENCE ON CORREGIDOR

Editorial

After five months of firing, after twenty-seven days of concentrated attack by a foe outnumbering the defenders perhaps twenty to one, after air attacks increasing in frequency and violence until they howled over the little island thirteen times in one day, after incessant bombardment by the heaviest siege artillery, after semi-starvation, sickness and uncounted casualties, after the invaders had actually landed in force—after all this the guns of Corregidor stopped firing yesterday morning at about 4 o'clock, Eastern war time.

The silence that fell over Corregidor must have deafened the remnants of the 6,500 soldiers, sailors and marines—men no different from their comrades, whom we see daily on the streets of this city—who had lived through those weeks of roaring hell. It might be fitting if all of us, now safe at home, kept silent too for perhaps the two minutes that we give on Armistice Day to the dead of the older war. We might keep silence, for that time, for the newly dead and for the brave living men who have fallen into captivity: all of us, the hesitant, who thought this was not our war; the provincial, who could not see beyond our continental shores; the unimaginative, who accept this war but do not yet understand what it

means in valor and in agony. Not one of us is wholly guiltless of Corregidor. From the high command to the most obscure citizen we stand at this tribunal whose judges are the captive, the wounded and the dead.

This is not the time to ask who was most to blame. We know that the fighting men who bore the burden of battle, aware that for them there could be no victory, were unafraid and blameless. It is for us to hope that never again will American soldiers be compelled to fight such a battle, and that from this time forward their naked courage will be clothed with force, with airplanes, with ships, with tanks, with the reasonable chance—and that is all they ask—of victory. It is for us to resolve that none of the small sacrifices by which we can help them shall be omitted, that no work whose fruits will succor them shall be left undone, that no jealousies, no intolerances, no greeds, no ambitions shall rob them of the least thing that they need.

Let us be silent for a little space before the living and the dead. Then let us take up our work again, each man to his task—each woman too—committing ourselves to it until the cause for which some died and others still suffer has won the day.

"The jig is up. Everyone is bawling like a baby."

Final word from Corregidor

Pvt. Irving Strobing tapped out the final message received from Corregidor before its surrender. Picked up by a listening station in the United States, it was published widely in both newspapers and magazines. Meanwhile, Strobing spent the remaining thirty-nine months of the war as a prisoner of the Japanese.

They are not yet near. We are waiting for God only knows what. How about a chocolate soda? Not many. Not near yet. Lots of heavy fighting going on. We've only got about one hour, twenty minutes before.... We may have to give up by noon. We don't know yet. They are throwing men and shells at us and we may not be able to stand it. They have been shelling us faster than you can count.... We've got about fifty-five minutes and I feel sick at my stomach. I am really low down. They are around us now smashing rifles. They bring in the wounded every minute. We will be waiting for you guys to help. This is the only thing I guess that can be done. General Wainwright is a right guy and we are willing to go on for him but shells were dropping all night faster than hell. Damage terrific. Too much for guys to take.

Enemy heavy cross-shelling and bombing. They have got us all around and from skies. From here it looks like firing ceased on both sides. Men here all feeling bad, because of terrific nervous strain of the siege. Corregidor used to be a nice place but it's haunted now. Withstood a terrific pounding. Just made broadcast to Manila to arrange meeting for surrender. Talk made by General Beebe. I can't say much.

I can hardly think. Can't think at all. Say I have sixty pesos you can have for this weekend. The jig is up. Everyone is bawling like a baby. They are piling dead and wounded in our tunnel. Arms weak from pounding key long hours. No rest. Short rations. Tired. I know now how a mouse feels. Caught in a trap waiting for guys to come along finish it. Got a treat. Can pineapple. Opening it with Signal Corps knife.

My name Irving Strobing. Get this to my mother. Mrs. Minnie Strobing, 605 Barbey Street, Brooklyn, New York. They are to get along O.K. Get in touch with them soon as possible. Message. My love to Pa, Joe, Sue, Mac, Carrie, Joy and Paul. Also to all family and friends. God bless 'em all. Hope they be there when I come home. Tell Joe wherever he is to give 'em hell for us. My love to all. God bless you and keep you. Love.

Sign my name and tell Mother how you heard from me. Stand by....

40.

The Battle of the Coral Sea

May 1942

Although the Japanese pulverized the eight battleships they found at Pearl Harbor, all three aircraft carriers attached to the U.S. Pacific Fleet escaped damage because none was in port on December 7. The *Enterprise* and the *Lexington* were delivering planes to Wake and Midway Islands, respectively; the *Saratoga* was stateside, having just undergone repairs at the Bremerton, Washington, naval yard.

In the months after Pearl Harbor, the *Saratoga* returned to Bremerton for additional repairs after being torpedoed by a Japanese submarine. Meanwhile, the *Enterprise* was assigned to protect the *Hornet* and its cargo of B-25s. Therefore, only the *Lexington* remained available when, in mid-April, navy cryptanalysts discovered Japanese plans to invade Port Moresby, a strategic Allied port on the southern shore of New Guinea. Adm. Chester W. Nimitz, the new commander in chief of the U.S. Pacific Fleet, immediately sent the *Lexington* to join the carrier *Yorktown* in the Coral Sea. The link-up was accomplished on May 1.

Two days later, American scout planes discovered a small, secondary Japanese force landing on Tulagi in the nearby Solomon Islands. Rear Adm. Frank J. Fletcher, in command of the joint operation, attacked at dawn the following morning. The raid inflicted considerable damage, but it also alerted the Japanese to the presence of at least one U.S. carrier in the area. For the next two days, the Japanese and the Americans

stalked one another without contact. Then, late on May 6, U.S. scout planes found what they thought to be the main enemy force about 250 miles to the northeast. In fact, these ships were part of a convoy, protected by the light carrier *Shoho*, that was transporting invasion troops from Rabaul to Port Moresby. A much more powerful Japanese task force, led by the carriers *Shokaku* and *Zuikaku*, remained undetected.

Fletcher steamed hard toward the enemy all night, but his planes were still 165 miles away when they launched early the next morning. "Scratch one flat-top!," Lt. Comdr. Robert E. Dixon reported back when he saw the *Shoho* sink beneath the waves. The next day, however, planes from the *Shokaku* and *Zuikaku* evened the score, sinking the *Lexington*. Thus the battle of the Coral Sea ended in a tactical draw, yet it secured a place in history as the first naval engagement ever fought between fleets that never came within sight of one another. Carrier-based aircraft did all the damage.

Survivors from the USS Lexington *climb aboard one of the carrier's escort ships during the battle of the Coral Sea. The attack on the* Lexington *took place on May 8 between 1116 and 1132 hours.*

THE CORAL SEA BATTLE

Engagement Is Viewed as the Opening Clash in Decisive Phase of the War

By HANSON W. BALDWIN

The great Battle of the Coral Sea is the opening engagement in the decisive phase of the Battle for the World.

Prime Minister John Curtin of Australia correctly interpreted that action as the beginning of the days that will shake the world. The belligerents are commencing the operations that during the Summer will probably preface the way to victory or defeat.

In the exotic and island-studded waters off Northeastern Australia the initial success in the great campaigns that have now been joined has probably gone to the United Nations. We appear to have had the advantage in the sea-air clash that late yesterday was reported in some dispatches to be continuing.

The Japanese almost certainly have lost a considerable number of naval units and of planes, and it seems certain that their losses in this engagement are more important than those they have suffered in any previous action.

Our own losses are not yet given, though they are described by a communiqué from General Douglas MacArthur's headquarters in Australia as "relatively light" compared with those of the Japanese. We must be prepared, however, for losses; perhaps for heavier ones than this phrase seems to mean, though the Navy Department's communiqué last night [May 9], saying no reports yet received substantiated the loss of any American carriers or battleships, was an encouraging one.

There is no clear picture of the Battle of the Coral Sea, and none may be available for some days. But, judging from the fragmentary reports, the action was not fought between the main bodies of the opposing fleets, but between large task forces.

The fact that the communiqués about the battle have been issued by General Douglas MacArthur's headquarters in Australia indicates that the United States naval forces participating were under his command. Most of our Pacific Fleet is under command of Admiral Chester W. Nimitz, with headquarters in Hawaii. It is, however, possible that forces of our main fleet might have been temporarily attached to General MacArthur's Southwest Pacific command. If the operations in the Southwest Pacific should be intensified it is probable that a large part of our main Pacific Fleet might have to be concentrated there.

The Battle of the Coral Sea seems to have been a prelude to greater actions. Official and unofficial comment still stresses that even our most optimistic claims yield no ground for hope that the strength of the Japanese Fleet has been broken.

Large parts of that fleet, including capital ships and carriers as well as light forces, have been concentrated in the mandated islands in the vicinity of Truk since the war started, and from the approximate vicinity of the battle in the Coral Sea to Truk is only 1,300 to 1,500 nautical miles. Japan probably will—if her mind is set upon Australia or New Caledonia or the islands in the vicinity—readily reinforce her naval units in the Coral Sea.

One characteristic of the Japanese is tenacity; they will keep trying until they win or are dead. For them there is no middle ground. Nevertheless, if Japan has lost two carriers and the other units claimed, she has suffered her most severe setback of the war.

The sparse information from the scene of action makes impossible any logical deduction as to whether or not the Japanese task force was really attempting invasion of the New Hebrides, New Caledonia or Australia. The Japanese intentions in the Battle of the World are not yet clear.

Vice President Wallace has warned of a Japanese attempt against Alaska and the Aleutians and even our West Coast—a step that is possible, but until other things are accomplished by the enemy, improbable. Reports from London and China indicate the enemy is massing troops in Manchukuo opposite the Russian frontier for the "inevitable war" for the Maritime Provinces.

Meantime, the Japanese are still fighting along the Burma Road in Southern China, and from Akyab airport they have raided the railhead and port of Chittagong in India, a step that might be a possible precursor to full-fledged invasion. With typical Hitlerian technique they are threatening everywhere, thus masking their real intentions.

But the naval battle in the Coral Sea may soon force the showing of their hand.

In Europe, Adolf Hitler still marks time as the ground dries on the Eastern Front. His armies might have marched against the Russian guns in the south at nearly any time after April

Members of the USS Enterprise *crew stand by to receive an encapsulated message from a scout plane returning from a two-hundred-mile mission in the Coral Sea area, May 18, 1942.*

20, but if the German intention is to strike for Moscow and also in the north, it will be some days or weeks before the terrain is dry enough after the Spring thaws to permit extensive operations. Any time between now and June 15 may be the deadline in Russia.

But this is an indivisible war and what happens in Russia is closely linked to what has happened in the Southwestern Pacific. For the wrecks of ships littering the waters of the Coral Sea may typify—if they are Japanese ships—the wreckage also of Herr Hitler's hopes.

"At 1456 the *Lexington* signalled for help."

An excerpt from the Battle of the Coral Sea Combat Narrative

The Office of Naval Intelligence prepared a confidential report, excerpted here, on the battle of the Coral Sea as part of its Combat Narratives series. These reports were intended "for the information of officers," who were reminded to "be guarded in circulation and custody of the Narratives and in avoiding discussion of their contents with or within the hearing of any others than commissioned or warrant officers."

When all planes of our attack groups had either returned or been given up for lost, Admiral Fletcher made a quick estimate of the situation. Consideration was given to making another air attack or sending the attack group in for a surface engagement. There was reason to believe that one Japanese carrier had escaped damage, and at 1422 Admiral Fitch reported that there were indications that an additional carrier had joined the enemy forces. Damage had reduced the *Yorktown*'s maximum speed to 30 knots and the *Lexington*'s to 24. Furthermore, both our carriers had lost a great number of planes in action and others had been rendered unserviceable by damage. This last consideration caused Admiral Fletcher to abandon the idea of another air attack. The idea of a surface attack also was rejected because it was felt that our ships might be subject to a strong carrier air attack before dark.

The decision was to retire to the southward for further investigation of damage to the ships and to give the air groups time to put sufficient planes in service for a strong attack the following day.

The sudden breakdown of the *Lexington* prevented the planned transfer of her operable planes to the *Yorktown*. When she lost headway the planes on deck could not take off, and 35 of them went down with her. However, 16 planes, 4 fighters, and 10 SBD's were saved. These were in the air when the *Lexington* came to a stop, and were landed aboard the *Yorktown* about 1535.

A combat patrol was maintained until darkness fell.

Admiral Fletcher reassumed tactical command at 1510. Conditions aboard the *Lexington*, meanwhile, had been growing worse. It was planned to take her serviceable planes aboard the *Yorktown* and send her back to Pearl Harbor for repairs. Of course she never got there, but the decision to retire was responsible for the saving of a large number of *Lexington* personnel. "Although probably based on incorrect information," Admiral Fletcher stated, "[the decision] resulted in saving the lives of 92 percent of *Lexington*'s personnel, a large portion of which would have been lost if the attack group had not been present when the ship sank."

As Task Force Fox proceeded southward, Comdr. Morton T. Seligman, executive officer of the *Lexington*, made an inspection of the ship. He found the damage control parties functioning smoothly, and "there was no apparent cause for concern." After reassuring himself as to the fires, Commander Seligman was making his way to the sick bay when a "terrific" explosion below decks blew him through a hatch scuttle. This occurred at 1247, and was followed by severe fires in the C.P.O. passageway and at other points on the second deck, being especially bad near the gunnery office.

Where the explosion occurred or what caused it was not immediately known. Some thought it was caused by a "sleeper" bomb. Eventually it was concluded that small gasoline leaks resulting from the heavy pounding the *Lexington* had absorbed caused an accumulation of vapors in the bowels of the ship, where they were set off by sparks of unknown origin. "In any event," Captain Sherman related, "from this time on the ship was doomed."

Hoses from the after section of the fire main were led out and strenuous efforts were made to combat the fires, which were spreading aft. As the fires gained headway, frequent additional minor explosions occurred below decks, either from hot 5-inch ammunition or gasoline vapors. The fires gradually ate through more and more communications. All lights forward went out. The fire main pressure dropped to 30 or 40 pounds. The telephone circuit to the trick wheel went dead and Captain Sherman steered for a while with the engines. Smoke filled spaces below decks. Commander Seligman concluded that the original explosion had occurred below the armored deck and that subsequent blasts and fires were incidental.

At 1452 the task force commander was informed that the fires were not under control, and at 1456 the *Lexington* signalled for help.

Heat, smoke, and gas conditions were such that men not equipped with rescue breathers could not participate in fighting the fires. The ship's allowance of these breathers was soon exhausted, but many men, equipped only with regular gas masks, which were inadequate, persisted in going back into the dangerous areas.

Excerpts from Commander Seligman's report of succeeding developments give a vivid picture of the scene. He wrote:

"Lt. Comdr. Edward J. O'Donnell, the gunnery officer, had procured two additional hoses from aft. These were led into the scuttles of the 5-inch ammunition hoist to starboard, and the last available hose was led into the dumbwaiter of the food distribution room in an attempt to flood the C.P.O. country. Good pressure was maintained on these hoses for a short time and it was hoped that sufficient water could be gotten below to flood the area on fire forward of the quarter deck and check the spread of the blaze. Under existing conditions it was impossible to combat it otherwise.

"Lt. (j.g.) Raymond O. Deitzer, who was in charge of the gasoline system, had determined shortly after the completion of the attack that the system on the starboard side was functioning satisfactorily. The gas system on the port side had been secured just subsequent to the attack as a precautionary measure. Well before the terrific blast at 1247 he had ordered that the gas control room on the port side be flooded with water and smothered with CO_2.

"It appeared that the situation, while extremely grave, might not be hopeless if sufficient water could be obtained.

"I proceeded to the flight deck, considerably weakened by smoke. Shortly afterward another explosion occurred. The forward elevator was jammed up and sheets of flame could be seen below it. A hose from aft was obtained and seemed to have some effect.

"I asked Carpenter Nowak to insure that all hangar deck sprinklers were on, and Lt. Comdr. O'Donnell saw that the 'ready' torpedo warheads on the mezzanine were sprinkled.

"It soon became necessary to evacuate the hangar deck aft and many wounded were brought from the fuselage deck to the topside. Lt. (j.g.) John F. Roach (MC) and Lt. Morris A. Hirsch led rescue personnel in evacuating all these wounded with utter disregard for their own safety.

"The forward part of the ship was ablaze, both above and below the armored deck with absolutely no means left to fight the fire, which was now spreading aft on the flight deck. It was inevitable that the 20-odd torpedo warheads on the mezzanine of the hangar deck must eventually detonate.

"One sound power phone to main control still was functioning, but communication was not good and it appeared that the heat might ground it out at any moment. Accordingly I sent word to the chief engineer that it might become necessary to abandon ship, and ordered that the life rafts be placed in the nettings and unoccupied personnel distributed forward and aft on the starboard side, as the ship was listing about 7° to port.

"I then proceeded to the bridge and reported the situation to the commanding officer. [He] immediately ordered that the engineering department be secured and personnel evacuated to the flight deck.

"I must again comment on the heroism of personnel. It was an inspiration. The first thought of all was for the wounded."

The engineering plant was secured at 1630, and the *Lexington* soon lay dead in the water.

"I ordered life rafts made ready and preparations made to abandon ship," Captain Sherman related. "Fire fighting efforts were still being made until the engineering plant was abandoned, when all water pressure was gone. At this time I asked Admiral Fitch for destroyers to come alongside and pass over fire hoses, thinking we might control the fire if we got water. The Admiral directed DD's to come alongside and also directed me to disembark excess personnel to the destroyers. The *Morris* passed two hoses over, which were put to work, and excess personnel went down lines to her deck. However, by this time the fire was beyond control. Additional explosions were occurring; it was reported that the warheads on the hangar deck had been at a temperature of 1400°F; ready bomb storage was in the vicinity of the fire; and I considered there was danger of the ship blowing up at any minute."

At 1707 Admiral Fitch directed Captain Sherman to abandon ship. Thereupon Admiral Kinkaid was directed to take charge of rescue operations. The *Anderson* and *Hammann* joined the *Morris* alongside the *Lexington*, while the *Minneapolis* and *New Orleans* stood by.

The *Morris* secured the hoses that had been passed to the carrier at 1714 and made preparations to move clear. All available deck space was crowded with survivors, and several hundred men were in the water between the destroyer and the *Lexington*. There also were many life rafts in the vicinity and a motor whaleboat from the *Minneapolis* with about 40 survivors aboard. The *Morris* backed her propellers several times, and when her stern was clear began backing away. A section of her bridge wind screen was carried away, a searchlight was damaged, and a foremast stay was snapped as she eased away from the carrier.

At 1737 the *Morris* went alongside the *Minneapolis* and transferred about 200 survivors to the cruiser. The *Morris* then relieved a ship screening the *Yorktown*.

While the *Morris* was alongside the *Lexington*, the *Anderson* and *Hammann* were circling the stricken carrier clockwise. At 1657 the *Anderson* proceeded to the *Lexington's* port side but experienced difficulty, largely because of the carrier's pronounced list to port, in making fast. Unable to stay alongside, the *Anderson* moved ahead to pick up survivors from the water. Before moving off she launched two small boats. These were filled with personnel from the water, who subsequently were taken aboard the *Dewey*. The *Anderson* proceeded to join the *Yorktown* and transferred to the carrier 17 rescued officers and 360 men.

At 1536 the *Hammann* was ordered to relieve the *Phelps* in standing by the *Lexington*, and soon afterward took station on the carrier's port quarter. Many men were taken aboard after lowering themselves down ropes and nets. Others were picked up by two small boats, a whaleboat and gig, which towed life rafts to the *Minneapolis*.

At 1720 Admiral Kinkaid directed the *Hammann* to move around to the *Lexington's* starboard to pick up many men still in the water. The *Lexington* was in the trough of the sea, drifting at one or two knots with the wind, and the men in the water on her leeward side were having difficulty getting clear. The *Hammann* moved carefully in among the many men in the water, and only by skillful maneuvering was able to come alongside without crushing men between herself and the carrier. About 100 men were taken from the water and life rafts on the leeward side. As the *Hammann* backed clear at 1750 a heavy explosion within the *Lexington* showered the destroyer with flaming debris, but no one was injured.

Debris fouled both of the *Hammann*'s main circulating pumps, causing a loss of backing power, so instead of transferring those rescued to the *New Orleans* as she had been directed to do, the destroyer circled back to recover her small boats at 1845. Ensign Theodore E. Krepski and Ensign Ralph L. Holton, who were in charge of the *Hammann* boats, were recommended for award for their excellent performance during the rescue work.

At 1739 both the *Phelps* and *Dewey* were ordered to close the *Lexington* and assist in the rescue. They took station 1,000 yards to windward and launched small boats to pick up survivors. Neither went alongside the carrier, as it was obvious by this time that most if not all hands had left the ship.

At 1810, after it was quite dark, Lt. Comdr. John C. Daniel, in a *Phelps* whaleboat, made a hazardous turn around the *Lexington* and along her lee side to make certain no more people were in the water there. The carrier had just been rocked by a particularly heavy explosion which tossed planes from her deck high into the air, was afire from stem to stern and listing about 30°. No more survivors were found.

Captain Sherman and Commander Seligman made a final inspection before leaving the ship. They found several men manning a gun mount on the starboard side aft who would not abandon ship until ordered to do so.

Sometime after 1800 the executive, followed by the captain, slid down a line over the stern. A small boat took them to the *Minneapolis*.

More than 92 percent of the *Lexington*'s crew were saved. It was believed that not a man was lost by drowning during the abandonment. A preliminary check accounted for all but 26 officers and 190 men of a total complement of 2,951.

To list the names of all officers and men who performed tasks above and beyond the call of duty would fill several pages, and would not be complete at that. In the words of Commander Seligman, "All of the individual cases of heroism and devotion to duty will probably never be revealed." Suffice it to say that there were many.

Admiral Fletcher particularly commended Admiral Kinkaid's direction of the rescue work.

At 1853 the *Phelps* was detailed to sink the *Lexington*. Five torpedoes, four of which detonated, were fired between 1915 and 1952. The *Lexington* sank very suddenly at 1952 in 2,400 fathoms of water. The position was latitude 15°12' S, longitude 155°27' E.

A few seconds after the *Lexington* disappeared two terrific explosions occurred underwater. The shock was distinctly felt by ships of the main body, which by this time were 10 miles away. The captain of the *Phelps* thought momentarily that he had been torpedoed.

Women recruits cross an obstacle course at the Third WAAC Training Center at Fort Oglethorpe, Georgia, in May 1943. The exercise, voluntary rather than mandatory, was intended to keep the WAACs fit.

41.

The Enlistment of Women

May 1942

Before Pearl Harbor, the idea of women serving in the U.S. military seemed ridiculous to most Americans. Yet with the war came chronic and deepening shortages of manpower. The new defense plants needed more and more workers, and so did the armed forces. It didn't take a statistician to understand that there wouldn't be enough men to fill all the jobs.

Early on, private industry began hiring women to replace men who had shipped off to war. The U.S. Army, however, was slower to find roles for women volunteers: Would they be trained for combat? Would they give orders to men? To the generals, the institutional fit seemed problematic.

However, to Rep. Edith Nourse Rogers of Massachusetts, the solution was obvious. As early as 1941, she had introduced a bill creating the Women's Army Auxiliary Corps (WAAC), a quasimilitary organization authorized to recruit up to twenty-five thousand women volunteers. Once enlisted, these volunteers would be trained to fill army clerical positions currently held by men, freeing the men for combat duty. Appreciating the benefits of this exchange, army chief of staff George C. Marshall endorsed the bill and began planning for its enactment. Unfortunately, Rogers's proposal languished in a House of Representatives otherwise occupied with Lend-Lease and its aftermath, and the bill died before reaching the floor.

In January 1942, Rogers reintroduced her bill, this time amending it to include authorization for up to 150,000 women and the granting of military status to WAACs. Because the latter provision generated a great deal of opposition among legislators who didn't want WAACs to receive veterans benefits, it was eventually dropped. This, in turn, allowed Congress to pass a compromise measure in May 1942 authorizing the army to begin enrolling women between the ages of twenty-one and forty-five and organizing them into WAAC units commanded by WAAC officers. To direct the new corps, Marshall chose Oveta Culp Hobby, who had helped plan for the WAACs as chief of the Women's Interest Section of the War Department's Bureau of Public Relations.

In late July, the first 440 officer candidates arrived at the new WAAC training center at Fort Des Moines, Iowa. Thereafter, new classes, averaging 150 women each, arrived every two weeks. After completing the six-week course, graduates were commissioned as third officers, the WAAC equivalent of second lieutenants. Meanwhile, enlisted women also began arriving at Fort Des Moines for their own four-week basic training course.

10,000 WOMEN IN U. S. RUSH TO JOIN NEW ARMY CORPS

By LUCY GREENBAUM

The Woman's Army whizzed into being with a spectacular start yesterday [May 27]. Shoving aside prospective masculine soldiers, more than 1,000 women surged through the doors of staid Army Recruiting Headquarters, 39 Whitehall Street, as enlistment in the first officer-candidate school of the Women's Army Auxiliary Corps began officially.

From ocean to ocean, from the Rio Grande north to Canada, women poured out of homes, offices and colleges to roll up a total of 10,000 for all the recruiting stations of the nation.

From Brooklyn, the Bronx, Long Island, New Jersey and Westchester, by subway, ferry, train, bus and "El," women beat their way to the Battery.

As early as 8:30 A.M. 250 women had shouldered their way into the offices seeking application blanks. Army figures late in the afternoon put the total requests at 1,400 by person, 1,200 by mail. The latter did not include 1,500 received previously.

Mild brute strength was used to combat the feminine forces. A guard's broad shoulders held back the tidal wave of patriotic pulchritude that lessened during the noon hour, when women sat down to enjoy lunch served on the house.

Side by side stood glamour girls and grave young mothers. Fur coats and $2.98 cotton dresses. Blondes, brunettes, redheads and gray-topped women. Single women, wives, widows, divorcees—and one grandmother.

All races, colors and creeds turned out. There were colored women, members of the American Women's Voluntary Services. There was a Chinese woman, Mrs. Leo Gum of 54 Elizabeth Street, whose husband is in the Army.

And there was an Indian woman. Even the Army did not believe its eyes when Laughing Eyes, a full-blooded Creek, appeared. She was dressed for a war dance, in tribal outfit complete from beaded band around her straight black locks to white buckskin dress and bright-colored Indian blanket as shawl.

Army officials questioning her authenticity were convinced of it when she produced a document testifying that she had been born on a reservation in Muskogee, Okla.

Asked Laughing Eyes: "Don't you think I have more right to join than some of the other women?" Her brother, Straight Arrow, she said, was in the Navy. As she was explaining that she owns a store in Brooklyn, where she sells Indian novelties, but yearly visits Muskogee, a young soldier stationed at headquarters grabbed her hand, shook it warmly and introduced himself as Morris Meyer of Sapulpa, Okla., thirty miles from Muskogee.

Private Meyer, a Dartmouth graduate, was homesick. His first question was: "Did you get home for Christmas?" As she walked away he said, "That's terrific. Gee! Imagine meeting her!"

Although there were many women who obviously had never held jobs, the majority were working girls. Stenographers looked eager to exchange the command "Take a letter" to "Company halt!" Young actresses appeared pleased at the chance to give up thoughts of occupying the spotlight in order to set the stage for others.

WAACs arrive at Bolling Field, the air force's District of Columbia headquarters, to take up clerical and other duties there.

Telephone booths kept clanging with nickels as calls were put through with excuses as to why the women would be late to work.

"My boss thinks I've got a toothache," admitted Miss Wally Borysevicz of 309 East Ninth Street, who is a stenographer for a laboratory house.

Some brave souls even defied parents. Miss Carolyn Waring, blonde 21-year-old social registerite of Plainfield, N. J., was alarmed at what her family would say.

The daughter of Mr. and Mrs. Edward J. Waring confessed, "Dad thinks it's all right, but mother is practically in hysterics."

There were women who made their minds up ages ago that they would enter the Army, were one created for them, and those who decided only recently to tackle warfare tactics.

"I joined the A.W.V.S. with the thought in mind that we'd have a woman's army some day the way England has, and I would serve in it," declared Miss Patricia Schepps, 23.

A first lieutenant in the A.W.V.S. Motor Transport Corps, she said that her rank would no doubt disappear—"I'll probably be Private Schepps for the duration."

Comparatively recent was the decision of Mrs. Celia Weinberger of Middle Village, L. I. A bride of seven months, her husband is in the Army in Mississippi.

"I'm joining to see what he's doing," she said, putting down for a moment her copy of Thomas Wolfe's "You Can't Go Home Again." She added, "I want to do the sort of thing he's doing."

A directly opposite reason was given by Miss Verda Newberger of Brooklyn. "I've got no relatives in any of the armed forces," she declared. "That's why I'm joining up."

Women with children said they felt their mothers could adequately care for them while they were gone.

Mrs. Maureen Evans, 43, of Brooklyn, has no home problem with her son, Donald. He is an aerial gunner in the Air Corps, she said, "somewhere in the Philippines."

Fame for being technically the first arrival went to Miss Annabelle Barr, 27, of New Rochelle, N. Y., who left her warm bed at 4:30 A.M. to reach headquarters at 6:45.

She said that she had no alternative but to join the women's forces, as her employer, a doctor, is leaving for the Army today.

Actually, however, Miss Dorothy Klafter, 21, of 4716 New Utrecht Avenue, Brooklyn, beat every one to the gun. She said that she was so excited she had been awake all night, reading in bed.

"I got here a little after 5 o'clock this morning," she explained, "but it was so dark that I was afraid. I rode on buses and subways to kill time. When I returned at 7 o'clock I found someone was here before me."

Miss Klafter said that although she hoped the training would help her reduce, that was not her objective in applying. Miss Klafter is pleasantly plump.

"If a man can give up his life for his country, certainly a woman can give up her time," she asserted.

Sticklers might say that Mrs. Anthony E. Sclafani, an A.W.V.S. member, came before anyone. Her application, written on notepaper, was at the recruiting station three weeks ago.

"I'm here because I figure it this way," she said. "I was too young in the last war to realize its significance. I'm doing what is expected of me now." She lives at 3017 Eastchester Road, the Bronx.

Miss Lillian Fox, a member of the examining staff of the Civil Service Commission, said she obtained a leave of absence "for the duration" to join the Army.

A warning note was sounded by Miss Betty Lou Bregoff, 22, of Knickerbocker Village. Having lived at an Army post in Panama for five months, she said she knew Army life pretty well.

"I'm sure these women don't know what they're in for," she commented. "Camp life is pretty tough."

In the rush of the morning Colonel John F. Daye, executive officer for recruiting in the Second Corps Area, surveyed the women.

"They are a fine type of young women," he said "We could use 90 per cent of them in this building right now to replace men."

Sixty candidates will be sent from this area to the officers' training school at Fort Des Moines, Iowa. Enlistments for privates will take place when the first batch of officers has completed the eight-week course. When that starts in New York the Army had better call out the Marines.

"None of us knew just what was coming next."

A letter home from WAAC boot camp

This letter belongs to a collection of correspondence donated to the U.S. Army Women's Museum by WAAC veteran Andrea M. Aiken. After completing her basic training at Fort Des Moines, Aiken was assigned to Camp Pickett in Virginia, where she was promoted to the WAAC equivalent of sergeant.

January 18, 1943

Dear Dad and Evie,

At long last, what I've been waiting for...time of my own to write to you. We really are settled in now and I don't mean maybe. It's been one hustle and bustle, from one thing to another, but in spite of it, I've found myself thinking of you and Baby Jim at odd moments now and then.

Want to begin at the beginning and try and cover the whole trip, and bring things up to date.

As you know we had pullman accommodations from New York to Chicago, three girls to a section...which gave us all plenty of room. It was fun, too. Just like a sorority house, because the car was all women, with plenty of privacy. Slept off and on, but I can assure you it was rather fitful. We pulled into Chicago at 8:30 in the morning, after breakfast on the train. We changed to a local, which carried just WAAC's to Des Moines. Honestly it was one of those trains that go about as fast as one could dogtrot along side. The one saving factor was the dining car which served us very delicious meals.

We reached Des Moines at 6:45 Monday night and Moon came through the car after we were parked and waiting and it was like seeing a face from home. I was so tired that I could have wept with joy at seeing a familiar face. Finally we were all loaded into trucks, canvas covered, and driven out to the Fort. We were left in a reception (incoming) center, and some of us had gotten together and made up our own group, so we had a bit of a scramble keeping together, but did manage it. Of course none of us knew just what was coming next. In one respect Army life seems to be "hurry up and wait"!! But anyway to get on with my story, after we were signed up, we were taken to a dining hall, fed, rushed to a building where we were issued men's overcoats and knit hats. I wish you could have seen us. We looked like birds in the wilderness, because none of them fit any too well. They did this just so that we would all be dressed alike, and we found out that they were not permanent issue. They really did give us all quite a laugh! Now we have uniforms that are swell. These do justice to our figure. (Just skip the last line or so, Daddy, one of the girls came along and dictated it, and I humored her because she's a trifle homesick, having received no mail since arrival.) Anyway they moved us into a barracks, which had been renovated from a stable, but it is a nice setup. All the conviences but of course none of the comforts of home, except a day room (lounge), that is done up pretty nicely. We were rushed around until 11:30 when we had to be in bed for bed check and so I didn't even have time to get a smell of water to clean up after our long train trip. I was so exhausted at that point that it didn't matter anyway and I think I went to sleep immediately my head hit the pillow. I pulled an upper bunk of double decker too, and wondered if I'd roll out, but woke up safely in the morning, but quite lost for the moment.

We got up at 6:05 by the way, washed, made beds, went to breakfast and worked on general cleanup of the barracks.

Later in the morning we went or rather were taken to the cloth warehouse where we went through line in booth after booth, and were fitted for clothes. They fit beautifully, and we have a complete issue so that means just as soon as I can get to it I'll be shipping my bag home UNPACKED. Makes me mad to think I lugged it all this way, all to no avail, because now there seems to be no clothes shortage. We all like the uniforms and they do fit, and that's no lie. They are slick. When I send my case home Evie, will you unpack it and put my things away? Wrap my woolen sweaters in bags or papers and they could go in the box with my shoes. Send my suit skirt and bathrobe to the cleaners, and they should be put or fixed so the moths won't get into them. I'm sending a check, and use that to cover any of my bills and keep the rest for future use or do what you like with it. I think that you have a key on that bunch I gave you that will open the case if not I'll send mine. But try it out anyway. Of course you know that I'm thanking you for it, and hate making you the extra work if you're moving, but I do hate leaving it in the bag.

Tuesday afternoon we had several tests, and what they don't know about our IQ won't be worth knowing. Wednesday morning we went for personal interviews and signed to buy bonds. As soon as I pay for one they will send it to you to hold for me. That afternoon we had shots for typhoid, small pox and tetanus. All at one clip and we have three more sets coming at weekly intervals or so.

Thursday we had informal classes and pictures at the theater, to sell us on winning the war. Thursday night we spent scrubbing and cleaning up for formal inspection Friday morning and I guess it was worth it too, because we tied with the barracks that has won for the last five weeks. I wish you could see my hands though! No polish, and sort of roughish at first but now they aren't in such tough shape.

Friday was spent in out first formal drilling, and it is a lot of fun. By the way the shoes are tan, and as comfortable as any of my own. I haven't had a blister or even a hot foot, yet.

Saturday we all donned our full kit and turned in our men's GI. We packed up (everything goes into duffle bags) in preparation to move to BOOM TOWN, the section of the Post where we get our basic training. Moon is here and I've seen her almost every day. Anyway after moving in I was more fortunate and got a lower this time. But I drew KP (Kitchen Police), and went at six Sunday A.M. and stayed until 8 that night and had to be there at six this morning, but finished up at 10:45 A.M. I did every kind of dirty work there is to do and it sure was LOUSY. You know me anyway, but I made the best of it knowing that it had to be done…and furthermore I'd be damned if I'd shirk the job (by Goldbricking). They have a wonderful setup though for serving food in the individual mess halls and it's fascinating to watch preparations progress. No food shortages here though, Dad, and I kept thinking of you struggling along trying to serve the public a decent meal all day. Who couldn't with what we have here.

It's been terribly cold and Iowa is flat as a pancake and equally uninteresting so far. We have plenty of heat inside and have had no drilling out in the cold. We have lights out at 9:30 but have to be in bed at 10:45. We hop in too, because a wearier bunch you couldn't find. There are still a million things I want to tell you and will try to get to it soon. It's nearly lights out so I'll say good night to you all with all my love. Am still anxious for news of Bill. My letters were interesting, Evie, and will drop you a line and tell you more about them later. Give Jimmy a big hug and kiss for me, and regards to all. Night again.

Haven't smoked yet. Sent out a few cards. Want to get letters off to some of the other girls. More later.

Drea

42.

The First Thousand-Plane Raid

May 1942

In the view of British Air Marshal Arthur "Bomber" Harris, the Germans lost the battle of Britain because they unwisely used a tactical force to carry out a strategic mission. The Luftwaffe's numerous dive-bombers and fighters had played a crucial role in supporting the Wehrmacht's *Blitzkrieg* successes, yet they were no substitute for the long-range heavy bombers that Harris knew were the sine qua non of strategic bombing.

The concept of strategic bombing—as developed by Hugh Trenchard, the RAF's first chief of staff—held that a strong fleet of long-range bombers could decide the outcome of a war simply by razing an enemy's cities and breaking its civilian morale. Yet the RAF lacked the financial support necessary to construct such a fleet; and, once the war began, most aviation resources were diverted to the production of fighters, because of the imminent Luftwaffe threat. Furthermore, the few small daylight raids mounted by RAF Bomber Command early in the war proved to be failures, yielding much more damage to aircraft than to targets. Finally, in April 1940, the Air Ministry restricted all bombing to nighttime raids. These demonstrated that German air defenses were indeed weaker at night, but so was British navigation, which made it difficult to deliver bombs even remotely near their targets. During the next seven months, two developments turned the situation around: Harris's February 1942 promotion to lead Bomber Command and the introduction of Gee, a radio navigational system that allowed RAF aircraft to locate their targets with much greater accuracy.

Instead of precision bombing, which targeted specific facilities, Harris introduced area bombing, a strategy that concentrated firepower over urban areas, assuming that some military targets would inevitably be among those hit. Harris also pushed for much larger attacks, including the first thousand-plane raid, believing that concentrating bombers in time and space would reduce loss rates while dramatically increasing the damage done. The RAF's May 30 raid on Cologne seemed to prove his point. During the previous nine months, RAF bombers had flown 1,364 sorties over Cologne with a loss rate of 3.5 percent and little damage done. On May 30, the RAF flew 1,046 sorties with a 3.8 percent loss rate—and photographs taken the next day showed that the city center had been leveled. Even so, German war production, most of it located in suburban factories, continued with little interruption, leading some to question later the morality of Harris's area bombing.

1,000 BRITISH BOMBERS SET COLOGNE ON FIRE; USE 3,000 TONS OF EXPLOSIVES IN RECORD RAID

A 90-Minute Raid; R.A.F. Causes Havoc in the Rhine City—Nazis Admit 'Great Damage'

By RAYMOND DANIELL

LONDON, Monday, June 1—More than 1,000 British bombers dumped 3,000 tons of high-explosive bombs Saturday night on Cologne and elsewhere in the Rhineland and in the Ruhr.

"Cologne was the main objective," the Air Ministry said, and British officials asserted the raid was the biggest air attack in the history of warfare.

Prime Minister Winston Churchill, congratulating Air Marshal A. T. Harris, chief of the Bomber Command of the Royal Air Force, who planned and directed the devastating attack on one of Germany's largest and industrially most important cities, described it as "a herald of what Germany will receive city by city from now on."

It was indeed the heaviest blow the R.A.F. has delivered yet in its promised air offensive against the Nazis, and it will not be long now before the American Air Force joins the British. The shadow that two years ago was no bigger than a man's hand has grown to a huge cloud threatening the whole Reich.

Forty-four British planes failed to return to their bases from the Saturday night operations, which included heavy attacks on Nazi coastal bases and airfields and fighter action against enemy interception.

This was the largest number of planes the British have ever lost in one raid, but it was still little more than 4 per cent of all the planes that were used.

That the losses for an assault upon a German city defended, as Cologne was, by 120 search-lights and at least 500 anti-aircraft guns and big Nazi night fighter forces, were not heavier was due largely to new tactics used by the R.A.F.

The bombers went in over their target at the rate of one every six seconds to distract and confuse the searchlight operators and the German gun crews and prevent their concentrating long on any single plane.

At the same time at least 250 other planes were drawn from every command of the R.A.F. and swarmed over the Nazi airports, from which enemy fighters might have been drawn to intercept the Cologne attackers.

[The Germans claimed to have shot down forty-seven British planes, thirty-six over Cologne and eleven near the coast. Berlin, while reporting "great damage" at Cologne, tried to discount the size of the raid by saying only seventy R.A.F. bombers were over the city. At the same time, Nazi officials talked of "reprisals."

[British bombers were over Western Germany again last night, according to a Berlin broadcast recorded by The Associated Press early today.]

Saturday night's supreme effort by no means exhausted the R.A.F. In daylight yesterday British fighters made several sweeps over Nazi-occupied France and Belgium. They shot down four Nazi fighters and lost eight of their own planes.

Off the Netherland coast British planes set afire and sunk a German armed trawler and two other vessels were driven aground, according to the Air Ministry. It was reported also that in Belgium railroads and barges were attacked.

Firebombs are loaded onto a British Stirling bomber for an air attack against industrial Germany, July 1942.

Last evening more R.A.F. sweeps were made over Northern France.

Blenheims, Bostons, Havocs, Beaufighters and other planes from the Fighter, Coastal and Army Cooperation Commands of the R.A.F. formed an interference for the big four-engined Lancasters, Halifaxes and Stirlings and twin-engined Manchesters, Wellingtons, Whitleys and Hampdens that went to Cologne and back.

The British used at least twice as many planes as the Germans ever sent against this country when the Luftwaffe was trying to carry out Adolf Hitler's threat to "wipe out British cities."

In the biggest German raids against London and Coventry in 1940 and 1941, Reich Marshal Hermann Goering never used more than 600 planes. These, although they flew a much shorter distance, carried much smaller bomb loads than the bigger and more up-to-date bombers the R.A.F. is using now. [German losses over Britain sometimes exceeded the 10 per cent of planes used that is considered too costly for continuous operation.]

Air Marshal Harris said yesterday that his fleets of bombers had four times the carrying capacity of the largest air force ever before concentrated on a single objective. Many planes carried the heavy bombs of the new 4,000-pound type.

The whole force of the attack on Cologne was concentrated in the brief space of ninety minutes; and no one who has not lived through a bad raid can appreciate fully what that means.

This ruinous assault by the R.A.F., which makes even those recent devastating raids on Rostock and Luebeck seem like token bombings by comparison, is to be repeated whenever the weather permits. British officials said last night that it was operationally possible for forces five times greater than those used Saturday night—

that is, 5,000 planes—to take part in expeditions over Germany in the future, particularly when the American bomber forces are ready to fly against the Reich.

To strike an average of 1,000 bombers over Germany nightly is the Air Ministry's objective. That is what has been meant when British officials have talked recently of the coming air offensive. Its aim is to force Germany to withdraw both fighters and bombers from the Russian front and paralyze her industries and communications.

In that respect Cologne was an important target. The third or fourth largest city in Germany, this inland port and vital link in Nazi road and rail communications with the West turns out from its many factories synthetic rubber, explosives and engines for submarines and planes.

It is interesting to recall that Air Marshal Harris said recently that if he could send 1,000 planes over Germany every night the war would be over by Autumn. If he could send 20,000 bombers over Germany in a single night, he said, the war would end the next morning.

It is unlikely that Air Marshal Harris will have a chance this Summer to test the latter theory; but it is to insure the fruition of the 1,000-plane plan that Lieut. Gen. H. H. Arnold of the United States Army Air Corps is here now consulting with high officials of the British Government and the R.A.F. That will be this Summer's contribution by the United States toward carrying the war to Germany.

The pilots and crews who were over Cologne, resting at their stations yesterday, said fires started in the Rhineland city by the first wave of the attack were visible from over the Netherland coast.

A pall of smoke that they said looked like a lowering thundercloud hung over the city and rose to a height of 15,000 feet.

R.A.F. reconnaissance planes that revisited Cologne during daylight yesterday said a terrific cloud of smoke still hung over the city.

Air Vice Marshal J. E. A. Baldwin, who is chief of one Bomber Command group, was one of the senior British officers who flew to Cologne, officials announced.

It may come as something of a surprise to Americans, accustomed to reading of the exploits of generals of their own air force in leading attacks, to learn that such a risk to commanding officers is almost unheard of in the R.A.F. Air Vice Marshal Baldwin is the first officer above the rank of Group Captain officially to have been reported as taking part in a bomber operation.

"Only one in three got within five miles of their target."

Excerpt from a British analysis of night bombing

In August 1941, F. A. Lindemann, Churchill's chief scientific adviser, told the prime minister of his concern that few RAF bombers were finding their targets within Germany. Nighttime navigation was so poor, Lindemann said, that he wondered whether the raids were worth the losses in men and matériel. Specifically, he recommended that a disinterested official—not a member of the Air Ministry—be assigned to evaluate the photographs of drop zones taken by cameras recently installed in many bombers. The subsequent report, written by David M. Butt of the War Cabinet Secretariat and excerpted here, directly influenced Churchill to speed up the development of Gee.

Report by Mr. Butt to Bomber Command on his Examination of Night Photographs 18th August 1941

SUMMARY
Statistical Conclusions

An examination of night photographs taken during night bombing in June and July points to the following conclusions:

1. Of those aircraft recorded as attacking their target, only one in three got within five miles.
2. Over the French ports, the proportion was two in three; over Germany as a whole, the proportion was one in four; over the Ruhr, it was only one in ten.
3. In the full moon, the proportion was two in five; in the new moon, it was only one in fifteen.
4. In the absence of haze, the proportion was over one half, whereas over thick haze it was only one in fifteen.
5. An increase in the intensity of A.A. fire reduced the number of aircraft getting within five miles of their target in the ratio three to two.
6. All these figures relate only to aircraft recorded as *attacking* the target; the proportion of the *total sorties* which reached within five miles is less by one third. Thus, for example, of the total sorties only one in five got within five miles of the target, i.e. within the 75 square miles surrounding the target.

Recommendations

1. These results though fairly reliable should be checked by a thorough expert study of the day photographs, and by a comparative study of photographs of German and British towns.
2. In order to keep these figures up to date, and to obtain continuous records of the success of our navigation, staff should be set up to maintain statistical records of night photographs and any other evidence that may be available.

3. This staff should consist of at least one trained statistician, with a sufficient clerical staff. He should have authority to modify forms and questionnaires in order to make sample enquiries, e.g. to replace some existing questions for a certain period by others designed to elucidate some particular point.

1. Night Photographs in June–July 1941
A Statistical Analysis

1. Particulars sufficient for some rough statistical analysis have been collected for about 650 photographs taken during night bombing operations between 2nd June and 25th July. They relate to 28 targets, 48 nights, and 100 separate raids. All show enough ground detail for the position photographed to be plotted if previous photographs of the area exist.

Nearly half of these photographs were taken independently of bombing, but as in all these cases the position believed photographed was named, they are equally useful for measuring the accuracy of navigation and have been included.

The technique of taking night photographs is such that the area photographed is not necessarily the same as the area intended to be photographed. Changes of speed, height and direction, and any tilting of the aircraft will affect the result, as will delay in launching the flash. But the displacement is most unlikely to be more than a mile or two miles on a photograph which normally shows an area of over a square mile. As for the purposes of this enquiry the 'target area' is taken as the area within five miles of the aiming point, the possibility of error in the results from this source is allowed for. There is no reason to suppose that more photographs intended for points in the target area actually show points outside than vice versa.

2. Success of Attacks over Period as Whole

The total number of photographs purporting to represent the target, target area, or believed target area for which details were obtained was 633. Of these, 326, or 51 per cent, have not been plotted; 113, or 18 per cent, have been pinpointed outside the target area; and 194, or 31 per cent, within the target area.

The Photographic Interpretation Section are confident that all unplotted photographs must be outside the target area. There seems no doubt that, in view of the specialised skill they have developed in examining some 750,000 prints, this claim is perfectly correct.

There is no reason to suppose that aircraft equipped with cameras are particularly unsuccessful. These 650 photographs were taken on over 500 different sorties; a sample of more than 1 in 10 of the sorties recorded as attacking during the raids covered.

The conclusion seems to follow that only about $1/_3$ of aircraft claiming to reach the target area actually reach it.

Prolonged consideration has revealed only one real possibility of error in this result. It may be that violent evasive action by aircraft will give rise to complete photographic failures and it may be that such action has to be taken particularly often within the target area. If so the results would be biassed. It is difficult to say whether these conditions are fulfilled, but from the records of the Command Photographic Officer, it appears that some 75 intended photographs either failed to be taken or, if taken, to come out in the period concerned by reason of evasive action, searchlights and flak. It is most unlikely that these failures wholly occurred over the target area. Supposing, however, that they did, and that had they been taken all would have been successfully developed, about 700 photographs with about 275 in the target area would have been available, i.e. the percentage of 31 reached above would be raised to 39.

This figure represents the maximum possible consistent with the data. The rough ratio of $^1/_3$ given above is more probable. Two qualifications to this average result should be made clear:

(a) This figure of one third...relate to the aircraft recorded as having attacked the primary target, not to the total aircraft despatched. In the raids considered in this analysis 6,103 aircraft were despatched but 4,065 attacked, i.e. 66 per cent. Thus of the total despatched not one-third but one-fifth reached the target area.

(b) It must be observed also that by defining the target area for the purpose of this enquiry as having a radius of five miles, an area of over 75 square miles is taken. This must, at least for any town but Berlin, consist very largely of open country. The proportion of aircraft actually dropping their bombs on built-up areas must be very much less, but what this proportion is, however, cannot be indicated by the study of night photographs.

DIE SCHWERSTEN ANGRIFFE DER LUFTWAFFE VON DER R.A.F. WEIT ÜBERBOTEN

Mehr als 1000 Bomber auf einmal eingesetzt

IN der Nacht vom 30. Mai griff die Royal Air Force Köln mit weit über 1000 Flugzeugen an. Der Angriff wurde auf anderthalb Stunden zusammengedrängt. Der deutsche Sicherheits- und Abwehrdienst war der Wucht des Angriffs nicht gewachsen.

Premierminister Churchill sagte in seiner Botschaft an den Oberbefehlshaber des britischen Bomberkommandos am 31. Mai:

„Dieser Beweis der wachsenden Stärke der britischen Luftmacht ist auch das Sturmzeichen für die Dinge, die von nun an eine deutsche Stadt nach der andern zu erwarten hat."

Zwei Nächte darauf griff die Royal Air Force das Ruhrgebiet mit über 1000 Maschinen an.

Die Offensive der Royal Air Force in ihrer neuen Form hat begonnen

Translation

THE ATTACKS OF THE R.A.F. FAR SURPASS THE HEAVIEST ATTACKS OF THE LUFTWAFFE · MORE THAN 1000 BOMBERS IN ONE ATTACK

On the night of May 30th/31st, the Royal Air Force attacked Cologne with well over 1,000 planes. The attack was concentrated into an hour and a half. The German civil and anti-aircraft defences were not equal to the weight of the attack.

In his message to the Commander-in-Chief Bomber Command on May 31st, Churchill said:

"This proof of the growing power of the British Bomber Force is also the herald of what Germany will receive city by city from now on."

Two nights after this the Royal Air Force attacked the Ruhr with over 1,000 planes.

THE OFFENSIVE OF THE ROYAL AIR FORCE IN ITS NEW FORM HAS BEGUN

The RAF dropped thousands of these leaflets boasting of the success of the Cologne raid during the days and weeks afterward.

PERMISSIONS

We would like to thank the copyright holders listed below for their permission to reprint some of the documents used in this book:

ILLUSTRATION CREDITS

Photographs from the Library of Congress are indicated with image numbers that begin LC. Those from the National Archives are indicated with image numbers that begin NA.

244: NA-80-G-30549;

247: NA-80-G-32420;

250: NA-80-G-19948;

255: NA-208-MO-104DD-1;

259: LC-USZ62-91315;

260: NA-208-WP-22R-2;

263: NA-208-AA-203L-1;

269: LC-USZ62-114394;

273: LC-USW3-009923-E;

278: NA-210-G-2C-172;

281: NA-210-G-2A-35;

286: NA-111-SC-334265;

289: NA-127-GR-111-114541;

295: NA-208-PU-53A-3;

298: NA-111-SC-134627;

301: LC-USZ62-104971;

305: LC-USZ62-96100;

312: NA-80-G-7392;

315: NA-80-G-21128;

320: D.C. Public Library, *Washington Star* Collection;

323: D.C. Public Library, *Washington Star* Collection;

329: LC-USZ62-91112;

333: Agincourt Press;

334: NA-80-G-17054;

338: NA-80-G-21603

ACKNOWLEDGMENTS

We would like to acknowledge the contributions made to this project by Robin Dennis of Times Books; by Susan Chira, Mike Levitas, and Tomi Murata of *The New York Times;* and by Wendy Fuller and the staff of the Chatham Public Library.

INDEX

About the Editors

DOUGLAS BRINKLEY currently serves as director of the Eisenhower Center for American Studies and is a professor of history at the University of New Orleans. Three of his biographies—*Dean Acheson: The Cold War Years* (1992), *Driven Patriot: The Life and Times of James Forrestal* (with Townsend Hoopes) (1992), and *The Unfinished Presidency: Jimmy Carter's Journey Beyond the White House* (1998)—were chosen as Notable Books of the Year by *The New York Times*.

Brinkley's recent publications include *Wheels for the World: Henry Ford, His Company and a Century of Progress*, *The Mississippi and the Making of a Nation*, *Rosa Parks* (in the Penguin Lives series), and *The American Heritage History of the United States*. He is also a regular contributor to *Newsweek*, *Time*, *American Heritage*, *The New Yorker*, *The New York Times*, *The Wall Street Journal*, *The Atlantic Monthly*, *Foreign Affairs*, *Foreign Policy*, and other journals.

DAVID RUBEL is the president of Agincourt Press, a book production company in Chatham, New York. Specializing in American history, Rubel has edited (with James M. McPherson) *To the Best of My Ability: The American Presidents* (2000) and (with James M. McPherson and Alan Brinkley) *Days of Destiny: Crossroads in American History* (2001). He is also the author (with Allen Weinstein) of *The Story of America: Freedom and Crisis from Settlement to Superpower* (2002). Rubel's books for children include *The Scholastic Encyclopedia of the Presidents and Their Times*, originally published in 1994 and now about to appear in its fourth edition.